Religious Innovation in a Global Age

Religious Innovation in a Global Age

Essays on the Construction of Spirituality

Edited by GEORGE N. LUNDSKOW

McFarland & Company, Inc., Publishers
Jefferson, North Carolina, and London

LIBRARY OF CONGRESS CATALOGUING-IN-PUBLICATION DATA

Religious innovation in a global age : essays on the construction
of spirituality / edited by George N. Lundskow.
   p.   cm.
Includes bibliographical references and index.

ISBN 0-7864-1977-6 (softcover : 50# alkaline paper)

1. Religion and Sociology.   I. Lundskow, George N.,
1964–
BL60.R445   2005
200—dc22   2004022517

British Library cataloguing data are available

©2005 George N. Lundskow. All rights reserved

*No part of this book may be reproduced or transmitted in any form
or by any means, electronic or mechanical, including photocopying
or recording, or by any information storage and retrieval system,
without permission in writing from the publisher.*

Cover imagery ©2004 PhotoSpin

Manufactured in the United States of America

McFarland & Company, Inc., Publishers
  Box 611, Jefferson, North Carolina 28640
  www.mcfarlandpub.com

Contents

Preface   vii
Introduction   1

Part I. Theory

1. Surplus, Excess, Waste, Leftovers, and Remainders: The Dialectic of Productive Functions, Antisemitism, and the Vicissitudes of Social Forces
   Mark P. Worrell   7

2. The Open Dialectic Between Religious and Secular Values and Norms: The Course of Civilization in the 21st Century
   Rudolf J. Siebert   37

3. Spirituality and Social Character: The Case of New Evangelicalism and Neopaganism
   George N. Lundskow   69

4. A Critique of the Ambiguity of Bourgeois Religion: Max Horkheimer's Critical Theory of Religion
   Michael R. Ott   97

Part II. Research

5. Apocalyptic Unbound: An Interpretation of Christian Speed/Thrash Metal Music
   Charles M. Brown   117

6. Islamic Fundamentalism, Modernity, and the Role of Women
   Mahruq F. Khan and Lauren Langman — 138

7. Legion of Small Knights: Informal Movements within the Polish Roman Catholic Church
   Agnieszka Koscianska — 160

8. Religionizing Crime: Ethos and Action in the Construction of the Finnish Satanism Scare
   Titus Hjelm — 176

9. There's No Place Like Home.html: Neopaganism on the Internet
   Alyssa Beall — 199

10. Religious Conflict in the Periphery: Islam and Politics in Turkey
    Mustafa Saatci — 228

11. The Virgin Mary Versus the Monkeys
    Deana Weibel — 247

12. Martyrdom and Violence in Sikhism: The Transfer of Embodied Experience through Witnessing
    Rory G. McCarthy — 258

13. Catholicism Recycled: The New Age in Poland
    Dorota Hall — 270

About the Contributors — 283

Index — 287

Preface

In April 2001, I attended a conference organized by CESNUR (Center for the Study of New Religions) at the London School of Economics. Scholars filled the various sessions with remarkably interesting, insightful, and academically rigorous papers. So impressed by the range, insight, and collegial attitude of the presenters, I determined to collect essays from a diverse assortment of authors for a book. But what of a theme? Although not the official theme of the conference, one theme permeated nearly every session, on whatever topic, approached through whatever theoretical perspective or methodological style — the crisis of meaning in modern society. This issue, already present since the founding of the social sciences in the late 19th century, rises and falls as social conditions change. Presently, the crisis is rising, and scholarship has correspondingly moved to understand it.

This volume thus finds company alongside such recent and excellent publications as Amanda Porterfield's *The Story of Late Twentieth-Century Awakening: The Transformation of American Religion* (2001) and Douglas Porpora's *Landscapes of the Soul: The Loss of Moral Meaning in American Life* (2001). Although the latter title may suggest a call to reinvigorate religion, advocated from a religious perspective, Porpora in fact writes as a secular sociologist. He contends that the social sciences must broaden their view, and consider, as part of understanding society, questions that pertain to, in general, the meaning of life. Porterfield similarly argues that, whatever the overt changes we may observe in American religion, the underlying quest pertains to meaning — the democratization of American religion means in practical terms that people demand the right to shape their beliefs to correspond to their lived experience. This book examines theoretically and empirically how a diverse assortment of groups, at their core, are trying to restore a sense of meaning through religious innovation.

Overall, recent scholarship increasingly focuses on the loss of meaning as an issue of vital importance, alongside the longstanding social scientific variables of work, class, race, and gender. I don't pretend that the essays in this collection will provide an answer to the meaning of life, or even that the social sciences can ever answer such a question. My goal following the London conference has been much more modest. What can the social sciences contribute to understanding the ramifications of the loss of meaning in the lives of real people? In this regard, the essays here focus on observed attempts to regain meaning.

This work is also preliminary, as serious attention to the meaning of life is preliminary in the social sciences. I hope this book will prompt further inquiry into an emerging field I would like to call Existential Studies — the role and significance of meaning and purpose in social life.

Introduction

Certain questions of the ages, although always present, become more or less prominent in people's minds as social conditions change. The more uncertain the times, the more attention people direct to major existential questions. Who am I? Where did I come from? How should I live? Of course, one question above all others strikes every person who has ever lived, and although such things as wealth and power often enable a person or group to avoid many issues in life, one issue remains entirely unavoidable — death. What happens when I die? Can an individual and society prosper and progress without meaningful answers to these questions?

Certainly, the new global economy testifies to the material success of modern society — the age of industry, of finance, of capitalism. Yet this triumph also entails the destruction of tradition, of local culture, of familiar reference groups and values. In place of meaningful traditions and cultural variation, the corporate system offers a commodified form of culture, often sold to the consumer as a restaurant, an experience or activity with no social or transcendent importance, or as a tourist trinket.

If the values, traditions, beliefs, and nomoi of the old religions no longer integrate the individual into a larger spiritual community of meaning, what, if anything, does? Even the sacred, whether formal institutions or rituals and beliefs, compete against each other just as innumerable other commodities compete for buyers in the marketplace. Can we buy fulfillment in the marketplace, or does meaning require the individual to play some active part in its creation?

Simulated sacredness does not meaningfully answer the questions posed above, nor build community. Commercialized religion offers little more satisfaction than the latest car, or television show, or thrill-seeking sensation. Perhaps satisfying at the moment, the consumerist approach to life demands ever newer commodities, ever newer thrills to satisfy the ever greater desire —

and ever greater emptiness. Eventually, when the car has lost its luster, and the video game has become just pixels on a screen, and the latest gadgets turn into useless junk, and thrill-seeking has become routine, then a person can go no further, and comes face to face with a void of despair.

Still, people cannot long endure such conditions, and even as meaninglessness increases, so too does resistance. This volume assembles a series of essays that address the struggle to create meaning. Although most of the movements discussed here arose within established religious institutions, all are a direct reaction to the collapse of meaning within established religious or cultural systems, and thus each movement is essentially contemporary and purposefully innovative in order to address, whether through reform or revolution, the crisis of meaning in a rapidly changing world.

In the past, a crisis of meaning — an existential crisis — portended dangerous times ahead. The last great such crisis arose in Germany, after 1918, contributed to the rise of Hitler, and concluded with the destruction of Europe, 1939–1945. By no means can we deny the political fallout from World War I and the double economic depression between the wars that crucially configured World War II. Rather, I contend that the social-psychological and cultural factors present in Germany in the Weimar years provided a necessary precondition and corollary for the rise of fascism, that the way people see themselves and the world and whether people feel that life has meaning greatly shapes the extent to which people will embrace reason, or — in the absence of meaning — the emotional fanaticism that arises from utter despair.

Yet today, at least in the West, we do not live in a world of mass warfare, mass persecution, and catastrophic economic failure. Then why the religious and spiritual revival? Why is a more or less comfortable life not enough? Why are the established mainline churches less and less appealing? What tendencies may we observe in this new revival, and from what social forces do they arise?

This volume consists of two parts. In Part I, we consider new developments in theory as a means to frame critical inquiry into recent developments in religion and the larger quest for meaning. Part II examines grassroots emancipation movements, which collectively, however much the form and content may vary, seek an expanded role for the individual and intentional design in both belief and practice. The chapters focus on Christianity and Neopaganism, and how each utilizes culture as a corollary to belief and community unity.

Despite certain essential similarities, the movements differ significantly, although as mentioned the overt content is not decisive. Rather, the social-psychological and cultural ramifications of each movement distinguishes one from another. That is, the overt ideological difference between evangelical

Christianity and Neopaganism, for example, conceals the essential similarity that they both seek spiritual meaning within, and not in opposition to, modern society. At the same time, the movements differ in the way they build group identity — in simplest terms, one emphasizes free thinking, the other emphasizes submission. Identity and social cohesion can be accomplished on different terms, and it is these social-psychological factors, rather than the beliefs of Neopaganism or Christianity, that concerns the authors in this volume.

At the same time, not all movements of meaning that seek to build community are grassroots. Turkey today provides an interesting case, in which an officially secular government uses its political power to shape religion, Islam, in order to build a social culture that legitimates secular rule and to ensure the influence of the military behind the scenes yet also above the democratically elected government.

Religious innovation, of course, is nothing new. But in every era, new developments not only arise from, but also change and challenge, established churches and beliefs. As globalization continues, not only capitalism broadens its purview, but culture as well. Can religion, or perhaps only religion, make life meaningful in a truly global world? Or, should we expect, in opposition to globalization forces, increasing sectarianism and the exclusive attractions of tribe, of place, of ethnicity, of Das Volk, whether actual, or, as is more commonly the case, of purposefully created identity? This book offers early testimony that the outcome of globalization has not yet been decided, that we are entering a new era of conflict, but possibly also new awareness and meaning, that the globe and all it contains is all we really have.

PART I
Theory

1

Surplus, Excess, Waste, Leftovers, and Remainders

The Dialectic of Productive Functions, Antisemitism, and the Vicissitudes of Social Forces

Mark P. Worrell

Marx is surely the most well-known social theorist to dwell on the concept of surplus but an argument could be made that Freud, Weber, Durkheim, and before them, Hegel, each articulated theories of surplus — i.e. theories of social and mental surplus, or the surplus of society and consciousness itself. For practical reason, concepts like surplus, waste, excess, and so on stand juxtaposed to notions such as lack, deficiency, need, etc. Critical reason, however, confronts lack and waste, etc., as constituents in the theoretical matrix of fetishization, ideology, alienation, desire, enjoyment, and domination. My task here is not a guided tour of the various flavors of "surplus theory" but to make a plausible case for what we might call the dialectic of productive functions — the alienation, construction, projection, circulation, transfiguration, and extension of sacred and monstrous social forces.

To keep this exposition grounded in reality I will, following a brief conceptual interlude, examine the enigmatic logic of antisemitism among American workers during the Second World War. The point of all this is to comprehend what we might call, metaphorically, the "exchange relation" between the sacred and profane and lay bare the social logic of antisemitism, the vanguard form of authoritarianism, which, though it is not a "religious" phenomenon, nonetheless functions "as if" it were.

Surplus and Excess

Marx was concerned with commodities and capitalism so it comes as little surprise that his theory of surplus would concentrate on economic practices. Yet his philosophy of "conscious life activity" or the "productive functions" of collective interaction are by no means limited to labor processes. What appears in the exchange of commodities is more significantly the moment in which human beings (hidden behind a material veil) acquire mutual recognition and moral statuses. What is important here is that it is the other's physical, natural, analytic shape (the other's use-value, in other words) which embodies the moral and social appearance of the subject. The other's utility, in other words, becomes the body and form of my value. Value is a relational, normative, social substance (a shared way of thinking, acting, and feeling) that transcends merely the idea of labor. Human labor may "create value, but is not itself value" (Marx 1976, p. 142). Value is, as Marx points out repeatedly, a collective form of consciousness — a thing of thought yet a *sui generis* reality, self-moving social substance. It is, in Durkheim's language, a social fact. We could adopt, metaphorically, Aristotle's language of the "unmoved mover": "There is a mover which moves without being moved, being eternal, substance and actuality. And the object of desire and the object of thought move in this way; they move without being moved" (Hegel [1821] 1991, p. 435).

Hence, we find Marx evoking analogies of royal authority and the relationship between Peter and Paul to illustrate the core logic determining the circulation of commodities (Marx 1976, pp. 143–44). As the owner of a surplus labor product, if I desire to realize and have recognized its value, then I must alienate it, set aside (misplace) its sensuous and analytic properties so that it may assume an existence as a value whose magnitude is determined by the quantity of labor time it embodies. In this exchange relation defined by the dual moments of the relative [r] and the equivalent [e] a thing becomes both less than and more than itself.

The moral status of "commodity" (a thing of both fear and wonderment) is acquired only by virtue of standing in relation to another commodity; only within the exchange relation does value manifest itself. Outside the exchange relation commodities lose their value and decompose into mere labor products with utilities. They may re-acquire their form as values if we bring them back into an exchange relation. For the purposes of illustration I use a variation on Marx's accidental value form.

$$\begin{array}{ccccccc} \eta & S & u & LT & \!\!\!\!\!\!\!\!\!\!\!\!\!\text{———} & V & L \\ [r] & C & P & & & P & C \; [e] \\ L & & V & \text{———}\!\!\!\!\!\!\!\!\!\!\!\! & LT & u & S & \eta \end{array}$$

1. Surplus, Excess, Waste, Leftovers, and Remainders

Commodities (C) possess both use-value or utility (u) and exchange-value or value (V). To enter the exchange relation I ([r]) must have a surplus labor product (S) that no longer has utility for me but does have utility for some other person ([e]). This surplus utility is the property of a self, an objectification of consciousness or mind crystallized (cf. Weber 1978, p. 1,402 where the means of production and bureaucracy are "mind objectified" and "objectified intelligence") open to alienation hence convertible from a property of self to formal, legal property able to be disposed of in a transaction.

I must also have a need or lack (L) something that the other has. So that my commodity may be elevated to a value and that I may have my needs met, I must alienate the use-value (h), the analytic properties of my thing, in order to reduce it to a quantity of labor time (LT) which then marks the magnitude of the thing's value and is expressed as a price (P) which guards the utility-to-be as a moral force field. Price (P) is artificially introduced here into the accidental form which is essentially nothing but random barter. Here, instead of actual money prices we would have only an expression of how much socially necessary labor time was crystallized into the product. Could not the "severe and humiliating conditions under which the wives of usurers might be admitted" to the church (see Weber 1958, p. 260) not be considered a "price" even in the absence of money exchange?

The essential aspect here is that through alienation the commodity ([r]) finds its expression as a moral status in the physical body and shape of the other's ([e]) commodity. This seems all rather commonplace until we consider what is eclipsed in the diagram: the people hidden behind the exchange. The relation between people is reduced to a relation between things. If C[r] is the labor power of a human being and the C[e] is the wage offered by an employer, we venture into the world of science fiction in which vampires really do exist, where 2=3, and water may indeed be transformed into wine. The potential worker, in order to become a worker, must alienate a portion of his or her total self (what employer ever purchases the whole self?). The worker must rest content with appearing only as labor power (skill set, time, and energy) in the eyes of the other.

We might refer to this as the "socially necessary" use-value of the worker. Idiosyncrasies, surpluses of the worker which are not essential in the organic composition of capital for the creation of surplus value, are variables to be dealt with or, if the worker is unable to suppress them voluntarily, then eradicated through transformations in the means of production. Here the employee-to-be is a dismembered and disfigured husk of a total person, as in Hegel's discussion of *laesio enormis* ("excessive damage") within the unethical contractual relation (Hegel [1821] 1991, p. 107). To become Other I must become a thing. Undoubtedly, the leftovers not reducible to the concept of variable capital are reluctantly brought into the labor process, but this excess that the worker drags behind him into the employment contract is yet one more thing the capitalist must wage war on.

This all sounds rather grim. However, if one is "successful" in exchanging a part of onesself for wages one will acquire a new quality: the title of the employee. This does not sound like a cause for celebration but being employed, subordinating oneself to the "unity of the count," means *being someone*—literally counting. As Badiou (2003: 9–10) argues, "On the one hand, there is an extension of the automatism of capital, fulfilling one of Marx's inspired predictions: the world finally configured, but as a market, as a world-market. This configuration imposes the rule of an abstract homogenization. Everything that circulates falls under the unity of a count, while inversely, only what lets itself be counted in this way can circulate."

We focused on the commodity but a similar exposition could have taken the relation between clans and totems (Durkheim) or subjects and disciples in relation to their kings and prophets (Weber)—the empirical work of both derives conceptually from Hegel—"For since the rational, which is synonymous with the Idea, becomes actual by entering into external existence [*Existenz*], it emerges in an infinite wealth of forms, appearances, and shapes and surrounds its core with a brightly coloured covering in which consciousness at first resides, but which only the concept can penetrate in order to find the inner pulse, and detect its continued beat even within the external shapes. But the infinitely varied circumstances which take shape within this externality as the essence manifests itself within it, this infinite material and its organization, are not the subject-matter of philosophy" (Hegel [1821] 1991, pp. 20–21).

Thus, commodity circulation only conceals or fetishizes the social relation between owners of property, regardless of how diverse and extensive it may appear. So, if the "sublime objectivity" of a thing, i.e. its moral status, is acquired in relation to and in the material shape of a non-identical other (but quantitatively identical), the same can be said to obtain for people. We obtain our moral and second (social) natures by virtue of our alienating relations with others. Like the commodity, to be recognized and to be realized as a "value" (to become simultaneously less than and more than my self) I must alienate myself, become a thing, and desire the form of the other (my equivalent)—my identity is predicated on the non-identity between myself and the other; difference as the foundation for equivalence.

After this transubstantiation has run its course there is always a remainder, something left over in the wake of the transformation. The worker who exchanges labor power for wages experiences this remainder as the waste of his self not incorporated into the labor process. Of course, once we move beyond the accidental value form the social relations become dense and the other appears to us, on the one hand, as the infinitude of others and, on the other, an absolute, and universal Other. The circulation of commodities has moved well beyond a series of accidental encounters and totemic emblems have long since given way to gods and other transfigured historical extensions such as the transcendent force of money — the "visible divinity" of modernity. If *money* is the bond binding me to *human* life, binding society to me, binding me and nature and man, is not money the bond of all *bonds*? Can it not dissolve and bind all ties? Is it not, therefore, the universal *agent of separation*? It is the true agent of *separation* as well as the true *binding agent*— the [universal] *galvano-chemical* power of society. Shakespeare stresses especially two properties of money: (1) It is the visible divinity — the transformation of all human and natural properties into their contraries, the universal confounding and overturning of things: it makes brothers of impossibilities. (2) It is the common whore, the common pimp of people and nations. The overturning and confounding of all human and natural qualities, the fraternization of impossibilities — the *divine* power of money — lies in its *character* as men's estranged, alienating and self-disposing *species nature*. Money is the alienated *ability of mankind*" (Marx 1964, pp. 167–68).

The barriers and frontiers that separated the sacred and profane have receded with the development of money relations. Areas of social life that were formerly experienced as discrete "islands of meaning" (Zerubavel 1991) run together, and "all that is solid melts into air." As such, what Marx called the "ontology of passions" (1964, p. 165), our collective representations, myths, shared fantasies, and ideologies, always determined by concrete social relations and the limitations of the signifying regime, take the form of composites and distorted condensations (the language of dream-work *qua* ideology-work) that fuse the signs of power, god, and money. Modern antisemitism is perhaps the most "perfected," interdigitated ideological thought form in circulation. The antipode of theology, political economy, and sociology, antisemitism nonetheless functions as a distorted, synthetic, and authoritarian system of explanation capable of resolving all questions of power, god, and money by summing and condensing all excesses and leftovers into the image of "the Jew." Yet to fully understand "the Jew" as envisioned by the antisemite, we must first understand the conceptual terrain of which the vision is a part. For it is not in the observable, material world that the antisemite deduces the object of his hatred, but rather he conjures his "Jew" from the ether of a vivid imagination that fails to accurately interpret the real world. We must therefore turn to an imagined world, or perhaps more accurately, the real world perceived through imagination.

Power, God, and Money

The classical tradition clearly articulates a material position, but not exclusively. When the principle texts of classical sociological theory are considered as a totality, i.e., the works of Marx, Weber, and Durkheim, a clear center emerges in the conceptual nexus of *value, charisma, and mana*. A tremendous quantity of material has been generated dealing with these concepts in themselves but very little exists in the way of theorizing the relationship which involves, among other things, an ideational-material nexus. Marx, Weber, and Durkheim each pointed out, by way of analogy and intimation, the parallel logic of, say, in the case of Marx, the commodity and the king, or, as in the case of Weber, the identical nature of charisma and mana. As such we know each phenomena as a process and result: fetishized collective consciousness and alienation — "people have reposed their faith in social powers 'projected' into things and people — commodities, in which the powers of producers are reified or 'materialized,' and authorities, in who the powers of the social ensemble are personified or 'etherealized'" (Smith 1995, p. 114). Antisemitism represents one form of alienated subjectivity and process of fetishization. Assuming a demonological, confused, and dangerous form, antisemitism attempts to explain the interpenetration of power, god, and money. The representation of Jews that we find at the center of the antisemitic imagination distortedly signifies the nexus of what sociology approaches as value, authority, and sacred forces — the fantasy Jew is the personification and embodiment of that relation but in a manner that obfuscates rather than penetrates the truth of those social forces.

Charisma

Few concepts provide as much controversy and misunderstanding as "charisma." The term is as obscure as it is popular and many sociologists know little more than Max Weber "invented it" even though he did not (Smith 1998, p. 34). Charisma is an unstable, revolutionary, shared form of consciousness and relation born from "collective excitement produced by extraordinary events and from surrender to heroism of any kind" (Weber 1978, p. 1,121) and can form the basis of authority. The everyday understanding of charisma assumes that some people or social segments, institutions, etc., are naturally endowed with "supernatural" or *otherworldly* powers or that charisma is somehow an "automatic function" of some personality types (Smith 1998, p. 33). Authoritarianism is dependent upon this belief in otherworldly powers as typified in the writings of Ernst Jünger.

> I had often met eminent persons — I think of those involved with the innermost wheels of our machinery of state who are very close to the invisible axle ... they all had something in common, something imposing, which is recognized, if not by everyone, then by a great many people, especially those with simple rather than complicated natures. A philoso-

pher, for instance, a rearranger of facts and ideas, who is endowed with this spirit, can fascinate his listeners even when they don't understand a word of his lecture. Spellbound, they will hang on his lips. The same effect is possible in other fields. Apparently a direct recognition of greatness exists, wholly independent of intellectual comprehension. We react like magnets to an electric current [1960, pp. 61–62].

In Weber's sociology, charisma was *not* an analytic property of the bearer or a personal trait.

The bearer of power is always distinct from the power itself. As Marx observed in relation to the use-value of some commodity and its exchange value: "Value is independent of the particular use-value by which it is borne, but a use-value of some kind has to act as its bearer" (1976, p. 295). By this logic even an object with no value (i.e., no labor time has been embedded in it) can stand in and be treated "as if" it possessed value which is only one more form of collective moral energy (ibid., p. 223) so it should come as no surprise when we find "props" that by any account exhibit a gulf between their analytic or personal properties and the grandiose, "magical" power accorded them. The decisive aspects of charisma and charismatic authority are not the "gifts" of the leader but the *relation* itself. Followers standing in the radiated glory of their leader are only basking in their own reflected energies — conferred mental energy, or, in other words, their surplus of consciousness. Charisma is transposable and shares an identity with other social forces.

> [C]harismatic domination is by no means limited to primitive stages of development ... As far as we know the early stages of social life, every concerted action that transcends the traditional mode of satisfying economic needs in the household has a charismatic structure. Primitive man perceives all external influences that shape his life as the actions of specific forces which are inherent in things and men, living and dead, and give them the power to do good as well as harm. The entire conceptual apparatus of primitive tribes, including their nature-and-animal-fables, proceeds from such assumptions. Concepts like *mana, orenda* and similar ones, the meaning of which ethnography explains to us, denote such specific forces whose supernatural character is exclusively due to the fact that they are not accessible to everybody but linked to some definite carrier — person or object. Magic and heroic qualities are nothing but particularly important instances of such specific powers. Every event transcending the routines of everyday life releases charismatic forces, and every extraordinary ability creates charismatic beliefs, which are subsequently weakened again by everyday life [Weber 1978, pp. 1133–34].

Weber is in direct accord with Durkheim's analysis of mana:

> Man does not recognize himself; he feels somehow transformed and in consequence transforms his surroundings. To account for the very particu-

lar impressions he receives, he imputes to the things with which he is most directly in contact properties that they do not have, exceptional powers and virtues that the objects of ordinary experience do not possess. In short, upon the real world where profane life is lived, he superimposes another that, in a sense, exists only in his thought, but one to which he ascribes a higher kind of dignity than he ascribes to the real world of profane life [Durkheim (1912) 1995, p. 424].

It should be clear, as it was to Weber, that mana and charisma are not only synonymous but survive in multiple forms, including the transfigured extensions (sometimes we see in Weber the notion of "survivals") that wash up on the shore of the future, bearing in many cases, alien and contradictory features. Durkheim's phenomenology of absolute power traced the transfigured extensions of mana and, like Weber, placed the origin of those forces within the "collective effervescence" of society itself.

Mana

In *Elementary Forms*, Durkheim claims that "As regards social things, we still have the mind-set of primitives." Further, he says:

> But if, in matters sociological, so many people today linger over this old-fashioned idea, it is not because social life seems obscure and mysterious to them. Quite the opposite: If they are so easily contented with such explanations, if they cling to these illusions that are repeatedly contradicted by experience, it is because social facts seem to them the most transparent things in the world. This is so because they have not yet appreciated the real obscurity, and because they have not yet grasped the need to turn to the painstaking methods of the natural sciences in order progressively to sweep away the darkness. The same cast of mind is to be found at the root of many religious beliefs that startle us in their oversimplification [Durkheim (1912) 1995, p. 25].

The "real obscurity" of social facts lies in their dialectical nature — precisely in Marx's sense that the energies and creations of humans, once liberated, return like a nightmare upon the living. Put simply, mana and its equivalents: wakan, orenda, charisma, pokunt, manitou, mauala, yek, logos, and so on for every culture and society that has hitherto existed, all signify one thing: "Power in the absolute, without qualification or limitation of any kind" (Durkheim [1912] 1995, p. 195). Mana, or, the same thing, absolute power, power pure and simple, is nebulous and impersonal yet capable of being crystallized into a myriad of objects not limited to the totem but also in words, food, etc. — there is "nothing in the world [that] is without its own share of orenda...." (ibid., p. 196). As Bourdieu argues more recently, "Symbolic power works partly through the control of other people's bodies and belief that is given by the collectively recognized capacity to act in various ways on deep-rooted linguistic and muscular patterns of behaviour, either by neutralizing them or by reactivating them to function mimetically" (Bourdieu 1990, p. 69).

Mana is thus "a principle of universal explanation," "immanent in certain categories of men and things," unequally distributed, has sacred as well as profane and "secular aspects," the object of desire and struggle, oppressive, authoritative, held simultaneously in awe and dread, deadly, vitalizing, capable of specialization and differentiation, imprecisely symbolized, and it develops complexity and comprehensiveness along with the development of social organization to the point where, theoretically, all forces become consolidated. "The notion of one universal mana could be born only when a religion of the tribe developed above the clan cults and absorbed them more or less completely. It is only with the sense of tribal unity that a sense of the world's unity arose" (Durkheim [1912] 1995, p. 199).

Each social segment has unequal access to its own form of power including magical and evil forces. Yet, despite the spread of mana, its various faces are but moments of a totality. The essential point lies in the *consubstantiality* of particular forces. "Such is the basic material from which were made the various beings that religions of all times have worshipped and sanctified. The spirits, demons, genies, and gods of every degree are only the concrete forms taken by this energy ... as it became individualized and fixed upon some definite object or point in space, and condensed around some being that is ideal or legendary, yet conceived of as real in popular imagination" (Durkheim [1912] 1995, p. 201). Any "mythological constructions" that arise from society are but "secondary products overgrowing a substratum of beliefs — simpler and more obscure, vaguer and more fundamental — that constitute the firm foundations on which the religious systems were built" (ibid, p. 205).

I want to avoid suggesting that antisemitism is a religious system in the conventional sense of a system of life conduct and I certainly want to avoid the suggestion that contemporary demonology and authoritarianism are simply identical with totemism as other authors have done. However, with Durkheim, it is more than plausible that antisemitic ideology, in all its shapes, including the purely secular moments, represents a secondary formation rooted in earlier and obscure "substratum" of religious forces because religious forces are nothing but social forces *transfigured*. Of course, mana and its various analogs are only "social pressures" experienced and "felt through mental channels" (ibid, p. 211). People experience a collective force and social facts at work over and against them. This force is felt in "the most desperate realms" and it is this force that unites all the various social realms into one comprehensive social system. "In one sense, the force was fundamentally human, since, it was made of human ideas and feelings; at the same time, it could not but appear as closely akin to the animate or inanimate being that gave it outward form. The cause we are capturing at work is not exclusive to totemism; there is no society in which it is not at work. Nowhere can a collective feeling become conscious of itself without fixing upon a tangible object" (Durkheim [1912] 1995, p. 238).

Any secondary construct or "tangible object" filled with projected energy is but a transfigured representation of social dynamism itself. And the notion that the individual merely "invents" a thing as he or she sees fit in an arbitrary fashion should be avoided as with the idea that the empirically existing "envelope" that carries some moral status has anything to do with the status itself. As Durkheim insists, "social thought, with its imperative authority, has a power that individual thought cannot possibly have. By acting on our minds, it can make us see things in the light that suits it; according to circumstances, it adds to or takes away from the real. Hence, there is a realm of nature in which the formula of idealism is almost literally applicable; that is the social realm. There, far more than anywhere else, the idea creates reality.... The object that serves as a prop for the idea does not amount to much as compared to the ideal superstructure under which it disappears, and, furthermore, it has nothing to do with that superstructure" (ibid, p. 230).

If mana and charisma seem like remote or exceptional phenomena compared to the "routines of everyday life," it is nonetheless true that we are surrounded by "otherworldly" forces in our everyday lives (though they may appear to natural consciousness to be perfectly "natural" and normal) and that our most mundane activities contribute to the efficacy of these "otherworldly" powers. In *Elementary Forms*, Durkheim makes the claim that "Only one form of social activity has not as yet been explicitly linked to religion: economic activity. Nevertheless, the techniques that derive from magic turn out, by this very fact, to have indirectly religious origins. Furthermore, economic value is a sort of power or efficacy, and we know the religious origins of the idea of power. Since mana can be conferred by wealth, wealth itself has some. From this we see that the idea of economic value and that of religious value cannot be unrelated; but the nature of these relationships has not yet been studied" (ibid, p. 421). This idea was amplified by Mauss in his discussion of Simian's "La Monnaie RÈalitÈ Sociale" where he points out that in many clan cultures the concept of the sacred principle (e.g., mana, wakan, etc.) was identical with the category of money (Mauss 1934). And it is not surprising that Durkheim's analysis of mana (orenda, wakan, et al.) should appear so similar to Marx's analysis of the commodity even though totemic religious practices have, seemingly, nothing at all in relation to capitalism and have, in fact, disappeared almost entirely from the world. Compare Marx's theory of abstract labor with Durkheim's description of the Dakota's conception of orenda: "It is not a defined or definable power, the power to do this or that; it is Power in the absolute, without qualification or limitation of any kind. The various divine powers are only particular manifestations and personifications; each of them is this power seen in one of its many aspects" ([1912] 1995, p. 195). Now it is true that abstract labor and orenda are two qualitatively separate social phenomena particular to specific times and places but they participate in the same social logic. What makes labor abstract is a form of collective consciousness: value and the desire for surplus value. The same can be said of the conversion of a clan representation into the highest, most abstract representation of all clan representations taken together. Marx found that the commodity relation operated essentially the same as the political authority relation. The moral status of the king, prince, etc., was essentially the same possessed by the commodity.

What is this moral substance that penetrates the prince and the commodity and confers upon them both the quality of sacred or authoritative? Examining Marx's theory of the commodity and the value form reveals a deep connection between the collective consciousness of the clan and value as a way of acting, thinking, and feeling in the modern world.

Value

Value is a collective, social way of thinking about labor, time, and the exchange of commodities. Marx says that value is "purely ideal or notional" (1976a, p. 189) and "quite distinct from [the] palpable and real bodily form." Value acquires its existence as a social status or substance once labor products enter into a relation of exchange with each other. The value of a thing is determined by the quantity of socially necessary labor time that the commodity embodies. Value is borne aloft by material carriers, the utilities in which it resides in varying quantities — varying in proportion to the amount of abstract human labor that is congealed within them, but value itself is a purely abstract. People understand and talk about value in the language of prices and money and, indeed, many self-professed Marxologists are incapable of distinguishing between value and price. Price is how value appears to the natural consciousness. As such, sociologically, "value-forms must be grasped semiotically as core phenomena of structured cognition in a world of value-relations" (Smith 2001, p. 58) if we are to move beyond surface appearances.

Once value becomes the socially dominant form of thinking about labor and wealth, once it is "in the saddle" as Weber put it, then "By virtue of being value, it has acquired the occult ability to add value to itself. It brings forth living offspring, or at least lays golden eggs" (Marx 1976a, p. 255). As parts of nature, water is water and wine is wine and never shall the two meet. Yet within the commodity exchange relation transubstantiation is not only possible but magic, science fiction, and vampirism are all very real. Water can easily be transformed into wine or anything else for that matter, $X=Y$, $5 + 1 = 9$ is a rational statement, and the money you carry in your pocket or deposit in the bank is nothing short of the crystallized remains of human energy. Capitalism has made the most extreme, otherworldly, bizarre, and chaotic situations "normal." In the commodity relation, like the totemic ceremony, *anything* is possible; the otherworldly capacity for *transubstantiation* becomes the norm (Marx 1976a, p. 197). Money, like charisma or mana possesses the power of transubstantiation whereby the ugly and stupid is converted to the beautiful and brilliant. These social relations and realities demand to be represented no less than any other fact of society and it should, then, come as little surprise when we find within demonology a simplification of these social processes.

Mana, orenda, wakan, etc., have for all practical purposes vanished from the modern world. These were all premodern, specific clan representations regarding sacred and supernatural forces sustaining life. Where premodern concepts survive they are hybrids, on the wane, and in competition with contemporary concepts. Today we worship other objects that have no relation to the totem yet they retain a similar "sacredness" that rests on a productive effervescence and emotional intensity that is arrived at through generative practices. Does not the labor product bearing a price tag, a commodity, enjoy the same protective, moral force of any other sacred object? Indeed, is not the violation of commodity theft not potentially more severe than profaning a god? Gods and commodities are akin as are demons and heroes. What varies is not the social substance or the logic but the symbols and language that distinguishes each filed or modality of action and thought. The secret lies in the universality of generative social practices and the "ontological" facticity of our powers once they take on a "life" of their own. Zizek's psychodynamic sociology, borrowing from Hegel, Marx, Lacan, et al., approaches the problem with the notion of "enjoyment"— or *jouissance*. As he says, "*jouissance* is 'undecidable,' 'free-floating.' The enthusiasm of fans for their favourite rock star and the religious trance of a devout Catholic in the presence of the Pope are libidinally *the same phenomenon*; they differ only in the different symbolic network which supports them" (1997, p. 50). Gods and demons come and go but society is never without its gods and demons because it never lacks the ability, in one way or another, to externalize, fetishize, and organize people around the "enjoyment" of their own collective energies.

The Death of God, or, the Convergence Force

At the end of *Elementary Forms*, Durkheim said that "the former gods are growing old or dying, and others have not been born.... A day will come when our societies once again will know hours of creative effervescence during which new ideals will again spring forth and new formulas emerge to guide humanity for a time" ([1912] 1995, p. 429). One interpretation of this "death of gods" thesis posits that spirituality and sacredness have been pushed aside by the "iron cage" of commodity fetishism and technical rationality. Yet, simultaneously, the world has not been so disenchanted. The important connection between, say, Durkheim's inquiry into ancient religions and Marx's study of capitalism is the equal capacity of "primitive" and contemporary cultures for living in superimposed fantasy worlds of their own creation. There is a connection between the fetishism of the commodity and the logic of the totem that goes beyond simple analogy. The difference is that the totem's mana was the product of a frenzied effervescence created by intense group activity aimed at communal regeneration — a charismatic moment. The enjoyment of value, on the other hand, has been shifted to ritualized relations with commodities and the pursuit of money.

The idiocy of capitalist production is definitely not the kind of effervescence associated with the rite. In fact, the genius of capitalism lies in its ability to harness and capture social and individual energies in a supervised and joyless manner — unless, as in some cases, where people are working for purposes other than necessity. But, for the vast majority of workers, as Weber makes clear, "The Puritan wanted to work in a calling; we are forced to do so." Any moral virtue affixed to work today is a perverted survival of an earlier, religious conviction that was not to last long.

> For when asceticism was carried out of monastic cells into everyday life, and began to dominate worldly morality, it did its part in building the tremendous cosmos of the modern economic order. This order is now bound to the technical and economic conditions of machine production which to-day determine the lives of all the individuals who are born into this mechanism, not only those directly concerned with economic acquisition, with irresistible force.... Since asceticism undertook to remodel the world and to work out its ideals in the world, material goods have gained an increasing and finally an inexorable power over the lives of men as at no previous period in history. To-day the spirit of religious asceticism — whether finally, who knows? — has escaped from the cage. But victorious capitalism, since it rests on mechanical foundations, needs its support no longer [1958, pp. 181–82].

Money and the "inexorable power" of material goods, commodity fetishism, in other words, have captured the imaginations of those that in previous centuries would have been galvanized by a belief that their labor "counted" for something beyond economic survival. The point is not that money has pushed out the moral or the sacred, rather, purely economic and mundane activities take on a sacred, ritualized hue. Marx wrote in the "Paris Manuscripts" that the modern "ontology of passions" fixated on value arose only with the development of private property (Marx [1844] 1964, p. 165). Today, the preeminent form of authority is money and with Shakespeare, Marx refers to money as the "visible divinity" (ibid, p. 165–67):

> The meaning of private property — apart from its estrangement — is the *existence of essential objects* for man, both as objects of gratification and as objects of activity. By possessing the property of buying everything, by possessing the property of appropriating all objects, *money* is thus the *object* of eminent possession. The universality of its *property* is the omnipotence of its being. It therefore functions as almighty being.... If *money* is the bond binding me to *human* life, binding society to me, binding me and nature and man, is not money the bond of all *bonds*?

Money as the "visible divinity"? This theme of the historical emergence of money (really value, the "sublime objectivity," whereas money is only one expression of that substance) as a paramount authority displacing traditional divinities recurs frequently in Marx's writings perhaps nowhere more clearly than in *Capital* where he states that "It was the 'strange God' who perched himself side by side with the old divinities of Europe on the altar, and one fine day threw them all overboard with a shove and a kick. It proclaimed the making of profit as the ultimate and the sole purpose of mankind" (1976a, p. 918). Was this merely metaphor for Marx? Not only was money the functional equivalent of God in modernity, money *was* God. Literally, we see in Marx the movement away from spiritual authority to the command of capital. "Modern society," says Marx, "which already in its infancy had pulled Pluto by the hair of his head from the bowels of the earth, greets gold as its Holy Grail, as the glittering incarnation of its innermost principle of life" (1976a, p. 230).

The impression we get from Marx is similar to that worked out by Weber in the *Protestant Ethic*: from God to profits, from Protestantism to utilitarianism. However, the argument whereby God had given way to money, as a *profane* substitute (the profanation of the modern world), does not square with the overall analysis offered by classical theory nor with history. Rather, money and God were two distinct faces of the same moral, social substance — identical not in particularity but in the form. Marx wrote that "value suddenly presents itself as a self-moving substance which passes through a process of its own, and for which commodities and money are both mere forms. But there is more to come: instead of simply representing the relations of commodities, it now enters into a private relationship with itself, as it were. It differentiates itself as original value from itself as surplus-value, just as God the Father differentiates himself from himself as God the Son, although both are of the same age and form, in fact one single person" (1976a, p. 256).

The long and the short of all this is that social life is a complex fusion of forces that interpenetrate one another. The economic, political, sacred, etc., resist compartmentalization and collide to form an opaque web of confusion and spectacle — not only in money, now, do we find the "glittering incarnation of its innermost principle of life" (Marx 1976a, p. 230) but, rather, the entire social complex is populated by "magical" and "glittering" embodiments of the sacred — both sacred pure and impure. The social realm, now as always, is a realm of enchantment and enchanted representations. Thus, we move now to understand not the real Jews who actually live, the real people who are Jewish, but rather, and in sharp contrast, the mythical and enchanted Jew who does not and in fact cannot exist. The Jew of the antisemite is a mythical creation conjured within an entire pantheon of perceived supernatural forces — antisemitism.

Antisemitism

Norman Cohn shows us just how myth and belief systems never leap far beyond the material and technical foundations of life. Indra, the Vedic Indian god, was a "hero pre-eminent, powerful, triumphant, exercising might, above every hero, above every fighter, born in might — mount the winning cars, finding cows! Him, cleaving cow-pens open, finding cattle..." (1993, p. 61). By today's standards "plunging with prowess into cowpens" appears as a somewhat limited set of powers. All belief systems, all personifications of social forces unfold with changes in social organization, technology, and the material bases of existence. So, it comes as no surprise that hammer-wielding gods who achieve mobility via wooden carts pulled by goats gave way to planet-eating destroyers of the cosmos. In a world where military and political rulers are capable of wielding the power of miniature stars against their nemeses, representations of the divine must also keep up or evolve.

As representations of the sacred develop so do the faces and capacities of the nefarious other — the impure underside of the sacred pure. Weber provides a good description of the sacred monstrosity in his analysis of Calvinism and the notion of a "double God": The truth is that both Luther and Calvin believed fundamentally in a double God ... the gracious and kindly Father of the New Testament, who dominates the first books of the *Institutio Christiana*, and behind him the *Deus absconditus* as an arbitrary despot. For Luther, the God of the New Testament kept the upper hand, because he avoided reflection on metaphysical questions as useless and dangerous, while for Calvin the idea of a transcendental God won out. In the popular development of Calvinism, it is true, the idea could not be maintained, but what took his place was not the Heavenly Father of the New Testament but the Jehovah of the Old" (Weber 1958, p. 221). How could a god be anything other than double? If, according to Durkheim, gods are but transfigured and hypostatized social forms then they must be essentially dual. What society is not characterized by both the arbitrary execution of power and social order? And one of the central issues here is the victory of order over contingency once the doctrine of predestination was given up in favor of the idea that material success could reveal the "blessing of God." Essential for the Puritan was "the absolute difference of the renewed man from others" and the identification of contingency and arbitrariness with perdition, condemnation, and evil (ibid, pp. 270–71).

Antisemitism, too, has undergone significant changes. When the Institute of Social Research ("Frankfurt School") undertook its analysis of American workers during the Second World War (ISR 1945) it found substantial differences between the American and European patterns of thought (Worrell 2003). The Institute's unpublished, four-volume report was entitled "Antisemitism among American Labor, 1944–45." The principle authors were Arcadius Gurland, Paul Massing, Leo Lowenthal, and Friedrich Pollock. For a complete analysis of the Institute's wartime labor antisemitism study consult Worrell (2003) "The Dialectic of Solidarity: Labor, Antisemitism, and the Frankfurt School."

Among other findings, the unpublished study revealed that, for American workers, the idea that Jews participated in the ritual murder of Christian children, drank blood, poisoned wells, roamed primeval and dark forests, and engaged in unspeakable sexual perversities were basically nonexistent. Gone even, except for a small minority, was the cosmological notion that a secret cabal of Jews controlled the whole world. Sure, they thought, Jews "are everywhere" and "control everything" but that did not mean, in the minds of antisemitic workers, that Jews were engaged in a global conspiracy (a New World Order) the way the fringe, fundamentalist Right in contemporary America does. American workers just did not buy it. For them, the pressing issue was, generally, the unentitled possession of money. Jews simply had too much money and issues such as undue influence in politics and unequal access to educational opportunities were all routes that led back, in the end, to Jewish money. In short, the mind of the antisemitic American worker in the mid–40s was dominated by money, prices, and business.

The Institute classified 566 workers into eight distinct groups on the basis of their attitudes toward Jews:

Type A: Exterminatory. 10.6%. These people were actively violent, vicious antisemites who openly favored the extermination of all Jews.

1. Surplus, Excess, Waste, Leftovers, and Remainders   23

Type B: Intense Hatred. 10.2%. These were definitely and unwaveringly hostile toward Jews but avoided openly advocating the extermination of Jews. Taken together, Types A and B (20.8 percent) constituted beliefs that were proto-fascist or "Nazi-like."

Type C: Inconsistently Hostile. 3.7%. These people were outspokenly hostile to Jews and possessed a desire to see Jews regulated or controlled but were inconsistent in this attitude; they exhibited an inner conflict.

Type D: Intolerant. 6.2%. This type of person wanted to avoid Jews, get away from them, and to see legislative action taken to separate Jews from everyone else.

Type E: Ambivalent. 19.1%. These people could not make up their minds. While they were potentially antisemitic, they could have gone both ways in terms of their tolerance of Jews. This type felt that Jews had too much power or money, and that something should have been done about it, but they didn't know what should be done. They were undecided.

Type F: Consciously Tolerant/Emotionally Inconsistent. 19.3%. These types were opposed to antisemitism at the level of humanitarian ideals and distaste for injustice. The Type F worker may have been mildly intolerant of Jews but was opposed to it at the level of "conscious intentions" so they worked to control any emotional prejudice.

Type G: Anti-discriminatory/Tolerant but still prone to stereotypes visible in friendly criticism. 10.8%. These people did not harbor any dislike of Jews, were opposed to discrimination but did criticize some character traits commonly ascribed to Jews. Their criticism was based, said the Institute, on reasoning if not in facts.

Type H: Absolutely not antisemitic. 20.1%. No resentment, no criticism whatsoever.

That more than 20 percent of the interviewees were virtual Nazis vis-à-vis their hatred of Jews (and an additional 10 percent were clearly intolerant) came as a shocking surprise to the Institute and the organizations that helped to finance the research: the Jewish Labor Committee and the American Jewish Committee. Workers were not simply antisemitic in a vague sense but, on the contrary, they hated Jews for specific reasons.

The ISR found nine "areas" or ways in which workers expressed antisemitic prejudice. These nine "areas" were divided into three "complexes of accusations": Area I: Personal Attributes; Area II: Economic Attributes; Area III: Political/Power factors (see Table 1).

Table 1: Worker Dimensions of Anti-Jewish Hostility

Area of Anti-Jewish Criticism	% of Total Sample	% of Interviewees Expressing Criticism
Area I: Personal		
Clannishness	22.4	28.0
Aggressiveness	37.6	47.1
Sexuality	1.2	1.5
Area II: Economic		
Jews in Business/Too Much Control	22.1	27.7
Mercenary Attitudes/Money-Minded	55.1	69.0
Not Workers	15.9	9.9
Area III: Political		
Too Much Power	13.3	6.6
Education/Too Much Privilege	3.4	4.2
Weak War Effort on the Part of the Jews	34.3	42.9

Table 1 summarizes large quantities of data (the totals sum to more than 100 percent because workers expressed hostility toward Jews across the full array of accusational complexes) and point in many interesting directions only a few of which I can pursue here. First of all, 79.9 percent of workers interviewed (i.e., the total sample) expressed a criticism of Jews; 62.8 percent of workers who criticized Jews did so based on the perceived personal attributes of Jewish people; 80.1 percent expressed criticism of Jews based upon the perceived economic activities of Jews; and 51.6 percent did so from a political/power viewpoint. The level of antisemitic prejudice based on supposed Jewish economic conduct outweighed the other areas by roughly 17 percent (personal) and 28 percent (political). Aggressiveness (Area I), "money-mindedness" (Area II), and weak Jewish war effort (Area III) came to the foreground during interviews and dominated worker concerns about Jews.

Two points stand out in the ISR-offered interpretation: first, the supposed "sexual character" of Jews was insignificant for the vast majority of workers; this presupposes, however, that sexual motives were conscious and they may not have been. It is plausible that worker concern regarding "power" and "war effort," etc., were but transfigured manifestations of unconscious sexual materials. This is unknown. Nonetheless, only 1.2 percent had any criticism in this area. This fact set American workers apart from their European counterparts. The Institute theorized that Jewish stereotypes had not merged with sexual mythology due to the presence of blacks in the U.S. who had already been stigmatized with the notion of deviant sexuality.

Secondly, 16.6 percent of the workers critical of Jews for their perceived overabundance of political power intimated that they were resentful of a "mystical power attributed to Jews" or that they had "demonic qualities." This meaning does not come through clearly in the above tabulations but was derived from the ISR's interpretations. As they said,

> While only 4.2 % of those expressing critique take offense at the alleged higher educational status of Jews, four times as many [16.6%] are resentful of some mystical power attributed to Jews quite out of proportion to their share in the population.... Charges preferred against Jews because of undue control they are said to have seized or to be aspiring to are mostly characterized by inarticulateness and vagueness. They belong to the realm of myth. Jews are pictured as exercising or coveting tremendous power within society — either through control of economic life or in addition to the latter. Hostile or critical statements in this field claim that Jews run the world, or the country, or the country's government, or that they try to do so; that they have too much power; that they control public opinion, communications, amusement industries; that they are a destructive element which ruins the country or the world; that they have infiltrated the administration of countries, states, cities, that they strive for power through clandestine manipulations, through political radicalism, etc. [ISR 1945, pp. 194–95].

Most workers who criticized Jews did so not for their "demonic qualities" (and the "mythical powers" of Jews, in the mind of American workers, still did not extend beyond normal institutions) but out of concern for "down to earth issues." In other words, "Anti-semitic accusations, far from being limited to mysteries of Jewish power, are leveled at alleged facts" (ISR 1945, p. 203).

Table 2

Area of Criticism	ABCD	E	F	G
	% of interviewees in each type of intensity			
Area I: Personal	%	%	%	%
Clannishness	23.0	30.6	29.1	36.0
Aggressiveness	48.9	50.0	43.6	42.6
Sexual Behavior	2.9	1.9	—	—
Area II: Economic				
Jews in Business	38.5	28.7	15.5	16.4
Mercenary/Money-Minded	79.9	74.1	66.4	32.8
Jews not Workers	27.6	24.1	10.0	8.2
Area III: Political Power				
Power	30.5	14.8	5.5	—
Education	2.9	1.9	8.2	4.9
Diminished War Effort	59.2	42.6	33.6	13.1

Table 2 helps to clarify the relationship between the "types" of antisemitic workers and the way in which they thought of Jews. It also helps to illustrate the contours of ambivalence and the manner in which ambivalence was distributed in prejudicial terms. One of the most striking things to emerge from the data includes worker antipathy toward the perceived aggressiveness of Jews. Across different degrees of anti-Jewish sentiment, the emphasis on "aggressiveness" was strong, as was the feeling that Jews were interested only in money (the mercenary spirit). Two more things stand out significantly: the sharp decline in anti-Jewish sentiment in the political realm — specifically on the attitudes toward "power" and Jewish participation in the war effort. The political criticisms offered by antisemitic respondents (Type A through D) were, as the ISR concluded on the basis of other data,

> substantially mythical, irrational quality. Here ... we note a steeply ascending curve of resentment. It starts at zero in the least antisemitic group and climbs up to 30.5 per cent in the most antisemitic group. This indicates the change from more or less rational critique to highly irrational aggression. The less people reason about Jews, the less they rein their emotional aversions and dislikes, the more they are inclined to view Jews in terms of fantastic stories of 'Jewish Power,' 'Jewish control,' etc. [ISR 1945, p. 210].

There existed a "direct correlation between intensity of general anti-Jewish prejudice and critique of Jewish war effort." Likewise, the belief that Jews were all-powerful corresponded to high antisemitism and the belief that Jews did nothing to contribute to the war effort.

Table 3: Major Areas of Critique and Degree of Intensity of Prejudice Directed at Major Areas: Personal, Economic, Social-Political

(a) Extreme hostility, extermination	51.6	98.3	71.7
(b) Extreme hostility, elimination	63.8	87.9	69.0
(c) Active hostility, inconsistent	52.4	76.2	61.9
(d) Strong hostility, restrict	74.3	88.6	62.9
(a, b, c, d) antisemites	60.3	90.2	67.8
(e) Prejudiced undecided	63.9	83.3	49.1
(f) Non-discrimination, emotional bias	61.8	76.4	46.4
(g) Non-discrimination, rational critique	68.9	50.8	18.0
(f,g) Non-discrimination but critique	64.1	67.6	36.5
All expressing critique (a, b, c, d, e, f, g)	62.7	79.9	51.4

Expressions of Critique as Percentage of Total for Each Column

(a) Extreme hostility, extermination	10.9	16.3	18.6
(b) Extreme hostility, elimination	13.0	14.1	17.2
(c) Active hostility, inconsistent	3.9	4.4	5.6

1. Surplus, Excess, Waste, Leftovers, and Remainders 27

(d) Strong hostility, restrict	9.2	8.6	9.4
(a, b, c, d) antisemites	37.0	43.4	50.7
(e) Prejudiced undecided	24.3	24.9	22.7
(f) Non-discrimination, emotional bias	23.9	23.2	21.9
(g) Non-discrimination, rational critique	14.8	8.6	4.7
(f + g) Non-discriminating but critique	38.7	31.8	26.6
All expressing critique (a, b, c, d, e, f, g)	100	100	100

Workers who desired to see Jews exterminated, eliminated, restricted, or were actively hostile toward Jews were overwhelmingly attracted to the perceived economic practices over personal, political, and social factors. Only 20 percent of the sample held no criticism of Jews whatsoever. Of the workers who criticized Jews for their perceived personal or political-social qualities, roughly twice as many or more were inclined to see Jews exterminated, controlled, regulated, or exposed to active hostility (a, b, c, d) than subjected to "rational" or non-discriminatory criticism (f, g) and among the workers who had political-social criticisms of Jews, more than half wanted to see Jews exterminated, eliminated, controlled, or subjected to active hostility. But descriptive statistics tell only part of the story.

The hatred of Jews amounted to the problem of money: clannishness meant Jewish solidarity for the purposes of enriching Jewish access to money, jobs, and resources; Jews were aggressive as bargainers and demanders of higher prices; sexual practices was essentially an irrelevant concern; Jews were "all in business," i.e., they were rooted in the interstices and margins of the capital-labor axis as parasites and exploiters and they represented an anachronistic historical leftover from earlier forms of economic organization; Jews were interested only in money, were money-minded, and were mercenaries in their acquisition of money at any cost; Jews did not "work" for their money — Jews were "always running around" getting the "soft jobs" and if they were found on the shop floor it was only to avoid the draft; Washington was filled with Jews who were pulling the strings in order to put defense contracts into the hands of Jewish firms and to make sure that other Jews did not have to fight in the "Jewish war"; Jews were hyperintellectual and made too much out of education as a means of making money — education was yet one more way for Jews to avoid real work and make more than their fair share of money as parasites (especially lawyers) living off the sweat of real workers; and, finally, the war was used by Jews as a means to make more money — they had no interest in seeing it come to an end and they certainly were not going to contribute to its prosecution. Ultimately, Jews were money, commodities, and capital personified: Jews were synonymous with the opacity of the exchange process at the local store; Jews were condensed symbolic stand-ins for the mystery of the value-price relation; Jews were the personification of the labor-power-for-wages exchange relation; Jews represented the capitalist mode of production, and so on. Jews were value—the face of the self-moving mover.

Antisemitic workers did not participate in theoretical culture and, in fact, out of the hundreds of workers interviewed the Institute found none that fit the model of the left-wing revolutionary. When we return to the concept of the dialectic of alienation within the matrix of worker antisemitism we see the introduction of a mediating substance that intervenes between the worker and his or her other. The exchange relation between two owners of property is a relatively simple process compared to a worker standing in relation to the sum total of all vital social relations. That workers overwhelmingly saw the Jew as a money problem we can surmise that they were themselves money-minded; they were members of the "cult of the dollar" but they did not comprehend their "double god."

Being a worker meant, first and foremost, the sale of labor power. And antisemitic workers were hostile to the idea of Jews selling their labor power and finding work in defense plants. For the antisemite, the Jew was no worker at the level of pure being. A Jew on the shop floor was an abomination of the worker/craft concept (even if the worker had no skills of his own he still defended the sanctity of work). The presence of the Jew defiled the purity of the job. Why the concern with the sanctity and purity of something as mundane and gritty as the labor process? In the premodern world, transcendent and monstrous forces responsible for collective identity and solidarity were the product of religious rites. Work was a necessary evil to be avoided as much as possible (cf. Weber on the creation of the modern, formally free laborer). In modernity religious forces, if not irrelevant, have been eclipsed by the "visible divinity" of money, commodities, and capital—i.e., the three faces of value. The special function of the rite was the capturing and focusing of collective energies ("collective effervescence") and projecting those energies into totemic emblems. For the Calvinist, it was the doctrine of predestination that liberated the "active energies of the elect" and enabled them in their "struggle to rationalize the world" (Weber 1958, p. 224). Value is not created by rites and ceremonies but by the exploitation of living labor power—all things being equal—and the dynamics of the organic composition of capital that correspond, at the level of analogy, to the relation between clan member and rite. The means of production capture, focus, and project energy (labor power is, after all, energy) into the products of labor. If money (value) is the dominant form that the moral energy of society takes then the circuitous route to the generation, distribution, acquisition, and appropriation of money becomes the core preoccupation for members of a value society.

Jews as bosses perverted (as an impure mediation) the good worker—entitled boss relation. Antisemitic workers desired recognition but of an

1. Surplus, Excess, Waste, Leftovers, and Remainders 29

authoritarian form: to be neither outstanding nor one who could not carry their weight, neither rate-buster nor shirker. The antisemitic workers desired alienation, to become both less than and more than themselves through abandoning the excess of their selves, but what exactly did they stand in relation to? What exactly were they supposed to exchange their surplus energies for? The fact that labor power was exchanged for wages is not the answer because money was only the quantitative halfway house on the road to qualitative identity and recognition.

In the most simplistic terms it appears that antisemitic workers longed for transparency and simple yet hierarchic relations of authority. They did not want to be in charge and they did not want to be on the bottom of the social order. At work they wanted to be bossed but only by an authentic boss. They had no problem with wage labor but resented irregularities in pay. At the corner shop they wanted transparency in buying and selling. They valued stability and durability rather than "running around" which was completely contradictory because they upheld the American myth of the "pioneer" ethos of upward mobility and personal success yet, in the face of their own failure to advance, lashed out at Jews for "running around." In short, the ideals that workers held in esteem were elements of a worldview that aimed at order, respect, veneration, and stability. But the modern world offers only a plague of divergent opinions and values that threaten to reduce the existent to the level of contingency. The "Jew" marked the threat of contingency as well as the means to transparency.

The Jew was a sign pinned to every excess (anything could become Jewish in this way) and, as such, the sign "Jew" was synonymous with excess. As an "excess" the Jew also marked the coordinates of punishment: as Lowenthal posited, the Jew was that which enjoyed a surplus without paying, enjoyment that went *unpunished*. Socially necessary labor time was the right amount of time. Beyond that, rate-busting, was Jewish; shirking, (s)lack(ing) was Jewish. The average, prevailing wage was right. Excessive pay was Jewish and those that would grovel and willingly accept subaverage wages were Jewish ("garbage dealers"). Prices equilibrated with value were right. High prices and selling below market value were both Jewish. Jews, in short, were identical with every excess and deficiency. Every "obscene excess" (Zizek) of society, that which was arbitrary, was the mark of the Jew.

For the antisemite, the Jew was that mediating, arbitrary substance that frustrated and blocked the necessary and authoritarian moment of alienation in which the self could abandon every idiosyncrasy, every surplus and, in so doing, be elevated, acquire a moral status in the body of the Other: to assume a place in the symbolic order, to have existence eclipsed by the sign. Of course, society offers us nothing but contingency. It is the "Jew" as "quilting point," as "fantasmatic spectre whose presence guarantees the consistency of our symbolic edifice, thus enabling us to avoid confronting its constitutive inconsistency"—the Jew as the antisemite's Lacanian Real (Zizek 2002, p. 32). So, it was not the case that the "Jew" prevented antisemitic workers from properly disposing of their only property (labor power) but enabled them to arbitrarily dispose of their property (self) and "enjoy" it, in the Lacanian sense of *jouissance*. *Jouissance* is pleasure that can be derived from suffering, excitement from the repulsive and disgusting that structures the subject's fantasy (Fink 1995, p. 60). Jouissance is related to the concept of sadomasochism, which is the psychoanalytic underpinning of the theory of authoritarianism that animated so much of the Frankfurt School's wartime empirical work. For our purposes, here, the spectral, fantasy Jew is that which the antisemite enjoys; the Jew is an object of desire and an object that causes desire. As such, the disunity of subject and object, the breach between the antisemite and society leaves a remainder—the Jew. The image of the Jew, the desired object that causes desire, is the leftover that "can sustain the illusion of wholeness" (ibid, p. 59).

The "Jew," as the sign of contingency, enabled the antisemite to participate in the life of value in the only way one can participate in the life of value: as a pure contingency. Here the religious "function" of antisemitism appears: the antisemite is able to disengage "from the *real* order, from the poverty of *things*, and of restoring the *divine* order ... [the purely contingent] is restored to the truth of the intimate world; he receives a sacred communication from it, which restores him in turn to interior freedom" (Bataille [1967] 1989, pp. 57–58). In victimizing the empirical Jew an enjoyable surplus is created. "Once chosen, he [the Jew] is the *accursed share*, destined for violent consumption" (ibid. p. 59).

Antisemitism in Sociological Perspective

Studies of antisemitism typically fall along two analytic and interpretive lines:

(1) there is something about Jews that calls forth hostility and persecution and that if it wasn't for some peculiar, Jewish traits, there would be no basis for hatred and violence, as for example, with Fabre-Luce (in Finkielkraut 1994, p. 58): "With the intrepid pride of an iconoclast, a taboo-smasher, Fabre-Luce makes the daring claim that Jews are partly responsible for the hostility they provoke. Like a friend offering advice, he asks Jews to heal themselves of separatism as quickly as possible, before it's too late— before a new wave of hatred once again overwhelms our beloved land." The signifier "Jew" implicates the material carrier of a social status and calls for some examination of Jewish life as a precondition for eliminating hatred and

violence. Grosser and Halperin (1978, p. 328) say that interpretations of this kind find it impossible to move beyond the sentiment that "it is almost impossible to accept the overwhelming innocence of the Jews in on-going anti-Semitism.... They themselves must in some form be responsible, for they appear at first glance to be the only constant in the long story of anti-Semitism. The persecutors and persecutions appear too varied to be culpable" (cf. Ascheim 1982; Ragins 1980; Wertheimer 1987).

If this were so, the problem of antisemitism would be an easy problem to solve. "If antisemitism is partly a reaction to the conduct or character of living Jews," says Smith, "then Jews may be able to reform antisemites by self-transformation. This is, in fact, exactly what most currents of Jewry have believed in this century. Under various banners (assimilationism and Zionism, Reform and Orthodoxy, liberalism and socialism), Jews have claimed the power to dispel antisemitism by self-reform" (1996, p. 205).

(2) Opposite to the "blame the Jews" theory is the notion that antisemitism is somebody else's problem. Here antisemitism has nothing to do with Jews and everything to do with the mental disposition of those who hate "the Jew" for whatever reason. As such, the signifier "Jew" becomes synonymous with the projected constructions of individuals and groups. As Sartre famously maintained, "Far from experience producing his idea of the Jew, it was the latter which explained his experience. If the Jew did not exist, the anti-Semite would invent him" ([1948] 1976, p. 13). Stephen Wilson, as well, informs us that "antisemitism has an autonomy, a being distinct from its declared object of hostility, and serves many functions which are unrelated to the actual presence of Jews or Jewish communities.

This, it seems, is what Louis Golding meant when he declared in 1938: "The Jewish Problem is in essence a Gentile Problem" (1982, p. xiv). In isolation, these two moments do not help us to traverse the remaining problem: antisemitism is both right (in the Durkheimian sense of being rooted in reality) and totally wrong (while being rooted in the real of society it nonetheless departs from reality by transforming social processes into distorted, myth-like representations.

Foisting the problem of antisemitism, or any form of demonology, upon the victim is antisociological whereas calling antisemitism only a "Gentile problem" borders on psychological reductionism and needs to be elaborated such that we move beyond antisemitism being *merely* an issue of the inner subjective life of the antisemite. If we deny the first position, that Jews bear responsibility for the hatred and violence directed at them, and embrace the hard constructionist perspective we still have a theoretical problem to contend with: today "the theme of 'socially constructed' identities is widely applauded, in myriad idioms. But there is still very little agreement about the implications of this notion for 'the Jews' of antisemitic folklore. Are these

Jews pure phantasmagoric constructions? Or are they, perhaps, distorted but still recognizable reflections of real Jews?" (D. N. Smith 1996, p. 205).

Another perspective, one I have hopefully elaborated here, posits that the antisemitic representation of "the Jew" says (with Sartre, Wilson, et al.) nothing about empirically existing Jewish people yet is more than pure delusion or fantasy. We can neither blame the victim nor take the "hard" constructionist line. As Durkheim noted, even the most absurd and distorted fantasy is, despite its errors, rooted in some kernel of concrete reality. *The bedrock upon which antisemitism is rooted is not the empirical Jew or the mental aberrations of the antisemite but the primary contradictions of society.* To rephrase this in line with the above: the antisemite's constructed Jew is not a "pure phantasmagoric construction" and the "distorted but still recognizable reflection" is not of real Jews but of real social relations. In other words, antisemitism gets "something right" but we can not fall back into making excuses for the antisemite on the basis of, for example, Jews in retail trade or the concentration of Jews in finance.

Rather, by focusing on the *relation* between antisemite and the object of hatred as a fetish reflection of contingent social forces we arrive at a point beyond antisemite and Jew: not Jews in finance, for example, and not even finance itself but the fetishization of capitalism such that it takes on two ideological forms: the productive (Christian) industrial kind and the rapacious (Jewish) finance kind. This compartmentalization of capital, as Massing (1949) argues, was the hallmark of Nazi economic philosophy as well as the antisemitic propaganda of Father Coughlin and sprang from conservative, Catholic economic philosophy.

Antisemites do not understand the logic of "business" but they do understand Jews. "Jew" becomes a name for "business"—which is itself a mere fetish condensation of capitalism. To solve antisemitism we do not proceed to grasp the empirical Jew nor the antisemite—the two separate poles of the antisemitic relation. We do need to know antisemitism as a relation, symptom, and reflection of core social contradictions and relations that perpetuate the authority of a tiny elect over a mass of servants. In a sense, Marx was correct that workers could endure only so much before they raised themselves up to threaten the social order. However, it was not, as we all know, the revolutionary, class-conscious proletariat but the authoritarian mass that has, to date, raised itself up repeatedly.

With any demonizing ideology, personified evil is a transfigured and distorted representation of society and, as such, antisemitism conforms to this social logic. Here, we take antisemitism seriously as more than pure fantasy, "emotional disorder," etc., even though fantasy represents a significant moment in this problem and we avoid the delusion that antisemitism has anything to say about its "object of hatred." This was the approach that

1. Surplus, Excess, Waste, Leftovers, and Remainders 33

Durkheim expounded when he said that evil and the personifications of evil were "nothing other than collectives states objectified; they are society itself seen in one of its aspects" ([1912] 1995, p. 416). As Sartre noted, antisemitism represents a kind of distorted realism toward social facts. "If we attempt to formulate in abstract terms the principle to which the anti-Semite appeals, it would come to this: A whole is more and other than the sum of its parts ... each person is an indivisible totality ... the anti-Semite has chosen to fall back on the spirit of synthesis in order to understand the world" ([1948] 1976, p. 34).

Indeed, the antisemitic portrayal of "the Jew" amounts to an ensemble of representations involving, potentially, all fields of society and history — but the density, kind, and intensity of antisemitism varies with time and place; for example, during the Second World War German antisemitism was not the same as American antisemitism. The differences serve to highlight the truth that ideological forms follow the developments of the material foundations of a given society. The fantasy Jew is like any other god or demon: it is a form of consciousness and logic of representation, peculiar to some segment of society, devoted to explaining authority, wealth, and the workings of transcendental forces. In short, antisemitism is concerned with power, god, and money, and, as such, is characterized by the ambivalence, distortions, confusions, and contradictions found throughout society.

The contradictory nature of antisemitism "is perhaps better understood if [historical] antisemitism is regarded as a complex myth, whose function, like that of other myths, was precisely to contain and express contradiction, to map out the social universe in terms of polarities, such as Money versus Honour, Stock Exchange versus Land, Gold versus Blood, Jew versus Christian or Aryan. In this way, it expressed the experience, the cultural dilemmas of those living in a society whose traditional structures and values were being altered by the process of modernization with unprecedented rapidity" (Wilson 1982, p. 639).

Why antisemitism? There has been much research on why antisemitism exists and why Jews continue to be persecuted. Numerous explanations have been put forward. But, in a sense, there is no real reason. The choice of the Jew was contingent (it could have been otherwise) and antisemites do not even need empirically existing Jews to sustain their hatred. All that is needed are opaque and unjust social contradictions, the word "Jew," and an image to put a face on injustice. If antisemitism is a "social disease" it is because society itself is diseased.

Antisemitism exists because society has failed to achieve the form of an ethical order. To be a person means, necessarily, to alienate oneself to society; to become a thing. Regardless of whether society is good or a moral abortion people subordinate themselves to it. In the case of the unethical, arbitrary social order alienation comes with an excessive "price"— that which is leftover from the "exchange" is a "plague of fantasies," demonological hatred, violence, periodic destruction, etc. If a society has failed to raise itself up above the status of an ethical abomination then there will be antisemitism, or, in the absence of the "Jew" there will be its functional, demonological equivalent. In the end, Marx is probably correct:

> The religious reflections of the real world can, in any case, vanish only when the practical relations of everyday life between man and man, and man and nature, generally present themselves to him in a transparent and rational form. The veil is not removed from the countenance of the social life-process, i.e. the process of material production, until it becomes production by freely associated men, and stands under their conscious and planned control. This, however, requires that society possess a material foundation, or a series of material conditions of existence, which in their turn are the natural and spontaneous product of a long and tormented historical development [1976, p. 173].

Antisemitism will be a recurring problem for a long time and there is no logical reason to exclude from our mental horizon the possibility of mass death on a scale that surpasses anything seen before. If, though, we at some point liberate ourselves from Judeophobia without solving the problems of servitude, contingency of existence, and human life reduced to little more than instruments for the enjoyment of a privileged few, then we can only expect some other segment of the global population to take the place of the Jew.

Ultimately, antisemitism is not about Jews and it is not reducible to the antisemite. Antisemitism is about the contradicting inequalities of society. "The Jew" provides, oddly enough, a mystical transparency. The task ahead is anti-mystical transparency. The Institute of Social Research found that the leading factors responsible for dramatically reducing antisemitic hostility were education and age. They literally found no workers under the age of 25, with college experience, who embraced the extermination of Jews or anything remotely approaching the kind of authoritarian hatred that would threaten Jews. Education tends to melt authoritarianism and its extreme manifestations.

References

Ascheim, Steven E. *Brothers and Strangers*. Madison: University of Wisconsin Press, 1982.
Badiou, Alain. *Saint Paul: The Foundation of Universalism*. Stanford: Stanford University Press, 2003.

1. Surplus, Excess, Waste, Leftovers, and Remainders 35

Bataille, Georges. *The Accursed Share*, vol. 1. 1967. Reprint, New York: Zone Books, 1989.
Bougle, C. *The Evolution of Values*. 1926. Reprint, New York: Kelley, 1970.
Bourdieu, Pierre. *The Logic of Practice*. Translated by Richard Nice. Stanford: Stanford University Press, 1990.
Cohn, Norman. *Cosmos, Chaos and the World to Come*. New Haven: Yale University Press, 1993.
Durkheim, Emile. "The Determination of Moral Facts." Pp. 35–62 in *Sociology and Philosophy*. Translated by D. F. Pocock. 1898. Reprint, New York: The Free Press, 1974b.
———. *The Elementary Forms of Religious Life*. Translated by Karen E. Fields. 1912. Reprint, New York: The Free Press, 1995.
———. "Individual and Collective Representations." Pp. 1–34 in *Sociology and Philosophy*. Translated by D. F. Pocock. 1898. Reprint, New York: The Free Press, 1974a.
Fink, Bruce. *The Lacanian Subject: Between Language and Jouissance*. Princeton: Princeton University Press, 1995.
Finkielkraut, Alain. *The Imaginary Jew*. Lincoln: University of Nebraska Press, 1994.
Freud, Sigmund. *Totem and Taboo*. 1913. Reprint, New York: Norton, 1950.
Grosser, Paul E., and Edwin G. Halperin. *Anti-Semitism: Causes and Effects, Revised and Updated Second Edition*. New York: Philosophical Library, 1978.
Hegel, G. W. F. *Elements of the Philosophy of Right*. 1821. Reprint, Cambridge: Cambridge University Press, 1991.
ISR (Institute of Social Research). Antisemitism among American Labor, 1944–45. Unpublished research report, 1945.
Marx, Karl. *Capital*, vol. 1. Translated by Ben Fowkes. New York: Vintage, 1976.
———. *The Economic and Philosophic Manuscripts of 1864*. New York: International Publishers, 1964.
Mauss, Marcel et al. "Discussion a l'Institut Français de Sociologie." *Annales Sociologiques*, Série D, No. 1: 59–86, 1934.
Ragins, Sanford. *Jewish Responses to Anti-Semitism in Germany, 1870–1914*. Cincinnati: Hebrew Union College Press, 1980.
Sartre, Jean-Paul. *Anti-Semite and Jew*. 1948. Reprint, New York: Schocken Books, 1976.
Smith, David Norman. "Authorities, Deities, and Commodities: Classical Sociology and the Problem of Domination." Unpublished doctoral dissertation, 1988.
———. "The Ethnological Imagination: Making and Remaking History." Pp. 102–119 in *Ethnohistorische Wege und Lehrjahre eines Philosophen*. Frankfurt am Main: Peter Lang, 1995.
———. "Judeophobia, Myth, and Critique." Pp. 123–54 in *The Seductiveness of Jewish Myth*. Edited by S. Daniel Breslauer. Albany: State University of New York Press, 1997.
———. "The Social Construction of Enemies: Jews and the Representation of Evil." *Sociological Theory* 14(3): 203–40, 1996.
———. "The Spectral Reality of Value: Sieber, Marx, and Commodity Fetishism." Pp. 47–66 in *Marx's Capital and Capitalism; Markets in a Socialist Alternative. Research in Political Economy, Vol. 19*. Amsterdam: JAI, 2001.

Weber, Max. *Economy and Society*, vol. 2. Berkeley: University of California Press, 1978.
_____. *The Protestant Ethic and the Spirit of Capitalism*. Translated by Talcott Parsons. New York: Scribner's, 1958.
Wertheimer, Jack. *Unwelcome Strangers: East European Jews in Imperial Germany*. New York: Oxford University Press, 1987.
Wilson, Stephen. *Ideology and Experience*. Rutherford: Farleigh Dickinson University Press, 1982.
Worrell, Mark P. "Dialectic of Solidarity: Antisemitism, Labor, and the Frankfurt School." PhD dissertation, University of Kansas, 2003.
_____. "The Veil of Piacular Subjectivity." *Electronic Journal of Sociology* 4(3): www.sociology.org. 1999.
Zerubavel, Eviatar. *The Fine Line*. Chicago: University of Chicago Press, 1991.
Zizek, Slavoj. *Welcome to the Desert of the Real*. London: Verso, 2002.

2

The Open Dialectic Between Religious and Secular Values and Norms

The Course of Civilization in the 21st Century

Rudolf J. Siebert

Introduction

I would like to invite you to a short discourse about the problem of religious as well as secular notions of unconditional meaning and universal moral values and norms in relation to more or less possible, probable, and desirable alternative futures, as it appears in the perspective of the critical theory of society of the Institute for Social Research at the Johann Wolfgang von Goethe University in Frankfurt a. M., Germany: of the by-now globalized Frankfurt School. In our discourse, we want to explore and explain what the highly secularized critical theory of society of the Frankfurt School may have to say about religious or secular universal moral values and norms rooted in unconditional meaning and being present, or not, in subjectivity and intersubjectivity, marriage and family, civil society, political state, international relations and history, and in culture: particularly about the possibility of the project of a world ethos incarnated in all of them and directed toward a society in which personal autonomy and universal, present, and proleptic solidarity will be reconciled; a society which will be a discourse-mediated solidarity association — in short, a union of free, autonomous human beings.

The Religious and the Secular

In our discourse, we presuppose the insight that modern civil society has from its very start been characterized by a plurality of dichotomies: the more or less intensive and extensive contradictions between the religious and the secular, the genders, the generations, the races, the nations, the classes, facility and belief, theory and praxis, etc. For our present discourse the gulf between the sacred and the profane, religious and secular values and norms, is of greatest importance. We remain, nevertheless, aware of the fact that the dichotomy between the religious and the secular is always interconnected with all the other antagonisms in late capitalist society.

Throughout the past 500 years the modern contradiction between faith and reason, faith-values and norms based on reason, has continually deepened and continues to do so up to the present. From Galileo, Copernicus, and Newton through Darwin, Marx, and Nietzsche to Freud, modern science and philosophy have launched one attack on religion and religious values and norms after the other up to the present debates on war and peace, abortion, homosexuality, stem cell research and cloning, and a new liberal eugenics. The churches have answered with one rear-guard struggle after the other. All religious rear-guard struggles were lost and ended at best with a religious accommodation. The result was an enormous loss of credibility on the side of religion, which weakens its position in its present discourse with modern civil society and culture, particularly with science and philosophy.

Here, of course, must not be forgotten that the modern attacks of science against religion had been provoked in the first place by the Western church and its extreme not only religious, but also cultural and even political, power claims. After the Western church had helped philosophy and science to reach autonomy, it tried to prevent them from developing it further. It remains also true that the counterattack of secular science and philosophy against an oppressive religion has endangered their own truth claims. Nobody has seen that clearer than the great thinker Friedrich Nietzsche, the self-proclaimed anti–Christ and transvaluator of all values: setting the values of vitality over those of spirituality. Adorno wondered if Nietzsche, from whom he learned more even than from Hegel, did not have doubts sometimes, if it was such a good idea after all to elevate the values of vitality over those of spirituality.

Return of Religion?

The recent claims that religion and its values and norms have returned again in modern civil society in the past 30 years against all the predictions of thinkers from Nietzsche and Marx to Freud, Horkheimer, Marcuse, Fromm, and Habermas are indeed more than problematic. In the 20th century and still today, we have witnessed a central rope of religion in politics, under the Nixon, Reagan, and the two Bush administrations and which we can hear about every night on television, even on the self-proclaimed fair and balanced Fox Network news, and which in recent decades has justified one war after the other against the Eastern European socialism or against the so-called Near Eastern Islamic fascism and terrorism, all in the name of the purposes and plans of divine providence. Indeed, Max Horkheimer, one of the founders of the Critical Theory of society, was correct when he stated that only the atheist is the true believer! It is one most important role of atheism to clean up ideological religion, understood critically as false consciousness — a doctrine of control rather than of authentic meaning — and as the masking of national and class interests behind "faith" and public declarations of piety. Ideological religion is the essence of bourgeois "spirituality."

Such bourgeois religion cannot truly reconcile, but only ideologically, and therefore in an illusory manner, harmonize what Adorno has called the theodicy of suffering. Theodicy deals with the dichotomy between divine providence, purpose, law, plan and judgment, and especially mercy on one hand, and the slaughter bench of nature, society, and history on the other. A religion rises when it can offer an answer to the theodicy problem on a certain level of understanding, relevant to the time and place in history. A religion falls into crisis and declines, and maybe even dies, when its answer to the theodicy question is no longer plausible. After Auschwitz and Treblinka, Hiroshima and Nagasaki and the first use of the most advanced murder weapons, i.e. nuclear weapons of mass destruction, the theodicy answers of all still-living world religions have become less and less plausible. Thus, all these religions are in a crisis, which they may survive or not. The recent resurgence of fundamentalism in all of the world's major religions testifies not to renewed faith, but to intensified doubt and even fear that established theodicies have lost all plausibility.

Already for Thomas of Aquinas and Hegel the identity between divine providence and the sacrificial altar of society and history was extremely precarious and fragile when innocent victims were in question. That Hegel is contrary to Adorno's view, and not merely an unrelated philosopher of abstract identity, becomes manifest in his instrumental theodicy, which functionalized social and historical evils in terms of the unfolding of history, into abstract realms of the Divine and of Human Freedom, such that he subsequently attributes evil to the so-called *Riddles of Providence*. Hegel's philosophy is not one of abstract but rather in tone of concrete identity which leaves room for what Adorno and Horkheimer called the Non-Identical, the radically

New, the totally Other, something beyond the empirical slaughter bench of nature, society and history.

The Aristocratic Principle of Nature

On this sacrificial altar of history, on which the virtues of the individuals, the happiness of nations, and the wisdom of states have continually been sacrificed for centuries, almost everybody is programmed to eat everybody for his own self-preservation in terms of what the great bourgeoisie thinker Hobbes had called the *Bellum omnium contra omnes* (the war of each against all). On the basis of this Hobbesian principle Carl Schmidt, Hitler's specialist in jurisprudence and political theologian, based his definition of politics as the identification and definition of the enemy. Since that time psychological warfare, the demonization of the selected and identified enemy has never stopped. Bourgeois religion merely harmonizes the theodicy of human suffering, instead of truthfully and honestly trying to resolve the dichotomy between what the great idealists from Kant to Fichte and Schelling to Hegel had called the Idea on one hand, and the murderous reality on the other, out of which all other secondary ideological lies of modern civil society arise continually from one day to the other. Thus, Hitler's notion of providence justified the aristocratic principle of nature, which allowed the stronger predator in nature, society, and history, to exploit and even to annihilate the weaker prey.

That was the very core of the fascist ethics, on the basis of which one smaller and weaker nation after the other was attacked in the middle of peacetime against all international laws and even against the constitution of one's own nation. The constitution, of course, was suspended more or less in terms of immediate instrumental decisions, justified by one emergency or another, rather than grounded in established normative standards. The fascist eugenics drew further consequences from that fascist ethics. Also for neoliberal or neoconservative nationalism, providence affirms the principle that, as the older president Bush stated, there must be winners and losers. Out of this liberal principle arises the neoliberal nationalist ethical position: right or wrong; my country, love it or leave it! The younger president Bush initiated the second Gulf War in the name of divine providence, although God at the same time had not yet revealed his full plan to the president. Although some may be motivated by the quest for ownership of oil resources, Bush himself makes no distinction between providence and politics.

2. The Open Dialectic

From Lex Talionis to Golden Rule

Both neoliberal and fascist ethics subscribe to the Lex Talionis, the most widespread law of retaliation: eye for eye and tooth for tooth (Exodus 21: 24; Matthew 5: 38).

It is the very opposite of the Golden Rule, which most world religions subscribe to: Taoism, Hinduism, Buddhism, Jainism, Judaism, Christianity, Islam, Bahai, and others. We start from the conviction that the world's religions have an important role to play in the establishment of peace among nations. We are also convinced that the world's religions can have this positive function for peace only when they enter discourse with each other and explore together their interpretation of reality, their dogmas, and their related orientation of action: the moral values and norms which they may have in common, and the possibilities of their application to society and history. In such discourse, members of the different religions may find out that they share, if also in slightly different formulations, at least one ethical norm: the Golden Rule. It states in its Jewish formulation:

> Do not do to others what you would not want them to do to you [Rabbi Hillel, Shabat 31a].

It states in its Christian expression:

> In everything do to others as you would have them do to you; that is the meaning of the Law and the Prophets [Matthew 7: 12; Luke 6: 31].

It states in its Islamic form:

> No one of you is a believer until he desires for his brother that which he desires for himself [40 Hadith. Saying of Muhammad an-Nawawi, 13].

The Golden Rule reaches its climax in the fourth and fifth commandments of the Sermon on the Mount; the fourth commandment demands that the stronger one takes the first step in order to break the talion. In Matthew (5:38–42) Jesus expands the fifth commandment to demand not only the love of the neighbor, which is difficult enough in the totally atomized modern civil society, but also even the love of the enemy. In Matthew 5:43–48, the fifth commandment is spelled out in the parable of the good Samaritan, who puts oil and wine into the wound of a Jew, a member of a nationally and racially foreign out-group, his enemy, and thus becomes perfect (regarding the love of others) like the heavenly father is perfect, and thus achieves eternal life, and thus solves the theodicy problem if not theoretically then at least practically.

The Global Future

Our discourse is driven by the hope that solidarity can break the spell of the lex talionis. After September 11, 2001, millions wrote to the president and senators and congressmen in Washington, D.C., and in essence urged: not lex talionis, but policy change. Unfortunately, there was more eye-for-eye retaliation than policy change. Now, nearly every day American soldiers are wounded or killed by guerrilla fighters in Iraq in the name of the lex talionis, which is not legitimated by the Torah, nor by the Quran, nor by the New Testament. Retaliation always produces retaliation again. There is no end to it. In comparison to this extreme irrationality the fourth commandment of the Sermon on the Mount, which prohibits the eye for eye or, as the Quran says, free man for free man, or slave for slave, is the peak of rationality!

Furthermore, our discourse is motivated by the hope, that religious and secular people of good will can work together to minimize the possibility of futures I and II (below) and work toward future III:

Global Future I— the totally administered, bureaucratized, computerized, and robotized signal society. Yet even this is perhaps preferable to the most horrible alternative,

Global Future II— the totally militarized society preparing one war or civil war after the other and finally moving toward nuclear, biological, and chemical (NBC) wars. Instead, religion and secular humanists must together promote passionately alternative,

Global Future III— the reconciled society, in which friendly and helpful living together of all people will be possible.

The Functionalization of Religion

When members of our Sociology Department, for example, at Western Michigan University, assert that religion is good, but not true, then this is unacceptable for any genuine religious believer. A religion stands and falls with its truth claim. What our sociologists really mean is that religion is functional. It serves the survival of modern civil society by functioning, in Parsonian terms, as integrative, or balancing, or stabilizing subsystems of bourgeois society, and its constitutional state, and its culture. As Luhmann put it, religion functions as a contingency-experience-management subsystem.

The religion of a Mahatma Gandhi, a Martin Luther King, or the new political theology of a Johann B. Metz, or the related liberation theology of a Gustavo Gutierrez, or the basic Christian communities in Central and

2. The Open Dialectic

Latin America and Africa — not to speak of the original religious messages of a Moses, or an Isaiah, or a Jeremiah, or a Gautama, or a Jesus, or a Mohammed — certainly contradict most vehemently and finally explode such apologetically conformist, positivistic, functionalistic definitions of religion.

Yet, functionalist notions of religion have been accepted in late capitalistic society almost globally to such an extent, even in popular discourse, that it is not even discussed very much any longer. Parsonian or Luhmannian functionalism anticipates alternative **Future I** — the totally administered society, in which the existence of religion will at best range on the level of drugs which will be necessary because life will be very meaningless and consequentially very boring and which will have to be developed in such a way that they do at least not destroy the brains of users. While alternative **Future III** — the reconciled peace society, rooted in what George W.F. Hegel had called the human potential of language and memory, of erotic love, and the struggle for recognition, is indeed most desirable but unfortunately not very possible or probable under the conditions of advanced industrial society. **Future I** — the totally instrumental and functionalized society, rooted in the evolutionary universal of work and tool, and torn off from the human potential of language and memory, is not very desirable, but is nevertheless very possible and probable and seems to rapidly approaching. Ominously, **Future I** is also always inclined to turn seamlessly over into alternative **Future II** — the likewise highly instrumentalized *militarized* society preparing one conventional war after the other and aiming at the ultimate use of NBC weapons, or other as yet unimagined weapons of mass destruction, and the consequent social and environmental obliteration.

Functional bourgeois religion is bad religion in the sense that it affirms apologetically and is conforming to the status quo of what Parsons called the system of human condition, and the human action system, containing culture, society, personality and behavioral organism. The functionalist harmonizes these systems, which in reality reproduce themselves antagonistically. Particularly civil society causes great human suffering at home and abroad thorough its gender, generation, race, and especially its class dichotomies. Bad religion legitimates and justifies antagonistic bourgeois society, no matter how unjust it may be.

To the contrary, good religion demands that the system of human condition, specifically the human action system, must become otherwise and is to be changed toward alternative **Future III**, a society which for once is what it ought to be, and what it claims to be in terms of its own declared values: a free and just society; a society which has freed itself from its different forms of alienation and is at home with itself. This is not an abstract utopia, but a concrete one: i.e., the productive forces have been developed, or could be developed, in order to make it a reality.

Reconciliation

The great German idealists from Kant though Fichte and Schelling to Hegel discovered and affirmed the development of modern science and thus the radical modern dichotomy between the religious and the secular. But Hegel hoped in his philosophy of religion that the modern antithesis between faith and reason, religious and rational ethos, would ultimately be reconciled without either of the former antagonists losing its integrity in the new synthesis. Beethoven, who had tried with gigantic energy to emancipate music from its cultic roots and to secularize it, finally wrote his *Missa Solemnis* and even thought that it was his greatest work.

Out of despair about Beethoven's return to the mythos, Adorno could not finish his book about him and his work. Goethe's Faust ventured with the help of Mephistopheles out on the most extreme secularity in the first volume, only to be seduced into heaven by Mary at the end of the second volume. But at the end of his own philosophy of religion, Hegel had to admit that while the synthesis of faith and reason had been accomplished in the philosophical dimension, the new synthesis had as such no empirical reality, i.e., sociological universality. The intellectuals had found the solution of the problem, but the masses of the people living in civil society were lost without the mythos, in which their personal and social morality had been rooted.

With the demythologization and the replacement of the mythos by science and technology as the foundation of bourgeois and socialist society, the masses of the people were left without ethical orientation of action. In addition, their spiritual leaders, who found their own private and entirely subjective religious and moral solutions, betrayed the masses. To be sure, Hegel's own synthesis between religious faith and dialectical reason was as fragile as all his syntheses in all realms of reality. Again and again the elements, which are synthesized, have the tendency to fall apart and become independent again. It has not been possible so far to reconcile faith and knowledge in civil society or socialist society. The only possibility which remained after the collapse of the idealistic systems was to keep open the discourse between religious believers and enlighteners, and to prevent it from being closed up by dogmatists — whether religious or scientific. As Habermas has put it: the dialect of enlightenment, which started with the initiation of modernity, has to continue for some time.

Inversion, Migration, Translation

Hegel's materialistic heirs started from the failure of the idealists to try to really reconcile the religious and the secular in civil society. Among them, the critical theorists of the Frankfurt School presupposed (1) that religious values and norms, e.g., the Decalogue in the Torah, or the Sermon on the Mount in the New Testament, or the Islamic Five Pillars had indeed contributed to the humanization of the human species on its long march from animal instinct to social freedom. The critical theorists of society presupposed (2) that the secularization process would not, as the idealists had assumed, return to religion, nor could it be stopped. Out of this double presupposition the Critical Theorists, particularly Adorno and Benjamin, developed their *Other* theology in the early 1930s while working on the Island of Ibiza. Also referred to as an *Inverse* theology, this conceptualization developed in with modern literature, especially the works of Franz Kafka. That meant that the critical theorists would allow the semantic or semiotic material or potential in the depth of the mythos to be inverted, or to migrate, or to be translated into the secular discourse of the expert cultures, e.g., psychology, sociology, anthropology, economics, philosophy, and though it into the communicative praxis of the everyday life world and even into political actions and movements in order thereby to prevent new waves of rebarbarization from happening in Western civilization. Under all circumstances, the critical theorists wanted to keep open the dialectic between the religious and the secular. They did not want it to be closed either through religious fundamentalism or dogmatic science, no matter which problems were at stake.

According to the critical theorists, this open dialectic of the religious and the secular was to make possible the discourse between the cultures and the world religions in their struggle for recognition and thus maybe the universalization and reconciliation of religious and secular values and norms in the context of a global ethos: e.g., the Golden Rule, which can even be accepted by humanists who are committed to a presuppositional atheism, which does not therefore accept any inherently religious presuppositions, such as the possibility of revelation, and asserts that religious transcendence is really a longing without any real fulfillment: the prayers of the innocent victims in their greatest distress are not heard any more readily than Jesus' outcry on Calvary: Eli, Eli, lama sabachthani? (My God, my God, why have you deserted me?) (Psalm 22:1; Matthew 27:46–47).

The theodicy of human suffering remains unresolved.

In our discourse, we take seriously the assertion that there cannot be any peace among the nations without peace among the religions, and there cannot be peace among the religions without discourse among the religions; and that there can be no discourse among the religions without foundational research in the world religions. We add that there can be no peace without an open dialectic between the sacred and the profane, religion and modernity. If a world religion is denied its struggle for recognition in the realm of secular public discourse, it may turn to violence and may draw whole nations and whole civilizations into its conflict with the modern world. Let us now turn to the examination of different necessary aspects of the open dialectic between the sacred and the profane, particularly between religious and secular values and norms as it takes place in public discourse.

Public Discourse

We understand public discourse as argumentative dialogue taking place in an ideal speech situation and in a power-free zone. We determine discourse as future-oriented remembrance of human suffering, particularly the suffering of the innocent victims of society and history, with the practical intent to diminish it. Precisely, public discourse is the medium in which religious and secular values and norms, which originally belong to particular systems of human condition and action systems, that is, cultures, can nevertheless possibly be universalized on the basis of the better arguments. In our discourse, we shall differentiate sharply if moral values and norms appear as the object of research, as subjective value-basis of the researcher, or as integral part of the theoretical systematization process. In the process of our discourse we shall move on all three levels. In any case, we are concerned with sociologically factual, or at least intentionally and tendentially universal religious values like personal freedom and the love of the neighbor, or secular values like autonomy and solidarity and the related moral norms and positive legal laws.

Of course, all such religious or secular moral values are historical: they have found their recognition in a particular social and historical discursive situation or context. There is not only a long historical, mainly religious tradition of and discourse on right — personal and social morality — but also a secular enlightenment tradition of the critique of morality which failed to examine its own contradictions. There is not only a modern dialectic of the sacred and the profane, but also a dialectic in the secular enlightenment and dialectic in religion. Not only religious and secular values can be in conflict with and challenge each other, but also secular values can turn against themselves — rationalization into irrationality, integration into disintegration, and religious values can turn against themselves: religious love can be inverted into hateful persecutions of gentiles, pagans, heretics and apostates and into most fanatic and terroristic religious wars, be they directed against other religions or against the modern protest in its bourgeois or socialist form as we experienced on September 11, 2001.

Moral Value

We differentiate between morality and ethics. We call morality the structure of action, which guides convictions, values, goals, normative judgments, and feelings, which are dominant in a particular location at a certain time. Correspondingly, there are religious or secular scientific, i.e., psychological, sociological, or historical theories of morality, which are for the genesis and function of religious or secular forms of morality. Contrary to morality, ethics is synonymous with reflection on morality, i.e., with moral philosophy. Ethics gives reasons or justifies moral positions and thereby connects them with everyday moral attitudes and judgments, which it analyzes conceptually and develops further. The difference between moral theory and ethics corresponds to the observer and participant perspectives.

Of course, conflictual material relations corresponds to conflictual moral-ethical relations, and conflict may also be universal. The totality of modern society contains many and well-known universal conflicts: between the religious and the secular people, between the genders, among the generations, among the races, among the nations and ethnic groups, between the individual and the collective, and among the social classes. We consider moral values or norms to be universal when, in the now-globalized antagonistic totality of capitalistic society they have found or can possibly find recognition by religious and secular people, by both genders, by three or four generations living together at the same time, by all races, by all nations or ethnic groups, by the individual as well as by the collective, and by different social classes. In other words, values become universal when they reconcile former antagonisms.

Civil Society

In our present discourse we are mainly concerned with values and norms which operate, or do not operate, in modern civil society. We understand under civil society that social unit which has been developing already in its traditional form in the city-states of antiquity between the family on one hand, and the political state organization on the other. Only too soon civil society, which evolved from the productive aspects of the family, began to undermine and finally destroy both family and city state. Homer's Odysseus, i.e., Nobody, can be seen as the still semi-mythical prototype of the dominant member of civil society, the bourgeois, particularly concerning his attitudes toward them and concerning the motivations of his actions. These values, attitudes, and motivations belong to the very *genesis* of the traditional and the modern bourgeoisie in differentiation from the citizen as the dominant member of the political state.

In contemporary society, the bourgeois is emancipated from the guidance of more specific biological instincts as well as from the ethical norms of the traditional family, or the traditional state. He has separated production from the family and made it the center of bourgeois society and left to the former merely consumption and care. In bourgeois civil society economic values always predominate over and against moral values. Today, economic and moral values have united to define the standards of bourgeois society: fair return for one's investment; to get good value for one's money; purchasing power; the value of the pound or the dollar or the euro; the monetary equivalent of something; property to the value of $10,000; use and exchange value; surplus labor and surplus value, etc.

While the bourgeois as the dominant member of civil society is concerned with his private material goods, the citizen as carrier of the state is interested mainly and first of all in the common good of the community. The dichotomy between civil society and the political state reaches right into our present historical situation and finds its expression in the continual attempt of the federal government or the states to control monopolies and oligopolies and protect the consumers from the producers and the workers from the owners and the smaller corporations from the bigger ones and to keep the competition open under all circumstances.

The Bourgeoisie

From the very start the bourgeois was a solitary figure who viewed others merely as instruments or commodities, even in business friendships. He was more determined by instrumental or functional rationality than by mimetic or communicative rationality. Thus, through his science and technology the bourgeois demythologized and shaped the face of the earth for better or for worse more than any other human type or social character. As the bourgeois demythologized the world progressively, he also reified it and thus delivered it to amnesia. For the capitalist, only the events of the present, of the right now, matter. Thus, Henry Ford, the author of the fascist, anti–Semitic book *The International Jew*, based on the fraudulent *Protocol of the Elders of Zion*, and friend of the fascist radio preacher Father Coughlin, and supporter and friend even of Adolf Hitler, could state: History is bunk.

Social and historical amnesia, of course, is functional for the survival of antagonistic civil society. Otherwise, some day the workers could ask the surplus value back, which they had produced, but which they had not received and appropriated for all their productive years; recently, the workers from the concentration camps have done this, and some of the distant offspring of the former slaves in North America plan to do so. Historical memory of the slaves, serfs, or wage laborers is indeed dangerous for the masters. That is the material social revolutions are made of. Only too often world history has indeed been world judgment.

It is continually most painful for parents, who have done an excellent educational job in family and life world, which are still determined by mimetic and communicative rationality and steered over moral values and norms, to see their children and even their grandchildren morally deformed as soon as they enter civil society: particularly its economic subsystem, characterized by functional rationality and steered over the median of money; and its political subsystem, determined also by instrumental rationality, but steered over the medium of power and force. More generally, civil society is immoral in the sense that it cannot reconcile in itself the particular and the universal, the individual and the collective, the personal autonomy and the universal solidarity. In the atomized civil society the individual as well as the collective remain abstract and thus untrue. Their truth would be to be mediated within themselves through each other.

Civil society is based on arbitrary autonomy, but it has no solidarity. Like the core value of religious neighborly love so is also the secular principle of solidarity the foundation of all moral norms. If one is in solidarity with another person, one will not steal from him or her, one will not murder him or her, one will not lie to him or her. Without solidarity there is no morality and anything goes, regardless of declared moral values. Morals remain abstract ideals unless implemented in actual relationships.

Moments of Crises

At best, civil society knows of and practices solidarity in moments of crises or catastrophes, when the capitalist system is momentarily interrupted by floods, earthquakes, acts of terror, and so on in emergency situations. But as soon as the system is normalized again, the bourgeois returns into his arbitrary and selfish autonomy again and solidarity disappears. This shows, of course, that also the member of civil society carries in himself solidarity as a potentiality. But this very human potentiality cannot be actualized as long as the capitalist system, which reproduces itself antagonistically and rests on competitiveness rather than cooperation, continues to function properly.

Recently, President Bush has tried to keep alive the neighborly love on the level of national solidarity, which originated from the catastrophe of September 11, 2001. Bush encourages citizens to give two years of their lives to community service. The Enron Corporation, along with WorldCom, Adelphia, and others were obviously not impressed or bothered by the president's rather reasonable appeal and demand. Executives at these and other corporations manipulated stock prices, withheld energy from consumers, decimated workforces, and bankrupted pensions, all to make billions of dollars of personal wealth.

We shall see if the president's compassionate neoconservative demand of neighborly love and solidarity continues in normal times. But then it would not be a bourgeois society any longer. It would have changed its identity toward alternative Future III — a reconciled society. For bourgeois society, the antagonism of autonomy and solidarity is essential and chronic: it is built into its less than equivalent, in fact, exploitive exchange process.

Dysfunctional Social Character

Erich Fromm invented the concept of social character to describe the various characterological attributes that members of a society share in common, compared to individual character, which refers to those characteristics that differentiate people from one another. Depending on social conditions, society as a whole rewards or discourages some types of social character over and against other types.

In moments of crises, antagonistic civil society produces millions of what Erich Fromm has called authoritarian personalities, who find their idols in people like Hitler, or a Mussolini, or a Franco, or a Salazar, or a Ford; or a Coughlin, or a Reagan, or a Limbaugh, or a Savage, or a Newt Gingrich, or an Oliver North, or an O'Reilly of the "fair and balanced" Fox News channel, or a Bush, or a Rumsfeld, or a Schwarzenegger, and innumerable others. These authoritarian personalities are longing romantically back to the good old times wherever and whenever they may have been; they are nationalistic, my country right or wrong; they are procapitalistic because the masses cannot do without masters; they are sadistic versus weak individuals, minorities, or nations and masochistic versus strong individuals, majorities, and nations; and sometimes they are racist: often in the lower classes against the African Americans and in the upper classes against the Jews. Authoritarian personalities come in both a religious and a secular version — the difference lies only in what they perceive as the absolute superior power, either the nation, or God.

In addition, the history of Western civil society has reproduced a type of human being, a social character, which had an increasingly difficult time to become an adequate marriage partner, or family member, or citizen of the state. This is the self-centered, acquisitive bourgeois type, for whom, given the exaggerated sense of individualism, even the most immediate and direct social relationships become difficult. Not Christianity, or any other

Eastern religion, but the bourgeois and civil society destroyed the old traditional family systems and city-states and empires of antiquity, including the Roman Empire, and continue to endanger the modern ones as well. Daily we can observe how modern civil society destroys its own foundations not only in nature inside and outside of human beings, but also in the family and in the state and even in religion. To the extent bourgeois society triumphs, it makes an end of marriage and the family. When the bourgeois asserts himself in the citizen holding a high political office, that means corruption. When the bourgeois breaks though in the religious person, even religion turns into a business. Everything becomes based on personal gain.

Daily, modern states struggle with their bourgeois societies and try to impose on them social thought and moral values and norms in the form of positive legislation and laws, and thus to protect not only the consumer from the producer, the worker from the owner, and the smaller corporation from the bigger one, but also the family member and the citizen from the bourgeois, in order thus to prevent civil society from committing suicide, and from tearing down with itself its own natural social and cultural foundations as well.

Georges Soros, the Hungarian-born billionaire from currency speculations and founder of the widespread "Open Society Institutes," has explained the fact that the move of civil society back into Eastern Europe, which was a main intention and goal of his life's work, has come to a halt after 10 years, by pointing to a Mafia-capitalism which, unrestrained by ethical principles and state control, turned into a gigantic predator, like the American robber barons of a century ago, exploited the territory beyond measure, and thus lost the support of the people, just as Hitler had done in the Ukraine half a century earlier after half the population had waited for him as the redeemer from Stalinism. Eastern Europe simply does not want to become another colonized India or Latin America. Soros understands that. He is an enlightened capitalist, amidst a sea of ruthless half-criminal, half-capitalists who have seized control of the state.

Criticism of Civil Society

Jewish, Christian, and Islamic prophets as well as most philosophers from Plato and Aristotle through Hegel, Marx, and Freud to Horkheimer and Adorno, Marcuse, and Fromm have criticized civil society because of the absence of the right moral values and norms, be they particular or universal. Already the Jewish and Christian prophets condemned early city-states, like Sodom, Babylon, Rome, etc., the more so the more in them a civil society and its polytheism and its social immorality had developed.

Already Plato, who wanted to rescue the Greek city-state from the destructive tendencies of its intrinsic civil society, counseled, advised, and recommended that if one wanted to have a good son, one should make him the citizen of a good state, not a member of civil society dominated by sophistry. Plato took a converted sophist, Socrates, as an example of how the Athenian state could possibly be healed not only from sophistry, but also from civil society. Plato's remedy was to repress civil society. While Hegel saw and appreciated the historical necessity and productivity of civil society, he nevertheless predicted that it would concretely supersede itself though its own class contradictions, through the consequent colonialism, and imperialism, and through always more abstract and generalized wars into alternative Future III — the rational and free constitutional state — rather than into alternative Future I — a totally mechanized and automated society — or into alternative Future II — an entirely militarized society engaging in always more and more universalized warfare.

Of course, civil society has its proponents as well. Carl Popper, who equated civil society with "open society," singled out particularly Hegel, whom he called a Prussian court philosopher, and of course Karl Marx for attack. To the enemies of the open society Popper opposed the few philosophers who were friends of bourgeois society, particularly Hobbes, the spiritual father of Carl Schmidt, Hitler's jurist and political theologian. Hobbes had anticipated affirmatively the concentration camps for the so-called strangers or foreigners in civil society, which according to him was characterized by the *Bellum omnium contra omnes* (the war of each against all). Both thinkers, Hobbes and Schmidt, one of the fathers of the present neoconservatism and deconstructionism, concentrated on the Leviathan from the end of the book of Job, and used the monster as an image for civil society as — what Hegel called the *State of necessity and analytical understanding* in distinction from the real state of freedom and dialectical reason. The critical theorist Franz Neumann used the other monster from the end of the book of Job, Behemoth, in order to characterize civil society in its fascist form. Published in 1944, it is still the best book about the structure and organization of national-socialist Germany.

For most prophets and philosophers, civil society was not the right, but rather the wrong society. Civil society as the wrong society was not only the absolute contrast to what Jewish, Christian, and Islamic prophets hoped for as the ultimate theocracy, but also to what philosophers from Plato through Thomas More to Hegel and Marx anticipated as the great utopia: alternative Future III — the good state, the rational state, the realm of economic necessity, not only of the freedom of the one, or the freedom of the few, but of the freedom of all. Most prophets and philosophers have agreed concerning the negation of the negativity of civil society toward the affirmation of man, and sometimes even of God. To be sure, the modern bourgeoisie was never sincere and honest enough in relation to religion and morality in order to recognize and admit that the principle of civil society was the exact opposite to, for example, the principle of Christianity, or Judaism, or Islam, in order to develop a decent theoretical atheism, in spite of the fact that its economic and political practice had long become atheistic with the exception of a few ideological, understood in the critical sense, mainly decorative residuals.

In place of meaningful religion and its attendant solidarity, modern bourgeois society knows only individual autonomy void of even the most minimal social obligation. The modern bourgeoisie never understood the Christian axiom:

> No one can be the slave of two masters: he will either hate the first and love the second, or treat the first with respect and the second with scorn. You cannot be the slave both of God and of money.

Since the modern bourgeoisie did not comprehend this axiom when it reached its cultural climax in the time of Hegel, in whose dialectical philosophy it reached its highest level of consciousness as much as in the great music of Beethoven and Mozart, it will forever escape bourgeois awareness.

While one may not know what the right society is, one always knows what the wrong one is: the antagonistic one. The wrong society is one in which either solidarity suffocates autonomy, initiative and personal freedom, or one in which arbitrary autonomy does not allow universal solidarity to develop in the first place or destroys it again in the process of normalization. The Soviet Union collapsed because of the familiar lack of individual autonomy. In contrast, the American empire is endangered by the lack of solidarity. The more war-oriented a society becomes, the more antagonistic it becomes — toward both outsiders and nonconformists within, and the more militarism increases, the more narrow the boundaries of conformity become. That means of course the total negation of human solidarity, since only a few will fit within the boundaries, and in the absence of other unifying principles, the few will seek to dominate the many.

While for Hegel the rational state, legitimated by religion, still included in itself family and civil society, one century later for the structural-functionalists Parsons and Luhmann the family, state, and religion were all placed as specific functional subsystems that in turn serve as pattern maintenance, goal-attainment, and integrative subsystems. Cumulatively, these various subsystems constitute civil society, as part of the overall modern human action system which included in addition culture, personality and behavior at the individual level. As merely functional subsystems, family, state, and religion had to serve the survival of civil society first and foremost.

This theoretical paradigm change from Hegel to Parsons and Luhmann reflects in itself a real historical development. Any discourse about universal values and norms and their relationships to alternative futures needs to take this theoretical and practical historical development into consideration. Soros does so, when he blames rightly the lack of socio-ethical thought and state and governmental control for the failure of the reintroduction of civil society into Eastern Europe since 1989. Russian president Putin does so when he states that the Russian Federation does not want a civil society but rather a civilized society.

There is indeed a great difference: a civilized society would be in compliance with universal moral values and norms, the civil society is not. If the bourgeoisie would conform to its own universal values, norms, and positive laws, e.g., human and civil rights, the Geneva Convention, the code of the United Nations, etc., nationally and internationally, the world would already be a somewhat better place, and not the brutal and exploitive place it really is presently.

Religion and Science

For Horkheimer, the decisive discoveries of the Renaissance transformed the earth as the center and foundation of the cosmos into what his great teacher Arthur Schopenhauer called "a tiny ball with a coating of mold on top of it, rolling around in the infinity of space." Modern philosophical-literary thinkers have tried to inscribe a moral meaning to the otherwise cosmologically void, invalid, trivial, and insignificant activities of human beings which would transcend the mere limited purpose human experience and its survival. Since morality — including all universal values and norms — can only with great difficulties, if at all, be grounded and legitimated without reference to generally binding, ultimately divine commandments, thinkers have since the 17th and 18th centuries engaged the philosophical task of coping with and possibly the overcoming of the contradiction between religion and science.

Particularly on the European continent, in France and Germany, philosophers from Descartes to Kant and their successors took refuge in the thesis that the notion of the almighty God was immanent in human reason, or that the certainty of his existence followed with necessity from constant concepts and sentences which belonged to it. Since also the science was referred to maxims of reason, namely the logic, such rationalistic theories seemed to be sufficient to satisfy the psychologically and socially compelling and cogent need for divine imperatives. The great period of bourgeois enlightenment was at least partially connected with the conscious or unconscious assumption that the binding nature and validity of moral duties and obligations was based on the idea of the perfect being, yet in no way on the traditional, supposedly already obsolete, old-fashioned, out-of-date teachings and narratives and stories and legends and myths, on what the German enlightener Ephraim Lessing had called the flood of arbitrary sentences of the positive religions. In modernity, universal values and norms can be discovered only in and through the dichotomy between the religious and the secular, between faith and reason, between religion and science.

Critical Theory offers a means of reconciliation between faith and reason, religion and science. The critical theory of society belongs to and concretely supersedes in itself the great secular traditions of the bourgeois, Marxian, and Freudian enlightenment movements. Thus, the critical theory of society remains at least partially connected with the conscious or unconscious assumption that the binding nature and validity of moral duties and obligations, including the possibility of universal values and norms, or even a global ethos, is based on the idea of the totally Other. That is, what once had been called heaven, beauty, or eternity, as the determinate negation of that which in nature, society, and history is called injustice, human abandonment, alienation, loneliness, meaninglessness, fear of illness, aging, dying, and death. In other words, Critical Theory seeks universal norms and values through actual negation of injustice, abandonment, alienation, and so on in the real world, rather than idealized negation in some far-off, transcendent replacement (such as heaven) for actual changes in the real world. Only by reconciling the totally Other with the real world, which is to say reconciling the age-old problem of theodicy, can universal values arise. This became the project of Critical Theory.

Unfortunately, contemporary society has yet to achieve much success in making the transcendent real. As a result, we live in what Kierkegaard had described as a "sickness toward death," of a repressed despair, which then stepped over the threshold of the consciousness and which finally forced, or compelled, the inversion of the modern and secular ego-centered consciousness. These forms of despair were as many manifestations of the missing of an existential foundational relationship, which alone could make possible an authentic self. Kierkegaard portrayed the worrying condition of a person who was admittedly conscious of his or her destiny that he or she had to be a self, but whom afterwards escaped into alternatives: desperate not to want to be oneself, or still lower, desperate not to want to be one self, or the lowest, to want to be another than oneself. The desperate person finally recognized that the source of the despair did not lay in the circumstances but in his or her own escape movements. Then the desperate person would undertake the defiant, but likewise unsuccessful and vain attempt, to want to be oneself.

The desperate failure of this last act of strength, of the wanting to be one self which stiffens and hardens itself completely in itself, moved the finite spirit toward the transcending of himself or herself and toward the recognition of the dependence on an absolute Other, in whom his or her own freedom was grounded. Kierkegaard's stages of despair remind us of the dialectical movement of consciousness in Hegel's *Phenomenology of Spirit*. Precisely here lay the roots for Adorno's and Horkheimer's notion of the longing for the totally Other — the desire to escape into the arms of a omniscient and omnipotent being.

Turning Point

This inversion of consciousness demanded by Kierkegaard was supposed to mark the turning point of his exercitium: the overcoming of the secularized self-understanding of modern reason. Kierkegaard nevertheless insisted that the human spirit could only through the consciousness of sin come to the right understanding of his finite existence. For Kierkegaard, the self existed truly only in the face of God. The self survived the stages of hopeless despair only in the form of a believer, who, as he related himself to himself, related himself to an absolute Other, to whom he owed everything. Therefore it may be rather hard to understand Kierkegaard's reference to a Power postmetaphysically in a purely secular way.

Kierkegaard emphasized, that we could not form a consistent notion of God: neither *Via eminentiae* nor *Via negationis*. In Kierkegaard's perspective, every idealization remained connected with the finite fundamental predicates from which had started the operation of increase or intensification or enhancement. Out of the same reason also the attempt of understanding had to fail to determine the absolute Other through the negation of all finite determinations. According to Kierkegaard, the understanding could not think the absolute difference because it used itself for this and thought the difference in itself. According to Kierkegaard, the gulf between knowledge and faith could not be bridged or reconciled.

In spite of the fact that Adorno did still stand in the tradition of negative theology and believed that no formulation of the truth was possible without it, he nevertheless — or precisely because of it — agreed with Kierkegaard that no consistent notion of God could be formed. Precisely therefore he and Horkheimer spoke merely of the longing for the totally Other. In place of a transcendent being, namely God, Adorno and Horkheimer longed for the totally Other in the form of nature and history as the source of unconditional meaning, of absolutely binding ethical validity claims, and of possible new theodicy answers.

For us the question is of course if such linguistic deflation of the notion of the totally Other, the destruction of the divine, still allows and grants to the individual person the ability to truly become one-self, and the motivation for this and for the solidarity with other human beings and even other living beings in a civil society. Given that humans do not have access to or control over divine powers, whether they exist or not, means that reliance on such power is inherently problematic. The problem lies, to a large extent, not necessarily on a lack of theoretical knowledge, but rather as Kierkegaard had put it, by the corruption of the will.

The issue of the corruption of the will, by many names, was argued by Socrates and Kant among others, who agree with Kierkegaard in that the dependence on an unavailable Power was not to be understood naturalistically, but that it concerned first of all interpersonal relationship. In order to make man's self-realization possible, with Kierkegaard's or Benjamin's God in time, or with Adorno's and Horkheimer's imageless and nameless totally Other, or with Metz's God as the end of time, how is such a dilemma to be resolved postreligiously and postmetaphysically in order to make the right life and the right society possible under modern, secular conditions?

Adorno would answer in conformity with the great enlightenment thinkers of the past that he could not simply say, although not ready to categorically deny the existence of God, that there was in fact a God and that he was just and good. This was so, because Adorno and Horkheimer had already in their common work, the *Dialectic of Enlightenment*, explained and expounded that the words "just" and "good" or even "God" could not at all be formulated positively. They could be formulated only negatively in terms of an *Other*, which could be signified only through this word *Other* and though nothing else.

It is the longing for this entirely Other which so far has prevented the Critical Theorists from reducing the notion of society to a categorical index, as positivists in sociology have done, or reducing the notion of the soul to emotional longings, as psychologists have done. The longing for the totally Other also has prevented so far a Critical Theory of society from falling victim to atheoretical empiricism, or narrow psychology, or biological reductionism, or any other form of positivism and its apologetic, harmonizing, and conformist tendencies. The longing for the entirely Other hindered the critical theorists from yielding to the bourgeois resignation: the refusal to make any significant statement on the crucial questions of human existence today and to simply setting up house in the finite world and exploring it with methodological intensity but theoretical insignificance, or to relegate this theodicy problem to art or religion, which are at the same time not recognized as genuine forms of knowledge.

The longing for the entirely Other also prevented the Critical Theorists of society from subscribing to a radical atheism of some philosophers of the bourgeois enlightenment, such as Helvetius, or La Metrie, or Holbach, who really did give negative answers to the God-question, and in whose thought reason was sufficiently confident to make even abstract negative statements about the Absolute. Like Kant, the critical theorists of society are rather guided by the conviction that reason is denied the right to stray into the realm of the Absolute: to move into the intelligible worlds. This explains why the critical theorists can stand with both feet firmly planted on the ground and that they really know what it is that they can positively and definitely know and what not. It is the longing for the totally Other which keeps the critical theorists from falling for the theodicy of bourgeois life, which is conscious of its own practical activity while despairing of the fulfillment of its own universal values and norms, and its own utopia. Finally, the longing for the entirely Other has enabled the critical theorists of society to participate realistically in the global discourse on universal values and norms.

Negative Theology

Adorno could never hide his opinion that a formulation of the concept of the truth was impossible without a determinate notion of negative theology. The critical theorists could not speak equivocally or univocally about the Absolute. However, they also could not speak analogically—as did the great medieval Jewish negative theologian Maimonides or the Christian negative theologian Thomas Aquinas, particularly in his *Summa Contra Gentiles*—against the Muslims—because they overemphasized, exaggerated, and radicalized—out of the horrible experiences of the 20th century—the difference between the finite and the Infinite to such an extent that they exploded the analogy and ended up with the *totaliter aliter*. However, even when this negative theology and its core concept of the totally Other as the absolute truth or the unconditional meaning was abandoned as lying in ruins or linguistically transformed in the second generation of critical theorists, particularly Habermas' universal pragmatic theory of communicative action, discourse ethics, and discourse theory of right and the democratic constitutional state, constructed in terms of facticity and validity and of the basic principle of the unlimited communication community, it still continued to function, nevertheless, at least as a motivating force for a communicative practice realizing universal moral principles, values, and norms, toward a world ethos.

The first generation of the critical theorists of society searched for global ethos not on the basis of any positive religion and its stories and sentences, not even of Judaism, which Hegel had called the religion of sublimity, from which they came, but rather on the foundation of their fundamental longing or hope for the totally Other in nature and history: the real driving force of the critical theory of society. Ethos meant originally in Greek the features of individual character, or of will. Later on, ethos signified the universal element that informed a literary work, its irony, or its melancholy, etc., as distinct from the subjective details of its maker. Finally, ethos meant the spirit of a people, of a civilization, or of a national system of human condition, including its telic subsystem, its natural environments, the human organism, and the action system as expressed cultures, institutions, ways of thought, philosophies, and religions.

Here we are concerned with a possible world ethos: the spirit of a global system of human condition or action system, as expressed in a diversity of cultures, the spirit of social systems, i.e., types of families, of economies, of political subsystems, of religious subsystems, as well as the spirit of different personality types and forms of behavioral organisms. The Critical Theorists do not only aim at the disintegration or decay of prebourgeois or bourgeois values and norms and laws and attitudes, but also and most of all at a postbourgeois value transformation, what Nietzsche had called the transvaluation of all values. The critical theorists are not concerned with post- or countermodernity, or ultramodernity, but rather with the concrete supersession of modernity. They aim at a global minimum of common values, norms, and attitudes: e.g., a secular equivalent of the Golden Rule, which has been present in most world religions.

New World Order

The Critical Theorists are convinced that there can be no really new world order without a new world ethos. They stand for common moral responsibility in mutual recognition and respect. They are aware of the dialectic of enlightenment in civil society and the difficulties which therefore even a communicative rationality has with personal and social morality, and ethics and social ethics, and with the binding nature and validity of and commitment to and motivation through values and norms in a postmetaphysical age, which sometimes even announces the end of religion as such, which supposedly is nothing else than a human projection. In the perspective of Horkheimer, to rescue an unconditional meaning was utter vanity without God, without the Unconditional, the Absolute, the entirely Other in nature and history. Otherwise, what remains is a crude biological truth, that the world is a food chain, or food web, in which almost everything must eat anything it can in order to maintain itself.

Therefore, it seemed to the Critical Theorist that in order to unite people at a higher level, only the Unconditional could justify unconditional unity in moral terms. Even for Habermas, at least an effective moral motivation of communicative acts in conformity to moral values and norms legitimated by the unlimited communication community and the corresponding necessary renunciation of opposing instincts and drives may very well still presuppose the rescue of an unconditional meaning, which is not possible without God, the Absolute, the Infinite or the totally Other.

In any case, no survival of humankind is possible without such a world ethos, which is deeply rooted in the Unconditional, the Absolute, the totally Other, and which precisely therefore can make possible the reconciliation of the fundamental antagonisms in late capitalistic society: between the sacred and the profane, between the genders, among the generations, among the races, among the nations, between the individual and the collective, between the classes, between freedom on one hand and brotherhood and justice on the other, between equality and plurality, between productivity and the solidarity with the human as well as the natural environments and the different economic systems, etc.

Of course, precisely those unreconciled contradictions stand in the way of a universal ethos, because religious people have different values and norms from secular people, the older generation from the younger one, one race from the other, one nation from the other, the individual from the collective, etc. Most recently the stem cell controversy between Pope John Paul II and President Bush has been showing in Rome once more clearly the modern dichotomy between religious and secular values already before the al-Qaeda attack against the World Trade Center and the Pentagon. The stem cell controversy divides also completely secularized positivists, who always think they ought to do whatever they can do scientifically and technologically, on one hand, and still negative-theologically motivated critical theorists, who recognize fully the great value of scientific and technological progress, but who also know of the dialectic of enlightenment and therefore cannot cease to ask for the human price to be paid for it.

Precisely these such unreconciled social and ethical antagonisms prevent the arrival of the right society. Therefore our discourse must not only reflect on the last four generations of Critical Theorists, but must also develop further the dialectical theory of society in terms of a contextual praxis to mitigate as much as possible the trend in late bourgeois society toward alternative global Future I — the totally administered society; to prevent under all circumstances the tendency in modern political states toward alternative global Future II — endless conventional wars and civil wars, NBC wars, and the consequent ecological disasters; and to promote as passionately as possible the tendencies in modern culture toward alternative global Future III — the right society, in which the fundamental modern antagonisms will be reconciled and a friendly, cooperative, and helpful living together of free human beings will be possible.

Love of the Neighbor

But how can leaders such as George W. Bush represent purely secularized and acquisitive values? Does he not publicly proclaim his Christian faith? There are many politicians today in Europe and in the Americas and elsewhere who belong to large political parties which carry the name "Christian," or confess to be committed to Christian values, norms, laws, attitudes, and policies. The question is, of course, if one can indeed engage at all in Realpolitik — not necessarily in reality politics — in most secularized advanced capitalist societies if you also place supreme value on foundational Christian virtues, such as you must love your neighbor, or even that you must love your enemies and turn the other cheek to those who persecute you. Can one follow a Christ who requires a love that breaks through all racial, national, and religious in-group–out-group boundaries and antagonisms, and still fulfill the role of leader at the top of a ruthless and exploitive hierarchy? Clearly, actions speak louder than words; saying one thing does not prohibit entirely opposite action, provided that the population offers no resistance, or even accepts the obvious contradiction as practical and necessary. Once the enemy is defined as evil incarnate, one is free to use any means necessary to destroy it.

To be sure, part of this fundamental value of neighborly love and the norms and laws derived from it, is not limited to, but rather more universal than Christianity. It can be found already in Judaism, in the Torah, and again in Islam, in the Quran. In the Torah it says: "You must love your neighbor as yourself. I am Yahweh." As a matter of fact, the Christian value of neighborly love originated from Judaism in the first place, as did many of its other values, norms, laws, and attitudes as well. In its Jewish and Christian form the love of the neighbor aims ultimately together with the love of God at eternal life and at the arrival of the kingdom of heaven. For both Jews and Christians and for Muslims as well there remains of course the most painful open flank: the *parousia* delay, the *apousia* — the nonappearance of the messiah.

More specifically, there arises the question of how, in an extremely atomized and alienated and now almost globalized late capitalistic system, neighborly love can possibly be practiced at all when there is no neighbor any longer and everybody moves as far away from the other as possible, and where one can die in a huge apartment building in the metropolis without it being noticed by anybody, and if values premised on love have not become obsolete.

However, one thing at least is for sure, namely that the religious value of neighborly love, which is not yet sociologically universal, but which is nevertheless shared at least by several world religions, cannot be practiced without losing its abstract form and without being particularized into specific moral norms, and without being concretely superseded into positive laws to steer the administration of justice of secular modern or postmodern states. Private charity can hardly deal adequately any longer with the massive social problems of industrial societies. This does of course not mean that private charity should not be practiced, where there is opportunity, as did for example Mother Theresa in Calcutta.

Of course, the Jewish and Christian core value of neighborly love has never remained merely private and abstract, but has from the very start in all three Abraham religions, in Judaism, Christianity, and Islam, been differentiated, and thus has been concretized into the commandments of the Mosaic law or the Decalogue, and into many enforceable positive laws. Thus to love the neighbor means concretely not to violate the seventh commandment and not to steal from him or her, or not to violate the fifth commandment and not to kill him or her, or finally not to violate the eighth commandment and not to lie to him or to her. The three commandments protect the values of property, life, and truth, which may have a good chance to be universally recognized in discourse with good reasons far beyond the boundaries of the Jewish, Christian, or Islamic community, at least in theory. But now it happens that even when, for example, capitalist leaders affirm in theory the value of neighborly love, they seem nevertheless to have the greatest difficulties practicing it through its differentiation and concretization via the norms of the Decalogue. There is not only the possibility of individual, but also of collective, or structural, or systemic deviations from the value of neighborly love and the norms through which it is to be actualized. The liberation theologians speak of structural sins. Secular people may speak of guilt, or if they are further secularized, of mistakes.

There is still an advantage for the capitalist to speak in a religious language, since it has still a certain appellative quality, which the entirely secularized positive social sciences, be it social psychology, sociology, economics, political science, or anthropology, have lost. That precisely is one important reason why, while magic and fetishism have been replaced by scientifically mediated technology, the positive social sciences have not yet been able to take the place of religion. There are, of course, other reasons: so far the fully secularized positive social sciences cannot give us an unconditional meaning. The positive sciences cannot even tell us why it is better to love than to hate, except that it may be better for business.

But sometimes it is even better for business to hate than to love, e.g., in fascist Germany to hate the Jews, or in the American South to hate the

African Americans, or the Chicanos. Contrary to positivism, the Critical Theory of society allows, in spite of its extreme secularization, semantic potentials — e.g., the universalizeable religious commandment of neighborly love and its differentiation and concretization in specific moral norms against idolatry and for the protection of property, life, and truth — to migrate from the depth of the mythos, which as such is considered to be obsolete, into the secular discourse among scientific expert cultures, like social psychology, or sociology. At least these disciplines offer the possibility of discourse, and through them into communicative and political actions in order thereby to prevent the further rebarbarization of Western civilization which seems to occur the more so when there is less chance that alternative Future III — an egalitarian or classless society — is possible or probable. The NATO bombardment of Yugoslavia three years ago, which imitated Hitler's attack particularly on Belgrade half a century earlier, and which cost the lives of 10,000 civilians in comparison to 400 soldiers and 200 policemen, a proportion of casualties of combatants to those of noncombatants seldom seen before, was just another symptom of this rebarbarization process, even before the current wars in Afghanistan and Iraq.

Class Exploitation

Conservative politicians seem to have great difficulties with several of the moral norms of the Decalogue, through which neighborly love is to be differentiated and concretized. Here we leave out the obviously difficult sixth commandment directed against committing adultery and protecting the moral value of marriage and family. There are three other moral norms with which capitalism seems to have even greater difficulties. Thus, reactionary Christian politicians, for example of the fascist Arena Party in El Salvador, or from other Central or Latin American states, have a great problem with the seventh commandment. The Christian politicians are in the habit of protecting and promoting the native or foreign owners' large private appropriation, or more precisely stealing of surplus labor or surplus value from their workers. If the workers organize themselves with the help of social workers, or labor unionists, or priests, or nuns, in order to defend themselves against such robbery and try to increase their wages, in order thus to be able to feed their children, they of course lower the surplus value of their domestic and foreign masters.

Precisely therefore, they are all called Communists, no matter if they are really Communists, or if they are rather Christians of the Roman Catholic liberationist affiliation. Communists are of course people who want to replace capitalism as the *private* appropriation of collective labor with Communism as the *collective* appropriation of collective labor. Communists are people who challenge the right of the owner to appropriate and to keep the surplus value, for which he has not worked, from those who have worked for it and don't get it.

Christians may very well support the private appropriation of collective labor as long as the owners are willing to pay a living or family wage. While the Christians of the Jewish-Christian paradigm were indeed often Communists, those of the Orthodox, Roman Catholic, Reformation, Enlightenment, and Ecumenical paradigms of Christianity were and are generally not, with the exception of the monastic orders and individuals like Thomas More in his *Utopia,* or also Thomas Münzer, one of the leaders of the farmer wars of the 16th century who applied the most revolutionary Sermon on the Mount in the service of the liberation of the oppressed and exploited masses, and who was finally captured by Charles V, and was decapitated after the Battle of Mühlhausen, Thuringia. I found Thomas Münzer's picture on the 10-mark bills of the former German Democratic Republic, the so-called worker and farmer state. When I used this bill the last time at the East German border shortly before the fall of the Berlin Wall, I murmured to myself: poor Thomas, you have lost another revolution! Despite obvious historical and contemporary clashes between theisms and secular humanism, certain possibilities exit for unity, a fact that totalitarian leaders have recognized, perhaps more readily than many more well-intended activists on both sides.

From Stealing to Killing

Today, conservative Christian politicians in North America have particularly great problems not only with the seventh but also with the fifth commandment of the Mosaic Law. Eighty percent of American corporations had been engaged in business in Central and Latin America already before the recent wave of globalization of the deregulated, neoliberal market and the establishment of free trade zones. Without massive private appropriation of surplus value from the South, the North American owners would have to lower greatly the salaries and wages of their own workers at home. The North American way of life would be fundamentally threatened.

Thus, the conservative politicians move from difficulties with the seventh commandment to trouble with the fifth commandment. They turn from stealing of surplus value to the killing of social workers, unionists, nuns and priests and even bishops and all other so called "communists" with the help of commandos and death squads trained in what once was called the School of the Americas, and which today is named by its opponents the

School of the Assassins situated in Fort Benning, Georgia. It specializes in training indigenous soldiers to violate in their own nations what the bourgeoisie itself has called human and civil rights and which it has developed out of its own modern, individualistic natural law position and to which today it binds everybody else except itself and its helpers, who are free to do as they please.

From Stealing and Killing to Lying

Yet they can only do as they please in the absence of public oversight and concern. Thus, the conservative Christian politicians move from difficulties with the seventh and the fifth commandments to trouble with the eighth commandment. They turn from stealing of surplus value and the killing of all those who defend the human and civil rights of the poor classes and try to empower them, be they Communists or Christians, to the cover-up of stealing and killing through propaganda, advertisement, and diversionary philanthropic or charitable public relations.

More concretely, the Christian politicians turn to lying often in the form of linguistic acrobatics and sophistry and the generation of euphemisms. That the School of the Americas has recently received a new official name makes no difference concerning its structure and function. In spite of all linguistic acrobatics, the school's cruel function remains the same: to terrorize Central and Latin American workers into accepting minimum wages, with which they can barely feed their families, but which allow the native and foreign owners to maximize their surplus value and profits. Regardless of the how the workers feel, whether loyal or committed, oppressed or liberated, their material fate lies entirely in the hands of the corporation.

Revolution or Counterrevolution?

After the fall of the Berlin Wall and the later collapse of the Soviet Union, it might appear that capitalism is not only rigorous, but eternal, that its very triumph over Soviet communism proves its superiority. That it outlasted and even defeated its main political-economic rival is apparent, and in the sense that one combatant triumphs over another, we may say it is superior. However, the success of capitalism as a global system does not necessarily equate with the triumph of the people of the former Soviet Union.

Since 1991, Russia has developed into a country with the highest social inequality in the world. If one takes the difference between the income of the richest 20 percent of the Russian population and the poorest 20 percent as a measure then Russia takes first place according to the *Human Development Report* (2003). In Russia the richest fifth of the population earns 14.53 times more than the poorest fifth, while this relationship is in the USA 8.91 times, in Germany 5.76 times and in Japan 4.31 times. The new Russian capitalists since 1989 have not been engaged in a revolution for the equality and freedom of all, but rather in a bourgeoisie counterrevolution for the freedom and the profit of the few at home and abroad. Despite their best efforts, no linguistic acrobatics, sophistry, euphemism, or ideological inversion can make a reactionary counterrevolution against social inequality into a true revolution for alternative Future III — a society characterized by the actualization of the universal moral value of social equality, which is no longer in need of organized stealing, murdering or lying.

Of course, if the workers do not want to, or cannot unite and emancipate themselves globally, and when they betray even their leaders for a few million dollars paid by the bourgeoisie, as it has happened recently again in Yugoslavia and Iraq, then they cannot expect anything else than the return to a very unequal and therefore not very civilized civil society. In secular terms, equality is not a matter of grace and of being given as a gift, but rather the result of a long and very extensive and intensive public discourse and struggle for recognition. It took the bourgeoisie 500 years until they freed themselves from the feudal lords. One can only hope that it will take the workers somewhat less time to emancipate themselves from the bourgeoisie.

In this sense the last decade has not been a very good period for the workers of the world. Inequality has reached an all-time high, and more workers now work for wages than under any other system — wages having replaced subsistence farming as the primary means of support in the world (McMichael 2003). However, the bourgeoisie also went through many such reverses before it defeated medieval feudalism and erected the modern civil society. Maybe the time has come that we could stop talking about negative growth in the capitalist economy as most of the population faces stagnant or declining incomes even as the top one percent increase their wealth beyond the wildest dreams of avarice. One recognizes the decay of a social system by — among other things — the degeneration of its evolutionary universal of language and memory.

Conclusions

What is needed is a union of morality and legality. While the praxis of the love of the neighbor is mediated through the praxis of the specific norms of the Mosaic Law and through them it points to alternative Future III, the violation of neighborly love or solidarity through the nonconformity to the norms of the Decalogue points to alternative Future I, in which collective stealing, murdering, and lying would be further institutionalized and perfected, or to alternative Future II, in which — like cancer — the war machine would destroy itself through the depletion of natural resources and the killing of its own and enemy populations. Although this would mean the end of the late capitalist system, it would also mean the end of humanity.

To reduce the possibility of this scenario, the possible universalization of the value of neighborly love beyond Judaism, Christianity, and Islam could happen only through the generalization of the norms of the Mosaic Law, which have validity already at least for Jews, Christians, and Muslims. Of course, these already specific norms would have to be differentiated and concretized further by being transformed into secular positive laws to guide the administration of justice of modern or postmodern societies and states. Thus, for example, the German Federal Republic has a so-called Samaritan Law, which translates the Christian value of neighborly love and its objectification in the fifth commandment of the Decalogue and the parable of the good Samaritan into a positive, enforceable law, which prohibits passing of an accident on the highways without stopping and helping the victims. Violation of the Samaritan Law means imprisonment.

It would be the task of truly Christian politicians to transform the universal value of neighborly love as well as its differentiation into the fifth, seventh and eighth commandments into even more concrete positive laws. Of course, moral norms cannot be reinforced by the power of the state. To the contrary, positive laws are by definition reinforceable. Thus, morality is definitely not legality. Maybe only a minimum of morality can turn into legality as long as the antagonisms of civil society are far from reconciliation. As long as the morality of accumulation predominates, for example, the morality of brotherly love cannot ascend.

But even this minimum of morality, a basic mutual respect and assistance, is nevertheless decisive for the further humanization of man at the beginning of the 21st century and for the avoidance of further rebarbarization: for the mitigation at least of alternative Future I — the totally administered society; for preventing alternative Future II — an all-consuming war machine; and certainly and most of all for the realization of alternative Future III — the reconciled society, in which the antagonisms of modern civil society would have been fought through and resolved.

Of course, we know that while alternative Futures I and II are not desirable, they are nevertheless very possible and probable; and while alternative Future III is most desirable, it is nevertheless at this time not very possible or probable. But the possibilities and probabilities or the impossibilities and improbabilities should not prevent us from fighting most passionately for what is most desirable: the right life in the right society.

References

Dirks, Walter. "Ein völlig abseitiger Vorschlag." *Die Neue Gesellschaft* 32 (February 1985): 100.

Flechtheim, Ossip. "Die Herausforderung der Zukunft und die Futurologie." *Die Neue Gesellschaft. Frankfurter Hefte,(NG)*, 32 (February 1985): 152–160.

Habermas, Jürgen. *Zur Rekonstruktion des Historischen Materialismus*. Frankfurt a.M.: Suhrkamp Verlag, 1976. Parts I–IV.

Habermas, Jürgen. *Die nachholende Revolution*. Frankfurt a.M.: Suhrkamp Verlag, 1990. 9–18, 179, 204.

Hegel, Georg W.F. 1986. *Grundlinien der Philosolphie des Rechts*. Frankfurt a.M.: Suhrkamp Verlag, 1986. Parts I, II, III; esp. 465.

Hegel, Georg W.F. *Vorlesungen über die Asthetik III*. Frankfurt a.M.: Suhrkamp Verlag, 1986. 352.

_____. 1986. *Vorlesungen über die Philosophie der Geschichte*. Frankfurt a.M.: Suhrkamp Verlag, 1986. 11–141; Parts One to Four; esp. 107–115, 422.

Hitler, Adolf. *Mein Kampf*. 1926. Reprint, New York: Houghton Mifflin, 1998.

Horkheimer, Max. *Zur Kritik der Instrumentellen Vernunft. Aus den Aufzeichnungen seit Kriegsende*. Frankfurt a.M. : S. Fischer Verlag, 1967. Parts I and II.

_____, and Theodor W. Adorno. *Dialektik der Aufklärung. Philosophische Fragmente*. Frankfurt a.M.: S. Fischer Verlag, 1969. Chs. 1–8.

_____. *Vorträge und Aufzeichnungen, 1949–1973*. Frankfurt a.M.: S. Fischer, 1985.

Kierkegaard, Soren. *The Sickness Unto Death, Collected Works Vol. 19*. Princeton, NJ: Princeton University Press, 1983.

McMichael, Philip. *Deveopment and Social Change: A Global Perspective*. Thousand Oaks, CA: Pine Forge Press, 2003.

Marx, Karl, and Friedrich Engels. *The Communist Manifesto*. New York: Appleton Century Crofts, 1955. 1–46, 47–64, 65–94.

United Nations Development Programme. *Human Development Report and Millennium Development Goals: A Compact Among Nations to End Human Poverty*. Oxford: Oxford University Press, 2003.

3

Spirituality and Social Character

The Case of New Evangelicalism and Neopaganism

GEORGE N. LUNDSKOW

Currently and over the past decade, the United States has been in the midst of a major religious revival in which the most popular revival movements embrace beliefs that combine reactionary models of personal conduct and family life with messages of universal brotherhood (Bainbridge 1997; Lundskow 2002, 2000). The reasons for this, of course, include, as Sara Diamond (2000; 1995) argues, mass political and economic changes.

At the same time, Diamond's excellent analysis overlooks the importance of social-psychological factors that configure the type of reaction that individuals or groups might have to political-economic changes. Furthermore, the resurgence of reactionary revivalism takes forms beyond politics, in mass movements like the Promise Keepers and the Fellowship of Christian Athletes, in popular best-sellers like the Left Behind series, and in public declarations of piety, as with the combined United States House and Senate standing on the steps of the Capitol and yelling out "under God" as they say the Pledge of Allegiance.

Thus, a political-economic analysis alone cannot approach the question: why are the movements that embrace a reactionary belief system increasingly popular? What sort of person finds this ideology appealing, and why? Why do others find a progressive orientation appealing? Alongside reactionary resurgence, we find also, although on a much smaller scale, progressive religious revival, although often not Christian in essence. Specifically, Neopaganism demonstrates considerable, if difficult to measure, popularity in sharp contrast to the conservative values of fundamentalism.

This chapter considers the social-psychological aspects of reactionary fundamentalism versus progressivism.

Neopaganism and New Evangelicalism in Overview

From a demographic standpoint, Neopaganism and neofundamentalism are quite similar. Both are almost totally white; middle to upper middle class; suburban; college educated, often with advanced degrees; concerned about social issues; and looking for emotionally gratifying religious experience. All feel alienated, fragmented, and without spiritual direction or enthusiasm in life; both movements formed and continue to develop as reactions against the spiritual dissatisfaction of modern life or in short, against the alienation of modernity (Dawson 1998). Furthermore, both identify various social problems, often the same social problems, especially poverty and violence, and self-destruction, such as alcohol and drug abuse, as indicative of an essential and underlying problem — spiritual vacancy. Of course, the particular doctrines and rituals are very different, but this is not the decisive difference from a sociological standpoint. Rather, the significant differences are twofold: each reinforces a different social character, which in turn reinforces very different social practice.

Neofundamentalism and Neopaganism are both, as social movements, forms of religious revival. The former is the latest in a series of Christian revivals in the United States since the Great Awakenings, which have been at various times reactionary and progressive. The current manifestation is, although perhaps not reactionary, definitely conservative. In contrast, Neopaganism is the latest in a 20th century history of progressive forms of revival, although none prior to the 1970s have been "pagan." Let us look briefly at the essence of neofundamentalism for comparative purposes with Neopaganism.

In the US, evangelical revival since the First Awakening (late 18th and early 19th centuries) has crossed denominational lines, with new alliances forming along lines other than particularities in denominational doctrine. Over time, a basic "conservative" compared to "liberal" social orientation now distinguishes movements that doctrinal differences previously separated (Hunter 1991), such that, for example, Catholics with conservative social values find more in common with conservative Baptists than with other Catholics. Similarly, progressive practices, such as Neopaganism or American versions of Eastern religions — Buddhism especially — find enthusiasts among mainline Christian churches, among Catholics and Protestants. Given the inclusive and flexible nature of religions such as Neopaganism and Buddhism, a person can be pagan or Buddhist (or both) and still remain faithful to mainline Christianity. Today, both fundamentalism and Neopaganism draw substantially from mainline churches and equally from nonaffiliated individuals (Perrin, Kennedy, and Miller 1997; Zinnbauer and Pargament 1998).

Fundamentalism began just after 1900, from diverse Christian movements, although many, such as the Pentecostals (founded January 1, 1901) did not intentionally read the Bible literally as the basis of social identity and social change (Barkun 1994). Only later, in the 1920s, did various congregations unite around fundamentalist principles as a direct reaction against secular modernism, and especially against the theory of evolution. Beginning in the 1950s and through to the present, fundamentalism has aligned itself strongly with American patriotism and anti–Communism (Ahlstrom 1972), and with conservative policy agendas (Guth 1996). Through formal and informal movement organizations, fundamentalism has, past and present, sought to engineer social life along principles of conservative Christian values, as in the temperance movement (Gusfield [1963] 1986), in the anti-pornography and anti-gay movements (Herman 1997), and in the rapidly strengthening creation science movement. Fundamentalists focus on and often mobilize in favor of prayer in public schools, censorship, the primacy of Christianity in the United States, and faith-based education, especially creationism, all as means to address social problems such as poverty, violence, and immorality, especially sex outside of marriage and homosexuality.

Whether highly organized politically as the Christian Coalition, for example, moderately organized as the Focus on the Family, loosely organized as the Promise Keepers, or minimally organized as Bible study groups in established local churches or factions of the local PTA, fundamentalism and other conservative evangelical faiths greatly outpace any other religious belief in the United States in terms of growth and geographic ubiquity both historically (Finke and Stark 1992; Heyrman 1997) and presently (Crapanzano 2000; Miller 1997).

In contrast, the central history of Neopaganism cannot be traced so readily. Although Ronald Hutton (1999, 1991) has produced a fairly detailed history of Neopaganism in the United Kingdom, no similar work exists for the United States. A curious book by Randolph (1947) indicates that a non–British version of paganism may have existed in the United States well before the publication and import of *Witchcraft Today* by Gerald Gardner — the source often cited by many contemporary practitioners. Of course, the nonwhite cultures of New Orleans embody many pagan traditions as well, such as Voodoo, none of which have been academically documented.

In general, Neopaganism refers to individuals or groups who practice pre–Christian religions, which may or may not be historically or anthropologically verifiable. In other words, Neopagans, like New Evangelicals, construct their beliefs within and in response to modern life. Neopaganism typically emphasizes female and goddess-centered beliefs, such as Wicca, and also nature-worshipping Druidic traditions, as well as ancient beliefs from the Middle East and Native America, and syncretic versions with Buddhism and even Christianity. Neopagan spirituality seeks balance and harmony between humans and nature and between diverse cultures. Neopagans focus on and often mobilize against environmental degradation, violence, racism, and sexism. They favor a live-and-let-live ethical system.

In general, Neopaganism encompasses a variety of what enthusiasts believe are pre–Christian beliefs which speak to people struggling with the uncertainties of modern life and the selfish and exploitive values of modern capitalism. Neopagans do not inherently reject science and modernity, but accept science as one source of knowledge and modern rationalism as one type of knowledge and one way of living, but neither addresses spiritual knowledge or spiritual living. Thus, neopaganism offers a set of values and a lifestyle that seeks to fill in, so to speak, the spiritual vacancy of coldly calculating and often exploitive modernity.

Similarly, fundamentalism calls its enthusiasts to a lifestyle and values that predate modernity, especially the reign of modern science and secular values. In contrast, Christian fundamentalism rejects syncretic inclusiveness and seeks to eradicate immoral beliefs and practices which its adherents feel predominate in modern life. Granted, conservative movements like the Calvary Church — which establishes parishes at the local level — or the Promise Keepers — which exists as a national movement without its own local parishes — both welcome interdenominational discourse and participation, but only to a point. More specifically, they welcome people with similar conservative values, regardless of denomination. As Lundskow (2002) shows, the Promise Keepers, Calvary, and similar neoconservative Christian revival ministries have minimal doctrine that consists of general yet typically fundamentalist and emotionally forceful statements of belief. Within this general framework, enthusiasts are "free" to fill in the specifics.

Belief and Character

However, this particular sort of "freedom" requires careful specification. The initial requirement is substantial — acknowledgement of rigid fundamentalist doctrine which at least sets narrow boundaries on belief and values, and depending on the particular movement or congregation may also set strict and specific boundaries on beliefs, values, and behavior. Once acknowledged, these new movement churches offer exuberant and contemporary services: sermons in common language with contemporary references, Christian rock and rap music, extensive casual conversation, and individual worship that may take many forms, from charismatic speaking in tongues to group prayer to quiet personal prayer. Many such movements are thoroughly enmeshed in popular culture, and parishes are often found in strip malls and suburban commercial thoroughfares. Although doctrinally narrow and sometimes harsh, they are also often exciting services.

For neofundamentalists, humans who would receive salvation must serve God, who is a superior power. The obligation is handed down from God — God calls everyone to fulfill particular tasks — and an individual can choose to accept the calling, and thereby submit to God's designs, or choose to reject it. Very differently, progressive revival holds that obligation arises from mutually recognized responsibility, and a more dynamic sensibility that individuals face a series of choices that have both personal and social impact. Decisions and actions are good or bad depending both on intention and effect on others, and not whether an action offends a higher power, i.e., God. Thus, religious belief and practice is not simply a matter of accepting and submitting to a higher power, but rather is a matter of choosing a path in relation to others. Humans can approach spiritual issues better when in conjunction with each other as dynamic, thinking, and interactive individuals who are also part of a community of their own making.

This difference in belief and practice points to a crucial difference that emerges at the social-psychological level. As with any religion, both movements reinforce the dominant values of the society in which the members live; as Durkheim discovered long ago, to celebrate religion is to celebrate the idealized social order. Thus it should not be surprising that neofundamentalists embrace conservative political platforms, and Neopagans embrace tolerance and progressive platforms.

But these two very different revivals indicate a much more profound difference: neofundamentalism represents negation of the self, whereas Neopaganism represents fulfillment of the self. The former calls for self-negation in service of absolute beliefs and the priorities of an outside and superior presence (in this case God) and whatever the person perceives to be God's earthly intentions (no gay marriages and no alcohol are common dictates). Neopaganism calls for and reinforces self-realization, that beliefs are created by and in the service of the human members; they are negotiated, and thus in turn, the terms of social life and the ideal order are likewise a process of negotiation in which all voices are relevant. This inherently produces a social ethic premised on diversity and pluralism. In contrast, the conservative doctrine just as inherently produces a closed social order; one either accepts the correct beliefs and the true will of God, or not. But to accept the social order is really an act of submission to a higher and nonnegotiable order, so I conceptualize conservative revival as self-negating. The individual surrenders his sense of self, his ability to make autonomous discernment concerning important matters of faith and practice. Thus, the apparent uniqueness of everyday living, the sacredness of the everyday, actually conforms to a rigid model based on a rigid morality. This orientation can only tolerate difference because difference corresponds precisely to right and wrong. Different is the same as wrong, and wrongness can only be tolerated, not cherished.

Furthermore, the need for spiritual meaning in both movements arises form social conditions, yet the particular approach, self-negation or self-realization, results from a particular social character orientation. This is, to be sure, not a psychologistic theory, but a social theory premised on commonly shared values and experience, which altogether produce a particular outlook or worldview that similar people share in common. Thus, social character overlaps with other collective variables, such as gender, ethnicity, and class. However, the scope of this chapter does not permit close attention to all the interconnections. Instead, I will concentrate on the particular types of social character as evidenced in self-negating and self-realizing movements respectively.

Stated succinctly: Neopaganism alleviates alienation not with exact answers about life, but rather, by offering a means, in close association with other people, to seek answers. In contrast, neofundamentalism seeks to alleviate alienation with exact answers and strict doctrine that demands obedience. Triumph over alienation thus comes at a great price — sacrifice of the individual self. Neopagans celebrate diversity and creative renewal of their faith; neofundamentalists celebrate submission to an external authority. Neopagan community practice thus depends on individual creativity, commitment, and critical reasoning. Neofundamentalism depends on moral enforcement — being on guard against moral violators who deviate from established authority.

In turn, the process of socialization instills a structure of feeling and tendencies that shape the way they approach situations and experience in general according to the values that dominate the group. It guides their actions, whether cautious, suspicious, bold, courageous, selfish, or selfless. As people grow, they develop characterological traits that become the basis of how they interact with other people. In this way, we may think of it as social character. In close friendships, family life, or romantic interests, character perhaps becomes most manifest as the person drops pretensions and whatever other façade he may project to a more anonymous relation. As other studies have found consistently, attachment between people at intimate levels depends on character orientation, not on abstract principles or rational choice from one moment to the next. Whether a person is aggressive, manipulative, and cold, or on the other hand cooperative, considerate, and warm "are not merely abstract philosophical preferences. Rather, they reflect a key dimension of the personality — the way people characteristically relate to others and their sense of commitment to them" (Oliner and Oliner 1992: 171).

In the case of religious devotion, devout belief usually creates strong integration and commitment within the same religious identity, but simultaneously reinforces division and exclusion from nonbelievers. A recent and thorough study found that the degree of devotion and separation from nonbelievers among Americans is decisive, and predicts most strongly the degree of intolerance and aggression (Beit-Hallahmi and Argyle 1997: 229). Furthermore, the greater the intensity of religious devotion, the more prejudiced a person becomes (Batson et al. 1993: 296). This aggression is not always directed against outgroups, but often against deviants or sinners within the group, and potentially parental discontent against their children in the form of corporal punishment, which as Danso (1997) and Straus (1994) show with contemporary data, and Greven (1992, 1977) shows with historical data, is extremely high and held in high regard among conservative evangelicals and fundamentalists. Therefore, the level of submission and aggression among the Promise Keepers, and what form it takes, may cover much of the decisive elements of their social interaction, but we must at the same time remain cognizant of socially positive influence from their beliefs as well. Still, if both movements seek a sense of meaning in a vacant world, why are the beliefs, values, and practices so diametrically different?

Self-Affirmation versus Self-Negation

To answer such questions, numerous scholars in the United States and Europe have revitalized a venerable theory and its associated research tradition — Critical Theory and the study of authoritarianism. Bob Altemeyer's (1997) award-winning book provides a detailed summary of five decades of empirical study on the topic, and offers fresh data. To date, Altemeyer has administered his RWA (Right-Wing Authoritarianism) scale to nearly 15,000 respondents, which posts a strong .90 alpha reliability (Leak and Randall 1995) and an astounding .98 construct validity (Altemeyer 1998, 1997, 1988). Altemeyer also deserves credit for noting the differences between authoritarianism and a related but unique occurrence, the social-dominator orientation (Altemeyer 1998). Other important contributions recently include theoretical work from David N. Smith (1998, 1996, 1992) and Lauren Langman (1998), and the extensive empirical research of Jos Meloen (1999, 1998, 1993), Meloen and Middendorp (1991), and Meloen et al. (1988).

Authoritarianism is in simplest terms the desire to dominate and control anyone (or anything) perceived as weaker or of lesser power, and at the same time to submit to anyone (or anything) perceived as stronger or of greater power, status, or whatever other criteria a person cherishes. A person with identifiable authoritarian tendencies bases his worldview on hierarchy, which usually has at its core some form of belief system — frequently religious — that legitimates the order in the hierarchy and in the process makes it appear as normal, natural, sacred, and in all cases immutable and unassailable. The source of this order, and usually the order itself, derives from or is believed to be ordained by the ultimate power, usually an abstract force — God, nature, the market, whatever else.

Crucially, Meloen (1999) has found that, through a comparative study of international data, the Netherlands exhibits the lowest levels of authoritarianism, with a corresponding decline in religious intensity and conservative political power. In general, Meloen and others, such as Lederer (1995, 1993) Lederer and Kindervater (1995) find that authoritarianism has declined in Western Europe generally since the end of World War II, and this decline correlates strongly with a decline in religiosity, whereas Altemeyer (1997) finds that authoritarian tendencies have remained comparatively high or increased in the same time period in North America, and that religiosity has remained correspondingly high. Furthermore, dogmatic religion in particular (Christian as well as other faiths) correlates directly with reactionary politics, intolerance, and aggression, all of which are expressions of authoritarian character tendencies (Altemeyer 1997; Batson and Burris 1994; Batson, Schoenrade, and Ventis 1993; Batson and Schoenrade 1991; Hunsberger 1996, 1995). Leak and Randall (1995) refine this still further, and found that authoritarianism correlates most strongly with "imperialist" versions of Christianity — those which require not only dogmatic adherence to moral absolutes, but also stipulate that others must also adhere to the same moral dictates, as well as reject reflective thought about one's own beliefs. In general, the more devoutly a person embraces dogmatic religious devotion, the more intensely one embraces an authoritarian worldview.

Yet let me add an element of sociological refinement. Daniel Bell ([1978] 1996) proposes that, to fully understand the disjunction of modern society, we must distinguish social role from the individual. In modern society, people for the first time develop differently as an individual, compared to their place in society, their role. An individual can have many roles (parent, supervisor, friend, worker, etc) which may or may not correlate with one's personal sense of identity. A person may fill any given role in a more or less mechanical manner; one invests no emotion nor derives any sense of self from that role — it holds no meaning other than practical necessity. Thus, the sense of self develops separately from, and sometimes in conflict with, a social role. After all, roles are determined by society, some of which we conform to willingly while others are thrust upon us. In contrast, personal development usually results from conscious choices — how to dress, where to vacation, what sort of friends to have, what movies to see, what to read, what political positions to hold, and a wide, nearly infinite array of consumer choices through which, based on the commodities we buy, we hope to create a unique definition of who we are as individuals. It is precisely this separation of person and role that will serve as the basis to understand contemporary religious revival, which is an attempt to create a meaningful sense of self, in contrast to increasingly meaningless social roles we find thrust upon us.

In response, religion seeks to mend this disjuncture, to offer a unity of belief and practice or, in sociological terms, to create continuity between person, role, and society. Yet disjuncture requires a free individual with the capacity to imagine life differently than one currently lives it. In other words, people must exist who feel unfulfilled as a result of separation from their individual self and the social world around them. Reunification with the social world can take two essential forms. The first corresponds to progressive revival, or progressivism in general, that the self must be made stronger, more dynamic and more resilient, but this requires the support of nothing less than a free and diverse community in which people continually question the answers, yet nevertheless maintain social cohesion by recognizing the inherent right and necessity to remain critically aware of one's own life, and the lives of those in our society. In the case of Neopaganism, society often includes nature as well. Self-affirmation consists not only of individual critical awareness, but also active participation in a community that affirms the individual self as a vital part of a collective identity.

In contrast, reactionary revival corresponds to self-negation, that unity with society occurs by removing the self. Without an individual self, there is no personal lack of fulfillment. Yet as we will see, this leads to new forms of dissatisfaction. Yet the issue at present is self-affirmation versus self-negation. The first depends on collective authority and empowerment. The second depends on submission to external authority.

Although not working in the Critical Theory tradition, the prolific Robert Wuthnow (1998) observes that self-discipline as an aspect of religion and authority is central to conservative evangelical rebirth at the turn of the 21st century. But this related and instructive insight is only the beginning of an analysis that seeks to understand American religious revival today. For a thorough understanding, we must turn to an extensive and detailed research and theory tradition that explicates the relationship of discipline and self-determination.

Religion and Authority

Discipline is simply the behavior that submission to any authority requires. Whether religious or otherwise, a person disciplines himself in accordance with the directives of the authority one recognizes as present, whether legitimate or illegitimate. In this case, I speak only of willingly chosen beliefs and thus only of legitimate authority. Peter Berger ([1967] 1990), in his classic statement on sociology and religion — *The Sacred Canopy* — and following Durkheim and Marx, sees the surrender to God as surrender to an idealized social order; when a person worships God, one worships the world as it ought to be. Although this holds true for all religions, modern societies are characterized by diversity in beliefs, cultures, lifestyles, and so on. Thus, many different world visions may coexist and some will likely conflict. For any particular group, the world as it ought to be may not be as it is. Those worldviews that address issues of ultimate importance, that address the very meaning of life, of death, of how to live, often exist as religious worldviews. The movements they inspire typically organize around a utopian vision (Gusfield 1973) of how the world ought to be.

In this way, neorevivalists of various persuasions "see their experience as an experience with and in a society, rather than as a set of isolated and unrelated events" (Gusfield 1973: 31). Yet their unity does not depend only, or even mostly, on unity of belief. Rather, neorevival movements offer a particular social relationship that the members find familiar and expected in the case of neofundamentalism, or intriguing and provocative in the case of Neopaganism. Thus, it is not the specific content of the beliefs only, but the particular social relationship between the beliefs, the adherent, and other members of the community that provide comfort and belonging — though in very different ways.

Recent empirical research is suggestive, because as Altemeyer (1997: 161) finds, authoritarianism correlates (.68) with fundamentalism and (.53) with ethnocentrism. Leak and Randall (1995) provide further quantitative corroboration, and find furthermore that authoritarianism correlates with an immature personality, one that seeks childlike submission to authority and avoids "mature" traits, in particular, self-reflection, responsibility, and critical reasoning. In qualitative research, Aho (1994, 1990) finds in Christian Identity groups that absolute devotion to moral codes seen as superior and beyond reproach inherently leads to intolerance and sometimes aggression. Bitterness, hostility, suspicion, and anger characterize their worldview. Historically, American evangelicalism has been both progressive (such as abolitionism and later, the center of the civil rights movement) and also reactionary (such as the Moral Majority), which suggests that religious devotion itself does not lead automatically to intolerance, but that some more specific social-psychological relationship must exist, or that the two tendencies may coexist and draw people in conflicting directions.

As Altemeyer found in his studies, "fundamentalism can therefore be viewed as a religious manifestation of right-wing authoritarianism" (Altemeyer 1997: 161). In my research on the Promise Keepers for example, I found that the men support the concept of racial reconciliation, yet they see minorities in highly idealized and generic terms — that all men have all the same hopes, dreams, values.

The Promise Keepers (PK) will serve here as representative of reactionary revivalism, although in comparison to other groups and organizations they are relatively mild.

Regarding distinctly progressive values and programs, the PK exhibit ambivalent tendencies at best. For example, Lundskow (2001) discovered hints of a concealed distrust of programs designed to bring about racial equality, such as affirmative action. The men wholeheartedly accept reconciliation as an ideal, but are less enthusiastic about policy and programs that might make material changes. On the issue of racial reconciliation, the PK men appear to be 10 degrees left of center in theory, and 10 degrees right of center if reconciliation will affect them personally.

Does PK faith and doctrine lead the men more toward a life predicated on power, control, and domination, however mild? Do the narrow parameters of the ideal PK gender roles liberate or further enclose the men? Or, does it free them from the routine they abhor, toward vital emotional relationships? What countervailing forces might be present in their outlook? To understand the PK men and the popularity of the movement, we must understand the relationships between the men and the PK organization as a representative of their faith.

The PK, as representative of neofundamentalism, reinforce familiar and, to the men, comforting themes: the patriarchal nuclear family, submission to Christ, deferral of individual satisfaction. Of particular interest is the relationship of parents to children and methods of raising children. As with nearly all aspects of PK doctrine and the evangelical history it draws from, the belief that children, like all people, are weak and doomed to failure, and ultimately damned to hell without divine grace, requires that parents guide their children properly to accept Jesus. Sometimes, in evangelical tradition, guidance necessarily takes the form of punishment, often physical punishment. As the leader of the family, final authority for the children rests with Dad. In stark contrast, the Neopagans in this study abhor physical discipline, and actively encourage children to speak out and think for themselves. The parents maintain a firm set of values, but values, namely cooperation, that inherently reinforces friendship and community rather than challenges it. The children thus seek and are rewarded for harmonious interaction rather than competitive interaction or simple obedience.

Yet how is it that the PK men in my study, and the neofundamentalists in other studies (Miller 1997, for example) feel "liberated" and "freed" and "saved?" Sometimes they named specific problems, such as drinking, or loneliness, or anger, or a general dissatisfaction with life. At the same time, they also say that a person must "surrender" and "submit" to Christ, in order to be saved. The following exemplifies their attitudes:

> You can't be saved until you are willing to give up your own desires, your own wants in life. Jesus is there if you are willing to surrender to Him, and He will guide you to salvation, but only if you submit to His plan for you. And He has a plan for everyone, but a lot of people, and me included for a long time, think they know better and try to find their way without the Lord, and let me tell you something, you will fail without Him. Once I gave myself over to the Lord, my life started to improve immediately. I found my family again, I started to get along better with people at work, and I knew, for the first time in my life, that things will work out. Maybe not the way I want, but I know Jesus will not let me down, and whatever He wants is the best for me in the long run. I felt so free at that moment, when I declared myself for the Lord.

How can a person feel free at the same moment he surrenders and submits? There are important variations on this attitude, but the consistent element remains that the men see their relationship as a submissive one, yet one that, in the act of submission, produces a feeling of freedom. In what sense are they free, and from what? Does this freedom entail other forms of unfreedom?

Erich Fromm first recognized that some people feel a need to submit, that

> The desire for obedience and submission as such, whether conscious or completely concealed through rationalizations such as conformity, necessity, and sensibility, the decisive point remains that for the authoritarian character, situations in which he can be obedient become moments of gratification and thus he does not seek to end such conditions, but rather bind himself to them all the more tightly [Fromm 1936: 114 — all translations from this text by George N. Lundskow].

For the authoritarian character, submission feels pleasurable, in the sense that it relieves the burden of responsibility, of thinking, of uncertainty that arises from life's vicissitudes. However, not all forms of submission are authoritarian. For example, students submit to professors because they hope to learn from the professor's greater knowledge, and in so doing, become more like the professor. Eventually, the authority relationship dissolves itself as the students approach the professor's level. In a different way, colonial people submitted to European powers because the Europeans brought large armies; rebellion always carried the risk of death. Rather, the authoritarian form of submission occurs because the person feels an emotional compulsion to submit to something one perceives as greater, to surrender one's sense of self-identity, to give up the possibility of autonomous thought. In short, authoritarianism is the longing and desire to submit to anything perceived as stronger or superior, and the desire to dominate and control anything perceived as weaker or inferior. People usually do not experience their feelings as "the desire to submit," but rather, they usually rationalize their actions, according to the perceived will of God, morality, laws of nature, and so on.

How can a person feel free through submission? Beit-Hallahmi and Argyle (1997) who, like Fromm and Batson, focus on the relationship of the individual to religious beliefs, and how the person internalizes values and likewise contributes to the social construction of belief and behavior. Oliner and Oliner (1992) examine the altruistic personality traits that motivated some few people to defy Nazi power and actively help rescue Jews with no recognition or reward, and often at great peril to themselves. Why did a few act on their own initiative and to benefit others, while most surrendered passively to the given circumstances to benefit themselves? To understand this, and why some people find absolute authority appealing while others embrace interactive negotiation of authority, we must now turn to the second component of the revival community — social character.

Social Character

Depending on the exact combination of values, a person can be said to have an identifiable character type, and to the extent one shares characteristics in common with other people, they all together share a social character. Social character thus refers to the way in which people see the world and interact with each other as members of a social group. In Social Character in a Mexican Village, Erich Fromm and Michael Maccoby ([1970] 1996) established aspects of social character that includes both authoritarian tendencies and anti-authoritarian tendencies.

Social character is a complex set "of character traits which has developed as an adaptation to the economic, social, and cultural conditions common to that group" (Fromm [1970] 1996: 16). Furthermore, in Fromm's view, modern societies with a complex division of labor do not have a universal social character, but within the general structure of society, such as capitalist class relations, with which "each class demands different kinds of functions from the members" (Fromm [1970] 1996: 17) and thus, each class develops a different social character. As capitalism has advanced, the working class, for example, became both submissive, yet rebellious. They must submit to the decisions of managers and the labor needs of business in order to survive, but as employment becomes less secure, benefits decrease, and corporate capital relocates, the working class also becomes rebellious and potentially revolutionary.

Class relations combine with various elements of capitalism, particularly the commodification of everything, including people, personalities, and even thoughts (Fromm [1941] 1994: 123–133) which tends to separate, that is, alienate, from each other, and from themselves. Objects become more real than people; in a classic example, men treat cars as if they had a life and a real personality, and conversely, the women in their lives become idealized objects and commodities. More importantly, an emotional loneliness results, and this state of "moral aloneness is just as intolerable as physical aloneness" (Fromm [1941] 1994: 17–18) and perhaps more than anything else, neorevivalists want to belong, but not to just any group, but to one on the right path. They are not alone physically, nor threatened materially. Yet they are all looking for certainty in society where a person can buy anything except spiritual certainty.

Class, however, is not the only important factor. Perhaps equally important is family life and upbringing, especially the treatment that a child receives regarding justice. Fromm refers to the development of character as "adaptation" because the individual must adapt to social conditions, such as the guidelines (or demands) of the parents, the presence of love or aggression, the possibility of personal growth or the pressure to conform, and so on. Later, the child encounters institutions in formal education, and eventually through work and career. Depending on the circumstances in which a child is raised, the child develops different character traits, usually a combination of self-limiting (authoritarian) traits, and self-expanding (anti-authoritarian or productive) traits.

Fromm concludes that one's general character becomes set around the age of 13 or 14, as the youth adapts to both parents and the beginning of work in the public sphere (Fromm [1970] 1996: 189). However, the particular age depends on the particular society, and the particular class and family circumstances to which one belongs. A youth from a middle-class professional family in contemporary America, for example, may not develop a distinguishable character until he sets off to college. In this case, the trip to college is expected, and thus seen as a natural rite of passage. Prior to this, the youth remains close to the parents who support him both financially and emotionally. Thus the child need not face the demands of self-support in the public sphere until after college. Depending on the society, youth may be relatively free to experiment with different attitudes, beliefs, lifestyles, and modes of adaptation, as often happens in college.

In this case, the person comes of age, so to speak, over a longer period of time through exposure to diverse ways of life. As he enters a more cosmopolitan world, he may discover, for example, that a cooperative and productive mode is preferable to the bitterness and fear that often accompanies an immature and selfish authoritarian reaction. This process of adaptation is complex, and people often do not consciously realize the changes they go through. Altemeyer (1997: 85) finds that students "can be walloped by" their university experience. Almost nobody became more authoritarian between their freshman and senior years, and high RWAs dropped over twice as much as any other group. Although Altemeyer doesn't see it, he confirms the notion that character forms early, and, once formed, changes slowly, and only if social conditions nurture and reinforce a more cooperative and productive orientation. Most importantly, there must be a real and actual possibility for productive relations, not just the presence of humanitarian values.

Fundamentalist Character: Authoritarianism

Just as the productive personality corresponds to lived experience, so too does the authoritarian personality. In longitudinal studies, Altemeyer's research shows that, after college, those who initially scored high on the RWA scale mostly returned to high scores, although not as high as originally (Altemeyer 1997: 86). Similarly, moderates and lows tended to stay moderate and low. It appears that the high authoritarians stayed high, and merely responded the way they believed superiors (in this case professors) would want them to answer. After college, their direct authority figure gone, they expressed their authoritarian views more openly.

As the person develops, character forms according to one's social "relatedness" to the world, and not from some innate trait. As mentioned, these traits develop according to personal experience and the structure of society, especially the degree of freedom which a person has to develop as an individual. Also, any one person is typically a blend of different characteristics, and often competing characteristics that pull a person in different directions. This "pull" creates a tension that may lead to all sorts of erratic behavior. For example, many PK men discussed with me their desire for a closeness with their children, yet at the same time they feel unable to express intimate feelings. The men still hold a residual sense of masculinity that does not permit ready expression of tender emotion, and they fear the possibility (subconsciously) that their children may perceive them as weak or unstable. Yet their own desire for emotional connection, combined with the urgings from the PK to develop emotional sensitivity, compels them onward. The result for many men is an indecisiveness that results from the inability to resolve competing desires—until they "surrendered" to the Lord.

Batson et al. (1993) term this "freedom with bondage," in the sense that "devout beliefs free the person from existential concerns; at the same time, they bind the believer to themselves, preventing free critical reflection...." (Batson et al. 1993: 198). Based on thorough review on previous work and their own study, the Batson team finds that devotion to absolute religious beliefs, which in the authoritarian tradition scholars term submission to a higher power, the believer relieves himself of existential concerns, or in other words of uncertainty, yet in the process binds himself to a strong internalized moral authority. This moral authority, which appears as a burdensome set of rules to the outsider, usually prescribes behavior in absolute moral terms, and thus the believer need not critically reflect, but simply believe. Batson calls this "intrinsic" religion, because it emanates from the person's inner psychic state, and because it settles many existential fears (such as the fear of death) or fear of self-destructive behavior (depression, drinking, etc.) the person values his beliefs highly. As Batson finds though, "the freedom obtained by devout, intrinsic belief is obtained at a high price; it is freedom with bondage, bondage to the belief system itself" (Batson et al. 1993: 224). The more threats or challenges to his faith the person perceives, whether real or imaginary, the more tightly the person clings to his faith. In the case of the PK, I think the threats are, as Batson terms it, extrinsic, that is, social in the form of economic pressure and changing cultural norms. From the perspective of the PK men, however, they interpret the threat as intrinsic, that they have personally strayed from God's intentions. Thus, the men believe that the solution is internal, to accept the will of Jesus Christ (and thus to submit more fervently).

The power of belief in this case can be decisive. As Beit-Hallahmi and Argyle (1997) show, sex is consistently the most proscribed activity and usually indicative of the general degree of spontaneity or dogmatism. Sex is always controlled and typically condemned in all but narrow circumstances. With data for all major Protestant churches, Catholics, and Jews, they found that the intensity of belief, and not the denomination, determines behavior. For sex, those with fundamentalist beliefs have sex much less often, even in marriage, and experience sexual satisfaction to a far less degree. Rasmussen and Charman (1995) tested Freud's superego hypothesis (which Fromm and many other in the authoritarian tradition rely on). They found strong support for the idea that the fundamentalist has a strong superego, which means the person internalizes an idealized version of external authority, which one then projects out again; in the case of religion, he projects it as God.

In general, the more fundamentalist and committed to personal moral righteousness a person is, the more authoritarian and intolerant one becomes. Both the older research, such as Adorno et al. (1950) and more recently, such as Altemeyer (1997) and Hunsberger (1995) confirm the relationship between authoritarianism, intolerance, and aggression.

Others working separately from the Critical Theory tradition reach similar conclusions (Juergensmeyer 2001; Tibi 2002). In a different study, Hunsberger (1996) found that fundamentalism determines authoritarian submission and aggression among Jews, Hindus, and Muslims as well as among Christians. To my knowledge, no studies reject this relationship.

Still, neorevival in the U.S. does not address its enthusiasts in terms of authority. Rather, I contend that in fundamentalist revival, the individual seeks to become acceptable to others who represent an external authority, whereas Neopagans seek to interactively construct a consensual authority. The fundamentalist seeks to please abstract authority; the Neopagan seeks to please the community of which he is an active member. Fromm theorizes a social character type that perhaps typifies capitalist society and, in our case, the fundamentalist. He calls it the marketing character, which did not exist, he argues, to any great extent prior to the rise of capitalism, for reasons that should become apparent. The marketing type forms in response to the spread of market culture, which is to say that people become commodities for exchange, and to the extent people see others in this way, they evaluate one another based on their exchange value. As we know today, commercials, pageants, MTV videos, movies, our culture in general reminds us that superficial physical qualities are most important, and defined within very narrow parameters of body size, dress, even attitude and topics of discussion. Romance becomes a means to acquire an object, and "the difference between people is reduced to a merely quantitative difference of being more or less successful, attractive, and hence valuable" (Fromm [1947] 1990: 73). Self-esteem becomes dependent on whether a person can sell himself in the market. The familiar term that bars are often "meat markets" illustrates the point. Overall, the marketing character strives to become what they think others want them to be; they defer their own goals, interests, and desires, both in career and personal relationships, to what will please an abstract authority — whether the market or God.

In contrast, neopagan revival represents a very different social character, the productive orientation.

Neopagan Character: Productivity

The productive orientation more or less contradicts all the aforementioned tendencies. Does human character involve more than simply the absence of negative traits? How else does society develop? If people are capable only of submission, dominance, or at best, benign routine, how then can we explain progress in the area of civil rights, for example? Or innovation in literature, film, science? For Fromm, the productive character is central to the condition of humanity in general. That is, the emergence of the self-actualized, productive, self-aware yet socially oriented character occurs simultaneously with the struggle for freedom.

Historical societies impose various laws, social codes, and other forms of control and coercion that determine the degree of freedom or oppression. In turn, the structure of society determines the extent to which people may think creatively, and independently, and to what extent people may pursue their own goals, desires, and dreams. A society that does not allow for free time, for example, with access to resources and fulfillment of basic necessities limits the opportunity for personal growth and enrichment. Thus, the productive character is an unfolding type — an ongoing struggle. Thus, Fromm says that "in discussing the productive character, I venture beyond critical analysis and inquire into the nature of the fully developed character that is the aim of human development and simultaneously the ideal of humanist ethics" (Fromm, [1947] 1990: 83). It is all too easy to fall into the familiar, if limiting, authoritarian type. The emergence of productive traits comes only with struggle, and at times may challenge social conventions, at which point the person feels pressure to conform or submit, in short, to surrender his struggle for true individuality. Thus, the productive type is a phenomenon that is still emerging at this moment in history, even as different groups and classes struggle for greater equality and justice.

Therefore, Fromm theorizes that the productive type is necessarily more generally understood. The productive person is able to perceive the world as it is, but also can conceive of alternatives, of possibilities (Fromm, [1947] 1990: 89–90). However, this differs from the opportunistic nature of the exploiter, in that the productive person realizes he is interconnected with others. Thus, the productive person comprehends the world, through love and reason together (Fromm, [1947] 1990: 97) and applies his ability to work accordingly.

Reason and passion combine to form care and responsibility, which derive from active engagement with the world and with human relationships. This person shuns motives such as greed and other forms of self-preoccupation, because they conflict with the desire for self-emancipation from compulsion. The productive person prefers to work cooperatively, rather than competitively, because competition leads only to the success of one and the failure of another, such that competition traps a person in a repetitive cycle of each against all. The productive person cares for others when he understands the condition of others; the productive person does not possess others in love, but loves them because he appreciates the feelings and needs of others. Responsibility derives from this combination of love and respect; each person accepts responsibility as he understands his relationships and freely assumed obligations to other people.

If this discussion seems abstract and philosophical to an extent — it is. As I said, the productive character is one and the same with the unfolding of individuality and freedom, and continues to unfold as the struggle for freedom continues. Productiveness requires a level of civilization that we have not yet achieved, and like all forms of social character, it requires an active community to reinforce it in the individual.

In my own recently completed (but unpublished) study of three Neopagan communities, in Boston, New Orleans, and Lawrence, Kansas, I found three intentional communities. All centered around particular residences or sometimes businesses. Although the particular identity differed, for example, that in Boston the members were also a community of writers, artists, and musicians, whereas in New Orleans they were families and activists, and in Lawrence mostly students, the spiritual identity — Pagan — was very similar. Space does not permit extensive presentation of my ethnographic data, but suffice to say that the findings regarding the spiritual identity resembles very closely the ethnographic studies of Neopagan communities by Berger (1999) and Pike (2001). Jorgensen and Russell (1999) obtained similar results through quantitative analysis, that regardless of the particular name identifiers apply to themselves, whether Pagan, Druid, Wiccan, and so on, the core identity of progressive spirituality remains consistent.

The Neopagan communities in these studies are generally productive, and strongly premise their collective identity on productive character. Still, they are very small communities, and perhaps most importantly, lack an economic foundation separate from mainstream society, and thus, despite the collective economy of members who lived at the so-called Nature House in New Orleans, for example, full productive character faces substantial challenges outside the household. The other two communities both lack an organized household, and thus are even more dependent on conventional employment which, with few exceptions, inhibits if not directly negates the productive orientation. Yet the members in Boston and Lawrence actively seek employment that defies convention as much as possible. They work in cooperatives, or local record stores, or noncorporate restaurants, or any livelihood that they feel respects the workers as individuals.

The Neopagan communities create a social space that encourages open discussion and allows people to live much more directly based on their moral commitments, rather than according to the demands of external authority, especially conventionality. As a result, I observed only minimal ambivalence, or suppressed emotions in general. If anything, they are among the most stable and expressive people I have ever known, even those that continue to struggle with alcohol or other self-destructive behavior (especially eating disorders). All have shown considerable improvement since their involvement with their respective communities, and although not all have fully overcome their problems, all have at least shed any illusion about their own behavior. They no longer attempt to justify it or minimize the harm it causes. Perhaps most strikingly, they worry most about the harm they may potentially cause others, that their continued affiliation with the community supersedes their personal desire to indulge their problems.

Yet much of their lives are joyful. In addition to the conventional holidays, such as Thanksgiving and the Fourth of July, Neopagans celebrate numerous other holidays. Most pertain to the changing of the seasons, or important spiritual times, especially the three-day Halloween, All Saint's Day, and Day of the Dead. Although they may give these fall days different names, the point is consistent — contact with the afterlife, the beyond. All holidays are times of celebration for Neopagans, always energetic, only sometimes but never entirely solemn. Holidays are for feasting and cooking, for camaraderie and love. Life is to be enjoyed.

Belief and Possibility: Specified Living versus Ongoing Negotiation

From early in life, neofundamentalists grow up with their lives premised on their relationship to an all-powerful authority — parents and God — while others lacked a definitive authority. Neopagans came from similarly mixed backgrounds. The difference is that Neopagans seek to overcome problematic relations to authority by changing the nature and role of authority in life, while neofundamentalists attempt to reconstruct the authority of their past or the authority they idealize.

Fundamentalists in modern times face an additional conundrum: they find themselves in a society that increasingly denies the possibility of living the nuclear family model. The ideal becomes increasingly impractical if not impossible. In contrast, Neopagan households manage routine and resources collectively, according to beliefs which are to a great extent negotiable as the members see fit, so long as they continue to promote collective living.

In order to preserve a society and its members, people must "work and produce," and the way work actually gets done "is always concrete work, that is, a specific kind of work in a specific kind of economic system" (Fromm [1941] 1994: 16). In other words, the actual possibilities one finds for fulfillment of basic physiological needs depend on the opportunities that a given mode of production allows and a person's location in the social structure. In the case of modern capitalist societies, some people have more opportunities than others, and some find themselves squeezed out almost entirely, whereas they once held an important economic and status position. The Promise Keepers and neofundamentalism generally propose to solve the problem by helping couples accept their new position, and looking inward to the family for different and better (spiritual rather than material) rewards in life.

If the nuclear family requires great material sacrifice or proves impossible, at least enthusiasts can feel good about struggling forever toward it.

Still, without a viable material basis, and the less the servant-leader and nuclear family models match their real-life opportunities, and the less it fails to provide the authentic emotion they seek and the less it effectively resolves marital problems, the less credible fundamentalism will become over time. In this scenario, servant-leadership perpetuates rather than resolves their dissatisfaction. The more hopes and dreams they set upon the servant-leader ideal, or the more they devote their emotion to worship of charismatic leaders, the fewer hopes and dreams they realize in actuality.

Neopagans have no particular head of the household, but instead rely on self-motivation and varying responsibilities, such that a person who knows a lot about household maintenance, for example, becomes a sort of leader on repairs, but in turn might defer to others on child-rearing. The extended family allows far more intimate diversity and balance in the household, compared to the limited and strict hierarchy in the conservative family. Each thus reinforces very different types of attitudes toward authority, and instills very different types of social character. The conservative family member responds to authoritative instructions or orders, whereas the Neopagan member responds to mutual praise and cooperation.

For new fundamentalist churches, God's Word is the only legitimate authority, as represented in fundamentalist beliefs. Beyond the basic beliefs, God speaks directly to each person, and thus only the individual and God can legitimately say what God intends for any specific person. Thus, new fundamentalist churches have no religious authority system, only facilitators and parish managers. The Word of God is primary, and requires no expert interpretation and each individual must apply the Word in his own life and in his own way, as God speaks to him. Of course, in sociological perspective, this represents a particular interpretation of Christianity, but my point is not to argue doctrine. Rather, since the message is primary but basic, any means may be used to communicate that message, and then only the individual can know what God wants for him. In other words, the movement provides the general framework, and the individual fills in the details. Thus, for example, rock music can carry the fundamentalist message just as legitimately as traditional gospel music. Of course, these churches do not accept everything about contemporary culture, but in contrast to older fundamentalist movements, there is no inherent need to reject popular culture or a modern way of life.

Conclusions

Neopaganism has found enthusiastic popularity in the same revival period as neofundamentalist movements. However, their terms of participation are different. There are no particular doctrines, no required beliefs, no specific practices. Whereas neofundamentalist enthusiasts tend to be politically conservative, Neopagans are overwhelmingly "progressive" and tolerant of diverse beliefs and lifestyles. This makes them compatible (at least for Neopagans) with many established faiths, Christian and otherwise. Like neofundamentalism, Neopagan enthusiasts celebrate a type of religious rebirth, a sense that life has some kind of larger meaning and that how we live, the choices we make, and the values we hold actually matter and make a difference — both in the here and now, and in a larger spiritual sense.

In contrast, a central feature of what Miller (1997) identifies as New Paradigm churches, although he refers only to Protestant denominations, is an emotionally powerful theology that turns everyday routine into a sacred obligation. Yet progressive revivals also regard the everyday as sacred and a type of obligation, but with a crucial difference. The progressive obligation arises from the acknowledgement that each individual has a social obligation to others, regardless of race, class, religion, and so on. This applies even to strangers, to society in general, and to the nonhuman world. For conservative revivals, humans who would receive salvation must serve God, who is a superior power. The obligation is handed down from God, and an individual can choose to accept it, and thereby submit to God's designs, or choose to reject it. As Bruce (1990 1988) and Phelan et al. (1995) found, conservative evangelicals have little regard for the poor or anyone in distress, and instead trust that God will take care of them. One has responsibility to oneself only.

Very differently, progressive revival holds that obligation arises from mutually recognized responsibility and a more dynamic sensibility that individuals face a series of choices that have both personal and social impact. Thus, religious belief and practice is not simply a matter of accepting and submitting to a higher power, but rather is a matter of choosing a path in relation to others. Humans can approach spiritual issues better when in conjunction with each other as dynamic, thinking, and interactive individuals who are also part of a community of their own making.

This difference in belief and practice points to a crucial difference that emerges at the social-psychological level. As with any religion, both movements reinforce the dominant values of the society in which the members live; as Durkheim discovered long ago, to celebrate religion is to celebrate the idealized social order. Thus it should not be surprising that neofundamentalists embrace conservative political platforms, and Neopagans embrace tolerance and progressive platforms.

But these two very different revivals indicate a much more profound difference: neofundamentalism represents submission of the self, whereas Neopaganism represents fulfillment of the self. The former calls for self-negation in service of absolute beliefs and the priorities of an outside and superior presence (in this case God) and whatever the person perceives to be God's earthly intentions (no gay marriages, for example). The latter calls for and reinforces self-realization, that beliefs are created by and in the service of the human members; they are negotiated, and thus in turn, the terms of social life and the ideal order are likewise a process of negotiation in which all voices are relevant. This inherently produces a social ethic premised on diversity and tolerance. In contrast, the conservative doctrine just as inherently produces a closed social order; one either accepts the correct beliefs and the true will of God, or not. But to accept the social order is really an act of submission to a higher and nonnegotiable order, so I conceptualize conservative revival as self-negating. The individual surrenders one's sense of self, one's ability to make autonomous discernment concerning important matters of faith and practice. Thus, the apparent uniqueness of everyday living, the sacredness of the everyday, actually conforms to a rigid model, based on a rigid morality.

Furthermore, the need for spiritual meaning in both movements arises from social conditions, yet the particular approach, self-negation or self-realization, results from a particular social character orientation. This is, to be sure, not a psychologistic theory, but a social theory premised on commonly shared values and experience, which altogether produce a particular outlook or worldview that similar people share in common. Thus, social character overlaps with other collective variables, such as gender, ethnicity, and class.

Contemporary research shows that Americans are dissatisfied with the established churches. Mainline churches continue to lose members; new churches continue to gain members, sometimes from mainline congregations, but mostly from people who felt nonreligious or claimed no particular affiliation at the time. Of the New Religious Movements, conservative and fundamentalist Christian movements are easily the most popular, and appear under various names, including the Promise Keepers, Calvary, and numerous fundamentalist revival movements within established churches such as Assembly of God and Pentecostalism. Altogether, fundamentalist Christians, despite denominational differences, organize effectively at a national level around political issues, and have placed numerous candidates in public office. They even include the current president of the United States, George W. Bush, among their ranks. His administration has obtained legislation to allow government funds to be delivered to faith-based education and social services. The president has ordered the State Department to facilitate the activities of Southern Baptist missionaries as they seek to convert the conquered people of Iraq to Christianity (Caldwell 2003; Goodstein 2003).

Simultaneously, we see also a few progressive movements in the realm of spirituality, which include Neopaganism. In contrast to fundamentalist Christianity, Neopagan groups are diverse and locally organized, typically around friendship networks or a commonly shared interest (such as art or music). Their emphasis against hierarchy makes them inherently unsuitable for mass national organization, and thus, although they constitute a countermovement in the spiritual realm, and even perhaps serve as model for alternative communities, they do not constitute a counterpolitical movement. Moreover, in comparison with fundamentalist movements, they are very small in total numbers.

At this moment in history, the United States seems destined for a very conservative period; prayer in public schools and perhaps even replacing evolution with creation myths in science class should not surprise us. Whereas Neopagan movements are able to integrate science and faith without violating the integrity of either, fundamentalist Christianity seeks to control all of social life and create a theocracy. In the present day, the security that self-negation offers seems ascendant, and the American public presently seems unable or unwilling to embrace self-realization, in whatever form.

Yet the American public has in recent years proven very fickle, and support for the Bush administration may fade as quickly as it rose. Can the movement survive the political defeat of such a prominent authority figure? Yet I would like to leave the reader with a statement from Max Weber, a founder of sociology. Speaking just after World War I, and predicting the rise of totalitarianism, Weber writes:

> Not summer's bloom lies ahead of us, but a polar night of icy darkness and hardness.... When this night shall have slowly receded, who of those among us for whom Spring has finally returned will still be alive? And what will have become of all of you by then? Will you be bitter and banalistic? Will you simply and dully accept whatever form of domination claims authority over you? Or will the third and by no means the least likely possibility be your lot: mystic flight from reality.... In every one of these cases, I shall draw the conclusion that we have not measured up to their own doings. We have not measured up to the world as it really is in its everyday routine [Weber (1918) 1946: 128].

Consider then, which of the two movements — Neopaganism or fundamentalist Christianity — speaks more to the world as it really is, to the reality of daily routine, to the real needs and hopes of humans in the real world. Which offers a flight from reality? Where would each lead us, and what do they require to reach the destination?

References

Ahlstrom, Sydney E. *A Religious History of the American People*. New Haven: Yale University Press, 1972.
Aho, James A. *The Politics of Righteousness: Idaho Christian Patriotism*. Seattle: University of Washington Press, 1990.
_____. *This Thing of Darkness: A Sociology of the Enemy*. Seattle: University of Washington Press, 1994.
Altemeyer, Bob. "The Other Authoritarian Personality." Advances in Experimental Psychology, Vol. 30 (1998): 47–91.
_____. *The Authoritarian Specter*. Cambridge, MA: Harvard University Press, 1997.
_____. *Enemies of Freedom: Understanding Right-Wing Authoritarianism*. San Francisco: Bass, 1988.
Bainbridge, William Sims. *The Sociology of Religious Movements*. New York: Routledge, 1997.
Barkun, Michael. *Religion and the Racist Right: The Origins of the Christian Identity Movement*. Chapel Hill, NC: University of North Carolina Press, 1994.
Batson, C. Daniel, Patricia Schoenrade, and W. Larry Ventis. *Religion and the Individual: A Social-Psychological Perspective*. New York: Oxford University Press, 1993.
Beit-Hallahmi Benjamin, and Michael Argyle. 1997. *The Psychology of Religious Behaviour, Belief, and Experience*. London: Routledge, 1997.
Bell, Daniel. *The Cultural Contradictions of Capitalism*. 1978. Reprint, New York: Basic Books, 1996.
Berger, Helen. *A Community of Witches: Contemporary Neopaganism and Witchcraft in the United States*. Columbia, SC: South Carolina University Press, 1999.
Berger, Peter. *The Sacred Canopy*. 1967. Reprint, New York: Anchor Books/Random House, 1990.
Bruce, Stephen. *What Does the Lord Require? How American Christians Think About Economic Justice*. New York: Oxford University Press, 1988.
Bruce, Stephen. *The Rise and Fall of the New Christian Right: Conservative Protestant Politics in America, 1978–1988*. New York: Oxford University Press, 1990.
Caldwell, Deborah. "Should Christian Missionaries Heed the Call to Iraq?" *The New York Times Late Edition*, April 4, 2003, Sec. 4, page 14, col. 1.
Crapanzano, Vincent. *Serving the Word: Literalism in America from the Pulpit to the Bench*. New York: The New Press, 2000.
Danso, Henry, Bruce Hunsberger, and Michael Pratt. "The Role of Religious Fundamentalism and Right-Wing Authoritarianism in Childrearing Goals and Practices." *Journal for the Scientific Study of Religion* 36 (December 1997): 496–511.
Diamond, Sara. *Not by Politics Alone: The Enduring Influence of the Christian Right*. New York; Guilford Press, 2000.
Diamond, Sara. *Roads to Dominion: Right-Wing Movements and Political Power in the United States*. New York; Guilford Press, 1995.
Finke, Roger, and Rodney Stark. *The Churching of America, 1776–1990*. New Brunswick, NJ: Rutgers University Press, 1992.
Fromm, Erich, and Michael Maccoby. *Social Character in a Mexican Village*. 1970. New Brunswick, NJ: Transaction Publishers, 1998.
Fromm, Erich. *Escape from Freedom*. 1941. Reprint, New York: Henry Holt, 1994.

_____. *The Anatomy of Human Destructiveness*. 1973. Reprint, New York: Henry Holt, 1994.

_____. "Sozialpsychologischer Teil." My translation, "The Social-Psychology of Authoritarianism." *Studien über Authorität und Familie*. Paris: Alcan, 1936.

Gardner, Gerald. *Witchcraft Today*. 1954. Reprint, Auburn Press, 1970.

Goodstein, Laurie. "Missionaries: Groups Critical of Islam Now Waiting to Take Aid to Iraq." *The New York Times, Late Edition*, April 3, 2003, Section B, Page 12, Column 1.

Greven, Philip. *The Protestant Temperament: Patterns of Child-Rearing, Religious Experience, and the Self in Early America*. New York: Alfred Knopf, 1977.

_____. *Spare the Child: The Religious Roots of Punishment and the Psychological Impact of Physical Abuse*. New York: Vintage Books, 1992.

Gusfield, Joseph R. "Utopian Myths and Movements in Modern Societies." University Programs Modular Studies, Harold L. Wilensky and Leon Mayhew, eds. Morristown, NJ.: General Learning Press, 1973.

Gusfield, Joseph R. *Symbolic Crusade: Status Politics and the American Temperance Movement, Second Edition*. 1963. Reprint, Urbana and Chicago: University of Illinois Press, 1986.

Guth, James L. "The Politics of the Christian Right." *Religion and the Culture Wars*. New York: Rowman and Littlefield, 1996.

Herman, Didi. *The Antigay Agenda: Orthodox Vision and the Christian Right*. Chicago: University of Chicago Press, 1997.

Heyrman, Christine. *Southern Cross: The Beginnings of the Bible Belt*. Chapel Hill and London: University of North Carolina Press, 1997.

Hunsberger, Bruce. "Religion and Prejudice: The Role of Religious Fundamentalism, Quest, and Right-Wing Authoritarianism. *Journal of Social Issues* 51. (1995): 113–129.

Hunsberger, Bruce. "Religious Fundamentalism, Right-Wing Authoritarianism, and Hostility towards Homosexuals in Non-Christian Religious Groups." *International Journal for the Psychology of Religion* 6 (1996): 39–49.

Hunter, James Davison. *Culture Wars: The Struggle to Define America*. New York: Basic Books/HarperCollins, 1991.

Hutton, Ronald. *The Triumph of the Moon: A History of Modern Pagan Witchcraft*. New York: Oxford, 1999.

_____. *The Pagan Religions of the Ancient British Isles*. New York: Ballantine, 1991.

Jorgensen, Danny L., and Scott E. Russell. "American Neopaganism: The Participants' Social Identities." *Journal for the Scientific Study of Religion* 38 (September 1999): 325–338.

Jurgensmeyer, Mark. *Terror in the Mind of God*. Berkeley, CA: University of California Press, 2001.

Langman, Lauren. "I Hate, Therefore I Am." *Social Thought and Research*, Vol. 21, 1–2 (1998): 151–183.

Leak, Gary K., and Brandy A. Randall. 1995. "Clarification of the Link between Right-Wing Authoritarianism and Religiousness: The Role of Religious Maturity." *Journal for the Scientific Study of Religion* 34 (June 1995):245–252.

Lederer, Gerda, and Angela Kindervater. "Internationale Vergleiche." *Authoritarismus und Gesellschaft: Trendanalysen und Vergleichende Jugenduntersuchungen*,

1945–1993, Gerda Lederer and Peter Schmidt, eds. Opladen: Leske und Budrich, 1995.
Lederer, Gerda. "Authoritarianism in German Adolescents: Trends and Cross–Cultural Comparisons." *Strength and Weakness: The Authoritarian Personality Today.* New York: Springer–Verlag, 1993.
_____. "Die Authoritäre Persönlichkeit: Geschichte einer Theorie." *Authoritarismus und Gesellschaft: Trendanalysen und Vergleichende Jugenduntersuchungen, 1945–1993*, Gerda Lederer and Peter Schmidt, eds. Opladen: Leske und Budrich, 1995.
Lundskow, George. *Awakening to an Uncertain Future: A Case Study of the Promise Keepers.* New York: Peter Lang, 2002.
_____. "Promise Keepers Attitudes and Character in Interviews." *The Promise Keepers: Essays on Masculinity and Christianity.* Jefferson, NC, and London: McFarland and Company, 2000.
Meloen, Jos D. "Authoritarianism in the Netherlands: Mission Completed? Downward Trends of Authoritarianism in the Netherlands 1970–1992 with an International Comparison of World Data." *Social Thought and Research*, Vol. 22, 1–2 (1999): 45–95.
_____. "Fluctuations of Authoritarianism in Society." *Social Thought and Research*, Vol. 21, 102 (1998): 107–133.
_____. "The F-scale as a Predictor of Fascism: An Overview of 40 Years of Authoritarianism Research." *Strength and Weakness: The Authoritarian Personality Today.* New York: Springer Verlag, 1993.
_____ and C.P. Middendorp. "Authoritarianism in the Netherlands: The Empirical Distribution in the Population and its Relation to Theories on Authoritarianism." Politics and the Individual, 1, 2 (1991): 49–71.
_____, L Hagendoorn, Q. Raaijmakers, and L. Visser. "Authoritarianism and the Revival of Political Racism: Reassessments in the Netherlands of the Reliability and Validity of the Concept of Authoritarianism by Adorno et al." *Political Psychology*, 9 (1988): 413–429.
Miller, Donald E. *Reinventing American Protestantism: Christianity at the New Millennium.* Berkeley: University of California Press, 1997.
Oliner, Samuel P., and Pearl M. Oliner. *The Altruistic Personality: Rescuers of Jews in Nazi Europe.* New York: The Free Press, 1992.
Perrin, Robin D., Paul Kennedy, and Donald E. Miller. "Examining the Sources of Conservative Church Growth: Where are the New Evangelical Movements Getting their Numbers?" *Journal for the Scientific Study of Religion* 36 (March 1997): 71–80.
Phelan, Jo, Bruce G. Link, Ann Stueve, and Robert E. Moore. "Education, Social Liberalism, and Economic Conservatism: Attitudes towards Homeless People." *American Sociological Review* 60 (February 1995): 126–140.
Pike, Sarah M. *Earthly Bodies, Magical Selves: Contemporary Pagans and the Search for Community.* Berkeley: University of California Press, 2001.
Randolph, Vance. *Ozark Superstition.* New York: Columbia University Press, 1947.
Rasmussen, L., and T. Charman. "Personality and Religious Beliefs: A Test of Flugel's Superego and Projection Theory." *International Journal for the Psychology of Religion*, 5 (1995): 109–117.

Smith, David N. "The Ambivalent Worker: Max Weber, Critical Theory, and the Antinomies of Authority." *Social Thought and Research*, Vol. 21, 1–2 (1998): 35–83.
_____. "The Social Construction of Enemies: Jews and the Representation of Evil." *Sociological Theory* 14, 3 (1996): 203–240.
_____. "The Beloved Dictator: Adorno, Horkheimer, and the Critique of Domination." *Current Perspectives in Social Theory*, Vol. 12 (1992): 195–230.
Straus, Murray. *Beating the Devil Out of Them: Corporal Punishment in American Families*. New York: MacMillan, 1994.
Tibi, Bassam. *The Challenge of Fundamentalism*. Berkeley, CA: University of California Press, 2002.
Weber, Max. "Science as a Vocation." *From Max Weber: Essays in Sociology*. 1918. Reprint, New York: Oxford University Press, 1946.
Wuthnow, Robert. *After Heaven: Spirituality in America Since the 1950s*. Berkeley, CA: University of California Press, 1998.
Zinnbauer, Brian J., and Kenneth I. Pargament. "Spiritual Conversion: A Study of Religious Change Among College Students." *Journal for the Scientific Study of Religion* 37, 1, (March 1998): 161–180.

4

A Critique of the Ambiguity of Bourgeois Religion

Max Horkheimer's Critical Theory of Religion

MICHAEL R. OTT

In the past 40 years, an essential element of the entire Critical Theory has been overlooked, that being the theory's dialectical critique of religion (Riemer 1992; Siebert 2001, 1994). This chapter seeks to make a contribution to the further development of this dimension of the theory by giving expression to Max Horkheimer's analysis and critique of the systematically created ambiguousness of bourgeois religion in modern society by means of his critical theory of religion (Ott 2001, Siebert 1979).

Modernity's Diremption of the Religious and Secular

In terms of G.W.F. Hegel's dialectical analysis of history, the sacred and the profane realms of premodern or "traditional" society were dialectically interrelated, with the religious dimension providing a universalizing synthesis and purpose to the existing social totality. In modern society, however, this traditional psychological, social, and cultural unity has been shattered by the development and historical success of the logic, rationality, and historical praxis of the positive, analytic sciences and their technology. Notwithstanding the attempts by Rene Descartes, Blaise Pascals, et al., to hold religion and science together at the beginning of modernity, the progressive development and success of the natural sciences in explaining prior unknown natural phenomena, the explanation of which at that time was left to faith in God and religion, pushed the need of God further out of an increasingly instrumentalized, scientific, and secular world. With the continued development of an increasingly demythologized modernity, the concept of God, faith, and religion as a whole withered into being a private, "inner," personal affair of the individual, whereas the objective world was increasingly understood to be now the domain of human reason and the physical sciences. The gulf between these two human dimensions and their rationality, i.e., between the religious and the secular, faith and reason, the individual and the collective, and between a philosophic, nonstrategic, discursive rationality and an instrumental, strategic, purposive rationality has developed in modernity into an ever-widening contradiction. In place of the traditional society's understanding of God's unifying presence and involvement in the natural and social worlds, modern positivistic science and its instrumental rationality have succeeded in creating a godless world while also positing a worldless God, if a God is acknowledged at all (Metz 1973).

However, as analyzed by the Marxian and Freudian enlightenment movements, as well as by the so-called "post-modern" critique, the paradigmatic project of the 18th century's bourgeois enlightenment, which sought to supersede the superstitious, socially conservative and oppressive, feudalistic solidarity of the traditional society's socially powerful and corrupt religion through the progressive development of society by means of a secular, scientific, instrumental rationality toward a new, more free, just, and humane social totality, has inherent contradictions. Through its rationalization, functional and cybernetic utilization, privatization, or even abstract negation and thus loss of the religious, eschatologically transcendent dimension of human experience and history, modern society has become increasingly "one-dimensional," i.e., dominated by the dualistic and hypostatized, either-or, subject-object, instrumental rationality of positivism. In modern society, there are no longer any unifying universals. Fragmented, nominalistic, alienated and alienating particularity reigns. Modernity has lost its cohesiveness, its center. The particular elements of modern life that have been historically used to fill the unifying, identity-giving void of religion, e.g., the appeal to the patriotism of nationalism and racism; the self-centered, strategic pursuit of capital and the maximization of profit at all costs; the promise of a linear historical progress by positive science, have not produced the desired reconciliation and "progress" of humanity but have only succeeded in increasing the horrific antagonisms between the classes, races, genders, nations, etc., which is now being globalized. It is correctly said that in the history of humanity, the 20th century has been the most barbaric and bloody (Siebert 1994).

The inclusion of the traditional form of religion in the development of modern Western society, however, would not have prevented this collapse into particularity, antagonism, and the barbarism of neo-imperialism. It was

4. A Critique of the Ambiguity of Bourgeois Religion 99

because of religion's — more precisely Christianity's — role in the legitimization of the status quo of traditional society that modern societies have marginalized if not abstractly negated religion as an obsolete and thus irrelevant, infantile, inhibiting, reactionary social force against the development of humanity toward a more emancipatory, just, and reconciled society. However, with modernity's bifurcation of human experience into a religious and secular dichotomy, with its emphasis and reliance placed singularly on the development of secularity for the advancement of human society and wellbeing, a "dialectic of enlightenment" — a turning over of the enlightenment and its goals of human liberation and sovereignty, social equality and solidarity into their opposite — has developed in the modern world (Horkheimer and Adorno 1969).

This destructive dichotomy between the universality of religion and the particularity and singularity of the secular in human experience and society systematically and structurally continues in and through the historical development of modernity. Max Horkheimer, the founding administrative director and "spiritus rector" (Habermas 1993: 49) of the entire research program now known as the Critical Theory of the Frankfurt School, struggled with and sought to resolve dialectically the destructive dichotomy between the religious and secular realms of modern life and society. Embodying the dialectical logic and methodology of determinate negation derived from the prophetic religions of Judaism and Christianity, as well as the critical philosophical and scientific theories of I. Kant, Hegel, A. Schopenhauer, K. Marx, S. Freud, et al., Horkheimer's Critical Theory of society included in itself as an essential element a dialectical theory of religion. Horkheimer's critical theory of religion is a new and liberating reformulation of the form and content of religion — particularly the prophetic Judeo-Christian religions — into a secular force for the transformation of a one-dimensional, technologically oriented and capital dominated, unjust and oppressive modern society toward a more humane, reasonable, emancipatory future society.

The Ambiguity of Religion

Horkheimer's dialectical theory of religion, like the entire Critical Theory itself, is an interdisciplinary study of the contemporary social totality and its trends from a materialist perspective. As such, the critical theory of society and religion is not an abstract philosophy that hovers over and beyond the concrete life world and social system of humanity. Horkheimer's dialectical theory of society and religion is, rather, deeply rooted in and critical of the existing social totality and its material conditions by which human beings live. The critical theory thereby belongs to and is an expression of the modern, bourgeois antagonistic society. This society is antagonistic due to the capitalist reification of the relations of its economic production and reproduction process, i.e., the relations of domination between the owners of the means of production and the workers, the rich and the poor, and the subsequent antagonisms between the classes, races, genders, ages, etc. This systematically and structurally produced antagonism in the capitalist social totality's base structure infiltrates and parasitically infects the cultural and psychic realms of society. According to Horkheimer, it is from the midst of the antagonism of the bourgeois social totality, "whose inner forces are driving it towards destruction" (Horkheimer 1969: 53) despite all cultural pattern maintenance efforts, that he understands religion in an either-or, ambiguous sense.

According to Horkheimer, religion can be either a liberating human expression of critique of the existing conditions of life and of hope for a better future society, or it can function as a conservative, reactionary force of social integration and legitimization of the existing status quo. Religion is a human creation, the content of which is conditioned by one's location in the society's class hierarchy. As Horkheimer states, neither the socially dominant representatives of bourgeois society's base structures nor of its cultural realm give any expression to the exploitation and suffering of the masses. Such complaint is voiced by the society's poor and dispossessed, and with their critique develops the critical religious and eschatological idea of eternity. The idea of eternity, according to Horkheimer, "manifests itself with greater purity and sublimity in the most naïve, the most crudely sensuous hope, than in the most spiritual metaphysics and theory" (Horkheimer 1978: 111). It is this earthy and raw type of religious complaint against social injustice and the resulting hope of an eternity, expressed in Christian form as the resurrection of the dead, a last judgment, the new creation of God — where the innocent victims of the injustice and horror of this world can receive justice, that dialectically contains a critical, materialistic potential for the praxis of social change and human liberation.

Such religious, dialectical materialism is not the approach to nor the purpose of the official religious theorists' expression of eternity, which has been stripped of its critical human and social content and made into an abstraction, a myth which mediates and rationalizes the critical distinction between the idea of eternity and an unjust social totality from which it arises. In bourgeois deistic terms, the socially critical notions of God and eternity become completely separated from human history. The notion of God becomes now not merely transcendent to the natural and social worlds, but totally emptied of any concrete sociohistorical substance or relevancy, e.g., the cries of the innocent victims of the horror produced by nature, society, and history. Such nominalistic disemboweling of the originally critical social

4. A Critique of the Ambiguity of Bourgeois Religion 101

concepts of God and eternity leaves this world in the hands of the dominant, capitalist class, and can thereby be filled in with the standards and practical expectations of the exploitive capitalist system. Another critical theorist of the Frankfurt School, Walter Benjamin, described this same social process in terms of a competition between two "religions": capitalism itself and Christianity (Benjamin 1996: 288–291). According to Benjamin, the religion capitalism—which is pure cult without any dogma—has attached itself parasitically to the history of Christianity in Western civilization. In so doing, capitalism has replaced not only the history but also the critical, liberational, messianic, eschatological future of Christianity with its own exploitive history and pursuit of more and more profit. In terms of the right-wing Hegelian, Francis Fukuyama, such a parasitic assimilation of religion and its hope and praxis for a better future world into the cybernetic service of capitalism brings about "the end of history" in the form of a totally administered capitalist dominated class society, and "the last man"—the bourgeois (Fukuyama 1992).

According to Horkheimer, the ambiguity of religion is a consequence of this antagonistic society, since the entire content of religion is derived from "the psychic elaboration of earthly data," (Horkheimer 1972: 58) which is produced, experienced, understood, and systematically reinforced by the structures of a class society. However, in this psychic projection of social class position and experience of life, the dominant class's religion and their "interests" becomes an objective force of the existing society itself, which dialectically turns around and influences the development of the human psyche as well as the entire social totality. Thus, as a fundamental form of mediation of the society's class domination and coercion to conformity, religion in the human psyche becomes an independent, specific power which can lead people to conform to or resist the existing social conditions. It is in this trifold, dialectical relationship between the foundational economic mode of production, the cultural and religious forms and institutions that are thereby created, and the human psyche that religion obtains its potential liberational, critical, good quality, as well as its reactionary, pattern-maintenance function. It is in the historical context of this dialectical relationship between these three realms of the modern antagonistic social totality of capitalism that Horkheimer's critical theory of religion is developed.

Thoughts on Religion

Horkheimer's dialectical theory of religion is not treated in a positivistic manner as an isolated, particular theme that is the focus of only one of his many theoretical works. Rather, as a fundamental element of his entire critical theory of society, his critique of religion is expressed in most of his writings and interviews. However, it was in his 1935 essay entitled "Thoughts on Religion" that Horkheimer gave precise expression to the inherent dialectic and thus, ambiguity of religion as well as to his materialist critical theory of religion (Horkheimer 1972: 129–131). As he states, religion is understood to express different, transcendent yet very concrete and historical values as the realm that possessed different norms, e.g., love, justice, peace, solidarity, hope, mercy, truth, than those of either nature or society. Religion, thus, contains the voice of accusation against the worldly conditions that produce the antithesis of these values as experienced by the masses of humanity for countless generations. Since these religious values were not experienced in the natural or social worlds, they were thought to exist in a transcendent place, e.g., heaven, or with a transcendent God. At the same time that Horkheimer was writing this article in exile in the USA, these very unjust norms of nature and society that such a dialectical theory of religion condemns were being forcibly institutionalized in Nazi Germany. Reminiscent of Schopenhauer's notion of the universal "will-to-life" as the inner nature of the world that produces all the antagonisms of life, Adolf Hitler glorified these ruthless social Darwinistic, worldly norms in his *Mein Kampf*, by calling them "the aristocratic principle[s] of Nature" (Hitler 1971: 65). Hitler's aristocratic law of nature, which according to him is expressive of the will of God, eternalizes the privilege of power and strength of the one or the few over the resulting oppressed masses. It is this barbaric aristocratic principle of nature, where the predator has every right to tear to pieces the weak for its own survival if not greed, that is the real religion of capitalism, from which it gains its legitimization and strength. Knowing better than most the religious foundations of his socialist enemy, Hitler condemned the "Jewish doctrine of Marxism," which in his terms would replace the eternal privilege of exploitive power and right through the negation of such socially produced antagonisms and horror for the masses of humanity, since its realization would result in the chaotic destruction of human civilization and the world as a whole (Hitler 1971).

According to Horkheimer, in counterdistinction to people's experience of injustice and oppression, suffering humanity's religious projection of justice, truth, righteousness, etc., to a transcendent God originally served a critical and negative function. However, as Horkheimer asserts, it was Christianity in both its Catholic and Protestant forms that perverted religion from expressing the critical ideal of justice — an ideal which according to materialism can never be identified with reality — into a religious harmonization of this ideal with the existing power structures of the status quo. Christianity, in its modern bourgeois religious Constantinian form, gave up its prophetic and Messianic function of social critique and took on the positive function of legitimating the domination of the socially powerful class in the form of the state. This turnover from its negative function to a positive one expresses the inherent dialectics and ambiguity of religion.

The Ideology of Nation and Religion

Horkheimer asserts that just as there is the economic base structure of bourgeois society that does not change, i.e., the exploitive relations of production, so there are also certain cultural principles of the society that are guarded against any change. Throughout his writings, he gave expression to the developing ideological relationship between the two fundamental notions of domination in bourgeois society: religion and the bourgeois nation. According to Horkheimer, religion enters into a historical conflict with the bourgeois nation on the essential issue of whether it will act in a structural functionalist manner, in which it inculcates pattern maintenance and thereby legitimates the state's authority and the society's antagonism, or whether it will resist such an antagonistic state and become the voice of social change on behalf of the oppressed and exploited. Already in his *Notes of 1926–1931*, Horkheimer exposed the reactionary quality of a "positive" religion that performs a legitimating, cybernetic function of social control in bourgeois society (Horkheimer 1978: 27–28). According to Horkheimer, the bourgeois nation and religion serve the same master — capitalism, the exploitive social system in which the collectively produced surplus value of human labor is privately appropriated or stolen by the ruling class.

For bourgeois society, the concepts of religion and the nation are considered sacred and are thus placed under the ban of taboo since they are fundamental ideological tools for the domination of the masses by the ruling elite. As Freud explains, that which is labeled as taboo is considered to be something ineffable and unapproachable yet experienced as extremely real, and is thereby expressed in the negative terms of prohibitions (Freud 1950: 18). These prohibitions are not derived from the cultural realms of religion or morality. These socially constructed prohibitions appear to have no known foundation for their existence but are nevertheless generally accepted by the members of the society. This unknown origin of the taboo prohibition, such as that applied to the concepts of religion and nation, corresponds to the hidden antagonistic mode of capitalist social production and reproduction, the "Medusa's head" (Marx 1977: 91) that hides behind the veil of the social facts and cultural ideology of capitalism, that is the materialistic ground of the bourgeois social totality.

Through these religious and nationalistic notions, the social domination of the ruling class is legitimated and made into a national, collective ideology in which the individual finds his or her identity. This ideological identity formation dynamic can be seen quite clearly in the recent patriotic and religious fervor in the USA since the horrific, retaliatory strikes against the globalization of capitalism on September 11, 2001. Through these tabooed totems and their supportive ideological relationship, the psyche of the individual is incorporated as a dynamic force into the process of its own social domination. Thus, these notions of the nation and religion are to be taken with the utmost seriousness. As Horkheimer states, if these sacred social structures are criticized, the person doing the critiquing will quickly become "personally acquainted with the very direct interest capitalism takes in the inviolability of the concepts" (Horkheimer 1978: 28). Horkheimer further expresses the pragmatic, functional conception of religion by illustrating its change of importance in the historical development of bourgeois society. As he states, atheism was tolerated in the 19th century because of its strategic and functional use in helping the bourgeoisie break the religious legitimization of the traditional feudal society. Such atheistic critique, however, is no longer tolerated in the modern capitalist society now under the domination of the bourgeoisie. Such critical atheism has the capability of exposing the hidden exploitive reality of the capitalist social system and its structures, which bourgeois religion and culture is to obscure and protect. Particularly in post–September 11 U.S. society, where the official yet coded line of demarcation has been declared by President G.W. Bush, "Either you are with us, or you are with the terrorists," (Bush 2001) implies that you are on the side of good Christian society, or on the side of the evil Muslims and other non–Christians. Nationalism and piety thus become mutually reinforcing. As Horkheimer states, the person who criticizes these ideological concepts of religion and the nation "lays hands on (the society's) very foundation" (Horkheimer 1978: 28).

This functionalistic service of the positive world religions to the given social system of which it is a part is what Horkheimer calls the "profound pragmatism at the core of world religions, the lack of illusions" (Horkheimer 1978: 123). This is the transparency of positive religion, i.e., its lack of any real substance and depth that seeks to critically address the injustice of the given, capitalist social system for the purpose of envisioning and creating a more just, rational, free, and humane future society. The world religions' pragmatic lack of illusions expresses religion's real lack of hope for anything other than what is as it has capitulated to the historical masters of the world and conformed to the facts of reality. As Horkheimer states, even the most sincere believers today have no illusions that the purpose of their religion is just such pragmatism, such realism, such pattern maintenance and conformity to the social status quo.

For Horkheimer this "synthetic, artificial, manipulatory, and trashy" characteristic of world religions is why the form of religion has to change (Horkheimer 1978). Again, for Horkheimer, there is a dialectical tension between the form and content of reality that provides its historical dynamic and revolutionary potential. For Horkheimer's critical theory of religion, the anachronistic form of religion needs to be determinately negated in order to allow the dynamic revolutionary, emancipatory, and enlightening content of religion to be expressed in a new secular form of hope and motivation for the creation of a new future society. Horkheimer expressed the dialectic nature of his critique of religion by saying that such religious conformity to the national systems of human domination "was least true for the poorest and most naive believers, and perhaps for Jesus of Nazareth" (Horkheimer 1978). As Horkheimer also stated 20 years earlier, the liberating, historically empowering, critical hope of eternity, for the totally Other, is to be found amongst this world's "wretched in their despair" (Horkheimer 1978: 111). Giving a new, relevant and secular voice to the religion of the poorest is the purpose of Horkheimer's Critical Theory of religion.

Modern Form of Animism

Through his Critical Theory, Horkheimer expressed another ideological aspect of religion as the projection of humanity's autonomy to other people, events, or to a similarly viewed divine will that is active in all worldly events. This is religion as fetishism, i.e., the religious attribution of humanity's strengths, abilities, hopes, etc., to a finite or infinite "other," which disables and alienates humanity from its historical potential. As such a projection, religion is understood to be independent of the human mind and thereby outside the critique of reason and science, which furthers the bourgeois division of labor between religion and science.

Horkheimer described this modern, fetishized religion as a form of animism. Due to their innocently suffering the socially created and maintained horror of poverty, hunger, homelessness, loneliness, alienation, exploitation, and death, the suffering masses themselves wish for and create a transcendent, divine other who will protect and save them from the hard, cruel reality of capitalist society. As Marx had stated a century before, tormented people themselves create their own assuaging yet illusory "opium" in the form of religion (Marx 1964: 42). As Horkheimer states, although a more adequate, critical, and liberating understanding of people's innocent suffering is possible, an understanding which then could be turned into a social praxis to stop such socially created horror, the capitalist power elite, who are responsible for such suffering, make sure that nothing disturbs the animistic religious dreams of the masses.

Thus, on the psychological level, according to Horkheimer, religion is a survival mechanism — a projection of oppressed humanity's wish, desire, longing, hope of something totally other than what is — within an unjust, oppressive, and death creating society. On the sociological level, religion in capitalist society is used as a justification of violence and state terrorism. Horkheimer uses the biblical story of Jesus driving the moneychangers and sellers of doves — the sacrificial animal sold to the poor — from the Temple to illustrate his point (Horkheimer 1978: 42) That Jesus took a whip and drove the moneychangers from the Temple is used distortedly as a legitimating rationale of the dominant class's use of violence to realize their goals or to maintain the social status quo. Yet, as Horkheimer ironically states, "it is curious how rarely the purpose of the biblical act is discussed" (Horkheimer 1978: 42). By driving out the moneychangers and sellers of doves who cheated the poor, Jesus was destroying the religious legitimization for the continued exploitation of the poor by the religious system of his day. According to Horkheimer, this story of liberation is ideologically turned around to justify the continued exploitation of the poor by the capitalists. Such bourgeois religion and its morality, thus, sanctify the antagonistic class structure and horror of capitalist society by giving the rich and powerful the appearance of being religious and ethical according to the status quo of capitalist society. Those on the bottom of society — the proletariat, as well as those who seek the liberation of humanity from domination and who thus seek to overcome the injustice of capitalism — are seen as being irreligious and immoral for they resist and deny the divinely established and blessed laws of capitalist society. As Horkheimer states, "bourgeois morality and religion are nowhere as tolerant as when they judge the life of the rich, and nowhere as strict as toward those that want to eliminate poverty" (Horkheimer 1978: 54).

The Future of Religion?

According to Horkheimer, the question of religion can be addressed unambiguously only when it has been freed of its ideological social function. In the antagonistic social totality of capitalism, religion takes sides and can be either good or bad according to Horkheimer's analysis (Horkheimer 1978: 163). Religion as a means of explanation, rationalization, pattern maintenance, and legitimization of life in society and history is religion in a bad sense; it is ideology, i.e., a socially created false consciousness. For the thinkers of the bourgeois enlightenment, particularly those in France, who understood religion in this bad sense to be the metaphysical and superstitious attempt to explain the unexplainable and thereby keep humanity in infantile servitude to the masters of the feudal first and second estates, religion needed to be completely negated. Thus, religion became increasingly useless the more scientific reason explained the functioning of the natural world. Now, by the means of the myth of positivism, the modern, enlightened, administered society no longer needs religion as society itself has become self-sufficient. It is only in emergency situations, when the inherent contradictions of capitalist society cause the cybernetic system to break down, that contemporary society still returns to religion as an ideological form of social mystification, integration, and harmonization. According to Horkheimer, modern bourgeois society has experienced a failure of nerve and will in continuing the bourgeois enlightenment's revolutionary vision and project of creating a society that was autonomous and solidary, just, humane, and good. Modern bourgeois society has returned to the past form of this bad religion as its attempt to save itself from its own annihilation. However, as Horkheimer states, such a return to religion does not mean a belief or trust in God or anything transcendent of itself. Such a fearful return to an empty religious form is only an expression of the disbelief in and rejection of a better future.

Critical Theory of Religion

However, according to Horkheimer, there is another aspect of religion besides its structural, functionalistic role as bourgeois ideology of domination and social integration. Religion is also a concrete expression of human hope if not struggle for emancipation and justice. This is the good theory and praxis of religion. As Horkheimer states, "in its symbols, religion places an apparatus at the disposal of tortured men through which they express their suffering and their hope. This is one of its most important functions" (Horkheimer 1978: 58). According to Horkheimer, "a respectable psychology of religion" is needed to differentiate between religion as the legitimization of the capitalist system and structure of society, and religion as the expression and longing for human emancipation (Horkheimer 1978: 58). As he states, the religious, mythical form of humanity's cry against the world's injustice has to be transformed into a this-worldly, revolutionary praxis to overcome the causes of this injustice. This is the very purpose of Horkheimer's Critical Theory of religion. This sublimation of the truth content of religion — of humanity's cries and struggle for liberation, solidarity, happiness, redemption — from its inadequate, coopted religious form is based on the historical fact that religion did not always ideologically distract people from such praxis. At times throughout history, religion functioned to expose and resist the injustice done to people and nature. These dynamic, religiously cloaked impulses for justice, truth, goodness, love, etc., that arose out of people's experience of the antagonistic and brutal "ways of the world," are still very much alive in modern society, albeit in a more secular form. As Horkheimer states, the life and praxis of the revolutionary can be such an expression.

Horkheimer's revolutionary critique of religion as ideology seeks to free religion's emancipatory impulses from its limited mythological and religiously distorted form that is created by and for the legitimization of the antagonistic economic mode of social production. This socially assimilated and thus distorted form and content of religion is what distracts humanity from its purpose and goal of realizing its psychic, social, economic, political, cultural, and historical emancipation. Such critique of religion illustrates the dialectical process of determinate negation as the obsolete and repressive form of religion is negated so as to allow the dynamic, emancipatory content of religion to migrate into the modern secular struggle for human enlightenment and emancipation. According to Horkheimer, the truth content of religion is found in its concern with and historical praxis for the liberation of humanity from all forms of oppression, injustice, and alienation, for sociohistorical creation of a new, more just, free, solidary, humane, peaceful future society.

Unlike the critical theory, the bourgeois critique of religion — that does not contain this goal of human emancipation — is a lie; a dirty trick that gives the appearance of concern for the religious content of humanity's liberation while enslaving people even further to the exploitation of the capitalist system. This lie is the social function of the church in bourgeois society, according to Horkheimer, as it ministers to and classifies the poor. As Horkheimer states, "these days, Christianity is not primarily used as a religion but as a crude transfiguration of existing conditions" (Horkheimer 1978: 59). The most recent expression of this capitalistic distortion of Christianity is President G.W. Bush's "faith-based initiative" (Ott 2001: 131–133).

Bourgeois Christianity

Through his appeal to the very ideals professed by Western civilization Horkheimer exposes the cruel lie of bourgeois Christianity which legitimates the very misery, despair, injustice, imprisonment, torture, and death of the innocent victims that its professed founder sought to negate. At the very beginning of his ministry, Jesus identified the concrete subject of his prophetic and messianic praxis of announcing the coming of God's kingdom: the poor, the captives, the blind, the oppressed. The lie of religion, particularly that of bourgeois Christianity, in modern capitalist society is that this prophetic, messianic, revolutionary, emancipatory character of Christianity is compromised and thus destroyed by it being made into a soporific salve that dulls and soothes away the horror of existing conditions in capitalism rather than being a dynamic force that seeks to determinately negate these conditions. Through such class distortion of the content of religion, the concrete, historical, and religious distinction between the oppressed and innocent victims of society and their oppressors is thus erased. Quite abstractly then, Jesus becomes the Messiah the Christ, the Savior of all people. Through the class domination of the capitalist society and its ideological process of abstraction, now all people can be justified in their life-style with no concrete repentance or discipleship, as long as their actions are in accord with the interests of the dominant, capitalist class. As Horkheimer states, in this contemporary, capitalist society the very rich are thus also considered especially devout persons.

The Seriousness of Religion

According to Horkheimer, religion is not taken seriously in capitalist society. In this society, religion has a cybernetic, pattern-maintenance function to perform that helps keep the masses subservient in their own exploitation to the antagonistic capitalist mode of social production. Since the critical, prophetic, messianic, eschatological if not apocalyptic teeth of Christianity have been knocked out by capitalism, bourgeois Christianity has become merely another comforting support and justification for the systematic and structural domination of the few over the many, the rich over the poor, the powerful over the weak, the owners over the workers, the "wolves" over the "lambs." It is this compromising religious lie that grants religion a place in modern, capitalistic society. As Horkheimer states, it is also this compromising lie that prevents the critical "implementation of religion" or its "expedient abolition" (Horkheimer 1978: 91).

However, as Horkheimer states, this antagonistic, dehumanizing society and its religion contradict the essential teachings of Christianity, which this society professes as its foundational heritage. Horkheimer states that it was inevitable that the contradictory principle of Christianity to the economic and social way of life in bourgeois capitalistic society would be willingly sacrificed to the development of capitalism, as "the vulgar positivism of bare facts along with the worship of success" would be raised up as the highest truth. As Horkheimer states, the dominant intellectual and cultural concern over the past few centuries was not to expose this contradiction but to hide and mystify it. Through such evisceration and perversion of Christianity's dangerous prophetic and messianic content, religion became compatible with any and all practices in capitalist society—which Horkheimer called "this atheistic reality" (Horkheimer 1978a: 440).

Due to Christianity's betrayal of its prophetic and messianic content through its functional assimilation in the antagonistic capitalist social totality, Horkheimer held no hope for the church to become again as it was in its beginning a liberating agent of social change. Rather, Horkheimer asserted that the original dynamic and liberating content of religion had freed itself of its religious form and had taken on the historical, secular form of social praxis through lives of progressive people (Horkheimer 1972: 130). Horkheimer states that as humanity develops historically, religion is something that is left behind as no longer needed. However, this historical negation of religion is not something abstract but is a determinate negation, for in this historical movement, so Horkheimer states, religion leaves its mark. Those desires, wishes, longings, and accusations that first gave rise to religion and the concept of God are not only negated but preserved and furthered as they shed their religious, spiritual form and become forces of a critical social theory and praxis for the creation of a more just and humane future society. According to Horkheimer, this living, progressive dynamic is the essence of good religion, which is the spiritual force and motivation that "sustains ... the impulse for change, the desire that the [mythical] spell be broken, that things take the right turn. We have religion where life down to its every gesture is marked by this resolve" (Horkheimer 1978: 163). Thus, a truly progressive person takes the liberating truth content of religion and translates it into social action for "the happiness of people who come after them and for whom they know how to die" (Horkheimer 1972: 130).

As Horkheimer states, "true discipleship" (Horkheimer 1972: 130) does not lead back to religion but to social praxis for the creation of a happier, freer, and more rational future society expressive of human solidarity, a society for which such disciples know how to live and to die. Christians, Horkheimer states, who take the religious meaning of the love of one's neighbor seriously may once again be called as they were originally to such praxis by the increasing barbarism of a monopolistic, capitalist society (Horkheimer 1972: 130–131). This is even more so the case today as the antagonism and horror of capitalism are being imperialistically "globalized" by means of the neoliberal programs of the International Monetary Fund, the World Bank, the non-democratic rulings and procedures of the World Trade Organization, and by war, e.g., the "war on terrorism" in Afghanistan, the Philippines, and the threat of U.S.-led invasion of Iraq. This transformation of the original religious negative, emancipatory content into a secular, revolutionary form of resistance and praxis for a better future society is the very heart of Horkheimer's critical theory of religion.

4. A Critique of the Ambiguity of Bourgeois Religion

Second and Third Commandments

The fundamental and guiding notion of Horkheimer's critical theory of religion is the materialistic determinate negation of the second and third commandments of the Jewish Decalogue: the prohibition of making images and naming the Absolute. Adhering to this prohibition as well as to I. Kant's philosophical rejection of human reason knowing the noumenal, Horkheimer's dialectical theory of religion cannot identify the Absolute, the good. According to Horkheimer, that which is evil primarily in the social sphere can be identified but the good cannot. The concept of evil also implies by its very nature its opposite and the action one could take to resist or counteract the negative. Thus, the critical theory of society and religion focuses on the negative. The negation of the negative is the only quality of the good that can be said or known. This is the teaching of the entire Critical Theory: to define the good by the evil that is to be negated. Through this method of negative dialectics, or "inverse theology" (Adorno and Benjamin 1999: 67), the Critical Theory of society and culture seeks to avoid the dialectics of Enlightenment process inherent in the naming of anything as good.

It is in this that "the role of faith becomes central" for Horkheimer's dialectical theory of religion (Adorno 1978: 158). His notion of faith expressed in the concept of the unknown and ineffable Absolute, however, is not expressed as a positive dogma that is to be believed but as a longing that unites all people in the hope that the horror of history will not be the ultimate end of its innocent victims. The longing for this totally Other than what is is the materialistic determinate negation of the Jewish and Christian, prophetic and messianic teaching of the coming reign of God into hope and longing and struggle for a better, more reconciled and just future society.

This longing for the totally Other than the world that is a socially and historically conditioned representation — and thus changeable — is the right granted to theology in Horkheimer's Critical Theory of religion. The Critical Theory of society and religion rests on the thought that the Absolute cannot be made into an object and that the theological assertion of the existence of God should be transformed into the longing that such a God exists who will not allow injustice to ultimately triumph over the innocent victims of society and history.

Secular Mimesis

Throughout the centuries, the church in both its Catholic and Protestant forms has removed from its teaching the danger that the prophets and the Messiah might have caused society so that the masses would not be tempted to imitate the radicality of their love, hope for the totally Other God, and desire for justice in solidarity with the socially disenfranchised. However, as Horkheimer states, such mimesis of Jesus as the Messiah is the core of Christian teaching, by which the life of the Christian is distinguished from life that imitates nature's aristocratic law of conformity to what is for the purpose of survival at all costs. Mimesis of the Messiah is the motive and spirit for Christian ethics. Such mimesis sets people free from the limitation to what is — the myth of positivism — as it seeks what is possible from the facts of the present with an eye toward a better future. The church and its theology have given up the emancipatory power of the negative, which can break the mythic spell of domination. As Horkheimer states, "when a doctrine hypostatizes an isolated principle that excludes negation, it is paradoxically predisposing itself to conformism" (Horkheimer 1974: 87). The lack of negation in any theory, be it religious, philosophical, or scientific, implicitly if not explicitly identifies the Ideal, e.g., that which is good and true, with reality. There is then no hope and no transcendence but only conformity to what is socially and historically created. This sacrifice of its foundational prophetic and messianic dialectical negativity of society which thereby constantly pushes toward a better, more humane, just, free, happy, and reconciled future society is what Horkheimer calls the "weakness of theology."

This weakness is the ambiguity of religion itself, whose content in its Judeo-Christian form expresses both a revolutionary indictment of the existing society in the empowering hope for a better future society as well as the longing for absolute justice of the totally Other God, as well as a conservative if not reactionary sanctification of the existing social totality and its system of social domination. It is due to this ambiguity that Horkheimer seeks the determinate negation of the historical form of religion, i.e., its positive social form of institutional structure, dogmas, rituals, the role of priests and ministers, religious language, etc., which have become obsolete in the historical struggle for human emancipation so as to allow that religious prophetic and messianic content that is still relevant in the existing sociohistorical context to migrate into a new secular form. This new secular form of the emancipatory and thus negative content of religion is Horkheimer's Critical Theory of religion, which does not thereby become a new religion itself. As Horkheimer states, "the critical theory rests on the thought that the Absolute, that is God, cannot be made into an object" (Horkheimer 1985: 434). In a post-religious, post-metaphysical, positivistic society that is developing toward its fulfillment in a hermetically sealed, totally administered social totality, Horkheimer's entire Critical Theory becomes the secular heir of the critical, negative, emancipatory content of religion in the historical struggle for a better, more enlightened, just, and reconciled future society, in the light of and longing for a totally Other who will not allow those who grind humanity's life into the dirt to ultimately be victorious over their innocent victims.

References

Adorno, Theodor, and Walter Benjamin. *The Complete Correspondence: 1928–1940.* Cambridge: Harvard University Press, 1999.
Benjamin, Walter. "Capitalism as Religion." *Walter Benjamin: Selected Writings, Volume 1, 1913–1926.* Cambridge: Belknap Press of Harvard University Press, 1996.
Bush, George W. Speech before Joint Session of Congress, September 20, 2001.
Freud, Sigmund. *Totem and Taboo.* 1913. Reprint, New York: Norton, 1990.
Fukuyama, Francis. *The End of History and the Last Man.* New York: Free Press, 1992.
Habermas, Jürgen. "Remarks on the Development of Horkheimer's Work." *On Max Horkheimer: New Perspectives,* Seylas Benhabib, Wolfgang Bonß, and John McCole (Eds.). Cambridge: MIT Press, 1993.
Hitler, Adolf. *Mein Kampf.* Boston: Houghton Mifflin, 1971.
Horkheimer, Max, and Theodor W. Adorno. *Dialectic of Enlightenment,* New York: Seabury, 1969.
Horkheimer, Max. "Authority and the Family," *Critical Theory: Selected Essays,* New York: Seabury, 1972.
_____. "Thoughts on Religion," *Critical Theory: Selected Essays.* New York: Seabury, 1972a.
_____. "The End of Reason." *The Essential Frankfurt School Reader,* Andrew Arato & Eike Gebhardt, eds. New York: Urizen Books, 1978.
_____. *Dawn & Decline: Notes 1926–1951 & 1950–1969.* New York: Seabury, 1978a.
_____. "Zur Zukunft der Kritischen Theorie." *Max Horkheimer Gesammelte Schriften, Band 7: Vorträge und Aufzeichnungen, 1949–1973.* Frankfurt am Main: S. Fischer Verlag GmbH, 1985.
Marx, Karl. 1964. "Contribution to the Critique of Hegel's Philosophy of Right." *On Religion.* New York: Schocken Books, 1964.
_____. *Capital: A Critique of Political Economy, Vol. I.* New York: Vintage Books, 1977.
Metz, Johannes B. *Theology of the World,* New York: Seabury, 1973.
Ott, Michael R. *Max Horkheimer's Critical Theory of Religion: The Meaning of Religion in the Struggle for Human Emancipation.* Lanham, MD: University Press of America, 2001.
Riemer, James A. *The Influence of the Frankfurt School on Contemporary Theology: Critical Theory and the Future of Religion, Dubrovnik Papers in Honour of Rudolf J. Siebert.* Lewiston, Canada: Edwin Mellen Press, 1992.
Siebert, Rudolf J. *From Critical Theory to Critical Political Theology: Personal Autonomy and Universal Solidarity.* New York: Peter Lang, 1994.
_____. *The Critical Theory of Religion: The Frankfurt School.* Lanham, Maryland and London: Scarecrow, 2001.
_____. *Horkheimer's Critical Sociology of Religion: The Relative and the Transcendent.* Lanham, MD: University Press of America, 1979.

PART II
Research

5

Apocalyptic Unbound

An Interpretation of Christian Speed/Thrash Metal Music

CHARLES M. BROWN

Introduction

The music is loud and seemingly chaotic. On stage, a bass player, drummer, and two guitarists are wildly flailing about on their instruments, playing at breakneck speed. Meanwhile the vocalist screams and then growls into the microphone, his voice echoing Linda Blair's performance in *The Exorcist*. All of the members wear black jeans and T-shirts. The bass player's shirt has a picture of a grotesque looking corpse with an ax through its head, the name of a popular band blazoned across the top. The stage is chaotic as the band members run across it, trying to keep from colliding with the constant surge of audience members who are climbing onto the stage and literally diving back into the sea of wildly gyrating bodies. Audience members close to the stage catch the "stage divers" and pass them around. "Crowd surfing" is what these kids call it. A circle of kids close to the stage wildly gyrate counterclockwise in a large circle. Eventually the circle breaks and the kids begin running into and bouncing off of one another like atoms in a supercollider. All of the action is done to the frantic beat of the music that keeps pouring out of the large speakers on the stage. The music is so fast that one can scarcely discern the quick staccato accents of the guitarists as they continue ripping out heavily distorted music that makes Led Zeppelin sound like Barry Manilow in comparison.

The above description may sound shocking. The real shock, however, is the fact that this is not a band who has come to "corrupt children" with the "satanic," drug, sex, and suicide-laden messages typically associated with heavy metal music. This is Vengeance, a speed/thrash metal band of conservative Christian musicians who believe that they are "metal missionaries" for God to reach unsaved youth with an evangelistic Christian message. In fact, several times during the performance, members of the band preach between songs. After the concert, there is a 15 to 20-minute sermon that could pass muster in any conservative Southern Baptist church complete with an altar call. Many kids go forward to pray and accept Jesus Christ as their new Lord and Savior.

The fact that conservative Christians are now using such radical musical styles as vehicles for a decidedly evangelistic message may be shocking to some. On the surface, evangelical Christianity and extreme forms of heavy metal with its graphic imagery do not seem compatible. I argue, however, that it makes perfect sense that evangelical Christianity would use such graphic imagery and radical musical structures given its emphasis on both evangelism and eschatology. Furthermore, scholars have pointed out that coopting forms of popular culture for evangelistic purposes is not new for evangelicals (Flake 1984, Frankl 1987, Romanowski 1990, Howard 1992, Romanowski 1992, Moore 1994, McDannell 1995, Howard and Streck 1996).

The academic literature on popular culture is, of course, replete with studies about popular music. For example, there have been many on the subject of music from a social and historical perspective. Some authors have concerned themselves with the developmental and historical aspects of musical forms (Baker 1979, Carlin 1988), while others have focused on the sociological implications of music (Curtis 1987, Wicke 1987, Weinstein 1991). Others have written about the social organization of the industries producing popular music (Denisoff 1975, 1986; Cusic 1996) as well as the role music plays as a reflection of subcultural beliefs and values (Hebdige 1976, 1979; Frith 1981; Brown 1995).

Few studies, however, deal exclusively with Christian music. Those that do tend to deal with either the historical emergence of contemporary Christian music (Baker 1979, Cusic 1990) or the debate regarding the acceptability of Christian rock music as a vehicle for evangelism and worship (Miller 1993, Simone 1993). A few have studied how Christians have coopted secular forms of music and the resultant ramifications (Romanowski 1990, Howard 1992, Romanowski 1992, Howard and Streck 1996), but these researchers deal primarily with mainstream forms of Christian music rather than alternative styles such as speed/thrash metal.

Today, contemporary Christian music encompasses a myriad of styles. Rap, pop, ska, gospel, rock, heavy metal, and blues are just a few examples. Heavy metal is perhaps the most controversial of all forms of contemporary Christian music. With its loud pulsating beat and sometimes graphic imagery, this genre is often accused of being the devil's music, and therefore unsuitable for Christian worship or evangelism. Some authors have written about Christian heavy metal (Peters, Peters, and Merrill 1986; Seay and Neely 1986; Wicke 1987), but this musical form is treated in slight fashion. Speed/thrash metal, a musical form evolved from heavy metal, has received even less attention, possibly because it is a fairly recent musical phenomenon.

Christian speed/thrash metal is a synthesis of heavy metal and punk rock (Dome 1991). It is separated from secular speed/thrash metal in that the musicians' intent is to convey their individual relationship with God through Jesus Christ. These musicians place a priority on the role of ministry over musicianship and are doctrinally conservative. The phenomenon of Christian speed/thrash metal emerged in 1988 as a response to the growing popularity of secular speed/thrash metal. Bob Beeman suggested that "The kids that were into Stryper (a Christian heavy metal band) four or five years ago are into thrash right now (Van Pelt 1989, p. 20). To date, there are approximately 15 Christian speed/thrash metal bands in the United States who are signed to record labels with a national distribution. Since its inception, this specific subgenre has grown tremendously in terms of bands and listeners. Furthermore, the subgenre of speed/thrash metal is beginning to spawn other subgenres by fusing elements of speed/thrash with industrial and rap music. Christian industrial groups like Brainchild and Circle of Dust, for instance, rely heavily on speed/thrash rhythms and textures in their music.

In this paper I argue that Christian speed/thrash metal has an affinity for apocalyptic themes in its musical structures, visual presentations, and lyrics. Authors have viewed musical forms in their historical development and as cultural expressions of social groups. However, the fact that these musical forms contain affinities for particular behaviors and themes has not been directly addressed.

This study is divided into three sections. First, I present apocalyptic thought and identify the major themes that are central in apocalyptic thinking. Second, I provide a historical overview of the emergence of the phenomenon of speed/thrash metal and show that Christian speed/thrash metal's affinities find their context in Christian views of evangelism and eschatology. Finally, to interpret the phenomenon of Christian speed/thrash metal, I analyzed nine albums by eight recording artists. I also reviewed several magazine articles and interviews to investigate dress codes and views on ministry. I show how apocalyptic harmonic, visual, and lyrical dimensions have blended within Christian speed/thrash metal, and argue that this musical genre provides a distinct, coherent view of the world that is consonant with the social experience of the groups it represents.

Major Themes in Apocalyptic Thought

Early apocalyptic thinking can be traced to a corpus of Jewish literature written primarily between 200 B.C. and A.D. 200. All of this literature, with the exception of the book of Daniel, was written between the Old and New Testaments and reflects radical social and religious changes.

In apocalyptic thought, a revelation is always mediated by an otherworldly being to a human recipient. The importance of the mediator is not only literal but figurative as it implies that the message is otherworldly and in need of interpretation. The content of the revelation is both historical and transhistorical in nature. It contains information about a supernatural world apart from the recipient's world, while stressing the imminence of judgment within this world. This judgment differs from earlier biblical prophetic works in that it extends beyond death.

Apocalyptic literature can be viewed as unified in its interpretation of the world. Although the apocalypses vary in their revelatory messages, they share common themes. By emphasizing these themes, one sees that the genre explains the problems of the world as the result of a continuing struggle between good and evil. The genre also provides comfort in chaotic times by stressing the impending triumph of good over evil. Values are clarified and behavior is monitored on an individual and collective level by emphasizing the notion of a final eschatological judgment. The world is viewed as mysterious, hostile, and therefore in need of otherworldly wisdom to give it meaning. Angels and demons exert their influence in human affairs and affect human destiny. As Collins (1984) points out, human life is bounded in the present by these supernatural beings and in the future by an inevitable final judgment.

Apocalyptic visions serve as forms of revelation and a means by which life can be interpreted. The framework of apocalyptic visions provided by the three explored themes suggests that the writers view the world as a hostile place. Human sinfulness, disease, and war can be interpreted as a foreshadowing of the events to come. Sinfulness, disease, and war are often believed to be at a critical state and in need of divine assistance to be alleviated. The world is mysterious and divine intervention is needed in the form of judgments and angelic beings. Disease, death, and other events are beyond human control, and are explained in a framework that points to future intervention. Furthermore, the apocalyptic provides a means by which the authors can find a sense of comfort. The comfort comes in the belief that the sinful world of the present will eventually give way to blissful paradise where the righteous can live in peace.

While studying apocalyptic literature and movements, one becomes acutely aware of certain themes that appear consistently. These themes are important in identifying a coherent worldview expressed in apocalyptic thought. There are at least three major themes that find expression in most if not all apocalyptic literature and movements: (1) a focus on the battle between good and evil; (2) themes of judgment; and (3) an identification with a coming mediator (Koch in Collins 1984, Robbins and Palmer 1997). Although these themes may be interpreted in different ways, they always concern themselves with future events.

The most predominant apocalyptic themes are those that focus on the battle between good and evil and the themes of judgment. The worldview expressed in the apocalyptic can be reduced to the notion that an ongoing fight between good and evil exists, and that a judgment is required to restore the good and punish the evil. The themes of the fight between good and evil and judgment are crucial for two reasons. First, they place importance upon the role of individuals who live in such "chaotic" times. The individual has a responsibility to God to remain faithful despite the temptations and pressures of the evil world. This responsibility serves to empower individuals to make choices, thereby alleviating powerless feelings. Second, they serve as a warning to individuals who deviate from this role. Those who do deviate are to be punished.

The notion of an ongoing fight between good and evil has traditionally fostered an "us versus them" mentality among the faithful. Conservative Christians view themselves as God's chosen people; as a result, they have an obligation to remain faithful and "go therefore and make disciples of all nations..." (Matt. 28:19). As I shall show later, the drive for evangelism along with eschatological views provide the context of Christian speed/thrash metal.

The final major apocalyptic theme is an identification with a coming mediator that provides a way of escape from judgment for the faithful. The mediator is generally interpreted in an eschatological fashion. He is viewed as the figure that will lead his people to enjoy the fruits of everlasting life that is free from physical and spiritual hardships, temptation, and evil. In the conservative Christian tradition, the Messiah is the Son of God, warrior of truth, final judge, and ruler king. Believers are encouraged to prepare for his second coming, which will occur without warning, by abstaining from sin and living a righteous life. Those who have not accepted Jesus as their personal Lord and savior will be judged and cast into hell where there will be "weeping and gnashing of teeth."

Apocalyptic themes are not the exclusive territory of religious groups; they also find expression outside religion (Lamy 1997). The apocalyptic is often used to express the interpretation of the world that is shared by religious and secular groups. The interpretation of the world as hostile and evil encourages a radicalized view of the world itself. By "a radicalized view" I mean that events and images are treated in a radical fashion to convey the urgency of the apocalyptic message. Symbolic images such as skulls, monsters, and corpses are reflective of this radicalized thinking, and show up on T-shirts, movie billboards, magazines, and art. The radicalization of the world is a central idea of the apocalyptic in general, as rebellion, the breakdown of social order, and gory imagery often reflect this radicalized view.

Apocalyptic thinking, be it religious or secular, shares common general ideas. One such idea is that the world is a hostile and evil place. As a result, themes and images that reflect a radicalized view of the world play a large part in symbolically conveying apocalyptic thinking. The ultimate fight between good and evil is here, and will end in good defeating evil. A judgment that restores good and punishes evil is the final step that both forms of apocalyptic share.

The History and Social Context of Speed/Thrash Metal

The Historical Development of Speed/Thrash Metal Music

When exploring the history of Christian speed/thrash music, one must begin with secular speed/thrash metal, which set the foundation for the harmonic structure of its Christian counterpart. Secular speed/thrash has its roots in heavy metal, which as a specific genre evolved from rock music during the late 1960s and early '70s (Dome 1990, Weinstein 1991).

The 1960s was a time of social upheaval for many individuals. The emergence of the youth culture, the Vietnam War, and the civil rights movement challenged and impacted the social landscape of America. The Vietnam War and the threat of nuclear war were often interpreted as signs of apocalyptic times, especially by fundamentalist Christians (Enroth, Ericson, and Peters 1972; Lippy 1982). The indifference of the United States government and business world toward individuals was interpreted as a sign that the situation in the world was critical, and unless changed, it would lead to the end of the planet. Music in the '60s called on the youth to prevent the coming apocalypse by becoming activists. As the '60s passed and the '70s set in, the "we" generation shifted into the "me" generation. The idealism of an era turned into pessimism.

Investigations of American popular culture reveal the apocalyptic as an idea in secular mythology. Nelson (1982) discusses the emergence of apocalyptic themes in movies and television. Some of these themes include (1) Humanity versus the natural world (*Earthquake, The Poseidon Adventure, The Towering Inferno*), (2) Humanity versus technology (*Planet of the*

Apes, 2001: A Space Odyssey, Westworld, Star Wars, Battlestar Galactica), and (3) Political conspiracy paranoia (*Futureworld, Invasion of the Body Snatchers*).

Secular music, particularly heavy metal and its subgenres, also embody apocalyptic themes.

> The Book of Revelations, that unique apocalyptic vision in the New Testament, is a particularly rich source of imagery for heavy metal lyrics. Not only are songs such as Iron Maiden's *Number of the Beast* inspired by its verses, but it provides a resonance, a cultural frame of reference, for the imagery of chaos itself [Weinstein 1991, Pp. 1–2].

Apocalyptic themes reach their height in secular speed/thrash metal. Environmental concerns (*Inherited Hell* by Nuclear Assault, *Blackened* by Metallica, *Greenhouse Effect* by Testament), death (*Fade to Black* by Metallica, *Leprosy* by Death) and rebellion (*Be All, End All* by Anthrax) echo just a few of the apocalyptic themes. Many of these themes are closely related to the chaotic element of heavy metal itself.

Apocalyptic themes in speed/thrash are an important component of the subgenre because they explore the texts and the harmonics of heavy metal in extreme fashion. As Weinstein (1991) points out, heavy metal is serious about power, and any lyrical theme within the genre is empowered by the sound. Lyrical themes can be placed into one of two opposite categories: the dionysian and the chaotic. The dionysian seeks pleasurable experience through ecstasy, including sex, drugs, and heavy metal music itself, and focus on immediate gratification. Dionysian themes are generally associated with a subgenre of heavy metal known as glam metal, a lighter form of heavy metal. The second category, that of chaos, finds expression in speed/thrash. Weinstein suggests that dionysian themes are not unique to heavy metal, but themes of chaos are distinctive of the genre. Apocalyptic imagery, especially of the biblical kind, is a primary source of chaotic themes for speed/thrash bands. But the secular apocalyptic thinking of the countercultural movements of the '60s also influenced the genre. Apocalyptic and chaotic imagery is not relegated to lyrics, but also finds expression in visual and harmonic dimensions, each of which will be examined shortly.

Secular speed/thrash metal evolved from heavy metal and punk rock in California between 1981 and 1983. Several bands are mentioned when alluding to its early formation, including Metallica, Megadeth (sic), and Slayer (Dome 1990). These groups fused elements of late '70s and early '80s punk rock with the styles of English heavy metal bands such as Venom and Iron Maiden. According to Weinstein, this new subgenre "can be understood as an attempt to reclaim metal for youth and especially for males by creating a style that is completely unacceptable to the hegemonic culture" (1991, p.

48). The subgenre represents, in part, a rallying cry for the return to the unpretentious, stripped down heavy metal of the early '70s.

Although Weinstein's (1991) analysis is correct, it does not consider Christian speed/thrash metal that has emerged in America during the late 1980s. This form is identical to its secular counterpart in harmonic and visual dimensions, yet is often described as a "musical-missionary movement" (Rabey 1987, p. 10ff). While Christian speed/thrash was influenced harmonically and visually by other secular speed/thrash bands, its thematic dimensions were influenced by Christian heavy metal bands such as Stryper, Barren Cross and Bloodgood. Apocalyptic themes are an important component of Christian speed/thrash and find their context in the Christian fundamentalist apocalyptic movement that grew out of the 1960s counter cultural Jesus movement. This movement, which birthed contemporary Christian music, was decidedly apocalyptic in nature and was made up of youth who were largely disillusioned with the idealism and subsequent failure of the secular counterculture (Enroth, Ericson, and Peters, 1972).

The music of the Jesus movement provided an outlet for the apocalyptic thought of its adherents. Larry Norman's *I Wish We'd All Been Ready* is one telling example. The song laments that some individuals are not ready for the second coming of Jesus. As the Christian music industry began to expand, it adopted many musical styles, images, and themes of the secular industry only to recast them into a fundamentalist Christian context. Heavy metal for example, was adopted by Christians almost 10 years after it had been formulated by secular artists. With the development of this musical genre came the adoption of new dress codes and visual presentations of album covers. Christian album covers generally had pictures of the artists in friendly poses, smiling happily, conveying a bright, optimistic tone. Christian heavy metal album covers became more ominous beginning in the mid–1980s. The artists, when pictured, looked serious, and the artwork reflected this serious tone through images of weapons (the missiles on the cover of Stryper's first album), blood (the spots of blood on Bloodgood's debut album), and chaos (Messiah Prophet's first album cover showed people running from falling debris off mountains). The lyrics in Christian heavy metal centered on apocalyptic themes of judgment and the second coming of Christ. Apocalyptic themes have reached new heights in Christian speed/thrash metal music.

Christian speed/thrash music began in the late '80s with the 1988 release of *Human Sacrifice* by Vengeance. A group by the name of Deliverance followed suit with a self-titled debut album. Both groups were born from the Sanctuary church movement, a group of churches in California that were created for ministering to those who listened to heavy metal (Rabey 1992). These churches became an important part of the Christian speed/thrash movement because they lent credibility to the music as a form of ministry.

The churches also became centers of socialization by providing a place where other potential band members could meet each other and receive training in reaching the lost youth with their particular brand of speed/thrash metal. Many of the dozen or so Christian speed/thrash bands signed to Christian record labels today are involved in a Sanctuary church.

Christian speed/thrash focuses on themes of chaos, and has an affinity for apocalyptic imagery. The Bible is constantly used by Christian speed/thrash bands, much more so than their secular counterparts. The reason for this is obvious. Members of Christian speed/thrash bands are Christians with a fundamentalist evangelical slant. They believe in a Bible that is error free, and is therefore a guide for living one's life. Furthermore, the Bible speaks of the dire consequences of not accepting Jesus as a personal Lord and savior. Individuals and society are judged and punished for their unbelief. In the book of Revelation, the author speaks of the wrath of God on those who do not accept Jesus and continue to live a life of sin, and provides a glimpse into the future battle of the forces of good and evil.

Apocalyptic images lend themselves easily to Christian speed/thrash bands for two reasons. First, they can be used as links to those who listen to secular speed/thrash by using similar musical patterns and radical messages. This provides a common ground for Christian groups and secular audiences, allowing Christians musical and social credibility since they are using the same language (music and themes) as the audience. Second, Christian speed/thrash musicians can use this imagery in their preaching by pointing to its source and explaining its meaning within a biblical context.

The Context of Apocalyptic Affinities

Apocalyptic musical structures, visual presentations and lyrics were in existence before Christian speed/thrash metal. The Christian subgenre, however, focused these apocalyptic dimensions in a sharper fashion than its secular counterpart because of the unmediated religious connections.

Two dimensions of conservative Christian thought are relevant to Christian speed/thrash metal's elective affinity for the apocalyptic: evangelism and eschatology. Evangelism is a requirement for a faithful Christian. Not only does it function to spread the Gospel and create converts, it also provides a sense of purpose for the Christian by fashioning a role to play in the continued fight between good and evil. The Bible suggests that the world is the battleground for souls and that these souls can be reached and converted only through active evangelism (2 Cor. 4:3–6; Eph. 2:1–2; Rom. 10:13–15). Christian speed/thrash metal became a priority after it was discovered that many 15- to 21-year-olds who had previously been into heavy metal were giving up the genre in favor of something more aggressive. Christian musicians who enjoyed this intense style of music began forming bands in hopes of reaching these individuals. This was a perfect form of ministry for many of these musicians because they could put to good use the music they enjoyed playing.

The second conservative Christian viewpoint that is relevant to the affinity between Christian speed/thrash metal and apocalyptic themes is an eschatological view of history. According to The American Heritage Dictionary (1985), eschatology can be defined as: "The branch of theology that is concerned with the ultimate or last things...." Walvoord provides a more complete definition, suggesting:

> Among theological conservatives it is generally agreed that Biblical prophecies will be fulfilled and such events as resurrection from the dead, reward of the saints, punishment of the wicked, and the continued conscious existence of all human souls throughout eternity will eventuate. Biblical eschatology assumes that the Scriptures predict future events with infallible accuracy and constitute a divine disclosure of the future [Walvoord 1967, p. 258].

The reason the style of Christian speed/thrash fits so well with eschatological views is obvious. The apocalyptic imagery serves as a warning of the urgency of the music's message; namely, that a battle is being waged between good and evil and that judgment will come upon those who do not accept Jesus. The listener is encouraged to make a decision concerning personal salvation before it is too late.

The theme of accepting Jesus Christ is a recurrent theme in Christian speed/thrash metal music. The bands are using the medium of speed/thrash metal music to preach the Gospel. To them, the music is a form of language that acts as a carrier for the Gospel message. Guy Ritter, the lead singer from the band Tourniquet comments:

> We have Christian missionaries in this country that learn the different languages of other third world countries ... we're doing that in a similar way. We know about how the kids live. We can relate to the kids that listen to heavy metal and thrash and we're saying to these kids, you know, the Bible is cool. We're taking out the Bible and we're explaining it to them so they can understand it [*Hot Metal 4: The Video* 1991].

The musicians see themselves as missionaries who are attempting to reach a group who may not be approachable by other means. Evangelists Billy Graham and Bill Bright are admired by musicians, however musicians feel that kids who are into speed/thrash metal will not listen to them. The evangelists, although speaking the same message, are simply speaking a different "language."

Together, evangelism and eschatology form the context upon which the affinity of Christian speed/thrash metal for apocalyptic themes is constructed. Evangelism and eschatology are central to the appearance of the apocalyptic in Christian speed/thrash. Evangelism and eschatology's merge with the apocalyptic lead to the phenomenon of Christian speed/thrash metal. While evangelism and eschatology provide the context, the apocalyptic provides the form and the substance of the message.

The Apocalyptic of Christian Speed/Thrash Metal

In this section, I identify three major components of Christian speed/thrash metal music, (1) harmonic dimensions (2) visual dimensions, and (3) lyrical dimensions and their relationship to apocalyptic themes. The first two components deal with the form of Christian speed/thrash metal, the carrier of the message that the musicians are preaching. The third component is the content of this message, where apocalyptic thinking is most evident.

The Apocalyptic of Harmonic Dimensions

Christian apocalyptic perceives the world as a confusing and hostile environment that is in need of divine wisdom to give it meaning. This view of confusion and hostility is reflected in the harmonic dimension of Christian speed/thrash metal which is made up of radicalized, and seemingly chaotic, musical structures. Christian Speed/thrash employs what is known as root 5th power chords. Since only two notes are played (the root and the fifth notes), these are not true chords. At least three notes are needed to form a true musical chord. Furthermore, riffs, the short melodic phrases that are repeated constantly during a song, are faster and contain more variations than those found in heavy metal or rock music. Speed/thrash also incorporates power chords that are played in one of three intervals, the tritone, the minor 2nd, and the major 7th. These three intervals are the most disturbing to Western listeners and are used for an added rebellious dynamic (Bowcott 1991).

Another common trait of speed/thrash music is its use of changing rhythmic subdivisions. Eighth notes, sixteenth notes, and triplets are often used back to back, making the structure of the music seem to skip, hop, stop and start, conveying a continuous quirky feel. The effect is to render the music unpredictable and therefore exciting as well as chaotic. To the listener, the music becomes the embodiment of chaos and rebellion; it *seems* to follow no musical rules and can change abruptly at any given moment.

Speed/thrash also eschews musical rules to reflect a chaotic attitude in its willingness to incorporate odd meter bars. Often, the meter will switch back and forth from the standard 4/4 time generally used in heavy metal and rock to odd meters such as 5/4 or 7/8, giving speed/thrash music a schizophrenic feel by throwing the listener off the rhythmic track.

The affinity between apocalyptic musical structures and speed/thrash music is apparent. The musicians reflect a radicalized view of the world by using radical musical harmonics and eschewing musical rules. The tritone interval, which consists of a diminished 5th or an augmented 4th; is commonly used in speed/thrash metal and is also known as "Diabolus in Musica," Latin for "the devil in music." This interval was banned from church music during the middle ages because of its association with Satan. Church leaders felt that the interval sounded evil due to the extreme dissonance produced and therefore was not suitable for Christian worship (Routh 1973, Ultan 1977).

Speed/thrash metal exhibits rebellion in musical theory by using power chords and dissonant riffing. Rules governing musical theory are transgressed as musicians rebel against traditional harmonic structures. Furthermore, this transgression conveys emotionally a sense of an unresolved, confused view of the world. These feelings are played out through the apocalyptic chaos and rebellion of the musical dimensions of speed/thrash.

The Apocalyptic of Visual Dimensions

Christian speed/thrash displays an affinity for apocalyptic visual presentations in dress, videos, and album covers. Speed/thrash metal musicians generally dress in ripped jeans or long, knee length shorts. They may wear T-shirts that display gory imagery, or long-sleeved, dark colored shirts. Black, gray, and other drab colors are the norm. Most wear their hair long and unstyled or they may shave their heads clean. Earrings and hightop tennis shoes are also normal apparel. In short, members of bands do not "dress up" in stage costumes. Unlike glam metal in which the musicians commonly wear Spandex and makeup, the audience and musicians share the same dress code.

Videos consistently incorporate apocalyptic themes and images such as dark churches, lit candles, and skulls, interspersed with concert footage of the band. The band Vengeance uses this key imagery in their video entitled *Before the Time*. This video contains shots, images, and camera angles moving at a rapid pace, at times keeping pace with the rhythm of the music itself. Band members look serious, scowling and grimacing. Smiles are ominous in manner, to accentuate a serious point made in the song.

Album covers extend the fascination with apocalyptic images and themes. Most have at least one if not all of the following: demons, skulls, and corpses. Christian bands incorporate these macabre images to emphasize the issues of the afterlife. These images are used to shock the audience into thinking about the future by pointing to issues of mortality and punishment for the wicked.

The fascination with apocalyptic imagery can be viewed as direct rebellion and defiance toward society. The rebellion in dress is an extension of the perceived notion of speed/thrash music in general, as visual dimensions and musical structure become an extension of viewing the world in a radical fashion. The world is perceived as hostile and repressive in nature. Loose codes concerning dress and deviant musical structure are the responses to this world.

The apocalyptic imagery focuses attention to the issues of impending death and judgment of the wicked. Skulls and corpses remind the listener that death is impartial and certain, shocking the audience into the apocalyptic reality that this is the time to make a decision to follow God as the end is coming quickly.

The imagery as a whole projects a dark, gloomy mood. This mood seems to run contrary to the bright, joyful disposition often associated with the Christian message. But this is only because Christian speed/thrash musicians generally speak in the narrow terms of the afterlife; furthermore, the speed/thrash musicians often aim their message at non–Christians and seek to obtain maximum impact on their audience.

The Apocalyptic of Lyrical Dimensions

As I have shown, harmonic and visual dimensions reflect apocalyptic thought in form. As with any musical form, these dimensions are important in identifying the genre. The apocalyptic harmonic and visual dimensions provide the carrier for an apocalyptic message, setting the stage for the substantive dimension I will now consider. The lyrical dimension carries the content of the message itself and is therefore the single most important dimension in understanding a musical subgenre such as Christian speed/thrash metal. With lyrics, the artist can explore apocalyptic themes in great detail.

In Christian speed/thrash metal, musicians have produced detailed visions of the apocalyptic that may not be possible to convey in an album cover or video alone. Bands explore many of the major themes of apocalyptic thought in their albums' lyrics. The band Sacrament explores two major themes in their debut album entitled *Testimony of Apocalypse*: judgment and preoccupation with physical disaster. Mortification, Vengeance, and Believer also explore the major apocalyptic themes on each of their debut albums.

Bands may explore the same apocalyptic theme several times on the same album, giving the listener a different perspective in each song. Vengeance, for example, in their album *Human Sacrifice*, explored the theme of final judgment in the songs *Burn* and *White Throne*. In *Burn*, Satan is the object of the eschatological judgment, while in *White Throne* individuals who have rejected Jesus are judged and condemned.

All three major apocalyptic themes find expression in Christian speed/thrash metal; in fact, apocalyptic themes are one of the most common throughout Christian speed/thrash metal lyrics.

1. Judgment

This apocalyptic theme is one of the most dominant in Christian speed/thrash. The lyrics approach the subject of judgment from various directions. In *Testimony of Apocalypse*, the band Sacrament speaks of judgment in general using graphic imagery: darkness descends, Judgment Day, general decay. When the end comes, the wrath of God's apocalyptic riders will avenge the righteous against the wicked.

The band Vengeance speaks specifically of the Great White Throne judgment mentioned in the book of Revelation. This judgment includes all the wicked dead who were killed in the ultimate battle between good and evil, as well as the wicked dead who were killed in all the ages before the battle and are temporarily held in Hades. In the end, there will be nowhere to run, nowhere to hide at the Great White Throne.

The band Deliverance focuses on death and judgment. In this example, the final age is viewed in terms of the judgment, while the age in which we are living now is viewed in terms of death. It has been appointed once for a man to die, but after this the judgment. Once the appointment has been made, nothing can be done to change it.

The theme of final judgment expresses the immediacy and inevitability of the event. Commonly used phrases such as "You're taken by surprise," and "nothing can be done to change it" reflect this thinking. The conservative Christian view of evangelism provides the context for the affinity between Christian speed/thrash metal and apocalyptic themes. For the Christian speed/thrash musician, judgment is something to be feared if you have not accepted Jesus Christ. It is the point at which it is too late for an individual to make a decision. The decision must be made in this lifetime or the individual will suffer the consequences.

The band Believer, in a song entitled *Vile Hypocrisy*, warns that "For rejection of Christ, (there will be an) eternal consequence." Mortification also warns that "destructive consequences befall the denier" in their song *Satan's Doom*. The apocalyptic theme of judgment is used by the bands to warn of the perils of unbelief. Listeners are reminded to "cross over or you will die" and to "seek God with all your heart (and) listen to his voice."

According to the musicians, an individual is placed in one of two locations after the judgment. Those who have accepted Jesus Christ are allowed to spend eternity with God in heaven; the wicked, however, are assigned to eternal punishment in Hell. Consider the following theme from Betrayal: Enter to the kingdom, the almighty God will say, or live forever in eternal torment because the kingdom of God is not for you. The prince of peace has shed his blood. What will you do with it?

The lyrics pose a rhetorical question to the listener. It is hoped that this approach will cause the listener to question the need for a personal relationship with Jesus. The lyrics remind the listener that a relationship is indeed needed if he wishes to escape eternal punishment.

The theme of a movement from this world to another world is even more graphic in a song by Deliverance. In this song, lost souls who have died and gone to Hell are shown. Millions may scream in dreaded harmony, and the shrieks of pain will be neverending. The faithful will never die, and no matter what they suffer in this world, God will redeem them through Jesus.

The apocalyptic theme of a spatial movement from this world to the other world is certainly evident in this type of song. The musicians remind the listeners that this event marks the end of the age. The punishments and rewards are for eternity. Damnation is forever while the faithful will live eternally. This scene is straight out of the book of Revelation. The earthly age is concluded and the wicked are separated from the righteous. For the righteous, there will no longer be any pain or sorrow. There will be no more tears. This marks the final victory of God and the faithful. No longer will the faithful have to fear the wicked or put up with Satan and his demons. God is glorified while Satan and this world are destroyed.

2. The battle between good and evil

Christians believe that a battle is being waged between good and evil. Christians are constantly encouraged to "Rise up with the sword of God and put your armor on," and "not grow weary in doing what is right, [for] God shall renew our strength." Christians are reminded that the battle being waged is not with other people, but with Satan and his demons. Stand against the devil. We are not fighting men, but evil forces of a dark age.

This means that Christians must use immaterial weapons. The armor in the song above is a direct reference to the armor listed in the sixth chapter of the book of Ephesians.

> Stand firm therefore, having girded your loins with truth, and having put on the breastplate of righteousness, and having shod your feet with the preparation of the Gospel of peace; in addition to all, taking up the shield of faith with which you will be able to extinguish all the flaming missiles of the evil one. And take the helmet of salvation, and the sword of the Spirit, which is the word of God [Ephesians 6:14–17, NASB].

Angelic beings also fight in the spiritual realm. Deliverance speaks of Angelic forces fighting the battles, unseen warriors, and although mighty, there is no place where angels fear to tread, drawing swords of God's awesome power.

This battle between good and evil escalates until the final battle of Armageddon which is recorded in the 16th chapter of the book of Revelation. Here, the forces of good defeat the forces of evil. After the battle, the evil are judged and punished while the faithful are rewarded.

The musicians rely on the apocalyptic imagery of the ultimate battle to remind every individual that (1) God exists, (2) evil will be defeated by God, and (3) individuals must choose whom they will serve. Christian speed/thrash musicians remind the listener of the fate of Satan and of the non–Christian. This message seems to serve two purposes. The first is to encourage the Christian with the message that Satan will soon be thrown in Hell by God. This means that he will no longer have the power to tempt Christians into sin, and that all forms of evil will be eradicated. The second is to warn the non–Christian: Satan will be conquered by God and is therefore not worth serving. In the end, Satan is stripped of strength and power and left helpless to burn forever.

Sacrament echoes this sentiment when they encourage Christians to follow God which leads to eternal peace. Satan will be destroyed.

This mocking tone toward Satan is also reflected in the Vengeance song *Burn*. The opening lyrics begin with the singer chanting "Burn Satan Burn." The tone of animosity is grounded in the fact that the singer blames Satan for blinding the eyes of friends from following God. The singer reminds Satan as well as the listeners that God's judgment will come swiftly. The tone of the lyrics reinforces the belief that ultimately good will triumph over evil. Satan and nonbelievers will be cast into Hell where they will no longer be a threat to the righteous.

3. The coming mediator

An identification with a coming mediator is another theme that is an expression of the apocalyptic theme of the world as hostile. The sinfulness and hostility of the world can only be overcome only by the mediator who is savior and judge. For this reason, the second coming of Jesus is an event that Christians look forward to. At the same time however, two warnings are given, one to Christians and the other to non–Christians. Christians are encouraged to keep themselves "unstained by the world" to meet Jesus without shame. Meanwhile, non–Christians are encouraged to prepare for the second coming by turning from sin toward God. Vengeance in their piece entitled *Mulligans Stew* argue that Jesus Christ is coming so we've got to get ready. Jesus hasn't come to call the righteous but rather the sinners, because all have fallen short of the glory of God. The second coming is an inevitable event. Those who are found to be without a personal relationship with Jesus will be punished, while those who know Jesus as their lord and savior will be rewarded.

For Christians, including the speed/thrash musicians, the world is viewed as hostile because it is at odds with Christian morals and beliefs. Passages abound within the New Testament that reflect this thought. Jesus himself suggested that since he chose his disciples out of the world, the world would hate them (John 15:19). The author of the book of James suggests that "whoever wishes to be a friend of the world makes himself an enemy of God" (James 4:4). This attitude is reflected within speed/thrash lyrics that suggest that the world will soon come under judgment.

Although the world is viewed as hostile, speed/thrash musicians encourage their listeners to realize that the world can only harm physically. After death, however, the spirit lives on either in Heaven or Hell. This being the case, the listener is urged to accept Jesus as Lord and Savior and repent from wickedness.

Conclusion

Christian speed/thrash metal displays an affinity for apocalyptic themes in three dimensions: harmonic, visual, and lyrical. The affinity between Christian speed/thrash metal and apocalyptic themes finds its context within conservative Christian views of eschatology and evangelism. In order to carry out and relate their ideas and interests, Christian musicians readily appropriated speed/thrash metal because of its inherent affinity for apocalyptic thought. In this conclusion, I want to recover more fully the meaning of Christian speed/thrash. The affinity of Christian speed/thrash metal for apocalyptic themes is based upon the conservative Christian views of evangelism and eschatology. These views are important because conservative Christians perceive this world as a continuing struggle between good and evil, a struggle that will eventually end in an apocalyptic manner. Evangelism is imperative and this is why so many of the lyrics serve as warnings to accept Jesus. The apocalyptic imagery is used because it is a very graphic way to convey effectively the urgency of the message.

Christian speed/thrash metal reflects an attempt by alienated youth to make sense of the chaotic and irrational world. The apocalyptic themes signal that soon there will be a time when this earth, and all that are in it, will cease to exist. Order and peace will be restored while Christians will be rid of the confusion of this world. Christian speed/thrash metal explains the chaotic world and its irrationality by interpreting it in terms of the ultimate battle between God and Satan; it proclaims this world as confusing and hostile because of Satan and because of the initial sin of Adam and Eve that is passed on to all humans.

Since Christian speed/thrash metal views the world as hostile, rebellion ensues as a counteraction. Musical structures convey rebellion through dissonant riffing and power chords, breaking with accepted traditional musical theory. The visual imagery of speed/thrash music rebels by transcending accepted norms: album covers and dress shock outsiders while providing a focal point for social solidarity with insiders. Finally, the lyrics reflect rebellious apocalyptic themes, whereby individuals feel that they are able to make sense of an irrational world and dismiss it altogether.

Apocalyptic radicalization stems from the view that the world is a hostile environment; as a result, events and images are treated in a radical fashion to convey the urgency of the apocalyptic message. In Christian speed/thrash metal, many radical images are used to convey the necessity for a relationship with God. Jesus is referred to as a "human sacrifice" whose "blood will atone our sins" (Vengeance/*Human Sacrifice*; Believer/*Not Even One*). Individuals are encouraged to "Fill this place with blood, and that of no other than the Lord Jesus Christ" as "there is a fountain filled with blood drawn from Emmanuel's veins" (Vengeance/*Fill this Place with Blood*; Deliverance/*Victory*).

The image of blood is used liberally in Christian speed/thrash metal because it has obvious religious symbolism, but it also reflects a radical means through which the evangelistic message can be communicated. Musicians do not just allude to blood; rather, they emphasize bloody graphic descriptions to convey the urgency of the message.

One may interpret the phenomenon in terms of a constellation of ideas and interests that, when viewed collectively, provide a unified, meaningful whole. In Christian speed/thrash metal, apocalyptic lyrics, musical structures, visual presentation, and speed/thrash metal seek one another out, coming together to form the musical phenomenon of Christian speed/thrash metal. Conservative Christian views of evangelism and eschatology do not cause apocalyptic musical structures and lyrics; rather, they merge like pieces of a jigsaw puzzle, which when viewed together provide a unified, meaningful social phenomenon. In the same way, apocalyptic musical structures do not cause apocalyptic lyrics; rather, the use of dissonant riffing, root 5th power chords, and high speed and distortion fit together with these lyrics better than conventional forms. The visual presentation of Christian speed/thrash metal and its album covers can also be viewed as incorporating apocalyptic themes as a piece of the larger puzzle. Visual presentations fit together with the musical structures and lyrics rather than being a cause or effect in themselves.

The musical style of Christian speed/thrash metal is a radical form of music in terms of its lyrical and harmonic content. However, this radicalization extends beyond surface observations of the music itself to the underlying social and cultural views of those who participate in this musical style. The affinity model is helpful in exploring these underlying views by showing us how, and to some extent why, Christian speed/thrash metal has attached itself to apocalyptic expressions. While this study does not represent the only interpretation of the phenomenon of Christian speed/thrash metal, it does provide a different way of interpreting the phenomenon, enhancing our understanding of our own culture and of ourselves.

References

Anthrax. "Be all, End all." *State of Euphoria*. Atlantic Records, 1988.
Baker, Paul. *Contemporary Christian Music*. Wheaton, IL: Crossway Books, 1979.
Believer. "Not Even One." *Extraction From Mortality*. R.E.X. Records, 1989.
_____. "Vile Hypocrisy." *Extraction From Morality*. R.E.X. Records, 1989.
Betrayal. "Plead the Blood." *Renaissance by Death*. Wonderland/Word Records, 1991.
Bowcott, Nick. "How to Play Thrash." *Guitar World*, 1991.
Brown, Charles M. "Musical Responses to Oppression and Alienation: Blues, Spirituals, Secular Thrash, and Christian Thrash Metal Music ." *International Journal of Politics, Culture and Society* 8.3 (1995): 439–452.
Carlin, Richard. *Rock & Roll: 1955–1979*. New York: Facts on File, 1986.
Collins, John J. *The Apocalyptic Imagination: An Introduction to the Jewish Matrix of Christianity*. New York: Crossroad, 1984.
Curtis, Jim. *Rock Eras: Interpretations of Music and Society, 1954–1984*. Bowling Green, OH: Bowling Green State University Popular Press, 1987.
Cusic, Don. *Music in the Market*. Bowling Green, OH: Bowling Green State University Popular Press, 1996.
_____. *The Sound of Light: A History of Gospel Music*. Bowling Green, OH: Bowling Green State University Popular Press, 1990.
Deliverance. "Awake." *Deliverance*. Intense Records, 1989.
_____. "Greetings of Death." *Weapons of our Warfare*. Intense Records, 1990.

_____. "If We Faint not." *Weapons of our Warfare*. Intense Records, 1990.
_____. "Slay the Wicked." *Weapons of our Warfare*. Intense Records, 1990.
_____. "Victory." *Deliverance*. Intense Records, 1989.
_____. "Weapons of our Warfare." *Weapons of our Warfare*. Intense Records, 1990.
Denisoff, R. Serge. *Solid Gold: The Popular Record Industry*. New Brunswick, NJ: Transaction, 1975.
Denisoff, Serge. *Tarnished Gold*. New Brunswick, NJ: Transaction, 1986.
Dome, Malcolm. *Thrash Metal*. London: Omnibus Press, 1990.
Enroth, Ronald M., Edward E. Ericson, and B. C. Peters. *The Jesus People: Old-Time Religion in the Age of Aquarius*. Grand Rapids, MI: Eerdman's, 1972.
Flake, Carol. *Redemptorama: Culture, Politics, and the New Evangelicalism*. New York: Penguin Books, 1984.
Frankl, Razelle. *Televangelism: The Marketing of Popular Religion*. Carbondale, IL: Southern Illinois University Press, 1987.
Frith, Simon. *Sound Effects: Youth, Leisure, and the Politics of Rock 'N' Roll*. New York: Pantheon, 1981.
Hebdige, Dick. "Reggae, Rastas and Rudies." *Resistance Through Rituals: Youth Subcultures in Post-War Britain*. Edited by Stuart Hall and Tony Jefferson. New York: HarperCollins, 1976.
_____. *Subculture: The Meaning of Style*. London: Methuen, 1979.
Howard, Jay R. "Contemporary Christian Music: Where Rock Meets Religion." *Journal of Popular Culture* 26.1 (1992): 123–130.
Howard, Jay R., and John M. Streck. "The Splintered Art World of Contemporary Christian Music." *Popular Music* 15.1 (1996): 37–53.
Lamy, Philip. "Secularizing the Millennium: Survivalists, Militias, and the New World Order." *Millennium, Messiahs, and Mayhem*. Edited by Thomas Robbins and Susan J. Palmer. New York: Routledge, 1997.
Lippy, Charles H. 1982. "Waiting for the End: the Social Context of American Apocalyptic Religion." *The Apocalyptic Vision in America: Interdisciplinary Essays on Myth and Culture*. Edited by Lois Parkinson Zamora. Bowling Green, OH: Bowling Green University Popular Press, 1982.
McDannell, Colleen. *Material Christianity: Religion and Popular Culture in America*. New Haven, CT: Yale University Press, 1995.
Megadeth. "Dawn Patrol." *Rust in Peace*. Capital Records, 1990.
Metallica. "Fade to Black." *Ride the Lightning*. Elektra/Asylum Records, 1984.
Miller, Steve. *The Contemporary Christian Music Debate*. Wheaton, IL: Tyndale House, 1993.
Moore, R. Laurence. *Selling God: American Religion in the Marketplace of Culture*. New York: Oxford University Press, 1994.
Mortification. "Satan's Doom." *Mortification*. Frontline Records, 1991.
Nelson, John W. "The Apocalyptic Vision in American Popular Culture." *The Apocalyptic Vision in America*. Edited by Lois Parkinson Zamora. Bowling Green, OH: Bowling Green University Press, 1982.
Peters, Dan, Steve Peters, and Cher Merill. *What About Christian Rock?* Minneapolis: Bethany House, 1986.
Rabey, Steve. "Big-Band Fan Turns Missionary to Metal Heads." *Christianity Today*, 1992.

5. Apocalyptic Unbound   137

———. "Heavy Metal Mania: In the Record Bins and on the Concert Stage Christian Heavy Metal is Hot. But What Hath Stryper Wrought?" *Newsound*, 1987.
Robbins, Thomas, and Susan J. Palmer, eds. *Millennium, Messiahs, and Mayhem: Contemporary Apocalyptic Movements.* New York: Routledge, 1997.
Romanowski, William D. "Rock 'n' Religion: A Socio-Cultural Analysis of the Contemporary Christian Music Industry." Bowling Green State University, 1990.
———. "Roll Over Beethoven, Tell Martin Luther the News: American Evangelicals and Rock Music." *Journal of American Culture* 15.3 (1992): 79–88.
Routh, Francis. *Early English Organ Music From the Middle Ages to 1837.* London: Barrie & Jenkins, 1973.
Sacrament. "Hellfire Denied." *Testimony of Apocalypse.* R.E.X. Records, 1990.
———. "Testimony of Apocalypse." *Testimony of Apocalypse.* R.E.X. Records, 1990.
Seay, Davin, and Mary Neely. *Stairway to Heaven.* New York: Ballatine/Ephany, 1986.
Simone, Angelo De. *Christian Rock: Friend or Foe?* New Haven, CT: Selah Production Agency, 1993.
Testament. "Greenhouse Effect." *The Legacy.* Megaforce Worldwide, 1987.
The Crucified. "Hateworld." *The Pillars of Humanity.* Ocean Records, 1991.
Tourniquet. *Hot Metal 4: The Video.* Intense Records, 1991.
———. "Spineless." *Psycho Surgery.* Intense Records, 1991.
Ultan, Lloyd. *Music Theory: Problems and Practices in the Middle Ages and Renaissance.* Minneapolis: University of Minnesota Press, 1977.
Van Pelt, Doug. "Mosh for the Master?" *Contemporary Christian Music*, 1989.
Vengeance. "Burn." *Human Sacrifice.* Intense Records, 1988.
———. "Fill This Place with Blood." *Human Sacrifice.* Intense Records, 1988.
———. "Human Sacrifice." *Human Sacrifice.* Intense Records, 1988.
———. "Mulligans Stew." *Human Sacrifice.* Intense Records, 1988.
———. "White Throne." *Human Sacrifice.* Intense Records, 1988.
Walvoord, John F. "Eschatology." *The Zondervan Pictorial Bible Dictionary.* Edited by Merrill C. Tenney Grand Rapids, MI: Zondervan, 1967.
Weinstein, Deena. *Heavy Metal: A Cultural Sociology.* New York: Lexington, 1991.
Wicke, Peter. *Rock Music: Culture, Aesthetics and Sociology.* Cambridge: Cambridge University Press, 1987.

6

Islamic Fundamentalism, Modernity, and the Role of Women

MAHRUQ F. KHAN
LAUREN LANGMAN

Introduction

For a variety of reasons, Islamic societies have remained quite stable, although this is not so much a virtue in that they have been relatively stagnant politically, economically, and culturally. Most Islamic societies have been ruled by single parties or dictatorial rulers who are typically intolerant of social changes that might limit or challenge their power. Without economic growth and opportunities, without political redress, and cultural isolation in face of major social changes that have nevertheless impacted vast populations, fundamentalisms, as seen in various forms of Islamism, with visions of restoring the past glories of the Caliphate, have found fertile soil and have taken root among wide segments of the population. Nevertheless, given limited infrastructures, limited transparency, unskilled work forces, *radical Islamisms indeed prove counterproductive, incapable of fostering ameliorative social change.* Instead, fundamentalism reinforces barriers to modernization in general and foreign investment in particular, thus intensifying the aforementioned negative conditions.

The Islamic world seems to have two choices: moving forward and embracing modernity while fashioning its own versions, or embracing fundamentalism of one type or another that is incapable of bringing amelioration (Esposito 2003). If we consider Iran under the ayatollahs or Afghanistan during the Taliban rule, Djibouti, Sudan, northern Nigeria, or even the

6. Islamic Fundamentalism, Modernity, and the Role of Women 139

deterioration of the Saudi economy, it becomes clear that societies run according to strict interpretations of Sharia (Islamic) law cannot much improve the life conditions of their citizens.

There is no consensus as to what constitutes modernity and indeed we can now speak of multiple modernities. In the West, post–Enlightenment modernity via the "rationalization of the world" can be characterized by 1) individualism, 2) critical thought and doubt, 3) freedom of action with personal responsibility for outcomes, and 4) a critical, reflexive stance toward oneself viewed a process of self-constitution. Modernity is rational and empirical, and sets itself apart from religious explanations of the world or human action. Religion becomes a personal matter and not a principle of social organization or political action (separation of church and state). The struggle to separate church and state, to create everyday life worlds apart from religious, magical, or mystical concerns was a long, slow process that began with the Renaissance (humanism), the Reformation (ending the hegemony of the Catholic Church), and the Enlightenment.

However, modernism does not necessarily equate with or singly define "civilization." When Europe in the Middle Ages sat mired in darkness and ignorance, Islam had forged one of the great civilizations, highly advanced in science; mathematics (inventing, for example, algebra); medicine; philosophy; and art, especially architecture, illumination, and pottery. By the time it reached its Golden Age, Islamic societies were tolerant, open to ideas, and curious about the world. But then, something went wrong.

Sociologically, we might ask the Weberian question, what were the barriers to rationality that in turn thwarted any pressures to modernity from within or without? More specifically, Weber (1978) argued that the Islamic legal system — *kadi* justice — based on the Quran gave rise to a system of charismatic jurists rather than rational technicians; more specifically, Kuran (2002) has argued that in the Hanafi commercial codes, for example, derived from Sharia law, many have been fair and just, but at the same time, *based on religious principles rather than rational considerations, and thus they limited the growth and prosperity of commercial venture.* Consequently, Islam could never foster the kinds of rational, commercial organizations that would develop in the West. Following the Amalfi codes of 1379, we might note the rise of the joint share organization, early versions of corporations, as distinct entities apart from the members per se. Such corporations could amass capital long after individual members died.

Despite the development of the joint share organization, which was neither widespread nor consistent, the West began its rise as an economic power. Much of this growth depended on trade with the Levant or Mahgreb. But as Islamic economic power began to wane, so too did its political and military power. Thus after the Ottoman conquest of Constantinople, the Inquisition forced Muslims out of Iberia. While Turkish siege cannon had once been the state of military art, they were rendered obsolete by European steel cannons with rifled barrels and explosive balls. European mobile field artillery decimated the horse or camel cavalry of Islamic armies.

Following its internal decline, waning political power, and weakened militaries, there was an ossification of its culture as well. In response, there emerged a *ressentiment* toward the West that in turn created barriers to its ideas, its science, and its medicine that has endured to this day. By the 17th century, travel to Europe was deemed immoral. These barriers to trade and the exchanges of ideas exacerbated the waning of Islamic power and indeed, by the 18th century, the weakened Islamic regions were easily conquered and colonized by Europe. The last to fall, the Ottomans, were able to maintain their empire into the 1920s, but with the defeat of their fleet by the Russians, their ultimate demise was foretold.

Ressentiment is more than simply disguised envy; as Nietzsche argued, it embraced a spirit of revenge that turned into self-hatred, and as such it thwarted the person from his self-fulfillment. Indeed, that very thwarting can lead to the love of death, decay, and petrifaction (Fromm 1961). With self-inspired development thus immobilized, the only remaining possibility is (typically violent) lashing out.

The Modernization of Islam

One of the problems with modernization theory has been its attempt to see a single pattern with the West as the model of both the process of modernizing and the goals of modernization. For example, Rostow's stage theory suggests a trajectory that moves from preconditions to mass consumption. But that model is less useful for contemporary developing societies, existing in a globalized world in which the major powers control the advanced technologies of production, transportation, and information. In most Muslim societies, lacking a modern, rational infrastructure, they are often highly dependent on agricultural or extractive exports and low-wage kinds of production (textiles, rugs, garments, toys). But so too did many other countries move from traditional agricultural or extractive economies to commercial or industrial, high-growth societies such as Portugal, Spain, China, the Asian Tigers, etc. We should note that political and economic factors, such as the geopolitics of the cold war and investment policies, have often played a crucial role in development. Nevertheless, we are suggesting that indigenous factors impact the extent to which external investors find a country favorable.

But at the same time, we often see that as individuals, Muslim scholars, scientists, doctors, lawyers, and indeed sociologists, are just as capable as any other group. In countries where Muslims are minorities, such as India or Malaysia, they often prosper and thrive. Moreover, those Muslim countries that have embraced modernity, such as Morocco, Turkey, and Indonesia, have shown higher rates of economic growth and qualities of life.

Resistance to Modernization

Modern economies foster vast wealth, technological sophistication, individual freedoms, and typically myriads of lifestyle options. It is often not clear why people would resist modernization to sustain "backward" ways, or those so labeled by modernists. But Marx, Weber, and Durkheim, charting the rise of modernity, soon observed its tolls and dysfunctions. For Marx, capitalist modernity turned people into exploited workers and consumers in impersonal markets. Wage labor led to alienation, exploitation, and immiseration. Workers were powerless in the face of a system produced by their labor; their communities were rent asunder and they were rendered bereft of humanity, little more than beasts of burden. Weber saw rational modernity locking people into rational systems devoid of humanity, lacking heart or feelings. Durkheim, no more sanguine, said that at moments of social transition society might face anomie; uprooted people, without constraining and meaningful ties, were more prone to suicide.

Thus the ascent to modernity has faced resistance ever since the "saboteurs" threw wooden shoes, "sabots," into the machines and the Luddites attempted much the same. We might easily note that modernization in developing countries, however considered, has generally had to face a number of obstacles ranging from a limited economic infrastructure, facilitating governmental or banking institutions (rationally organized), and cultural values. While this is true in many different countries, Islamic countries tend to have a number of cultural and religious values that, given the historical legacies we noted, *ressentiment* at the assent of the West, and genuine anger over colonization, imperialism, intervention, and supporting corrupt regimes, act as barriers to modernization. Further, as must be noted, there are wide ranges of variations between Turkey, a secular nation since 1920, and Afghanistan, one of the world's poorest, most economically backward countries.

The Power of Tradition

Islam became a world religion insofar as it provided strict ethical codes, sustained by dramatic punishments and promises of salvation; as such, it served to pacify and unite otherwise warring nomadic tribes (Turner 1984). It rapidly spread across North Africa, the Middle East, and Southeast Asia and would lead to one of the world's great civilizations. But at the same time, Islam created a seamless web in which there was little space for thought and action apart from the religious. While Islam would encourage universities where science, medicine, and mathematics would flourish, and even Greco-Roman philosophy was studied, *it did not encourage a secular, rational realm at the level of everyday life*, with the notable exception of Ibn Khaldun, who as a secular sociologist formulated various social theories based on observation rather than derived from religious interpretations. This does not detract from the argument that in societies where Islam predominated, with its commercial laws and its religiously based jurist system that together promoted stable markets at one time, were disposed to stagnation at a later time where devout Islamic traditions still prevail.

The *ressentiment* toward the West was so powerful that Muslim merchants were loath to travel to Europe and even more reluctant to embrace its crass, commercial ways. One might receive a *fatwa* for traveling to Europe. Thus while Europeans freely drew upon Islamic scholarship that was to be essential for the Renaissance, Muslims constructed barriers against Western ideas — some of which, such as separation of church and state, popular sovereignty expressed through elections, and the notion of unalienable civil might erode the power of political or religious elites. Democracy was said to be sacrilege; only Allah could make laws, even if he glossed over corporate laws, patents, contracts, intellectual property rights, and other key developments that promoted economic prosperity in the non–Islamic world. Beyond Western Christendom, for example, Japan converted its own feudal system into a modernized industrial system, although it was not Christian nor culturally Western.

Among the most important barriers to modernity are the powerful ties and bonds that link people and their families. While again noting variations, these ties to clan and family remain very strong in Muslim societies. Finally, we might also note that not only does modernity attenuate the bonds and familial ties between people, but also it challenges established patterns of authority between generations, especially parents and children, and between men and women. Thus younger, more educated children are likely to challenge parental authority, based in part on greater knowledge. Similarly, with greater education (see below), women are likely to interrogate male authority and gender prerogatives. What needs to be noted is that challenges to established authority systems lead to a great deal of anxiety, not only to those used to holding power and authority, but also for the newly freed and empowered who often fear their own freedom and seek mechanisms of escape to assuage their anxiety through submission to a higher power (Fromm 1941).

Fundamentalism

Fundamentalism is both reactive and *reactionary*; it would stop, if not reverse, the social changes brought about by the forces of modernity by re-creating a golden age of the past when people lived happier, more simple, and more moral lives. Of course, despite the merit of such lofty goals, the actual history of golden ages generally shows that most of the people were poor, uneducated peasants or even slaves with little connection to the intellectual and cultural elites of Athens, Rome, Beijing, or Damascus.

Fundamentalism tends to demand strict, highly idealized moral codes over behavior based on divinely inspired scripture that gives adherents a superior self-image based on a moral stance that provides a sense of calmness while repudiating a detested secular world from which the faithful must maintain their separation. Indeed there is often anger, if not hatred, of the infidel Other.

The growth and passion of fundamentalism throughout the world has been a reaction to the major changes of the last few decades that have taken place in such a short time. Given the emergence of contemporary globalization, many people have experienced dislocation either through migration and population movements (rural to urban), or experienced class mobility, typically downward as small merchants and independent artisans face competition from globalized companies. This is especially important, in that most Muslim societies are predominantly lower middle class, in the form of small merchants, crafts producers, and farmers — collectively the class most aggressively squeezed by a global economy. Moreover, in many of the Muslim countries, there have been civil wars within (Algeria, Indonesia) and conflicts from without (Iraq-Iran, various wars with Israel). Attempts at amelioration though Western means such as socialism, nationalism, or even democratic elections have been undermined by Western (American or British) powers. Further, the secularism, with its privatized, hedonistic lifestyles and narcissistic preoccupations, and liberal social values challenges the traditional value orientations; that in turn fosters a radical embrace of a more radical, fundamentalist value orientation.

Fundamentalism then provides a stable sense of identity in a changing world, a cohesive community when social ties are fragile, and it grants a moral basis for dignity through piety when other sources of respect are waning. Fundamentalism, as a reaction to globalization, has adverse consequences, especially in Islamic societies that already have a number of grievances against Western governments. The irony is that these historical and ideological dispositions not only act against the culture of modernity, but also limit economic development that would in point of fact help people in their daily lives. Thus *fundamentalisms, as noted, reproduce conditions of adversity that engender their embrace.*

It might be noted that one of the major tropes of fundamentalism has been to embrace a theologically legitimated, biologically based, essentialist reading of gender. Men are seen as dominant, assertive, and protectors of their family, women as submissive and compliant — and often unable to constrain their sexual passions, thus needing men to protect their safety and honor. More specifically, as other aspects of social and economic life have witnessed major changes eroding traditional bases of male status and identity, with ambiguity of gender relations and authority, fundamentalism has been radically embraced as an attempt to sustain what has (been imagined to have) been lost. Assertions of female autonomy, from self-determination of dress to erotic choices have been strongly rebuked. Thus fundamentalism serves to provide a compensatory masculinity that is increasingly challenged by globalization from without and confronted from within by no longer docile and compliant women.

Given what has been said, in some few instances, Islamic fundamentalism has spawned terrorism, attacks on unarmed noncombatants by irregular military forces. More generally, insofar as globalized modernity has acted to thwart the fulfillment of human potential, one reaction has been to embrace death and indeed we have seen that the extreme response to globalization in general and perceived injustices has been martyrdom operations in various forms.

Pressures to Modernity

Despite the seeming growth of fundamentalist Islam, from the influence of al-Wahab in Saudi Arabia at an official level, to al-Qutb in Egypt and elsewhere, though popularly without governmental support, there are less visible, less dramatic forces at work that are clearly impacting Islam and dragging it into the 21st century. Indeed we have argued that fundamentalism is a reaction to various social forces within Muslim societies creating forces for modernity. This is not to ignore various inroads of Western ideas ranging from nationalism to socialism to parliamentary rule. Even various dictators, generals, presidents for life, etc., stage rigged elections in the Islamic world for the sake of the veneer of democratic legitimacy.

But all the same, historically, ever since contemporary (mostly 20th century) anticolonial struggles, modernization movements have taken a progressive, if not left-wing, stance and have been suppressed by Western nations with imperialist ambitions or in confrontations with the former USSR. With the emergence of a world market, there are external pressures to liberalize markets and democratize politics. Such conditions allow for the expansion of global markets, and the Islamic countries represent over a billion potential consumers. Thus, in *sotto voce*, unlike the fundamentalist rantings, there are pressures from both within and without pressing for modernization, not least of which is the desire for a better standard of living. The move toward modernization is thus not procapitalist or pro–Western as such, but rather derives from a desire for greater freedom and a higher standard of living, which modernization offers.

Globalization

The fundamental reality of the current age has been the emergence of a deterritorialized, globalized economic system, based on advanced technologies of information. This system has been decoupled from the nation-state system and instead has created a global market in which anything can be made anywhere and shipped anywhere — or at least almost anywhere. But if one observes a map of the world, there is a wide swath of primarily Muslim countries from Algeria to Pakistan that have seen very little foreign investment in productive industries. Rather there are marketing and distribution channels for goods made elsewhere. But Islam is not a monolith; a cursory glance shows much variation between countries like Morocco and Yemen, or between Turkey and Bangladesh. Moreover, this cursory glance also shows that those Muslim countries practicing more moderate forms of Islam, whose legal systems are consistent with international standards of trade and commerce, where there are some protections for human rights, generally fare much better economically, politically, and culturally. That said, Arab societies show the least freedom in the world and limited space for civil society organizations, NGOs (Non-Governmental Organizations), and INGOs (International NGOs). These conditions serve as a barrier to globalization.

Globalization, as a factor fostering modernization, works in a number of ways beginning with population movements seeking jobs, tourism, or even the Hajj. Historically, as people come into contact with others, they usually become more cosmopolitan, and surely most of the cosmopolitan centers of the world have been ports and trading cities like London, Paris, New York, or at one time, Cairo, Damascus, Baghdad, and Cordoba. When TNCs (Trans-National Corporations) employ nationals in local settings, they must often attend training programs and so on where they become exposed to greater social diversity. Further, whatever the differences, TNCs use rational methods to produce, distribute, and track goods and services. While a bit reductionistic, the social psychology of modernization suggests that people who worked in more modern settings themselves became more modern, that is, open, tolerant, future-oriented, and concerned with the larger world.

While not entirely true and oversimplified, Friedman (1999) suggested that countries with McDonald's don't go to war against each other. What he is suggesting is that countries that are integrated into the world markets do themselves great damage by war that disrupts such markets. Thus today, a war between France and Germany is unthinkable, and so too does the promise of integrated markets, dependent on modernizing economies, act as an incentive for modernization. Otherwise said, while on the one hand globalization has fostered radical changes that have deposed fundamentalism, it also encourages a variety of internal changes encouraging rational economic practices, openness, the rule of secular law, autonomous courts, and even channels for political redress.

Arab labor markets in particular, as they tend more toward strict interpretations of Islam, tend to be traditional, segmented, and dysfunctional. Markets tend to be too small to be viable. In other words, historically nationalist corporations, owned by traditional elites, could easily tolerate, if not encourage, dictatorships, authoritarian governments, and stagnant, compliant populations. But TNCs encourage modernization, not for altruistic or moral reasons, but modernizing countries make for good infrastructures, markets, and work forces. Thus TNCs create forces in which modernization should enable cooperation and coordination between Arab countries that would in turn enable regional markets and greater social opportunities.

Education

Perhaps the most important single factor that has fostered modernization has been the growth of education and, in turn, literacy. While a school curriculum generally serves the interest of the ruling classes, and often includes political indoctrination, so too does education foster greater awareness of diversity, toleration, open-mindedness, and the ability to learn for oneself beyond the official curriculum. This becomes even more salient at higher levels of education, especially in fields that require access to international information and innovation.

While most Muslim societies have done little to encourage economic growth, in almost every case the governments have encouraged public education and have both expanded school systems and often encouraged foreign study, especially in the natural sciences and medicine. But we might also note a caveat, as the recent UN commission observed, that while Islamic states have encouraged education, the content has often remained quite insular from the Western world. The Arab countries have the lowest rates of expenditure on science in the world, the lowest rates of ICT use, and the greatest insularity from international sources of data. The entire Arab world translates fewer books each year than does Greece alone.

In sum, there has been a rapid growth of education and literacy, but without other changes, namely liberalization of the economy and greater political freedom, the Arab states are likely to remain stagnant. Indeed one of the lures of fundamentalism is its compensation for such stagnation. Thus we can see how in recent years, without economic opportunities for the educated, their frustration and dissatisfaction greatly intensifies as their ability increases yet their real-life opportunities decrease, such that increasingly they are drawn to fundamentalism or terrorism. Muhammad Atta (the leader of the 9–11 World Trade Center attackers) was well-educated, in Germany no less, with a degree in architecture. Yet the Islamic world makes only minimal use of such innovative and advanced skills.

Globalization creates pressures and opportunities to utilize ever better educated populations. However weak and disempowered, there are growing classes of progressive intellectuals that in concert with other groups, such as more educated women, stand as spearheads to progressive social changes and modernity. As Eickelman (1999) has argued, the rapid growth of educated Muslim women, together with growing NGOs, suggests the emergence of a female public sphere that can and does increasingly challenge discrimination, human rights abuses, and the like. (see below).

Mass Media

In most of the Islamic societies, especially in the Middle East, information is tightly censored. The global mass media, from foreign books and magazines to pop culture, have had little impact in the Muslim world. Media, from print to sound to television, CDs and videotapes, tends to be very controlled — though the boundaries are increasingly porous in societies where smuggling has been a tradition. But not only is this beginning to change, but, with more information from the outside world, there are emerging pressures on governments.

In many cases, while local television is either produced or controlled by government, many people have satellite dishes where they can get a broad range of entertainment from BBC theater to porn to news. While often hidden, in places like Iran, they are as common as weeds. (And much to the consternation of the Islamic authorities, such dishes receive antigovernment propaganda from exile communities such as Los Angeles.)

One of the most significant changes in mass media has been al-Jazeera, the Arabic satellite news service for the Middle East. It was launched in 1996, supported by the emir of Qatar. It has adapted American techniques of journalism and has provided uncensored news — rare in most Middle Eastern countries. Unlike other channels of information, it has had interviews with American and Israeli officials and spokespersons. It has often featured "unflattering" stories of graft, corruption and malfeasance, not unlike *60 Minutes*, *20/20*, or *Dateline*, but critiques of political elites, typically quite corrupt, are typically quite rare.

The changing nature of media in a global age, from the availability of CNN to al-Jazeera, from smuggled CDs and magazines, is now an irreversible process that fosters moderation and, in turn, modernization. On the one hand, a great deal of foreign media, especially American films, stand as daily reminders of underdevelopment and stagnation; the spread of a "free" press, in lieu of partisan politics, fosters greater openness and, in turn, facilitates the spread of modernization. As Inkeles noted many years ago, one of the signs of modernization was reading the paper and showing greater concern with the outside world. Today, in Muslim societies, it might instead be watching al-Jazeera or logging on to the Internet.

The Role of Intellectuals

Muslim intellectuals, as members of an educationally elite class, have had exposure to Western thought and culture as well as Islamic values and principles. This opportunity provides intellectuals with the ability to critically reexamine the dialectic between Islam and modernity. However, now more than ever, Muslim intellectuals continue to find strong resistance toward modernity from Muslims around the world. Although a plethora of reasons exist as to why Muslims in Islamic countries perceive movements towards modernity as detrimental to their religious identity, Muslim intellectuals are carving out a special role for themselves by tackling structural obstacles in order for Islam and modernity to coexist successfully.

We witness Muslim intellectuals ushering in a new perspective on the current discourse of modernity, beginning with the rejection of a monolithic definition of modernity and an introduction of the notion of a plurality of Islamic modernities. Secondly, intellectuals are bridging the socially constructed rift between "Islam" and "democracy." Through their writings and lectures, intellectuals are illustrating that both Islam and democracy carry certain universal truths, such as all human beings are equal and that we should treat each other with respect (Martinovich 2003). Not only is the compatibility of Islam and democracy being propagated, but also the notion that democracy as a political system for Islamic societies may not ensure justice, but it is the best system for establishing a basis that pursues justice (Abou El Fadl 2003). Furthermore, the struggle to link the compatibility of the two is couched in the language of justice, which they believe plays a central role in Quranic discourse. It is with this legitimization — the incorporation of Quranic discourse — that the intellectuals are gaining more support among the masses.

Muslim intellectuals have discovered that further clarification and nuanced explanations of these key terms are necessary as a first step in responding to the way these profound concepts are misunderstood while being loosely tossed around. By laying this foundation, Islamic thinkers then adequately gauge the influence of the various historical, structural, and societal events over the Islamic world, which have fostered the prolific negative sentiment toward modernity. An in-depth analysis of these obstacles encourages the formulations of timely and effective responses on the part of Muslim intellectuals. Despite the residual negative sentiments, felt primarily on the part of conservative Muslim clerics, the shift in discourse brought about by intellectuals has created the space for potential for democratic governance and rational conduct in more parts of the Islamic world than ever before.

Feminism

With this potential for rational conduct and respect for democracy emerges a new sect of the Muslim population that is struggling for social and political reform. Standing on the shoulders of their progressive male counterparts are Muslim feminists, who are fighting for more democratic, modern political systems around the world. To counter some of the intolerance sparked by radical Islamists and narrow concepts of Sharia, some Muslim feminist scholars are working on reinterpretations related to human rights, religious freedom, and tolerance (Lampman 2003). Not only are they raising consciousnesses, but they are also spearheading progressive movements aimed against religious extremism around the world.

Discussions during this century regarding women and the family are constantly being shaped, reshaped, and changed by reference to internal as well as external factors. Internal factors include: (1) the consequences of economic, political, and cultural policies implemented by various nation-states; (2) legislation adopted by governments regarding personal status law that affects women's lives; (3) the availability of opportunities for women in education and employment; and (4) the dominant belief that national liberation should take precedence over liberation of women (Haddad 1998).

Notwithstanding political and economic stagnation, if not relative decline, as we noted, one of the most significant changes in the contemporary world has been the education of women in general and Muslim women in particular, which has served as a major factor in the amplified participation of women in the public sphere. The Arab countries spend a relatively large proportion of their GDP on education. On the one hand, the Arab region has shown the greatest increases in female education in the world, yet women have shown little empowerment through either work or political representation — and no society can prosper when it denies the creativity and participation of half its members.

But education does not simply fill an empty canister, it changes the recipient and encourages agency. In much the same way as the American civil rights movement depended on a more educated mass of African Americans, so too has greater levels of education had at least two consequences. Firstly, there has emerged a female public sphere where women find encapsulated realms where they can share personal experiences, debate various texts, organize action, etc. (Cf. Eickelman 1998). Much of this had become possible through the rapid growth of NGOs linked together by the Internet, which has had an enormous impact on the free access of information typically suppressed by most political authorities.

The increase in visible political participation and democracy advocacy on the part of Muslim feminists is a relatively recent phenomenon though. Although women have been the support for such movements throughout, they have not been as vocal and visually defiant as they are now. There are certain structural conditions that have contributed to the rise of Muslim feminists on the frontlines of the political arena.

During the 1970s, the cities of Iran were the center of the most drastic changes and visible social-political upheaval, while peasants and the rural population remained largely separate from the movement (Moghadam 1994). This may signify the importance of socio-psychological factors during rapid modernization: newly urbanized women and men experienced "relative deprivation" due to their exposure to new possibilities, in which they expected a share but which the system could not provide. "Literacy and education increased people's aspirations, but political repression, fierce economic competition, the conflict-ridden and stressful lifestyle of big cities resulted in incoherence, frustration, and anomie" (Moghadam 1994: 114).

During the 1960s and the 1970s, it was precisely the traditional strata of women (and men), particularly the better educated, younger generation, who constituted the principal economic and ideological constituency of Islamic fundamentalism in Iran. As the first generation from the traditional families, these younger women were being exposed to a high level of public education, a dramatically different set of ideas and values, and an occasional chance of a teaching career. Subsequently, with regard to women's roles, they were soon caught up in the midst of a double bind, two conflicting and competing role models — the traditional and the Western, which was defined as having low pay, fierce competition, too much stress, scarcity of child care, and the double day (Moghadam 1994). The younger educated female members found neither of those roles attractive. Instead they chose a political

6. Islamic Fundamentalism, Modernity, and the Role of Women   151

character that was nondomesticated, nonpassive, socially engaged, and politically militant.

Moghadam argues that women students, then and now, found alternate ways of resisting oppressive regimes. Some within this new movement adopted an alternative style of clothing called the *hijab-e Islami*, which consisted of a scarf covering the hair, a tunic over a long-sleeved shirt, loose pants, and flat shoes. It did not entail cosmetics and jewelry, thereby releasing women from excessive concerns over looks, fashions, and consumerism. Moreover, they believed it could enhance uniformity and reduce competition over class disparities and physical appearance among female students, and provide an asexual and serious image appropriate for political activism. These strata of women, who have now (unlike under the shah) gained status and a legitimate, respected identity, feel empowered and self-confident. Paradoxically, these women seem to have appropriated some of the political purposes of the veil to their own advantage. That is, the revival of piety and the Islamic dress code are being utilized by these women as a means of gaining access to the public sphere (Moghadam 1994).

In addition to the industrialization of certain Islamic societies, globalization and higher international standards as well as social accountability for women's roles in society are also playing a significant role in the rise of support for modernity, especially from efforts led by women. This, coupled with the diminishing role of clerics in most cosmopolitan cities, has also served as a supportive force. Finally, the increase in Muslim women attaining both secular and religious education has served as the gap bridging the changing tide of modernity and local customs and norms.

Eickelman and Andersen cite "new" media, that is, the Internet, law journals to which non-jurists regularly contribute, teenage romance novels, the popular cinema, and women's use of the telephone and the Internet as the new basis for political networking, which allows women's political participation to take on a more participatory character. The ability of state and religious authorities to control or filter what is printed or broadcast has been on the wane for decades. Thus, a leading Arab secularist, Syria's Jalla al-'Azm, can debate Shaykh Yusuf al-Qaradawi, a leading preacher and conservative religious scholar, on a Qatar-based pan–Arab satellite channel (al-Jazeera TV) (Eickelman and Andersen: 1999). Their novelty also comes from creation of new audiences through the exponential rise of mass education since the mid–20th century in Muslim-majority countries and the much greater ease of communication and travel, for religious, political, and educational goals, as well as labor migration and emigration (Eickelman and Andersen: 1999). These new media suggest emerging forms of public space beyond the conventional broadcast media and face-to-face communication among people who trust one another.

As modernity collides with religious traditions in Morocco, women have begun to demand reinterpretation of civil codes that presume a woman, in her private life, is a capricious creature in the need of a man's guiding hand. These emerging views emanate from female scholars who are confident in their religious judgments, and who use the Internet to promote an alternate vision of the rights of Muslim women. The views also are a result of ordinary women who fear legal strictures will prevent their country from integrating into the modern world. Recently, over 400,000 people took to the streets to support the plan for equal rights for women in support of a government plan to end inequalities in the kingdom.

In Pakistan, gender roles and expectations have been undergoing substantive change in the last decade with the introduction of new kinds of technology that free up women's time (such as running water from taps, gas connections for cooking, covered drains for more hygienic conditions, and accessible low-cost transportation), the availability of wage labor for women, women's increased exposure to higher education, and their growing attentiveness to mass media (Weiss 1998).

Gender relations have undergone their greatest shifts in the last quarter century. Two factors account for these changes more than any others: what has been official state policy toward women, and the subsequent rise in the intensity and power of the women's movement in the country (Weiss 1998).

As a result, in Pakistan, 35 out of 139 members of the National Assembly of Pakistan in Karachi that are women (Cowasjee 2003). Women in Pakistan are working to instill notions in the mainstream discourse that women are not divorced from humanity, that they must become better educated, and that the elevation in status of women in Pakistan is crucial in the steps toward democracy.

Fighting illiteracy, along with raising women's socioeconomic levels, preparing them to exercise their full rights as citizens, and developing bonds of friendship and understanding between Arab women and women around the world to improve their situation at home and to strengthen peace have become the forefront of women's initiatives in Jordan. These qualitative changes in the objectives of the Arab Women's Federation illustrate the changing shapes of feminism as a stepping stool toward modernity.

It could also be argued the major reason for change is rather the cumulative effect of work on women's issues at the national level, as well as the increased participation in international forums during the United Nations Decade of Women (Hijab 1998). There has been a qualitative change in the way women activists work at the national level. Many have moved beyond the elites in the capital city to undertake outreach activities at the grassroots level, where they are in contact with the reality of women's lives. And many Arab women participate in international conferences, where they learn from and contribute to the international debate, and they have therefore gained confidence and expertise in articulating the issues they face in international terms.

This evolution can perhaps best be illustrated through the experience of the Palestinian women's movement. It began as a nationalist response against colonialism. Palestinian women became involved in organizing and establishing many charitable activities, initially as a response to the need for education, health, and shelter. By the late 1970s, a change in approach was discernable. Several young Palestinian women established grassroots committees that sought to combine a nationalist, socialist, and feminist agenda. These committees heralded a new, politicized generation of women and new organizational techniques (Hijab 1998).

In the 1990s, there was a move to set up independent women's research centers in Iran. Five centers have been established that articulate a frankly feminist agenda and that are intent on keeping a distance from the political fragmentation that affected the women's committees. Such centers are tackling undiscussed issues related to women's social, legal, and economic status. Their agenda includes such topics as violence in the family, inequity in inheritance, school drop-out rates for girls, and women's economic activities in the economic sector.

It is important to note that last year there was a women's summit in Jordan that attracted women from all over the Muslim world. The hundreds of delegates from 18 Arab states called on Arab regimes to follow Morocco, which guaranteed 10 percent of its 325 parliamentary seats to women. In recent Moroccan elections, the number of elected female parliamentarians soared from two to an Arab-world record 35 — a level of representation akin to France.

As we have said, one of the central lures of fundamentalism has been providing compensatory masculinity to men rendered powerless by economic changes, especially when male roles and masculine power is challenged by ever more educated women, more aware of their marginality, but increasingly more likely to move from toleration to active confrontation. *The progress of modernization is at the same time a process whereby the female half of the population attains equality, justice, and freedom.* From what was said above, for intellectuals, male or female, to become relevant, progressive forces, they must build popular coalitions in order to challenge entrenched authority or fundamentalist voices. And the most natural allies of progressive intellectuals are newly empowered women, not simply as supporters, but as co-equal partners.

Toward Islamocracy: A New Synthesis

Muslim intellectuals and feminists alike are articulating a vision of a plurality of modernities that are compatible with the ideologies, lifestyles, and expectations of Muslims in the Islamic world. Because there is such a wide array of such perspectives, these movement leaders have selected a few key elements in fostering an Islamic democracy, or *Islamocracy* (Mazrui 2003).

For instance, in Iran, feminists have made rhetorical use of any available position to invent a female-friendly discourse on modernity. When pointing to the advancements of women in other countries, they are choosing not to be "blind imitators" and "inauthentic apers of the West" (Najmabadi 1998); rather they are employing the widespread acceptability of "new sciences" as the alchemy of civilizational progress. They argue for education of women, using modernist and Islamic justifications to inscribe and constitute their new selves as literate citizens.

As part of an ongoing effort to promote democracy in the region, they provided an opening in three Arab countries for both Islamic and secular democrats to come together for the first time to debate the compatibility of Islam and democracy. In Morocco, Egypt, and Yemen, government leaders, opposition members, and civic activists joined in frank private and public workshops on such hot topics as human rights, women's rights, and religious tolerance (Lampman 2003). A cross section of Muslim thinkers, religious leaders and mainstream Islamic movements from Egypt to Indonesia, Europe to America, engage in this kind of reformist interpretation of Islam and its relationship to democracy, pluralism, and human rights.

This Islamocracy, as articulated by feminists around the world, implies moral agency and ownership of women's own thought processes; awareness of community; and the ability to criticize any level of control, from the family to government — a process that is fundamentally democratic and necessary to revamping societies. An Islamocracy entails the people having a say in how their lives are run. Muslims in the Islamic world are responsive to the idea that democracy is the only system that gives that option. And it is feminists, and younger ones particularly, who articulate very well the compatibility of Islam and democracy, based on the Quran and Islamic experience (Lampman 2003).

Reinterpretations of Scripture: Critical Doubt versus Received Wisdom

A second key element of an Islamocracy entails free, open, and encouraged reinterpretation of Islamic law, scripture, and social governance. *Ijtihad*, or the concept of legal reasoning in Islam, had been closed off to Muslims around the world for centuries, with the exception of a few clerics (Esposito 2003). However, the push to open the doors to reinterpretations has made headway, mostly due to the "resurgence of intellectual vigor, moral courage, and political will on the part of feminists and intellectuals" (Lampman 2003).

Sisters in Islam, a feminist group in Indonesia, is under fire from clerics who charge them with insulting Islam, as they fight proposals for draconian state laws discriminating against women (Lampman 2003). The group has spurred debated through the media, challenging clerics over their failure to see Islamic law in a historical context.

Pakistani feminists are beginning to reinterpret quranic verses as the ideological basis for fighting for democracy. Believing that Muslims are currently in a state of paralysis and dormancy, they are driving women to be more vocal about asserting their views of propagating universal human rights and democratic societies. The loss of intellectual critique of Islam, for the most part, had historically served as the cause for Muslims' reluctance to start a debate on challenging patriarchal, irrelevant norms. However, tides have changed and feminists are encouraging Muslims around the world to rethink cultural mores.

Out of these early years of Islamic women's activism also emerged the drive toward rethinking gender in Islam in more radical ways. A number of women's institutes, as well as a variety of women's journals now published in Iran, attest to the significance of rethinking.

Zanan, one such feminist journal in Iran, has been established as a powerful and articulate new voice, challenging the earlier presuppositions and changing the terms of the debate. Furthermore, it provokes other women to engage in direct interpretations in their own right by asserting "it is time for *ijtihad*." It is this assertive move to take charge of the canon and thoroughly reinterpret it from a woman's perspective that has brought the fire of the more traditional Islamic advocates upon them (Najmabadi 1998).

The emergence of *Zanan* as a vocal women's position is a radical break from Iran's past feminist movements. The writers have opened up the domain of interpretation to nonbelievers and non–Muslims, insisted on equality of women and men in all domains, and disconnected natural and created differences between women and men from cultural and social constructions of womanhood and manhood. In doing so, Najmabadi argues that *Zanan* has opened up a new space for dialogue between Islamic women activists and reformers and secular feminism that is beginning to review a 60-year-old rift that constructed the two categories as mutually exclusive.

Islam on the Internet highlights not just new interpreters but also the presence of intermediate contexts that reflect a more nuanced diversity of views, settings, projects, and expressions of Islam today. These interpreters are part of a real diversity of opinion, interests, and variously formed programs, and part of a more general and diagnostic context shared with activists of sharper profile. The recency of the introduction of its interpreters to a more public realm brings out the priority of responsibility and how taking responsibility, particularly for interpretation, in public (instead of forming associations) is the intermediating step for "civil" society.

Women in Public Spheres

The third key element to an Islamocracy is the widespread acceptance of women's presence in every aspect of the public sphere. Women's own collective action and conscious participation are critical in the materializing of political achievements for women in any modern economic and political system. The centrality of gender and support for women to work, live, and produce outside the confines of the house has greatly impacted the way Muslim women view their roles in society (Najmabadi 1998). In particular, women are positioning themselves to take responsibility for the misogyny of their leaders. Some may deny or justify it, and others are challenging and opposing it, but it is definitely not being ignored.

In Iran, women are still not the legal equals of men. Nevertheless, the past decade has witnessed an incredible flourishing of women's intellectual and cultural productions in Iran (Najmabadi 1998). Not only have women not disappeared from public life, but they have an unmistakably active presence in practically every field of artistic creation, professional achievement, educational and industrial institutions, and even in sports activities. Others have turned the restrictions and limitations imposed by the government and by the dominant ideas about gender roles and ethics into wedges to open up new arenas for their creative energies. The most glaring example has been women turning to the production and directing of film, given the restrictions at the level of acting. In such fields as photography, painting, sculpture, literary production, and publishing, women have established themselves on an unprecedented scale. This creative outpouring cannot be accounted for as only oppositional reactive energy. The rise of the Islamic movement in the 1970s in Iran signified the emergence of a new political sociability and the dominance of a new political discourse within which woman stood for culture, occupying a central position (Najmabadi 1998).

A major step forward in the growth of presence of women in the public sphere was taken at an Arab regional meeting held in Jordan in 1994 to prepare for the United Nations' Fourth World Conference on Women. A key decision among Arab delegates of the region was to draw on the global 10-point agenda of the conference as the basis for their new draft plan of action. Secondly, from the conference, NGOs learned how to "lobby" governments to get their views reflected. In the fourth paragraph of the draft, it states: "The Arab plan of action draws on the features of Arab civilization, the values of revealed religions and human civilizations which respect woman's rights as a human being and her participation in development and its benefits as a condition for comprehensive and sustainable development" (Hijab 1998).

The effect of these two decision was a major shift in framework — from the ethos of the Arab-Islamic heritage to that of the international arena, and from the prescriptions of an Islamic perspective to that of a secular one (Hijab 1998). The final text called for women's right to participate in decision-making structures and authority; lifting the burden of poverty on women; increasing access to education, health, employment, and self-reliance; protecting women's rights in situations of armed conflict; recognizing and supporting women's roles in the environment; condemning violence against women; and calling for better reflection of women's roles in the media.

Conclusions

As the UN report on Human Development noted, the Arab countries of the world face a critical junction–they can continue economic stagnation, showing among the lowest labor productivity and in turn growth rates in the world while enduring authoritarian governments that tolerate no dissent But so too can Arab societies embrace radical reforms and move to modernization and democratization and prosper in many of the same ways as have other formerly poor nations. While the report was concerned with the 280 million Arabs, much the same can be said about other Muslim countries suffering poverty, stagnation, rapid population growth, etc. On the one hand, many of the problems faced by the Muslim countries are typical in most underdeveloped countries ranging from indigenous cultural barriers, economic dependency and exploitation, etc. But that said, *we have argued that Islam itself, or at least the ways it has been interpreted and practiced, has been a barrier to the kinds of economic, political, and cultural transformations that would indeed ameliorate the conditions that are creating the fertile grounds for extreme Islamisms and in the extreme cases, terrorism* in which martyrdom has become seen as an acceptable weapon of jihad. (Most Muslim clerics deplore suicide in any form.)

While we have noted a number of factors unique to Islam that have contributed to economic, political, and cultural stagnation, at the same time, dialectically understood, there are others within Islamic traditions, intersecting with the realities of the present age, fostering progressive reinterpretations of tradition that can and probably will foster an new and unique form of Islamic modernities. As was argued, this is indeed what is happening, various intellectuals, often trained in the West, stand at the forefront of these debates. Moreover, among these progressive voices we must also hear the louder and louder voices of newly educated and newly empowered Muslim women whose unique articulations of feminism are essential ingredient of the emerging project of Islamic modernity.

References

Abou El Fadl, Khaled. "Islam and the Challenge of Democracy." *Boston Review* (April/May 2003).
Cowasjee, Ardeshir. "Blackened Man, Blackened Woman ('Karo-Kari')." *Dawn*, March 9, 2003.
Eickelman, Dale F., and Jon Andersen. *New Media in the Muslim World: The Emerging Public Sphere*. Bloomington, IN: Indiana University Press, 1999.
Esposito, John L. "Practice and Theory." *Boston Review* (April/May 2003). http://bostonreview.net/BR28.2/esposito.html
Friedman, Tom. *The Lexus and the Olive Tree*. New York: Farrar, Straus & Giroux, 1999.
Fromm, Erich. *Escape from Freedom*. New York: Farrar & Rinehart, 1941.
_____. *Man For Himself: An Inquiry Into the Psychology of Ethics*. New York: Holt, Rinehart & Winston, 1961.
Haddad, Yvonne Y. "Islam and Gender: Dilemmas in the Changing Arab World." pp. 3–29 *Islam, Gender and Social Change*. Edited by Yvonne H. Haddad, and John L. Esposito. New York; Oxford: Oxford University Press, 1998.
Hijab, Nadia. "Islam, Social Change, and the Reality of Arab Women's Lives." pp. 45–56 *Islam, Gender and Social Change*. Edited by Yvonne H. Haddad, and John L. Esposito. New York; Oxford: Oxford University Press, 1998.
Huff, Toby, and Wolfgang Schluchter, eds. *Max Weber & Islam*. New Brunswick, NJ: Transaction, 1999.
Kuran, Timur. 2002. "The Islamic Commercial Crisis: Institutional Roots of Economic Underdevelopment in the Middle East." *Journal of Economic History* 63, no. 6 (2002).
Lampman, Jane. "Easing Into Islamic Democracy: Convinced By Their Experience in the U.S., American Muslims are Helping Form Democratic Coalitions in the Muslim World." *The Christian Science Monitor* (May 2003).
Lewis, Bernard. *What Went Wrong?: Western Impact and Middle Eastern Response*. Oxford: Oxford University Press, 2002.
Martinovich, Steven. "Islam and Democracy — Not an Impossible Marriage." *Christian Science Monitor* (May 8, 2003).
Mazrui, Ali A. "Islamocracy: In Search of a Muslim Path to Democracy." Presented at Center for Islam and Democracy Conference in 2003. Retrieved 15 June 2003. http://www.islam-democracy.org/4th_Annual_Conference-Mazrui_address.asp
Moghadam, Valentine. *Gender and National Identity: Women and Politics in Muslim Societies*. London; Atlantic Highlands, NJ: Zed Books, 1994.
_____. Edited by Nabil Khoury and Valentine M. Moghadam. London; Atlantic Highlands, NJ: Published for the United Nations University, World Institute for

Development Economics Research by Zed Books and United Nations University Press, Tokyo, 1995.

Najmabadi, Afsaneh. "Feminism in the Islamic Republic: Years of Hardship, Years of Growth." pp. 59–84 in *Islam, Gender and Social Change*. Edited by Yvonne H. Haddad, and John L. Esposito. New York: Oxford University Press, 1998.

Turner, Bryan S. *Capitalism and Class in the Middle East: The Theories of Social Change and Economic Development*. London: Heinemann Educational; New Jersey: Humanities Press, 1984.

Weber, Max. *Economy and Society*. Berkeley: University of California Press, 1978.

Weiss, Anita M. "The Slow Yet Steady Path to Women's Empowerment in Pakistan." Pp. 124–143 in *Islam, Gender and Social Change*. Edited by Yvonne H. Haddad, and John L. Esposito. New York; Oxford: Oxford University Press, 1998.

7

Legion of Small Knights

Informal Movements Within the Polish Roman Catholic Church

AGNIESZKA KOSCIANSKA

Introduction

The Polish Roman Catholic Church, both the hierarchy and the faithful, is not a homogenous institution or community. There are, for instance, movements connected with right-wing politicians, fundamentalist "Catholic bigots" movements, and very progressive movements, involving the so-called Catholic intelligentsia. Among the various factions, one central issue that divides the church is the phenomenon of private visions. In Poland (like in other Roman Catholic countries), many lay people have visions and claim that they are a medium, that God (personalized usually as the Virgin Mary or Jesus) uses them to communicate something important to the church, e.g., the apocalypse is coming, priests are not faithful, or people should pray more, etc.

The church does not recognize these private revelations officially, unless they fulfill certain criteria verified through an official inquiry. According to the Roman Catholic Church Canon Law, the vision first must be finished. Then the church convenes a special commission to investigate. The commission analyzes the essence and results of the vision, based on canonical law. If the vision proves consistent with Catholic faith, and the results positively influence the church membership or institution, for example the faithful more often attend mass, the church hierarchy may recognize the vision as legitimate. The most famous example is Fatima's Virgin Mary apparition.

In Poland, we have plenty of visionaries. Most of them are not recognized by the Roman Catholic Church, nor does the church conduct an inquiry, but a lot of people accept them as legitimate. They organize prayer groups, for example, or visitations to and audiences with a visionary. In general, these informal communities exist on the fringe of the Polish Catholic Church. Visionaries, who are leaders of these organizations, want to belong to the church, but the church hierarchy does not accept them as religious leaders, although the church simultaneously seeks to retain the visionary's followers within the church. The resulting situation is very complicated and full of conflict, since to openly discredit and condemn local visionaries would alienate their supporters from the established church, yet to openly acknowledge local visionaries lends at least tacit legitimacy, and in turn some degree of authority.

The issue has been divisive. Priests sometimes turn against their superiors to support visionaries. Some groups decided to leave the Roman Catholic Church and registered as new churches. The most famous Polish visionary built his own church without secular state or church permission. But some visionaries try to negotiate and discuss their visions with the established clergy. They have their own spiritual directors who help them find out if God or the devil is the one who initiates the visions. One of these movements, which was founded as a result of a private vision, is the Legion of Small Knights.

The Divine Mercy

One of the mystics who received visions was St. Faustina Kowalska. She was born in Glogowice in 1905 to a very poor family. As a child she was very religious, and in her 20s she entered the Congregation of the Sisters of Our Lady of Mercy. She devoted herself often to deep prayer, which often took the form of trances, communication with divine entities, and extended periods of isolation from the material world. She was considered to be crazy, and also lazy (in the convent nuns must work for the congregation). She wrote a diary in which she described all her visions and conversations with Jesus. Her diary was later published as *The Divine Mercy: Essential Features of the Devotion to the Divine Mercy*.

The main vision that would later constitute the basis of her own following occurred on February 22, 1931, in her cell in Plock convent:

> In the evening, when I was in my cell, I saw the Lord Jesus clothed in a white garment. One hand was raised in the gesture of blessing, the other was touching the garment at the breast. From beneath the garment, slightly drawn aside at the breast, two large rays of light emanated, one red, the other pale. In silence I kept my gaze fixed on the Lord; my soul was struck with awe but also with great joy. After a while Jesus said to

me: "Paint the image according to the pattern you see, with the signature: Jesus I trust You.... I want this image to be solemnly blessed on the first Sunday after Easter; that Sunday is to be the Feast of Mercy" [English translation in Siepak 1993: 27].

Her mission given by Christ was to reinvigorate a religious life. Her visions started a new form of devotion — devotion to The Divine Mercy, which is very popular now in Poland. But originally the church did not recognize her vision. In Vilnius (now in Lithuania) she met her later spiritual director, Michael Soporko. After her death in 1938, he became the main propagator of The Divine Mercy devotion. The image of the Merciful Lord became one of the most popular holy icons in contemporary Catholic Poland, and also becoming popular in other Catholic counties. Finally she was beatified in 1993.

Now Faustina is compared with other famous Catholic women-saints like Hildegarda von Bingen, Teresa of Avilia, and Catharina of Siena. She is also considered to contribute significantly to the leaders of the Roman Catholic Church in Poland to find the proper way to God (Obirek 2000, p. 32) and thus created a uniquely Polish version of Catholicism. Faustina is described as a saint who helps to find the grandeur of God in small, trivial, colorless things, in opposition to the ostentatious displays of wealth, power, and other manifestations of purely secular grandeur.

Most importantly for our study, Faustina was the predecessor of more recent charismatics, including Sister Zofia. Like her predecessor, Zofia leads a popular movement that is at once distinctly Catholic, distinctly Polish, and distinctly her own creation. At first glance, Zofia does not look the part of charismatic leader; she appears utterly conventional by Polish standards and, if anything, remarkably unremarkable. Of course, perception of charisma depends on the followers, not on the person or object itself. In the sections below, we explore her special status among her followers, and her significance in Polish Catholicism and culture.

Research Method

The data on the Legion of Small Knights were obtained through in-depth interviews conducted by students of the Institute of Ethnology and Cultural Anthropology, Warsaw University, between April 2001 and October 2002. I trained the interviewers in my workshop, "Women's Religious Leadership" in Warsaw and Tolkmicko. Altogether, we interviewed the leader — Sister Zofia — her followers, and inhabitants of Tolkmicko — Sister Zofia's town. In the interviews, I focused on their biographies, their activity in the legion, and also the history and organizational structure of the legion. In the interviews with inhabitants of Tolkmicko I asked them about their opinion of Sister Zofia. I also collected stories from and about Sister Zofia's life.

To reconstruct Sister Zofia's spiritual life story, I analyzed her mystic diary. I also met with her three times to interview her. She told me her spiritual life story. She said that her ordinary life was uninteresting. Her connection with the spiritual world, however, posed serious difficulty in fieldwork. During our meetings, she sometimes claimed to have contact with the Holy Spirit — that I in fact had the privilege to witness her communication with God. Consequently, she became as much a preacher as an informant.

Conducting fieldwork among a religious community requires participant observation. I participated in legion members' organizational and prayer meetings. Although I presented myself openly as a researcher, they also perceived me as a potential member of the legion. All of the members I talked to were trying to present what in their view constituted flawless moral and religious attitudes. Given their openness and willingness to converse with me, the situation gave me the opportunity to collect a lot of data. Given their open trust and forthrightness, I could not intentionally deceive them; I conducted the fieldwork among them always stressing that I was only an anthropologist interested in religiosity.

The Legion of Small Knights

The Legion of Small Knights of The Divine Mercy is a religious movement within the Roman Catholic Church that adheres to the aforementioned Divine Mercy devotion. They believe that even though the devotion to The Divine Mercy became very popular, Jesus still gives new signs of guidance. The faithful organize new prayer communities and new people may have powerful visions of the Merciful Lord. One of them is Sister Zofia, founder of the legion — just like St. Faustina a poor, un-educated, ordinary woman. Followers of The Divine Mercy believe that God chooses similar people to share new visions:

> Time of great happiness comes. Savior chooses man to found a praying community. This is not a specialist, not a theologian, nor an intellectual. This person is just like Helena Kowalska [Sister Faustina] non-educated, without experience, very weak [Krajewski 1994: 8].

The rules that regulate the activities of the legion were dictated by Jesus. In general, to be fully devoted to The Divine Mercy, one must be humble and truthful. Knights should attend to the "universal good," to love his enemies and be devoted to God and all people. Moreover, members should organize prayer communities in their parishes. Generally, people entering the Legion are already very religious, and the legion gives them the possibility to pray together. Prayer centers on three main intentions: to deliver guidance to the clergy and the Roman Catholic Church; to free souls suffering in purgatory; and to convert sinners and the nonfaithful. Moreover, members must commit to the following prayer and declaration:

> My Lord, I promise to serve You as a Small Knight of Your Mercy. I renounce my free will to let You reign in my heart. I want to obey Your Holy Will with all of my love and devotion. My Lord, please, bless me! [Zgloszenie: 4]

The legion also promotes a nationalistic ideology. In Zofia's diary one can read that the Polish nation is *the* chosen nation. The following hymn exemplifies the nationalistic attitude of members of the legion:

> Commander of the Polish nation, the brave Queen!
> You call us, Small Knights of The Divine Mercy, to fight at Your side.
> You give us Holy Rosary instead of armor and call for help for sinful world.
> Our dear Queen, You lead us. We are Your Small Knights [Zgloszenie: 3].

In Polish, all nouns are gender specific. Traditionally, there has been no female equivalent of the male "commander." In this hymn, the word "hetmanka" is used. "Hetmanka" is a neologism. It is a female form of the word "hetman" which is a historical term that refers specifically to a commanding officer in the Polish army in the 16th and 17th centuries. In this period the Polish army won a lot of victories, and is part of the glorious, nationalistic past of Poland. In this hymn, "hetmanka" equates also to the Virgin Mary in traditional religious usage. Thus, the legion hymn connects a traditional feminine ideal—the Virgin Mary—with a traditional masculine ideal—the commanding officer—to create a new term that applies only to Sister Zofia. She is thus at once the embodiment of tradition and revolution, or perhaps we could argue that she is a revolutionary who seeks to restore an idealized past as much as lead toward a new future.

Furthermore, nationalist ideology is deeply linked with the cult of the Virgin Mary as queen of Poland:

> In Polish history, the dominant discourses of gender are complex, and are inextricably linked to those of Catholicism and nationalism, with the fatherland, the patriarchal father figure and the male nationalist hero standing side by side with Mother Poland, nurturing mother/Madonna who saves and perpetuates the nation, and the mother who mourns, suffers, and endures [Pine 2000: 89].

Sister Zofia often invokes this image. In her diary one can find a description of the Madonna, who takes care of the Polish nation:

> Virgin Mary says: My Dear Children, I bring you to tell you about great danger to Polish nation. I am very sad, because I love Polish nation so much. I am the Queen of Polish nation, but they hurt my heart. Only you, my dear children [members of the legion] make me happy.... You will be responsible for the organization, which will save the world [Grochowska 1999: 113].

Although nationalistic at its core, at the same time the legion aspires to international influence. It works in 17 countries. Originally Zofia's followers abroad were Polish immigrants, but now her activity is also addressed to non–Poles.

Members of this emerging international community claim to be a part of the Roman Catholic Church, but there are differences between the doctrine of the Catholic Church and the legion. As mentioned, the church hierarchy does not want to recognize the legion, although outright rejection also carries risks. Sister Zofia tries to negotiate with priests to find an official place for the legion within the Roman Catholic Church. The legion is already established as a separate religious community, although members see themselves as faithful members within the Catholic Church also. Therefore the legion can best be understood as a spiritual community, like new religious movements. Eileen Barker asks: "Do we include movement within mainstream traditions (Opus Dei, Fokolare)?... There is, of course, no 'right' answer" (Barker 1999:16). She points out that new religious movements are

> ... new in so far it has become visible in its present from since the Second World War, and that it is religious is so far as offers not merely narrow theological statement about the existence and nature of supernatural beings, but that it proposes answer to at least some of the other kinds of ultimate questions that have traditionally been address by mainstream religions, questions such as: Is there a God? Why am I? How might I find direction, meaning and purpose in life? [Barker 1999:16]

In this sense, the Legion of Small Knights may be described as a new religious movement. Why do people seek membership in such a community? In my view, one salient reason presides: the need for community.

Community within the Legion

Members maintain very strong interpersonal relations with other legion members. As one respondent commented:

> Community links with people. During our meeting we pray a lot. And we learn a lot about praying. We desire to meet, but not only to pray, but also to meet each other, to talk, to discuss. We are very close to each other, we miss each other [woman, 67 years old, Warsaw].

This kind of relation can be described in terms of Victor Turner's communitas and liminality.

> In liminality, communitas tends to characterize relationships between those jointly undergoing ritual transition. The bonds of communitas are anti-structural in the sense that they are undifferentiated, egalitarian, direct, extant, non-rational, existential, I-Thou relationships. Communitas differs from the camaraderie found often in everyday life, which, though informal and egalitarian, still falls within the general domain of structure, which may include interaction rituals [Turner 1974:274].

Based on my interview data, members of the legion represent this style of religiousness, which Turner describes as "a try to create a communitas and a style of life that is permanently contained within liminality" (Turner 1974:261). In the legion, the style of life is very much monastic.

> Of course this conversion of liminality, in modified form, into a way of life, has also been true of monastic and mendicant orders in, for example, Christianity and Buddhism, but the religious state has been there clearly defined as an exceptional condition reserved for those who aspire after perfection.... The religious life is not for everyone, but only for those "elected by grace" [Turner 1974:261].

Next, the manifestation of communitas is "the Bank of The Divine Mercy." Each member of community can ask others for help in case of spiritual and material needs. If one, for example, has a spiritual crisis, one can ask for prayer. One can also ask for financial help. Also, the status of a leader in the legion is consistent with idea of communitas, yet the leader must also adhere to the basic principles of the community. According to Turner, one of the main characteristics of communitas is humility, and we find this as both a stated and understood aspect of life in the legion. Although Sister Zofia is a leader of the legion, she emphasizes that she is humble and unimportant. Liminality does not accord hierarchy. The leader of a community is also a paradigm of humility, especially in religious terms, because authority derives only from God, such that the leader is still a servant of a higher power.

"Divine Education": A Spiritual Leader's Spiritual Life Story

Sister Zofia was born in 1931. In 1950 she got married. She has three daughters. She lives in Tolkmicko, a small town on Wislany Bay in northern Poland. Her husband, like most of the men in town, used to work as fisherman. Now he is retired. Zofia has spent most of her life as a housewife. Her educational background is very modest. She finished only three classes of primary school. Her parents were illiterate.

Zofia says that she has instead "divine education." She remembers from her childhood that her parents argued all the time. She also remembers that they were very nervous. At the age of six she prayed to be different from her parents in the future.

> When I was six I prayed to be different than my mother. She was very quarrelsome. When I was fifty-six I heard the internal voice: "now you have this God's grace for which you asked when you were six." That was my turning point [Tolkmicko 2001].

Her "divine education" consists of three parts. First she was talking to the Virgin Mary, who healed her during her pilgrimage to Czestochowa, the main Polish pilgrimage center with a holy icon of Virgin Mary. Next she was a disciple of Jesus. Then she began her relationship with the Holy Spirit. This is a very important shift, because it changes the character of her organization. It starts to resemble a Charismatic Catholic movement or, even more so, the Pentecostals. Yet the similarity is only partial. The legion is more sincretic, and links at least three elements: The Divine Mercy devotion; Holy Spirit devotion; and New Age. Analyzing her vision, one mostly finds The Divine Mercy devotion, but in her healing practice she refers to the Holy Spirit and to the very New Age term "energy."

Zofia's devotion to The Divine Mercy manifests in her diary. By her followers, Zofia is seen as a successor of Sister Faustina. Also her diary is similar to Faustina's diary. Although neither received a formal education, both Zofia as well as Faustina say that Jesus wants them to write. In Zofia's diary Jesus talks about Sister Faustina. A few days after Faustina's beatification, Jesus said to Zofia:

> I took a liking to sister Faustina to tell the world about The Divine Mercy. She was my tool. She was quiet and humble. She suffered a lot to save the world. You should say like her "I am all yours to save the world" [Grochowska 1999: 110].

In the mystic diary Zofia describes her visions and talks with Jesus and the Virgin Mary. The diary, written from 1988 to 1999, was published

(Grochowska 1994, 1999), and these books are the most complete source of knowledge about her visions. She also uses her book (1999) to ask God about his opinion on various issues, major and minor. For example, when I met her for the first time and I asked for permission to conduct fieldwork among her followers she told me to open the book at random. Having done so, I read the fragment. Finally she said: "Yes, Jesus agrees, and I agree. You can talk to all members of the legion; you have my blessing."

In Sister Zofia's diary one can learn a lot about The Divine Mercy devotion. The most important characteristic of The Divine Mercy devotion is full commitment. Worshippers of the Merciful Lord should devote themselves to Him without reservation. Jesus says to Sister Zofia, "My dear daughter, be quiet and humble" (Grochowska 1999: 114). Worshippers of The Divine Mercy have a great mission to accomplish. The world is sinful, and the apocalypse is coming. Only deep prayer to the Merciful Lord and commitment to faith can save the world and its sinners:

> I miss God and I consider all future catastrophes. I am asking my Jesus and His Mother how to save the world.... When I pray to The Divine Mercy, God became merciful [Grochowska 1999: 115].
>
> You [Legion of Small Knights] have to be an example to all people. Keep praying! You will change humankind and the world will shine when I, Jesus Christ, come back to you in my Glory [129].

Generally The Divine Mercy devotion is based on millennial assumptions. The end times are coming and only the Merciful Lord can save people from punishment. In Sister Zofia's diary one can learn about future catastrophe:

> My dear daughter, write these messages to the whole world. The whole world should pray to The Divine Mercy for help, because war, which was prophesied, will break out all around the world. [Grochowska 1999: 85]
>
> My Dear Daughter, I will soon come and punish the world for all evil, which was done.... Before the end of second millennium, the world will see where is Love, Goodness and Mercy. No one who lived for his/her own can count on Mercy at the day of punishment. [123]

Sister Zofia also encourages prayer to The Divine Mercy. Prayer communities established by Zofia always meet the first Monday of the month at 3 P.M.

In the second part of Zofia's diary, the Holy Spirit appears: "Take care of Holy Spirit's Temple. This temple is, like net, linked with my heart. Only sin can destroy this net" (Grochowska 1999: 266).

During her meetings, Zofia calls upon the Holy Spirit rather than God or Jesus. Meetings of members with Sister Zofia are similar to meetings of Catholic Charismatics. She heals with help from the Holy Spirit.

In regards to "healing," Zofia claims also to have "energy." Sometimes she uses the term "divine energy." Her healing skill comes from God. She prays a lot, and God grants her the power of healing, in a seemingly miraculous fashion. She can also bless water, and this blessed water cures various kinds of illness. Last year she said that God granted her a new blessing, a new charismatic power. Now she can bless water via telephone. One can call her and ask her to bless water.

She also gives her blessing to individuals directly. During the act of blessing she keeps her hand on somebody's head and prays. After the act of blessing she says: "My heart is warmth like fire. This warmth from my heart flowed to you. Energy flowed to you" (Tolkmicko 2001).

At this point in her life, she is like a professional healer:

> Certainly you feel peace in your soul and your body is relaxed. I know that you benefit from this blessing. This is not my invention. This is Jesus' invention. He says: "Souls blessed by you will immerse within The Divine Mercy" [Tolkmicko 2001].

But originally the flow of energy was very harmful for her. In the early days, she was nearly overwhelmed by "bad energy."

> People received good energy from me and I received bad energy. But know I am only a donor. I am a medium. Energy can flow through me even to 300 people [Tolkmicko 2001].

Her use of "energy" can be compared to what is described as the Human Energy Field (HEF) (Hedges and Beckford 2000:177), a common New Age belief. In this belief, HEF is a subtle energetic field which is harmonized with natural energies. HEF regulates the physical body as well as mental processes. Furthermore, Zofia's healing of the HEF encompasses not only physical and mental health, but also restores spiritual health. In their article, Ellie Hedges and James A. Beckford give examples — they quote their respondents — of the coexistence of the flow of energy and bright flashes of colors. Also Zofia links these phenomena:

> I have a connection with electromagnetic fields. There are divine energetic fields and bad fields. I can connect to energetic field and I can pass to other person some energy. Energetic fields are colorful. Most often beautiful pink appears. Pink is the color of the Holy Spirit [Tolkmicko 2001].

Hedges and Beckford's respondents refer to other New Age elements: "The success of a treatment depended on preventing distractions and on evoking the appropriate atmosphere through a ritualistic lighting of candles and burner, dimming of lights and the playing of New Age music" (Hedges and Beckford 2000:181).

However, Zofia adheres firmly to Catholicism, over and against "upstart" New-Ageism. Zofia puts her healing practice and concept of "energy" completely within the context of Catholicism. She uses a crucifix. She meets her followers and patients in church or at her apartment, which is full of holy icons. This arrangement is typical of new religious movements, in that "women religious leaders, more than men, seem to straddle the public and the domestic spheres. They used their homes as ritual spaces" (Sered 1994: 237). She says that she is only a medium and it is God or the Holy Spirit that actually heals. In sharp contrast to New Age beliefs which seek to empower the individual, Zofia holds that only through submissive and humble devotion to God, through Catholicism, can a person receive healing, salvation, and so on.

Social Perception

Sister Zofia is a very successful spiritual leader, but her neighbors from Tolkmicko treat her in a very specific way. Although usually respectful, most of them consider her to be crazy. They remember her when she was an ordinary housewife. Her husband used to drink a lot of alcohol. He spent most of his life working as a fisherman and consequently was away from home for extended periods. People said that she was very lonely, and this contributed to her madness.

Sister Zofia did not begin as a charismatic. When she organized prayer meetings in Tolkmicko in August 1999 and 2000, her neighbors were shocked that people came from all around Poland to meet her and pray with her. One woman who came here for a prayer meeting told me

> "God takes care of our town, and it is extraordinary to have such a person in town." And I said, "What are you talking about?" And she said that God speaks via Sister Zofia. I was shocked [woman, 67 years old, Tolkmicko 2001].

Generally people in Tolkmicko don't believe in Sister Zofia's charismatic visions and healing skills. They say that it is impossible that an uneducated, ordinary woman can get in touch with God. They remember her when she was young. She was very nervous, and not very religious.

They are also very critical about members of the legion:

> This lady who belongs to the legion used to have a very bad reputation. When she was young she prostituted even for a piece of lard or tomato.

And her grandson is imprisoned for murder. And her daughter also spent some time in prison. She has very bad reputation. Maybe even the worst sinner can convert! [woman, 67 years old, Tolkmicko 2001].

Only a few people say that Sister Zofia is very religious and helped them when they were ill and they believe in her God-given grace.

My mother believes in her healing skills. She reads her books. Sister Zofia spends a lot of time in church praying. My mother says that Sister Zofia has charisma of healing. My mother was very ill, she had horrible pain in her hand. I think that she has some kind of energy. Sister Zofia sat down close to my mother and she said, "Sit down close to me, give me your hand." And my mother felt flow of energy. And she never had any problems with her hand again [woman, 46 years old, Tolkmicko 2001].

Fundamentalism and Gender — Women's Leadership

The Legion of Small Knights can be described as "ethnocentric Catholicism." Janusz Marianski argues that Polish "ethnocentric Catholicism" is both a fundamentalist religiosity and also culturally specific (Marianski 1997:175, Bronk 1995:21). The full meaning of the phrase, however, is specifically Polish. The term "dewocyjny katolicyzm polski" has three elements: "dewocyjny" means full of piety, yet at the same time bigoted against those of different piety; katolicyzm — Catholicism; polski — Polish, but in this context it stresses the nationalistic character of this kind of religiousness. That is, the ethnocentric legion member, although not necessarily supportive of the Catholic Church as a formal religious institution, still upholds Catholicism as a cultural identity, that consists of recognizable rituals and doctrine particular to local culture or particular ethnic groups. Furthermore, the legion subscribes to a specifically Polish version of Catholic religiosity, over and against other Catholic cultures and non–Polish cultures. The movement, like others of its type, is thus nationalistic as well.

According to Alfons Skowronek fundamentalist movements within today's Roman Catholic Church first and foremost reject most or all of the Second Vatican Council. This is a kind of internal opposition which is, in fact, a bigger problem for the church than clergy who officially exit from the church, like Archbishop of Dakar Marcel Lefebvre (Skowronek 1996:39). Skowronek identifies the main watchwords of Catholic fundamentalist movements: (1) tenacity (our way is the only way); (2) isolation (community spirit, group is chosen to accomplish a special mission); (3) authoritarianism (need of charismatic leadership); (4) dualism (world seen as black and white); (5)

reductionism (salvation depends only on one factor); and (6) inability of dialog (Skowronek 1996:40–41).

These watchwords are also familiar to members of the legion. As I pointed out above, they think that devotion to The Divine Mercy is the only way to salvation; they have a very strong community spirit and consider themselves as chosen by God; they see the world divided between the Small Knights and the rest. Sister Zofia is also a charismatic leader in the classic Weberian sense — somewhat perceived to hold genuine supernatural powers or authority. According to Zygmunt Bauman (1997:182), religious fundamentalism is an effect of the uncertainty of postmodernity. People lost in the contemporary world look for a clear explanation of reality. The message, as one can read in Sister Zofia's book or hear her speak about, is very clear. The world is presented as black and white, good and evil. We (the good ones) have to fight against evil (everyone else). Yet evil in this sense is not embodied in specific people or groups necessarily, but rather, evil is omnipresent and unpredictable. Evil can be everywhere. Only the true believer — the devoted follower of the charismatic leader, i.e., People who believe in Zofia's visions — are chosen by Jesus. All others are at best suspect.

The true believers have a divine mission to change the "evil" world. Bauman argues that the absolute quality of fundamental religiosity, which stands in opposition to today's uncertainty, has a great chance for development. This process can be observed also in Poland, especially in the present time of social and economic transformation from a formerly Eastern Bloc nation to something more closely resembling the capitalist democracies of Western Europe. Many Poles feel that, although many reforms, especially in the area of greater political freedom, have been a substantial improvement, changes may only be different from, rather than better than, the problems of the earlier socialist system. The current economic crisis and fears concerning integration with the European Union create a favorable situation for development of radical attitudes.

Religious fundamentalism can go together with nationalism. In Poland many of the movements founded around private revelations are nationalistic and xenophobic. Visionaries often make "anti-alien" statements. Members of the legion are patriots and fundamentalists; the latter often becomes specifically antisemitic. They stress a close connection between God and the Polish nation which should consist only of "true Poles," even though in Sister Zofia's diary one will not find any xenophobic nor antisemitic statements.

The legion is a religious community founded and led by one woman, and about 90 percent of the followers are women. It happens very rarely that women are founders and leaders of religious organizations. However, Elizabeth Puttick points out that Christianity in some periods has given possibilities of various religious roles (Puttick 1997:188). Also parachurch fundamentalist millenarian organizations offer women special opportunities (Brasher 1999). Puttick provides a typology of women's leadership: masculine or "male-oriented"; feminine; or non-gendered or androgynous (Puttick 1997:192). What is Zofia's style of leadership? I would argue a feminine charismatic type. According to Puttick, the main characteristic of this style is motherliness:

> Most women in religious life hitherto have acquired the title "Mother," including those such as nuns who are debarred from biological motherhood. Women who identify with motherliness as a defining characteristic will tend towards a more feminine style of leadership [Puttick 1997:193].

Also, Zofia is treated as the mother:

> [Members of the legion] respect her very much. They love her. They look forward to meeting her. Because she has so much divine love in her. She can make people together. She can hold them. She is so joyful and she has God's grace [woman, 46 years old, Tolkmicko 2001].

She also acts as mother of the community. In her speech to her followers she said: "Come to Kalisz to attend the retreat. I will take care of you. I am your mother. I will cook for all of you."

Exploring female leadership, Susan Starr Sered points out that women who run religious organizations frequently deal with cooking (Sered 1994: 237). Cooking is also an important part of Zofia's activity. She organized a meeting of her followers in her town of Tolkmicko. She cooked for all of them. While conducting my fieldwork, I participated in cooking lunch for a priest. Sister Zofia was visiting Warsaw in April 2001. She stayed at the apartment of the chief of Warsaw's legion community and they invited a priest — a professor of theology. Zofia was the one who says for how long pasta should be boiled and so on.

Zofia also claims to have a special role in the Catholic Church. She also acts like "the mother of the Church." She takes care of priests: she buys vestments and takes care of the church in Tolkmicko. She claims that they cannot exist in proper ways without her. At the same time she gives them spiritual guidance. She believes that she can improve even the worst clerical incompetence or misconduct. That is her mission. God chose her — an ordinary, noneducated woman — to improve the Catholic Church and convert sinners, and to show them The Divine Mercy. In her diary one can read that she was chosen to improve the church (and world):

> I am calling you to pray for the Holy Catholic Church. My dear children, pray for whole the clergy. The Church needs your prayers, Satan will

attack the Church with great power. Satan will possess young priests. Only your prayers can save the clergy [Grochowska 1999: 262].

Sister Zofia and her followers also discuss the role of women in the Roman Catholic Church. She points out the fact that she is a woman, which creates problems in cooperation with the clergy. Priest should listen to women as equal members of the church community. Generally, Zofia believes that women have an extraordinary role in today's world. Namely, women should be the caretakers of moral values, but contrary to the traditional Catholic concept of family they should not limit themselves only to the domestic sphere.

Simultaneously, other characteristics of women's religiosity are discipleship and serving as a medium between God and the people (Puttick 1997). Puttick describes the typical master-disciple relationship as patriarchal. Exploring interpersonal relations within the community of Small Knights, I would argue that there is no master-disciple relationship within the community. Although Zofia is the founder and leader of the legion, she is "sister" at the same time. Members say that they are like a family, that all are equal. Moreover, Zofia is not the author of the messages in her diary, but only a servant of Heaven, a conduit through which God speaks. She is only a medium. Jesus, the Virgin Mary, the Holy Spirit, and even King David of Israel are the authors. Zofia says that these heavenly personages told her: "My dear daughter, write down what I said. I am the Author, you are only a tool. Don't hesitate. It can't be unreal" (Grochowska 1999:85).

Final Remarks: From "Ethnocentric Catholicism" to Sincretic Spirituality

In my opinion the activity of the Legion of Small Knights is an illustration of a very important trend in the Polish Roman Catholic Church. Catholic religiosity is not homogenized. The fundamental movements acting on the borders of the Catholic Church become significant in today's religious culture. The Legion of Small Knights is only one exemplification. May we discern any common elements among the various movements which we collectively term ethnocentric or fundamentalist?

They are all sincretic, and they are all reactions to social change propelled by global economic and cultural forces that intrude upon and transform local economies and social life.

Sincretically, they link different forms of devotion and cultural elements, despite their sometimes overt testaments about specially Catholic devotion or Polish-centered practice. Previously "ethnocentric Catholic" organizations, like communities established to pray to the Virgin Mary, or movements devoted to charismatic visionaries, were localized prayer communities established through friendship networks, and focused on local issues particular to a specific community. Now, movements like the Legion of Small Knights work in the whole of Poland and in Polish communities abroad. In its own way, the legion takes part in a growing worldwide fundamentalist movement across many of the world's major religions.

References

Barker, Eileen. "New Religious Movements. Their Incidence and Significance." *New Religious Movements. Challenge and Response.* Edited by B. Wilson and J. Cresswell, London and New York: Routledge, 1999.

Bauman, Z. *Postmodernity and Its Discontents.* New York: New York University Press, 1997.

Brasher, B. "Women at the End of the World: Christian Fundamentalism as an Engendering Machine." *Journal of Millennial Studies.* (Summer, 1999).

Bronk, A., "Typy fundamentalism." *Zeszyty naukowe KUL*, no. 3–4 (1995) p. 3–25

Grochowska, Z. Czas ostaniej szansy, Warszawa (1994).

_____. U _róde_ Bo_ego mi_osierdzia, Tolkmicko (1999).

Hedges E., and J.A. Beckford. "Holism, Healing and the New Age." *Beyond New Age. Exploring Alternative Spirituality.* Edited by S. Sutcliffe and M. Bowman. Edinburgh: Edinburgh University Press, 2000.

Krajewski, Tadeusz. "Introduction." *Czas ostatniej szansy*, Warszawa (1994).

Mariaski, Janusz. *Religia i Ko_ció_ mi_dzy tradycj_ i ponowoczesno_ci_*, Kraków: Zak_ad Wydawniczy Nomos, 1997.

Obirek Stanis_aw. *Ludzkie oblicze nowej _wi_tej, Siostra Faustyna Kowalaska*, Kraków: Wydawnictwo WAM, 2000.

Pine, F. "Kinship, Gender and Work in Socialist and Post-socialist Rural Poland." *Gender, Agency and Change: Anthropological perspectives.* Edited by V. A. Goddard. London and New York: Routledge, 2000.

Puttick, E. *Women in New Religions: In Search of Community, Sexuality and Spiritual Power.* London, Macmillan, 1997.

Sered S. S. *Priestess, Mother, Sacred Sister: Religions Dominated by Women.* New York & Oxford: Oxford University Press, 1994.

Siepak, Sr. M. Elzbieta ZMBM. *Blessed Sr. Faustina.* Translated by the Rev. Seraphim Michalenko MIC and Maciej Talar, Warszawa, Kraków: Congregation of Our Lady of Mercy, 1993.

Skowronek, A. "Fundamentalizm wyzwaniem dla tolerancji." *Wi__*, no. 7 (1996). p. 37–51.

Turner, V. *Drams, Fields and Metaphors.* Ithaca: Cornell University Press, 1974.

Zgoszenie, date and place of publication unknown, Declaration of the Legion of Small Knights.

8

Religionizing Crime

Ethos and Action in the Construction of the Finnish Satanism Scare[1]

TITUS HJELM

Introduction

Some scholars have indicated that Satanism scares in America are a remnant of the late '80s and early '90s (e.g., Degh 1995:38). That the major studies and evaluations in America were published at that time indicates at least that the heyday of public (and academic) interest in Satanism dates from the same period (see Richardson, et al. 1991; Victor 1993). Other countries have followed in different succession, but generally it could be concluded that major Satanism scares have been a phenomenon of the '90s.

Finland experienced its major Satanism scare only at the end of the millennium. Most commonly Satanism has manifested itself in different forms of crime that are allegedly Satanically inspired. The most common of this type of crime has been cemetery vandalism. This paper analyzes the way the image of Satanism is constructed in public discourse, notably the media. Attention is specifically paid to the ways that the media construct a link between ethos (Satanism) and action (cemetery vandalism).

Satanism has been presented in the media especially in the form of various criminal acts. Cemetery vandalism in particular has become a typical act of crime committed by alleged Satanists, headlining Finnish newspapers throughout the 1990s. Pictures of overturned tombstones and chapels scribbled with Satanic graffiti have been regular news material, especially during the summertime. At times cemetery vandalism has generated national waves of concern, when an incident in one locality has been followed by a similar incident elsewhere in the country. The fear of Satanism spreading to the locality has aroused public discussion in numerous local newspapers, and the nationwide occurrence of the phenomenon has been a topic of discussion in the national media. Cemetery vandalism has commonly been regarded as the first sign of Satanism gaining ground in the locality.

Cemetery vandalism, the desecration of graves to be precise, is an act of crime. What makes it exceptional is the motivation brought forward in the definition process of the problem: Satanism. Because of this, cemetery vandalism as a crime places itself not only in the traditional criminal discourse, but also in a wider discourse related to common social values. It is my intention to study how this discourse is structured and who the parties are defining the problem in the media.

There is an obvious distinction between newspaper reports on cemetery vandalism and other types of criminal acts: Satanism is an *explanatory* qualifier in the headlines. Whereas a headline "a man killed his friend" only recounts the actual event, a headline "Satanists stormed the cemetery" also relates the underlying reason for the actions. A description becomes an explanation also (Bodily 1994). In other words, it is assumed that the persons who vandalized the cemetery possess a certain kind of ethos which guides their actions. In this context the word ethos is used to refer to an individual philosophy of life.

However, Satanism as a phenomenon makes the question somewhat different here than, for example, in a study of Islam or the Hare Krishna movement, because it seems reasonable to doubt whether acts labeled as Satanism have anything to do with religion in the first place. Yet Satanism is presented as a religion in a large number of newspaper articles. Satanism has been presented in the media also from other points of view and religious discourse is not the only one present at the coverage. I have elsewhere studied the image of Satanism presented by the media more generally (Hjelm 2000). In this study the research material is examined particularly from the perspective of the relationship between ethos and actions, and how it is constructed in the media.

Public Image and the Construction Process of Social Reality

The subject of the study of social problems is defined as "the definitional process in which morally objectionable conditions or behaviors are asserted to exist" by Malcolm Spector and John I. Kitsuse in their classic work *Constructing Social Problems* (Spector & Kitsuse 2001, 1977). This signifies the fact that social problems are not an absolute concept, instead each given culture and society defines the social problems specific to it. Therefore, it is a process attempting to generate action, regardless of whether that action is introducing the subject matter to public discussion or attempting to influence decision-making.

In a late modern society, the role of the media in exposing social problems has constantly increased. Especially when it is a question of new phenomena, which are still alien to a culture and unfamiliar to the general public, the capability of the media to produce certain kinds of information to shape public opinion toward a desirable direction is considerable (Thompson 1995:213–214).

John B. Thompson, who has developed a social theory of the media, employs the term "mediated sociality" in his study. By this he refers to a development by which a larger and larger portion of our mutual knowledge is transmitted through the media. As a consequence, the groups and communities with whom people identify themselves are more and more constructed through the media (Thompson 1995:35). In the definitional process of social problems it is important to draw attention to any abnormal behavior and to define "we," a group of which this behavior is not part of. News reports on criminal acts are one of the most explicit examples of news reporting in which the media exposes any deviant, morally objectionable action and in this way reinforces the division into us and the others (Fishman 1998).

The focus of attention in a discursive study is in particular on the devices with which social reality is produced from a certain point of view. In determining these devices the following questions emerge when examining the media material related to cemetery vandalism:

1. How are the perpetrators portrayed in the article? Are they active or passive?

2. How can we know the identity of the perpetrators; who functions as a determiner of the problem?

3. How does the article explain the motivation of the perpetrators? And in connection with the previous: whose voice is used to explain the motivation?

Cemetery vandalism has been presented as a phenomenon that has in many contexts been given features of a crime wave. The concept of a crime wave means a conception of crime that has been brought into public awareness (Fishman 1998:53). Although crime waves are not necessarily connected with the actual crime rate, they generate action by inflicting fear. "Crime waves may be 'things of the mind,' but they have real consequences" (ibid). In his study, Mark Fishman has examined the origins of crime waves on the basis of the interaction between newspaper reporters and the police authority. The present article, however, is not concerned with the actions of individual parties external to the crime report itself. Instead, it concentrates particularly on examining the way in which cemetery vandalism is constructed as a crime wave in public discourse.

Cemeteries and Vandals

In their simplest form, newspaper articles on cemetery vandalism are concise reports that recount what happened and where. The articles describe the events and make some reference to the suspected perpetrators:

> Funeral crosses and tombstones were overturned in the Orthodox cemetery of Hietaniemi during Friday night in Helsinki. A total number of eight crosses and 15 tombstones were overturned on the Porkkalankatu side of the cemetery. The act of vandalism was committed between 11 P.M. and 9 A.M.... There is no information on the perpetrators for the time being ["Tombstones down in Hietaniemi," *Uutislehti* 100, October 25, 1999].

The short report relates the nature of the crime (the desecration of graves) with which the Finnish public was already fairly familiar by 1999. However, when compared to the large majority of newspaper articles on cemetery vandalism, reports like the one above are in the minority. Irrespective of whether there is actual information on the perpetrators, the majority of the articles point out a connection between the actions and Satanism:

> Over one hundred tombstones were overturned in the Old Church cemetery of Espoo.... In addition, graves and buildings located on the burial ground were scribbled with paint.... Altogether over 140 tombstones were overturned in the cemetery of the church and chapel. There were also inverted crosses and five pointed stars, symbols used by Satanists, sprayed on the tombstones and buildings located in the cemetery. According to the chief inspector Pekka Partanen, the police are investigating the case as an aggravated vandalism ["Tombstones overturned in Espoo," *HS* June 15, 1993].

Especially during the wave of cemetery vandalism in the summer of 1999, the actions were linked to Satanism usually already in the headline. The fact that a naturalization (2) of the association between the events and Satanism had already taken place culminates in a worried headline of *Iltalehti*, a Finnish tabloid: "Satanists strike once again?" (*IL* July 26, 1999). Especially the acts of vandalism that occurred in cemeteries all over Finland at the end of July were readily put down as the activity of "a cult familiar from horror flicks," a cult explicitly thus named even before 1999 ("Satanism emerged in Finland not until 1998," *IL*, December 29, 1998). At times when there is no information on the perpetrators and no marks characteristic of Satanism has been discovered on the crime scene, a potential connection is introduced:

> More than ten tombstones were overturned in Sonkajärvi during Friday night. It is possible that there is only one person responsible for the vandalism. He has not been found yet. According to the police, 13 tombstones were kicked down. Evidently, no serious damage was done. Nothing suggesting Satanism has been discovered ["More tombstones overturned," *Uutislehti* 100, September 27, 1999].

Occasionally the viewpoint of the caught grave desecrators themselves, based on police interrogation records, has been presented in public as well. One example of this is the case of a man who stormed the cemetery of Karttula in the summer of 1999. In this case, the motivation for cemetery vandalism is obvious: "During a police interrogation the man told that he was a Satanist" ("The man suspected of the grave desecrations in Karttula confessed," *HS* August 6, 1999). The article, which could be characterized as being moderate, leaves the relationship between Satanism and the actual events somewhat vague by adding that "according to senior constable Jari Kolari the police have no knowledge on the man's possible connections to the previous grave desecrations. There is no certainty on the role of alcohol in the case" (ibid).

Although in this respect it seems that Satanism is almost without an exception connected to cemetery vandalism, there have also been some skeptic statements. These statements have, however, been in the minority in the entire coverage of cemetery vandalism during the 1990s. Before 1999 it was mostly the police who, due to the nature of their work, could not give any definite comments without credible evidence and who doubted the connections. During the first years of the phenomenon Satanism was simply seen as one possibility. "A part [of cemetery vandalism] can be put down to drunken hooligans, but it does seem that in some of the cases the perpetrators have apparently been inspired by Satanism" ("The police increases the surveillance of cemeteries," *HS*, September 22, 1993). The doubts of the police are the most apparent in a case from 1996, where two underage girls were caught overturning 360 tombstones in Jyväskylä:

> [T]he girls could not specify a rational motivation for their actions. The execution of the crime was accelerated by the fact that the girls were intoxicated that night. Myllymäki emphasized that speculations linking the events to Satanism are false. "The person who claims that Satanism was the motivation, speaks with too large a mouth" ["Two young girls caught on overturning tombstones in Jyväskylä," *HS*, August 1, 1996].

However, the nature of police work has not prevented the members of the police force from confirming the prevailing image of the connection between cemetery vandalism and Satanism. Even if there has been no reliable information available on the perpetrators or their motives, the police may have stated, quoting chief inspector Osmo Perkkiö, that "the adolescents themselves have accounted for their actions but at this point it is still difficult to say whether this is Satanism or not. In my opinion it is" ("Seven youngsters suspected of cemetery vandalism," *HS*, July 27, 1999).

As in the latter half of 1999, and also in the most recent news coverage, the question is perhaps not so much about skepticism. Instead, the media has adopted a new approach on reporting cemetery vandalism, an approach where the question of motivation is not brought out without dependable information from the police sources.

Thus it seems that in the vast majority of reported cases a cemetery vandal is profiled to be a young Satanist. There exists some variation on how uncritically explicit the presented connection is. However, the identification of the actions and perpetrators alone does not satisfactorily explain the nature of cemetery vandalism coverage and the process in which a certain type of crime is constructed. In constructionist study of social problems the foremost method of approaching the construction process of the phenomenon is the examination of the claims presented above. In the next stage, it is necessary to also examine the claimsmakers, as well as their backgrounds and their influence on public discourse. Many different parties interpret cemetery vandalism: the police, employees of the church, journalists, and a variety of experts. Each one of these parties defines the problem in its own exclusive way. The reciprocal relationship of the different definitions and their influence on the overall picture is considered next.

The Definition Process of the Phenomenon

What devices are used to create an image of a connection between cemetery vandalism and Satanism? How can the readers be sure that it actually was Satanism that was in question? Although the examples presented above do reveal the nature of the problem, they fail to reveal how and by whom the nature of cemetery vandalism is defined. The role of the police as the primary source of information has already been brought up. However, on what grounds can the police say and a journalist write that overturning tombstones is a sign of Satanism?

At the first glance it seems safe to argue that sufficient proof can be obtained from the evidence left in the cemeteries by the vandals. Inverted crosses and five-pointed stars found on the crime scenes, the primary symbols representing the ethos of the perpetrators, have been interpreted as signs of Satanism. However, this cannot be satisfactory for a critical examination. How can we know that these particular symbols are connected with Satanism? Also, on what grounds can we say that the appearance of these symbols on the crime scene is somehow related to the ethos of the perpetrators? In order to be able to answer these questions, it is necessary to examine how and by whom the interpretations are made. Next, I will examine the parties who all have introduced their own interpretation in the coverage, as well as the relationship between the different interpretations.

Journalists and the Motives of the Vandalism

When studying cemetery vandalism and crime reporting in general, it is also important to take the various genres of news reporting into consideration. Newspaper articles can be roughly divided into short, concise news flashes, more comprehensive news reports accompanied by background information, and news commentary, which resembles opinion writing (Bruun, et al. 1986:55–56). All these types are present in the news reporting on cemetery vandalism. The role of journalists in providing a perspective is accentuated in concise news flashes, where it is usually a choice of the journalist and the newspaper whether to bring forward the connection with Satanism or not. Both types do occur. More comprehensive news reports provide, virtually without an exception, the comments of the police and background information, featuring experts who often comment on the phenomenon of Satanism in a broader sense and are uninvolved in the case itself.

However, it is obvious that the way in which journalists lay out their questions influences the comments given by outside parties. In addition, the newspaper production process may significantly alter the original content of the article (see Fairclough 1995). News reports on cemetery vandalism endeavor to adopt comments given by the interviewed parties, those of authorities in particular. However, even if the police had expressed uncertainty on the motivation, a news report can nevertheless be constructed on a discourse based on Satanic ethos. This is the case in the article cited above, "Tombstones overturned in Espoo" (*HS*, June 15, 1993). In the article, the police are quoted only when relating the information on the nature of the crime and the suspicion that the perpetrators are adolescents. Making a connection between the incident and Satanism appears to be the decision of the newspaper; at least the article fails to identify a justification or the source for the allegation. The contradiction is also evident in the articles in which the police speak primarily on their own terms and on grounds of actual information. After the police, the other associated parties are interviewed, employees of the church or other experts who confirm the connection between the incident and Satanism. It is ultimately a decision of the journalist and the newspaper as to which voice to emphasize in the finished article.

The Perspective of the Police on the Crimes

The stir created by the fear of Satanism in the United States has also given birth to a special group of so-called "cult cops." The cult cops serve as experts especially when investigating crimes that are presumably related to Satanism (see Hicks 1991 for more on cult cops and their criticism). In Finland, the role of the police in public discussion on crimes has mostly been traditional commentary of the "who, what, where" type (Chermak 1998:178). However, the perspective of the police is to a certain degree influenced by the news genre. For example, the police are quoted in the form of indirectly stated facts, such as "there is no information on the perpetrators" "the police are investigating the case as aggravated vandalism" or "the adolescents have confessed to vandalism." Quotes like these are common in short news flashes. More comprehensive news reports feature more direct quotes in which the police outline the actions and perpetrators. Also, in this case, the comments of the police are concentrated on their special field, i.e., describing the incident using specific criminological language.

The connection created by the police between cemetery vandalism and Satanism becomes apparent in the articles that examine the background of the phenomenon in a more comprehensive manner. Articles such as these want to present the viewpoint of the police, and other experts, on presumably criminal actions. They also seek to receive some kind of synthesis of the nature of the phenomenon from police representatives. What is interesting is an article dating from the early days of news reporting on Satanism, in which the deputy chief of the National Bureau of Investigation, Kari Rantama, is quoted:

> According to Rantama, the crimes committed in the name of Satanism are an extremely dangerous type of crime for which there is no Finnish name yet. The crimes belong to a category for which the most severe punishments are given in the United States because they are aimed at breaking the morals of the society. Rantama promises that the matter will be firmly resolved also in Finland ["Satan arrives in Finland," *IL* September 25, 1993].

Although it is confirmed by a police officer in a leading position that the police take the matter seriously in Finland, it remains unclear exactly what kind of phenomenon the police consider Satanism and the crimes connected to it. Between the quotes of Rantama, the journalist has positioned a clause which intensifies the vileness of the crimes: *the morals of society* are jeopardized if we want to follow the example set by the United States. Although by its placement the clause is attached to the statement of a police representative, it remains unclear whether it represents the viewpoint of the police.

Police representatives are bound to concise comments on the quality of the crimes primarily due to the nature of their work. Regardless of this, statements given by police representatives may be positioned in such a way that they support the discourse of Satanic ethos presented by other sources. The viewpoints differ only in situations when the police explicitly deny any connection between Satanism and the vandalism that has taken place in cemeteries.

Attack Against the Church?
The Viewpoint of Church Employees

In addition to the police, the chief commentators on cemetery vandalism have been the employees of the churches that have been the targets of vandalism. These include vicars, pastors, and caretakers of the church. The voice of the church is transmitted through its employees in more comprehensive articles. The alleged connection between cemetery vandalism and Satanism is presented very explicitly:

> It is a question of guesswork no more. The act of vandalism had an unmistakable reference to Satanism," says the vicar of Espoo's Swedish Church, Carl-Gustav Henricson.... [A]n inverted cross represents mockery of the Cross of Christ and professing the Devil's faith ... it can no longer simply be a question of misbehavior of intoxicated adolescents because of the fact that similar vandalism has occurred even before ["All distinctive marks of Satanism: Doors of the church scribbled and graves desecrated," *IL* June 15, 1993].

Even if there is no certainty of the connection, representatives of the church take the possibility of Satanism very seriously:

> [Vicar Arno] Toivanen is hesitant to make any guesses.... In any case we have received information that Satanism has arrived also in Iisalmi.... The vicar has played a very active part in erecting an anti–Satanism league in Iisalmi. According to him, it must be possible to do something about the matter ["Satanists in an intense surveillance of the church and authorities," *IL* March 30, 1998].

8. Religionizing Crime

Cemetery vandalism appears to church employees as an attack against church itself and the values it represents. Especially in the early days of the phenomenon, church employees were eager to bring up a view that the activity posed an actual threat against the basic values of society. The experts who appeared in the media were also employed by religious circles. It was often emphasized that Satanism is real, a phenomenon that was now actually also in Finland and a consequence of which was cemetery vandalism. This view was also shared by Harri Heino, head of the Research Institute of the Evangelical Lutheran Church of Finland, who served as a semiofficial commentator on the events of 1993 in particular.

> According to researcher Harri Heino, contemplating Satanic philosophy is not enough for adolescents. Instead, the cult stirs up a desire for direct action and violence in them ["Rituals are not enough for children and adolescents," a caption in *IS*, November 22, 1993].

Also based on the interview with Heino, Helsingin Sanomat sorts out the motives of Satanists and the criminal nature of Satanism:

> Satanists completely reject the values and ideals of society. They seek to establish a counterculture where morals opposite to those of a normal society prevail. Wrong becomes right and evil becomes good. There is no need to feel guilt for acts of crime ["The police increases the surveillance of cemeteries," *HS*, September 22, 1993].

In both the articles commenting on single events and the news reports with background information the explanation for cemetery vandalism is presented through a Christian frame of reference in the interviews of church employees. However, the viewpoint of the church representatives is not exhausted merely by making an unambiguous connection between cemetery vandalism and Satanism. The viewpoints of the church representatives presented in the media have been influenced by a shift in both the way the phenomenon is comprehended and the manner in which the way of comprehension is illustrated in the news articles. An interview with the vicar of Pieksämäki, Juhani Kaipiainen, in connection with the outbreak of cemetery vandalism in the summer of 1999 illustrates this approach:

> This is some kind of national boom. It is the relatives of the dead that will suffer most because of it.... Kaipiainen also wonders what the reason is for adolescents becoming socially marginalized. On the other hand, overturning tombstones reflects the malaise of the offenders ["Grave desecrators struck in Pieksämäki. 'It feels terrible,'" *IL*, August 16, 1999].

Similar to exposing other social problems, in the first news reports on Satanism the church in particular possessed an urge to bring out a viewpoint emphasizing the reality of Satanism and the seriousness of the phenomenon.

At first Satanism was interpreted as an activity aimed specifically against the church. Obviously this interpretation was further reinforced by anti–Christian symbols found in cemeteries. Soon after, more interpretations began to appear in public in which the center of attention was shifted from mystical and terrifying Satanism more to those adolescents themselves who were at the focal point of the phenomenon. The social malaise among the youth and the consequences of it became part of the discussion. At this stage, even the Evangelical Lutheran church commented on the matter from a fresh point of view. One single comment that probably had a great influence was made by Archbishop Jukka Paarma. The interview of Paarma begins with a statement that "according to Archbishop Jukka Paarma, Satanism in Finland is not an attack against the church and religion in particular, but is a protest against the common values of society in general" (in, e.g., "Social marginalization of the youth leads to extremist phenomena," *Aamulehti* August 15, 1999; "The church traces underlying reasons for Satanism," *HS*, August 16, 1999, etc.).

Paarma particularly brought out the subject of vandalism that has taken place in cemeteries: "The majority of the recent acts of vandalism are most likely a consequence of alcohol and lack of consideration" ("The church traces underlying reasons for Satanism," *HS*, August 16, 1999). Although Paarma is quick to add that the marks of Satanism, which have been more and more frequent in connection with the acts of vandalism, force the church to investigate the matter thoroughly, making an automatic connection between cemetery vandalism and Satanism has decreased in statements given by church employees.

Christian and Social Scientific Expert Discourse

In news reports on cemetery vandalism the police and church employees serve as primary sources of information. At times when multiple cases of cemetery vandalism have occurred within a short period of time, the media have employed researchers (both academic and nonacademic) who have specialized in Satanism to serve as their source of information. These individuals have been presented as experts in the subject in an even wider sense than the police or church employees commenting directly on a particular case. What is noteworthy in these expert discourses is that as their starting point they try to answer the question "what is Satanism?" In this way being a expert in itself defines cemetery vandalism as being a consequence of Satanic ethos. Although this view is not supported by every expert, the articles

8. Religionizing Crime

intended as background information on the phenomenon of cemetery vandalism almost exclusively use the term Satanism, not juvenile delinquency, for instance.

At the early days of cemetery vandalism the most often quoted expert was Harri Heino, whose views have already been presented. Shortly thereafter, Keijo Ahorinta, a special education teacher from Rauma, emerged as the most often employed expert in the media. Ahorinta has also written a book on Satanism entitled *Saatananpalvonnan monet kasvot* (*The Many Faces of Satanism*, Ahorinta 1997). The central ideas introduced in his book have been frequently presented in newspaper articles:

> According to Ahorinta, Satanism is ruthless abuse of people, absolutely criminal activity to which drugs and sexual abuse are related. It is sacrificing yourself to Satan, and it generates gang addiction with which the members are chained to community through earthly goods ["The interest in Satanism among young girls awoke Jyväskylä," *HS*, April 16, 1998].

The status of Ahorinta as an expert is largely built on his long experience and his academic interest in the subject matter: "He has studied Satanism for 11 years and is now working on his doctoral thesis on the subject" (ibid). A closer inspection of the views presented by Ahorinta reveals a strong Christian influence on his views that is also evident in his book (Ahorinta 1997:9). His view on the personal evil underlying behind the phenomenon varies depending on the context.

Although Ahorinta does state in *Helsingin Sanomat* that there is no distinction between Satanism and worshipping Satan on "the final frontier" ("The interest in Satanism among young girls awoke Jyväskylä," *HS*, April 16, 1998), his views are best presented in publications aimed at Christian readers. One of these publications is *Kotimaa*:

> A Satanist is a distressed, misled teenager, but we must make no mistake to disparage the underlying personal evil. "What is most important is that we do not bury our heads in the sand because Satan does exist" ["A scholar warns not to underestimate Satanism," *Kotimaa*, November 11, 1994].

Expertise and the term "expert" are used ambiguously in connection with cemetery vandalism. One of those who have appeared as experts in the media is the often quoted ex–Satanist Päivi Niemi. Her personal experiences on Satanism together with their terrifying details have received coverage in national tabloids.

Besides Ahorinta, Niemi has been a central figure expressing concern toward the extent Satanism has spread among the Finnish youth. "People do not seem to believe how numerous Satanists are. They do not want to believe it. Maybe it is because the subject is so unfamiliar to them" ("Ex-Satanist Päivi Niemi: My parents would not have believed the deeds I did," *IS*, April 18, 1998). In the same article, Niemi tells how she was redeemed from the clutches of Satanism by "switching lord," that is to say, by becoming a born-again Christian.

An academic survey of the situation had to wait until 1999, when a memorandum on Satanism (Kuure 1999), commissioned by the Ministry of Education and conducted by the Finnish Youth Research Network, was published. The survey was carried out by Tapio Kuure from the Department of Political Research of the University of Tampere. In spite of the shortcomings of the brief memorandum, it was the first academic survey of the situation. The memorandum did not receive much attention in the media, and its academic language was employed as such. In comparison with the deterrent views presented earlier by experts, the conclusions of the study are presented in less explicit terms:

> Kuure describes youth Satanism as a working project of evil. The foundation of Satanism is the wickedness of man. This is a rhetorical method with which the responsibility for own actions is transferred to that what is beyond, "Satan" ["A Survey: Youth Satanism is a middle class phenomenon," *HS*, August 31, 1999].

The views of experts on cemetery vandalism and Satanism can be therefore divided into interpretations made on a Christian basis and on a social scientific basis. A notion of personal evil which has influence on the world and a concrete struggle between good and evil are behind the interpretations made on a Christian basis (see Arnold 1997:4–12).

Although the religiousness may not be immediately evident in connection with news articles, the religious viewpoint can be said to be an underlying factor for all experts with a Christian frame of reference (see Rikkinen 2000). Religious interpretation is not necessarily in any way related to the status or position of the expert, as in the case of the late Harri Heino. He attempted to approach the phenomenon from a social scientific point of view, in spite of his position as the director of the Research Institute of the Evangelical Lutheran Church of Finland.

Interpretations that could be characterized as being social scientific have inevitably been overshadowed by visions painting nightmare scenarios. Academic language seems to lend itself poorly to the media looking for concise and pithy statements. What is fundamental in the case of cemetery vandalism is that in spite of their critical attitude, the views of academic experts who have appeared in public (one of whom is the author) have dealt with the question "what is Satanism?" As mentioned earlier, despite the critical statements this further develops an image that there is a connection between cemetery vandalism and Satanism. However, it does seem that the connection has weakened in the more recent news coverage, and Satanism is not necessarily brought up in connection with cemetery vandalism.

The Voice of the Youth

What is striking when trying to define cemetery vandalism is the silence of the perpetrators themselves in the whirlwinds of the media. Young age, alcohol, and Satanism all emerge as rationalizations for the acts of cemetery vandalism. However, the definition is made by the parties mentioned above, who in all of the cases have had only second-hand information of the actual events. At times when the voice of the perpetrators themselves has been heard, it has been filtered through a police interrogation process. For instance, in the following citation the statement given by a perpetrator in a police interrogation functions as a device with which to reinforce connections with Satanism: "According to the police, one of the teenagers has been interested in Satanism and has acquired information on the field from books and the Internet" ("The vandals of the cemetery in Kauhajoki were released," *HS*, July 30, 1999).

Although the fact that there is correlation between cemetery vandalism and interest in the "field" does not necessarily tell anything about the motivation, the connection made in the newspaper article is based on this. The choice of words in a news flash published in *Helsingin Sanomat*, dealing with the overturning of tombstones in Joensuu, is also interesting: the headline of the article states that "a young *student* of Satanism overturned tombstones in Joensuu" (emphasis added). In the actual article, however, it is mentioned in a somewhat ambiguous way that "the man has denied being a Satanist, but has admitted studying occultism and Satanism" ("A young student of Satanism overturned tombstones in Joensuu," *HS*, February 10, 1999).

A step closer to disclosing the voice of the youth and finding out their motivation and ethos is made in an early article published in *Helsingin Sanomat*:

> The two young men who overturned over hundred memorial plaques in Simo were inspired by a television program on Satanism. The 17- and 18-year-old teenagers have confessed to the vandalism inflicted on the Old Church of Simo.... The teenagers said that they had been inspired by a recently screened television program dealing with Satanism about the church burnings in Norway ["Satanism inspired to overturn soldier's graves in Simo," *HS*, September 15, 1993].

When analyzing the article it becomes clear that there is an obvious tension between the headline and the text itself. Although the headline implies that the motivation for the vandalism was Satanism, the voice of the teenagers themselves clearly indicates that the motivation was actually a documentary on Satanism. Even though the voice of the youth is once again filtered through the police, the article specifies the actual motivation and does not settle with only mentioning that the perpetrators were Satanists. The connection between the vandalism and Satanism is still there, but it is not as apparent as in the other similar cases.

Except for the cases that involve public figures (e.g., politicians) and the single cases that have received significant publicity, the voice of a perpetrator is rarely presented in the crime coverage of the media (Chermak 1998). The voice of perpetrators in connection with cemetery vandalism has been actually presented only once in the media. *Iltalehti* published an interview of the teenagers who stormed the cemetery of Kauhajoki in 1999 with a headline "'It was a relief to get caught.'" In the interview with the teenagers who appeared in public the connection between cemetery vandalism and Satanism is presented as follows:

> Although the teenagers had admitted their fascination for Satanism in a police interrogation, according to them it was just a question of sheer curiosity towards everything supernatural. Both of them stress that neither they nor the events that took place last summer had anything to do with Satan.... The vandalism could have been a subconscious feeling of malaise, although it is more likely that the actions were irrational foolishness of drunken teenagers ["'It was a relief to get caught,'" *IL*, February 28, 2000].

The last sentence of the extract is left open to interpretation whether it is the teenagers' own assumption of their motives or an estimation of the journalist. Whatever the case may be, the teenagers state, as presented in the introduction of this article, that "it was a sudden idea which had nothing to do with Satanism."

Obviously the statements given by the perpetrators of a single case do not exhaustively explain the motivation of dozens of other grave desecrators. However, it is worth noticing that the first time the voice of the youth is heard in public, it signals an altogether different message than the discourse emphasizing Satanic ethos that prevailed throughout the 1990s. It is possible that when entering the 21st century the media have become more receptive to different interpretations concerning the relationship between actions and ethos in connection with cemetery vandalism.

Cemeteries and Satanism: Examination of the Interaction Between Action and Ethos

This section summarizes the observations presented earlier of the connection between cemetery vandalism and Satanism in newspaper articles. There is a special emphasis on examining the relationship between actions and ethos presented in the beginning. I will also make a survey of the changes that have occurred in reports on cemetery vandalism since 1990 to the present day and examine what kind of crime cemetery vandalism has been presented as. Finally I will consider the manner in which the media explain the nature of a new, unfamiliar type of crime. In this connection I will also introduce the concept of religionization as a possible device to aid in the analysis.

Cemetery vandalism is brought up in the Finnish media as a consequence of a new, unfamiliar phenomenon that inflicts fear in the public: Satanism. The desecrations that have taken place in cemeteries since 1993 have been mostly associated with Satanism. Although Satanism has seldom been explicitly presented as a motivation for cemetery vandalism in the articles describing single incidents, the headlines and the actual discourse create a strong image of Satanic ethos which drives adolescents into committing acts of vandalism. More comprehensive articles meant as background information reinforce the references to Satanism that appear in shorter news flashes.

However, the connection between cemetery vandalism and Satanism is dynamic. The intensity of the connection depends on the party defining the problem. From the parties presented earlier in this article the strongest connection between cemetery vandalism and Satanic ethos is maintained primarily by church employees and experts commenting on the subject in a Christian frame of reference. According to their point of view, it is a question of either an attack against the church and the Christian values it represents, or outcast adolescents possessed by personal evil. Also, some of the statements given by the police reinforce the connection with Satanism.

The connection is, nevertheless, weakest in a large majority of the comments given by the police. Immediately after the occurrence of the crime the police have no information on the perpetrators or, in any case, their motives. Because of this, the police have often been unable to confirm the influence of Satanism on the crime, at least not in direct quotes. Satanism is mentioned, but based on the available information the police cannot verify the suspicions. In cases such as these, it is mainly a choice of the journalist whether to create the connection or not. However, there also exist other views in public discussion that represent a weak connection. According to these views, cemetery vandalism can and should be examined especially from the viewpoint of youth culture, as a means of expressing separation from conventional values that is typical of today's youth. Views such as these are brought together by the fact that they are still grouped together under the caption Satanism (e.g., "Insecurity and troubles lie behind Satanism," *Aamulehti*, July 30, 1999).

What is most notable is that the adolescents who have vandalized cemeteries have been conspicuous by their absence in the news coverage. Although there is only one example available in the present material, it is noteworthy that in the previously cited article ("'It was a relief to get caught,'" *IL*, February 28, 2000), the outspoken adolescents deny any connection between Satanism and cemetery vandalism, an interpretation which had already become natural.

The problem of front-end/back-end disproportionality (Wright 1997:107–109), which is related to crime reporting in general and to reporting on new religious movements, may be a contributing factor in creating a strong link between cemetery vandalism and Satanism. Front-end/back-end disproportionality means that a crime is reported immediately after it has occurred, but there is little attention paid to the later procession of the case, for example, in a court of law, except for the individual cases that have received significant publicity. As a consequence of this, remarks on the influence of Satanic ethos on cemetery vandalism survive, irrespective of whether they were justified or not. This is the case even if solving the case would not support the hypothesis of Satanism as a motivation. Also the rhetorical qualities of the Satanic ethos discourse have enabled its long-term survival as a primary version with which to interpret reality. However, the construction and development of the connection between cemetery vandalism and Satanism must also be examined in a chronological perspective, so that the dynamics of the development of the problem may be solved.

The Evolution of News Reporting on Cemetery Vandalism

I have previously made a reference to the change in news reporting on cemetery vandalism that has taken place during the almost 10 years that the subject has been under discussion. In a constructionist frame of reference, a chronological perspective and a change in the way a subject is processed play an essential role in determining the devices with which social problems are brought into public awareness (Lowney and Best 1995). A change can be seen not only in the ones who define the problem of the connection between cemetery vandalism and Satanism and the way it is processed in the media, but also in the influence of different discourses on what the approved way of defining the phenomenon is.

The first news reports in Finland on Satanism were about the suspected connections between Satanism and child abuse as well as other types of crimes outside Finland (3). The tone of the articles was mostly skeptical. For example as late as in 1994, by which time cemetery vandalism had already emerged in public as a new type of crime, *Helsingin Sanomat* published an article with a headline "FBI: Satanism is just an invented phenomenon" (*HS*, December 12, 1994). The article even included a statement given by the National Bureau of Investigation which confirmed that there is no evidence of Satanism in Finland.

Although news reports on Satanism were sparse during the following years, experts who had specialized in Satanism in particular made their appearance in public. The discourse of Satanism was dominated by views presented by these experts up until the turn of the millennium. A book which had a particular influence on this was *Saatananpalvonnan monet kasvot*, written by Keijo Ahorinta and published in 1997. The book became the first source of information on anything related to Satanism. Even before that there had been strongly religious redemption tales of those who had fallen into the clutches of Satanism but had since discovered Jesus (Rinne and Jääskeläinen 1994, Rinne 1996). The image of a solid connection between Satanism and crime was constructed mostly on the basis of these works, which approached the subject from a religious frame of reference.

There are still not many academic studies on the subject in Finland, and they have been introduced to the public even less. The previously mentioned memorandum on youth Satanism (a term used by Kuure himself) by Tapio Kuure is the only academic survey that has gained publicity in the mainstream media. The function of academic researchers in connection with news reporting on Satanism has been not so much to present the results of their studies, but to function as general commentators on the subject. In this role the views presented by academic researchers can be said to act as a certain kind of "sociological intervention" in increasing the sense of proportion of the parties participating in the discussion. Especially in comparison to the nightmare scenarios presented by experts with Christian views, the academic viewpoint has brought up alternative ways with which to interpret the phenomenon. The views based on social scientific research, which have received still more coverage in the media by the turn of the millennium, have quite possibly also influenced the way the media treats the connection between cemetery vandalism and Satanism. In the most recent articles, the cause-and-effect relationship has not been presented as the self-evident fact it used to be. At the time of writing of this paper it is still too early to point out the exact reason for this, and even more difficult to predict how permanent the change will be.

Religious Ethos and Religionization

Studying the relationship between action and ethos theoretically has been based on the concept of homology. A concept familiar from sociological language, homology refers to a correspondence which manifests itself between ethos, i.e., "internal orientation" (Lähteenmaa 1996:104), and action, i.e., external behavior. The theory was made well-known by the so-called Birmingham school in the late 1970s, especially in connection with youth subcultures. According to views presented by the later widely criticized Birmingham school, it can be specifically indicated that ethos is the guiding factor of actions (Lähteenmaa 1996:105). Transferring the theory into terminology used in the comparative study of religion, it can be said to signify a religious conviction of a certain group which manifests itself in, e.g., praying, giving alms, going to church, etc.

A strong homological connection has developed between cemetery vandalism and Satanism in the Finnish printed media. Cemetery vandalism, the action, has been usually seen as a consequence of Satanism, i.e., the ethos serving as a motivation. The connection between vandalism and Satanism has alternated from a strong, explicit connection to a weaker, almost nonexistent connection, possibly even questioning the theory. Except for the most recent news reports, the intensity of the connection has remained a choice of the journalist and the newspaper, at least on the headline level, in spite of the fact that in the article itself experts or other interviewed parties may have denied the connection. The discourse transmitting Satanic ethos in terms of critical discourse analysis has become a hegemonic way of comprehending the phenomenon of cemetery vandalism in the media (Fairclough 1995:38).This hegemonic view of cemetery vandalism on the media can be approached and criticized in two ways: First of all, by directing attention to the definitions of the problem itself, and secondly by directing attention to the definition process and the ones who define the problem. Like the Birmingham school theory on subcultures (Lähteenmaa 1996:105), reporting on cemetery vandalism can be primarily criticized because of the causal cause-and-effect relationship constructed in it between Satanism and the acts of vandalism that have taken place in cemeteries.

The way of reporting on Satanism can be criticized more widely as well because of the fact that it fails to distinguish between correlation and the cause-and-effect relationship. Even if the perpetrators admitted their interest in Satanism, as in some of the cases, it does not automatically mean that Satanism has been a motivation for the crime. In social scientific studies, actions and ethos are in general understood to be working in an interactive relationship, instead of an explicit cause-and-effect relationship (Lähteenmaa 1996:105). This is also the case with cemetery vandalism: it can be hypothetically argued that public discussion has given a name to the action which does not necessarily have any particular motivation. In other words, whereas car side mirrors could have been a target of vandalism earlier, now the same vandalism, which possibly has no explicit motivation, is exercised in cemeteries.

I use the term religionization for interpreting cemetery vandalism as an activity motivated by Satanism. By religionization I mean a definition process by which a phenomenon is constructed in a religious frame of reference. Religionization can be external or internal, depending on who defines the issue. Especially in the case of cemetery vandalism, where the actual motives for the actions often remain unsolved, the interpretation of the actions as being motivated by religious ethos is done by others than the perpetrators themselves. This is an example of external religionization.

The religionization of cemetery vandalism is related to the problems in the so-called typification process of social problems. Typification refers to the type of a social problem which is used to present the phenomenon (Best 1995b:8). The view according to which the problem appears as a consequence of religious ethos motivating a criminal lifestyle has become the mode of hegemonic typification of cemetery vandalism.

Religionization of the public discourse in Finland is clearly related to personal ethoses of the individuals who have been given expert status and the rhetoric originating from it. Religious arguments, were they explicit or implicit, have been presented in a remarkably uncritical manner as valid ways with which to interpret the phenomenon of cemetery vandalism. No doubt religious commentary has its place in a wider discussion, but especially the manner of speaking which portrays nightmare scenarios and mystifies the phenomenon has mostly replaced alternative interpretations because of its rhetoric qualities. A religionized discourse then classifies the problem as a moral one. Like anti-Satanist Keijo Ahorinta explicitly states, Satanism is a consequence of the youths' lack of ideals today, which is a distinctive feature of modern society ("A young person needs grown-ups, not Satan," *HS*, January 11, 1999). Also, the criticism aimed at the Finnish Evangelical Lutheran Church often comes from the inside ("Ex-Satanist visits schools to talk about values," *HS*, November 4, 1994).

It is ultimately a decision of journalists and newspapers who is given an expert status in the public discourse. In this regard the reason for the popularity of the religionized discourse can be found in the desire of the media to get a short, concise, and explicit explanation for cemetery vandalism. On the other hand, it is possible to find a crime wave-type phenomenon in news reports on crimes that have occurred in cemeteries, in which case a certain crime is established with a name and an explanation. In the material of this study the crime is cemetery vandalism and the explanation Satanism. When the explanation has gained sufficient ground in the media, similar crimes are associated with the same explanation even more promptly. This develops into a crime wave (Fishman 1998:68–69).

What is significant is that regardless of whether the crime waves brought up in the media correlate to actual level of crimes (or their motivations), they have real consequences. Crime waves cannot do any direct harm but they may inflict fear (Fishman 1998:53). Furthermore, they bring the chosen problem out into the open and thus make it easier to see that particular crime in the events that have taken place. This dynamic has also had an effect on the naturalization process of the connection between cemetery vandalism and Satanic ethos that has occurred in the media. In this situation it is, however, essential to realize the interactive nature of actions and ethos and instead of settling with a straightforward causal explanation, move to examine the interaction between all the involved parties: the youth, the media, experts, and the general public.

Notes

Abbreviations used
HS: *Helsingin Sanomat* (Finland's largest daily newspaper)
IL: *Iltalehti* (Tabloid)
IS: *Ilta-Sanomat* (Tabloid)

1) Throughout the article I will use the term Satanism, although the terms Satanism and Satan worshipping are used side by side in the Finnish news coverage. The media refer primarily to newspapers, but the results can be applied to TV news and documentaries made on the subject as well, naturally each with their own emphasis.
2) The discourse analyst Norman Fairclough employs the term "naturalization" when referring to processes in which one particular discourse becomes dominant, perhaps replacing all other discourses as a way of presentation. Such discourses appear as so-called "common sense" expressions. Fairclough 1989:91–93.
3) The news articles refer to the Satanism scares and the alleged Satanic child abuse in Britain at the turn of the 1990s that has been excellently documented by J.S. LaFontaine in her book *Speak of the Devil* (LaFontaine 1998).

References

Ahorinta, K. *Saatananpalvonnan monet kasvot*. Helsinki: LK-kirjat, 1997.
Arnold, C. *Spiritual Warfare*. London: Marshall Pickering, 1997.
Best, J. ed. *Images of Issues. Typifying Contemporary Social Problems*. New York: Aldine deGryuter, 1995a.
_____. "Typification and Social Problems Construction." In *Images of Issues. Typifying Contemporary Social Problems*, edited by J. Best, 3–10. New York: Aldine deGryuter, 1995b.

8. Religionizing Crime 197

Bodily, C. "Ageism and the Deployment of 'Age': A Constructionist Perspective." In *Constructing the Social*, edited by Theodore R. Sarbin & John I. Kitsuse, 174–194. London: Sage, 1994.
Bruun, M., I. Koskimies, and I. Tervonen. *Uutisoppikirja*. Helsinki: Tammi, 1986.
Chermak, S. "The Presentation of Drugs in the Media: The News Sources Involved in the Construction of Social Problems." In *Constructing Crime. Perspectives on Making News and Social Problems*, edited by G.W. Potter and V.E. Kappeler, 161–192. Prospect Heights, Illinois: Waveland Press, 1998.
Degh, L. What Is a Belief Legend? *Folklore* 107 (1996). 33–46.
Fairclough, N. *Language and Power*. London: Longman, 1989.
_____. *Critical Discourse Analysis*. London: Longman, 1995.
_____. *Media Discourse*. London: Edward Arnold, 1995.
Fishman, M. 1998 (1987). "Crime Waves as Ideology." In *Constructing Crime, Perspectives on Making News and Social Problems*, edited by G.W. Potter and V.E. Kappeler, 53–72. Prospect Heights, IL: Waveland Press, 1998.
Hicks, R.D. *In Pursuit of Satan. The Police and the Occult*. Buffalo, NY: Prometheus, 1989.
Hjelm, T. "The Making of a Media Panic, Satanism in the Finish Press." In *Beyond the Mainstream. The Emergence of Religious Pluralism in Finland, Estonia and Russia*, edited by J. Kaplan, 289–297. Studia Historica 63. Helsinki: SKS, 2000.
Kuure, T. NuorisoSatanismi ilmiönä Suomessa. A memorandum commissioned by the Finnish youth research network 30.8.1999. >http://www.alli.fi/nuorisotutkimus/nuoriso-www/index.html>, 1999.
LaFontaine, J.S. *Speak of the Devil, Tales of Satanic Abuse in Contemporary England*. Cambridge: Cambridge University Press, 1998.
Lowney, K.S., and J. Best. "Stalking Strangers and Lovers: Changing Media Typifications of New Crime Problem." In *Images of Issues. Typifying Contemporary Social Problems*, edited by J. Best, 33–57. New York: Aldine deGryuter, 1995.
Lähteenmaa, J. Alakulttuuriteorian nousu ja tuho? In *Näin nuoret. Näkökulmia nuoruuden kulttuureihin. Tietolipas 143*, edited by L. Suurpää & P. Aaltojärvi, 95–128. Helsinki: Suomalaisen kirjallisuuden seura, 1996.
Potter, G.W., and V.E. Kappeler. *Constructing Crime: Perspectives on Making News and Social Problems*. Prospect Heights, IL: Waveland Press, 1998.
Richardson, J. T., and J. Best, and D. Bromley, (eds.) *The Satanism Scare*. New York: Aldine deGryuter, 1991.
Rikkinen, M. "The Christian Frame of Reference in the Interpretation of Satanism." In *Beyond the Mainstream: The Emergence of Religious Pluralism in Finland, Estonia and Russia*, edited by J. Kaplan, 299–307. Studia Historica 63. Helsinki. SKS, 2000.
Rinne, R. *Pimeys väistyy*. Helsinki: Kuva ja sana, 1996.
_____ and Jääskeläinen. *Syvyyden kuilusta*. Helsinki: Kuva ja Sana, 1994.
Thompson, J.B. *Media and Modernity. A Social Theory of the Media*. Cambridge: Polity Press, 1995.
Spector, M., and J.I. Kitsuse. *Constructing Social Problems*. 1977. Reprint, New Brunswick: Transaction, 2001.

Victor, J. *Satanic Panic. The Creation of a Contemporary Legend.* Chicago: Open Court, 1993.
Wright, S. "Media Coverage of Unconventional Religion: Any 'Good News' for Minority Faiths? *Review of Religious Research* (1997). 101–115.

9

There's No Place Like Home.html

Neopaganism on the Internet

ALYSSA BEALL

It's August 1, the Wiccan holiday known as Lammas or Lughansad. In a religious calendar based on agricultural and fertility cycles, Lammas signals the change between summer and fall, from planting and growing to harvest. What are Wiccans doing on this holiday? Some will gather in ritual groups or covens to perform a variety of rituals; some solitary Wiccans will cast circles in their homes; still others will sign on to the Internet to discuss what an agricultural festival means in this day and age, or how to define the term "nature":

> We are of nature.
> We create things.
> What we create is thus in the scope of nature using what nature provided us in the first place.
> This is why all places and things have an element of the sacred to me — their form now is simply different now than it was, and different now than it will be.[1]

This statement brings together several of the ideas I will address in this article: That "nature" can mean different things to different people, and that discussing these ideas on the internet can be, for some Neopagans, an important form of participation in the religion.

Online communication has served as a huge part of my own participation in Wicca. In 1993, I discovered the internet and although some people I knew had been using it for several years, it was not a widespread phenomenon. When one of my roommates signed up for AOL, I was fascinated and spent hours online while he was in class. At the time, AOL was an almost self-contained world; not many people used it for internet access but rather they used it for the different bulletin boards and chat rooms.

Early on, I found a chat room called Pagan Tea House. At the time, "Pagan" meant nothing to me aside from the standard definition of "non–Christian," but after my first night chatting I was well aware there was something else going on: a nature-based religion that seemed to fit in with what I already believed. Over the next few months in Pagan Tea House, I chatted with a variety of people, received book recommendations, and eventually set up meetings with Wiccans in my area. Since I wanted to learn more about the religion and perhaps join a local coven, I had high hopes for these meetings. Unfortunately, none of the in-person meetings went very well, and I soon gave up the idea of practicing with a group.

This lead me back to the internet for information about solitary practice. Many of the people in Pagan Tea House practiced the religion alone, and we would discuss the benefits and drawbacks of being solitary Wiccans. When I moved to an area that had many more Wiccans, namely, Berkeley, California, I tried again to find a group, but again found that I preferred solitary practice.

During this period, I discovered that Wicca was a very diverse religion, and meeting people who had the same ideas about it as I did — ideas based very much on a scientific understanding of the world — was more difficult than I expected. For example, my view of the God and Goddess as personifications of natural forces — rather than as "deities" — met with resistance from some other Wiccans. Eventually I met a few friends and would occasionally do two-person rituals, but the bulk of my interaction came from online sources.

The Neopagan religion in general was, of course, growing steadily over these years. Wicca, as the most well-known of the Neopagan religions, was getting more and more coverage both in the news and in publishing. By the time I moved to Syracuse, seven years after I had started learning about Wicca, it was no longer uncommon to run into people who knew what it was, or practiced themselves. Around this time I also became involved with a bulletin board of about 30 people, several of whom were Neopagan. Since this board was not related in any way to the religion, I was fascinated by the fact that so many people on a "random" site were practitioners. Although I've met only one of them in person, the group regularly shares holiday celebrations, discussions, rituals and spell work online. While continuing to practice as a "solitary Witch," I also consider this group my unofficial coven; more recently, I have started my own board to discuss issues of science, nature, and Neopaganism.

All of this has sparked my interest in the formation of online communities in general, and in Neopagan communities more specifically. From the beginning, most of my information on Wicca has come from the internet; almost all of my interaction with other Wiccans has been online as well. Yet, Wicca is, at heart, a religion about nature: the holidays follow the cycles of the seasons, and the tenets are based in worship of natural forces. How does one take these basic ideas and get to a flourishing of the religion in cyberspace?

Neopaganism on the Internet

In movies and on TV, a "witch" is usually a young, sexy, well-dressed woman, fighting the forces of evil. Some Wiccans, I should clarify, do refer to themselves as Witches, depending on how they practice the religion and on their personal preference. The word is difficult, however, when trying to go back and forth between pop culture references and religious identification. Throughout most of this paper I have used "Neopagan" as the general term, and "Wiccan" when discussing more specific groups and people. Yet even in popular culture, witches and computers have overlapped: In its first season, *Buffy the Vampire Slayer* took a character raised in a "gypsy" family and combined her Romanian roots with a love for technology. As the character, Jenny Calendar, put it: "You think the realm of the mystical is limited to ancient texts and relics? That bad old science made the magic go away? The divine exists in cyberspace same as out here."[2] It is with the introduction of Jenny Calendar that the more traditionalist modes of presenting witchcraft become most clearly laced with contemporary notions. Jenny tells Giles that she is a "technopagan" and is part of a coven that meets online. It is her group which helps remove a medieval demon, Moloch the Corrupter, from the Web after he was uploaded during a library scanning session ("I Robot, You Jane," 1008). Jenny's computer skills help update the concepts of magic used in the show (Krxywinska 2002:187).

Because portrayals of Neopagans in the general media have contributed to a greater general awareness of this particular new religious movement, the addition of a technopagan to the mix was an interesting sign of the times. In reality, the sheer numbers of Neopagans online seems almost contradictory on the surface, as Neopaganism is, at base, a self-proclaimed "nature religion." How, and why, does a nature religion end up booming on the internet? It appears, as I will discuss below, that the internet is not simply a tool for the spread of the religion, but has become one of the primary ways Neopagans choose to both connect and practice. In addition, what constitutes "nature" is up for debate, depending on which Neopagans one speaks with. The internet itself is considered an entirely natural phenomenon by a portion of Neopagan practitioners.

Here I will explore the rise of Neopaganism on the internet by looking at three related topics: First, I delineate the makeup of the Neopagan population online, including identification with the feminist movement, activism, and general socioeconomic characteristics. Second, I will explore new studies on Pagan festivals. Emphasis on festival "time," information exchange, and issues of safety and community serve as parallels to the space of the internet and its role for Pagans. The correlations between festivals and the internet help to explain why the internet has become so popular in Neopagan circles. Third and more theoretically, I will show how the internet itself functions as an analogy for the overall worldview of Neopaganism.

The Neopagan Population

Obtaining accurate numbers of practicing Neopagans is a difficult task. Many Neopagans are still "in the broom closet" for a variety of reasons, including safety, which I will address below. Surveys that ask people to identify their religious preference seem to often end up inaccurate regarding this particular religious population. Several online surveys have attempted to come up with percentages, but these are skewed by several factors, including the diversity such a study would be able to encompass. ReligiousTolerance.org has been one of the sites exploring the growth of Neopaganism as well as the reasons numbers are difficult to come by. Commenting on the American Religious Identification Survey (ARIS) of 2001, Religious Tolerance.org states that:

> Some heavily oppressed and discriminated against groups, like Wiccans and other Neopagans, often refuse to reveal their religion to a stranger over the telephone because of safety concerns. So, the actual number of Wiccans is probably much larger than the survey indicates. In the ARIS study of 1990, 2.3% of those contacted refused to disclose their religion. In the 2001 survey, the number had grown to 5.4%. The latter number represents over 11 million adults. The reason for this increase in desire for secrecy is unknown."[3]

The implication here is that part of this large increase — more than double the numbers between 1990 and 2001— in the "refuse to state" category is tied to similarly increasing numbers of Neopagans. This, of course, cannot be proved, but must be taken into account as a possibility.

The categories used in this study are confusing on the surface, and are part of the problem in obtaining accurate numbers. As a result of the 2001 survey, ARIS estimates 134,000 Wiccans and 140,000 Pagans in the United States. However, as ReligiousTolerance.org points out, "many Wiccans describe themselves as Pagans. So, the number of Wiccans is probably larger than indicated."[4] The study was then expanded to include both self-identified religious practitioners and an "estimated refusal to disclose," leading ARIS to estimate "the number of Wiccans at 408,000 adults, making it the seventh largest organized religion in the United States."[5]

An earlier estimate by writer Eric Davis states,

> Though hard figures are difficult to find, estimates generally peg their [Pagan] numbers in the US at 100,000 to 300,000. They are almost exclusively white folks drawn from bohemian and middle-class enclaves. A startling number of Pagans work and play in technical fields, as sysops, computer programmers, and network engineers.[6]

Considering the time lapse of about five years between Davis' estimate and the ARIS study, the numbers seem about accurate. However, in this statement Davis brings up other points which should be considered in Neopagan demographics: race, class, and employment. Davis was not the first to point out the unusual number of Neopagans in technical or computer-based fields: Margot Adler, in the 1986 edition of *Drawing Down the Moon*, generalized from her own interviews and experiences with the Neopagan population to state that "a striking number of Neo-Pagans worked in scientific and technical fields, and all felt there was absolutely no conflict between their scientific work and their belief in, or use of, magic" (Adler [1979] 1986: 385). This is part of the apparent paradox of perceived "nature religion" and use of the most current technology within groups of Neopagans: how does one hold a scientific worldview and yet believe in magic? As I will discuss further in my final section, these two ideas are not as far apart as an outsider would generally perceive them to be. When "magic" is thought of as manipulation of natural forces — energy — then science and Neopagan practice are extremely compatible. Without further study of the Neopagan population, the idea of a proportionally large number of "techies" must remain a theory; however, the race and class estimates lend it some credence as well, especially as these figures relate to computer and internet use.

A study by the National Communications and Information Administration titled "Falling Through the Net: Defining the Digital Divide" used data from the 1998 census to explore which class and race groups are most likely to have both home computers and internet access:

> The 1998 data reveal significant disparities, including the following: Urban households with incomes of $75,000 and higher are more than twenty times more likely to have access to the Internet than rural households at the lowest income levels, and more than nine times as likely to have a computer at home. Whites are more likely to have access to the Internet from home than Blacks or Hispanics have from any location.

Black and Hispanic households are approximately one-third as likely to have home Internet access as households of Asian/Pacific Islander descent, and roughly two-fifths as likely as White households. Regardless of income level, Americans living in rural areas are lagging behind in Internet access. Indeed, at the lowest income levels, those in urban areas are more than twice as likely to have Internet access than those earning the same income in rural areas.[7]

If, then, the middle-class white American trend in Neopaganism holds true, the likelihood that Neopagans have at least greater access to computers and the internet follows from this study on race and class divisions. These divisions of race, class, and socioeconomic status must be taken into account in any study of Neopaganism, especially one that involves the use of the internet in religious practice.

Neopagan Community

Although I and the authors I use above have put Neopagans into certain categories — white middle class or those with jobs in the field of technology — Neopagans are also significantly outside the perceived American "norm," in several ways. Part of the ideology is an openness toward a variety of lifestyles and choices, as well as a lack of binding rules within the religion itself. As Margot Adler notes in *Drawing Down the Moon*, "Neo-Paganism, from its inception, has been less authoritarian, less dogmatic, less institutionalized, less filled with father figures, and less tied to institutions and ideas dominated by males" (Adler [1979] 1986: 208). An obvious part of Adler's point is that Neopaganism is often understood in contrast to mainstream Christianity, and to accepted social-religious behavior, although some versions of Christianity, of course, have their own movements with ideas similar to Neopagan ideas of equality, antihierarchy, and the like. Although not exclusive in this regard, this deviation from the "norm" is a central aspect of Neopaganism which can be seen in many guises, including issues of sexuality and gender roles.

In *A Community of Witches: Contemporary Neo-Paganism and Witchcraft in the United States*, Helen Berger draws a parallel between the lesbian community and the Neopagan community, saying that both "are defined by their participants' position outside of the mainstream, sharing a life world, and participating in some aspect of politics" (Berger 1999: 66). Both the lesbian community and the Neopagan community rely on concepts of safety *within their group*, as well as a recognition they rarely receive in outside society. The Neopagan or lesbian identity which is usually concealed or set aside in daily life can be embraced within the group. "Both lesbians and Witches are marginal groups within the culture; their members often keep their identity hidden" (Berger 1999: 68). There are, of course, overlaps between the two communities. As Sarah Pike points out,

> Neopagan festivals are one of the few public contexts where gay and lesbian relationships are affirmed and celebrated. Gay, lesbian, and bisexual [and a few transgendered] people made up a sizable and visible minority at every festival I attended.... While heterosexuals make up the majority of festival goers, heterosexuality is less emphasized as the norm in the Neopagan community than it is by most Americans [Pike 2002: 84].

While this overlap is important overall, it is the ideal of community that Berger sets forth for both groups that is most applicable to my focus on the internet. Neopagan and lesbian groups are, she says, different *kinds* of community from what we typically expect. "Both the Neopagan and homosexual communities have permeable boundaries. People may be considered members who do not have face-to-face interaction and who, in fact, do not know one another" (Berger 1999:69). Berger attributes this change in the makeup of community partly to internet technology, saying that it has created "an interactive national community, even if not always on a face-to-face basis ... this medium provides a venue for people to exchange ideas, make contact, and learn about the resources within the larger community" (Berger 1999:69).

While many other groups participate in online communities, there are particular issues that make the internet extremely attractive to Neopagans. Some of these issues are related to Berger's idea of being "outside the mainstream": anonymity, safety, flexible gender boundaries. A second set of issues are more intimately related to the Neopagan world view: interconnectivity and magic. To discuss the first, I will turn to the recent material on Neopagan festivals and show how the use of the internet reflects many of the same ideals found in these gatherings. For the second, I will discuss Neopagan Web use in general, and specifically the ideas that a variety of groups have put forth about the use of the internet as a manifestation of Neopagan religion.

Neopagan Festivals

All over the world, Neopagans gather to celebrate holidays, exchange information, and connect with other like-minded people. These gatherings range from small and local to large and nationwide; some of the largest can span several days and bring together thousands of people.

Some of the most recent books on Neopaganism have focused on specific groups and on the idea of festivals. Sarah Pike's *Earthly Bodies, Magical Selves* and Helen Berger's *A Community of Witches* look at the growth of specific communities in different geographical areas. Each of these books has a focus on "festival time," gatherings of Neopagans in areas outside their usual lives. It is my contention that the internet acts as a similar type of "space" for Neopagans as festivals do. The internet is similar to the liminal space of festivals, but is generally easier to access. When cyberspace is seen in the context of festival space/time, the growth of the religion on the internet makes a great deal of sense, because the same things which draw Neopagans to festivals are found in internet communities.

To explore these parallels, I will look at several different functions of Neopagan festival space/time: First, they are a place to exchange information of all kinds, ritual and philosophical ideas included. This can lead to the formation of ongoing friendships that continue both in future festival space and in the outside world. Second, they are a place in which it is generally "safe" to be Pagan, at least in theory. Third, the festival provides a way to change from "normal time" to "sacred time." I will address each of these functions in festival context and show how each can be related to the idea of online practice as well. It would also seem that internet use is contributing to the growth of the festival scene, by being a venue in which particular types of information can easily be accessed by those interested.

Information Exchange

The exchange of information at Neopagan festivals is extremely important. This exchange includes everything from dates of other festivals to workshops of various kinds, to intense philosophical conversations a practitioner might not get to have in the "normal" world. In the introduction to *Earthly Bodies, Magical Selves*, Sarah Pike states that:

> Festivals make available the material for creating ... new identities. At festivals, self-creation takes place within and alongside group activities: workshops on astrology, tarot cards, mythology, magic, witchcraft, Native American medicine, African drumming, large rituals, and late-night bonfires. Most of the workshops and rituals focus on healing and self-improvement "techniques" as well as the myths and beliefs of diverse world cultures [Pike 2002: xiii].

These are some of the very basic aspects of interaction which are not frequently available in the outside world, especially for solitary practitioners.

Festivals serve as networking time for Neopagans, allowing them to form new relationships and share information. People who want to share their knowledge or techniques lead workshops on standard topics such as astral projection, writing rituals, drumming, ritual dance, song, crystal magic, and healing through herbs. Some workshops are organized to discuss a topic of interest or concern, such as how to raise a Pagan child in the mundane world, coming out of the broom closet to your family and friends, Witches and technology, or the feasibility of creating an ongoing Pagan village or living site. Dialogues begun at these workshops are often discussed further in journals and newsletters and on the internet.

It is important to again note here that these are the topics Neopagans often cannot discuss in the outside world. Based on her "Pagan Census" Berger estimates that 42 percent of Neopagans had attended one or more festivals in the previous year, a number far greater than the earlier estimate by Margot Adler of 10 percent.

Whether or not the percentage of Neopagans attending festivals has grown by the estimated 32 percent—most Neopagans I know have *not* attended a festival—some of the information and relationships started at festivals are, as Berger points out, continued in the larger frame of the internet. Web sites for festivals serve both as informational (giving times and places for future festivals) and as community pages. Circle Sanctuary (www.circle-sanctuary.org) is hosting 11 different festivals in 2003, including the Pagan Spirit Gathering, one of the largest Neopagan festivals in the United States.

One of the main ways the Circle Sanctuary Web site functions to help bring people into festivals is by providing lists of Frequently Asked Questions (FAQs), guidelines for behavior, site maps, and "what to bring" lists. A large "memories" page[8] also allows newcomers and past participants to see what has gone on at the festival in the past. Included are photos, a history of the site, and personal experiences.

> I met the man who was to become my husband at that 1989 PSG and we conceived our first child while we were there. We have all been together for a decade and another little girl has joined us since. I cannot guarantee these exact results for everyone, but festival experiences are life-shaping. Many people will agree with me that you are never the same after your first gathering. How could you be? If you've felt odd in a world that doesn't make sense, you may feel that you have come home, that you once again have found your long-lost family.[9]

These ideas of homecoming and belonging, of transforming life, are found in many of the "testimonies" about festivals. The majority of these memory pages have e-mail links, by which one can contact the author of the piece. In this way, along with the variety of information, the internet is making it more likely new people will attend future Neopagan festivals.

However, aside from gaining new attendees, these sites function as community areas as well. Circle Sanctuary hosts a Pagan Academic Network and the Lady Liberty League, which "formed in response to the growing number of calls and letters to Circle concerning religious freedom difficulties. It is a referral network of volunteers affiliated with Circle Network interested in helping out with Wiccan/Pagan/Nature Spirituality religious freedom cases."[10] Reports from these groups are available online, making them accessible to the entire Neopagan community and not just those who attend the festivals or belong to the Circle Sanctuary group.

In her research on festivals, Pike also noted the exchanges which take place in the areas set aside for sales of ritual tools and other objects. These merchants rows were the places Pike felt initially most comfortable as a stranger to the festival scene:

> When veteran festival goers gathered at their friends' campsites, I sought out the ever-available merchants for company and conversation. In this way, like many other newcomers, I was gradually brought into the festival community by merchants introducing me to their friends and customers [Pike 2001: 80–81].

Here I see a "real-world" analogy, that of the New Age-type bookstore commonly found in larger towns across the United States. These often serve as jumping points into Neopagan communities, as they provide some workshops and meeting places as well as information. However, at these types of stores the interaction is usually limited; as a practicing Witch I personally feel uncomfortable in most of these stores, perhaps because they are heavily commercialized. This seems to fit with Pike's impression of merchant's row as somewhere to move on from rather than a place where veterans of the festival scene gather.

Similarly, commercial sites on the internet can serve as an introduction to other sites and groups. For example, Magickware (http://www.magickware.com/) sells a variety of ritual tools, touting itself as a place which

> provides the tools you need for witchcraft spells and rituals in Wicca, witchcraft, Santeria, and any of the occult arts, and earth-centered pagan religions. Here you will find herbs, essential oils, herbal incense, spell kits [love spells, protection spells, prosperity spells, Wiccan spells and more], ritual candles, glass candle holders, mojo bags, bath salts, Wiccan altar supplies, gemstones, Celtic and Wiccan jewelry including Celtic knot designs and pagan symbols, crystal balls, god and goddess statues, pagan supplies, occult tools, metaphysical books and more.

However, like many of these online stores, Magickware is also a gateway site to a nonmerchant site, in this case Branwen's Cauldron, a place to find "resources and opportunities for discovering and sharing knowledge about Wicca, witchcraft, spellcraft, shamanism, the occult and any of the Earth religions and magickal traditions."[11] Much like the festival merchant space, the sale of practical items is a jumping point into an extensive Pagan community.

The overall point here is that the internet has accomplished several different things as relates to information exchange. At the most simplistic level, it has increased the numbers of people who can find out about different festivals, and has probably in part led to the increase in attendance at those festivals. Secondly, the internet parallels the festival atmosphere in both type and variety of information exchange; it is easy to begin at a merchant-sales site and move further into the Neopagan community from that jumping point. Finally, the internet allows access to parts of the community which formerly were available only to those attending festivals, such as the Pagan Academic Network at Circle Sanctuary.

Issues of Safety and Acceptance

The relative safety of festival space for Neopagans also has parallels to online Pagan communities, in several different ways. Ideally, festival time not only serves as a way to be Pagan without fear of repercussions, but also as a place where gender and sexuality are less structured. In discussing these aspects of festivals, I will demonstrate how these ideas are also applicable to online settings, and can in some instances take the ideas to a new level, allowing for a *choice* of gender, for example.

While numbers of Neopagans in the United States are increasing, the religion itself is still less than fully accepted by society in general. To speak generally, any new religious movement (NRM) is usually portrayed in a negative light by the media; Neopaganism is no exception. In a collection of articles titled *Sex, Religion, Media*, Herman R. Foushee Jr. discusses the coverage of NRMs, including the Church of Wicca. He summarizes his findings by saying:

> NRM's are characterized as criminal, manipulative, and surrounded by controversy. References to New Religious Movements are more often negative than positive in tenor. The term "cult" is often used as pejorative label for New Religious Movements. Thus, New Religious Movements are portrayed as being deviant and sometime dangerous without any reference to social history [Foushee 2002: 155–156].

The specifics Foushee discusses are particularly applicable to this section of the paper, although it is difficult to separate out which groups are being portrayed negatively or positively in his study. Since the study includes groups like the Branch Davidians, it is easy to see how the results might be skewed by the inclusion of this particular group. It should, however, be noted that Foushee separates out coverage of Satanism from the articles on NRMs.

As the title of his article "Cult Sex" suggests, deviant sexuality is a primary concern; included are issues child sex abuse, polygamy, abstinence, and open sex partners. Far more surprising are his statistics about "calls for consequences":

> Almost four-fifths of the news articles [122 of 154] called for some consequence for the NRM. More than three times as many articles contained negative consequences than positive ones, 78% versus 21%, respectively. The negative consequences often involved prosecution of NRM members, the NRM's breakup, and making recruitment more difficult.

Using a news article search, however, proves interesting as an example of Foushee's theories.[12] The hits include an article "Ministers oppose gay camp: Prayer vigil set March 5 in Pollock" about a prayer vigil against the gathering of "radical faeries"—a Neopagan gay movement.[13] The overlap in this particular article between homosexuality, "nature religion," and safety for those involved is one topic of primary concern in publications on Neopagan festivals, and I will return to this article below.

Given the general negativity in the media, festival times certainly serve as places where being Neopagan is "safe" and accepted. Berger says that Neopagans "often live and work in communities in which their religious affiliation is either not known or is considered an oddity. They therefore enjoy being in a group in which they are practicing the 'state religion' even for a short time" (Berger 1999: 75). This aspect of the festival is also addressed by Pike, who says:

> Neopagans attend festivals to experience a sense of belonging to a community, but it is in part their experience of marginality that unifies them. Festivals become meaningful places as extensions of participants' own feelings of marginality. Many Neopagans see themselves as social outcasts and the Neopagan lifestyle as a rebellion against mainstream society. The separateness of festivals allows for a community-wide recognition and a communal self-affirmation of Neopagan marginality and its historical roots [Pike 2001: 31].

Pike cites several general problems Neopagans face in what she calls "mundania," that is, time and space outside festival.

One of the main areas of concern, religiously, is the critique of Neopagan religion and lifestyle put forth by conservative Christian groups. Some of these groups, she says, make Neopaganism one of several focal points [abortion is another] for conservative Christian critiques of contemporary American life and morality. Critics of Neopaganism range from Pentecostal ministers and conservative Protestant political lobbyists to Catholic priests and followers of Marian visions. They include southern Baptists who attacked an Arkansas occult bookstore, Pentecostal church members in southern Indiana who showered Bible tracts on ELF members worshipping the Yellowwood forest, and conservative Catholic writers who instruct their readers to avoid the danger of Satanism in its New Age and Neopagan guises [Pike 2001: 95].

What Pike does not add here is that, with the population of Neopagans heavily pro-choice as well, they fall into Pike's "other" focal group, making them doubly problematic to conservative Christians. For example, a page called The Champion[14] is subtitled "Witchcraft and Abortion" and lists articles "as a warning to Christians who stand for the sanctity of life. There are a small segment of Wiccans who practice abortion as a form of child sacrifice to their false gods." Citing the fact that several abortion clinics have Wiccans on their payroll and that Wiccan newsletters have encouraged Wiccans to act as escorts at Planned Parenthood, The Champion not only addresses the connection between Wicca and abortion, but goes further in saying that some Wiccans actively promote child sacrifice:

> [T]here is a strong connection between the Aware Woman abortion clinic and a cult of witches called Wicca. As we view the ties between the Wiccan organization and the abortion industry, the conclusion will become obvious: The promotion of abortion is not just a political issue for members of Wicca; it is part of a religious agenda — the religion of witchcraft and child sacrifice.[15]

The editor of the page says he has received many e-mails from Wiccans explaining that child sacrifice is *not* part of Wicca, but apparently continues to be concerned.

Another aspect of this safety and acceptance relates back to the concerns over "alternative sexualities" shown in Foushee's study of NRM-related media articles. Participants feel that they can be their "real selves" in the festival families they have chosen. They can dress as they please, worship foreign goddesses and gods, explore their sexuality, and express their sexual orientation as they are unable to do in their given families. Festivals also make possible a community space where political organization around issues of religious and sexual freedom or "alternative" families can take place. Starwood XIV (1994) offered workshops on "The Path of Polyamoury" and "Dysfunctional Families and Group Energies: The Gaia Conspiracy," and Pagan Spirit Gathering 1992 held workshops on "Bisexual Spirit, Bisexual Pride" and "Out of the Broom Closet: An Open Discussion of Craft

Homosexuality."[12] At festival I witnessed gay as well as straight handfastings, and a handfasting between two men and a woman. In the festival setting, invented families are a haven from the struggles of daily life, and they call into question accepted norms such as heterosexuality and monogamy (Pike 2001: 34). Since the worldview of Neopaganism allows for a variety of sexuality — a variety often frowned upon in mundania — it is not surprising that this manifests in the safe space of the festival.

Festival space as safe space is not always the case, however, as Pike details in a chapter titled "The Great Evil that is in Your Backyard." "As a result of unfounded rumors that they are carrying out satanic ritual, festival goers are harassed by neighbors and members of local churches; festival sites are vandalized by teenagers and searched late at night by local police" (Pike 2001: 87). This was seen in the previously mentioned news article on the Radical Faerie gathering: a similar gathering place called Camp Sister Spirit is mentioned:

> Violence against homosexuals occurred several years ago at a gay-friendly camp called Camp Sister Spirit, located in Ovett, Miss., near the city of Laurel. It is similar to Manitou Woods. Andrea Gibbs, Camp Sister Spirit's caretaker, said that when the camp opened 10 years ago, she and others associated with it were terrorized in a variety of ways. "We were shot at, run off the road, had acetylene bombs set off, had a car set on fire and rolled into our woods, dead animals [placed] at out gate," Gibbs said.[16]

Going to Camp Sister Spirit's Web site (www.campsistersspirit.com), it is interesting to note that many Neopagan festivals have taken place there, including Circle Celebration, one of the larger gatherings each year.

Being Neopagan on the internet — like attending a Neopagan festival — is still a relatively safe bet for those who feel uncomfortable with the repercussions in daily life, or those who cannot find a group near them. Kindlebee, a practicing Witch raised in a reformed Jewish household, says

> I have longed to find a good coven but don't think that would be easy.... I went to two pagan community meetings and just didn't connect to anyone. Most of the people were older and not particularly intelligent or interesting.... What I didn't like about that meeting was that no one seemed to want to talk about their beliefs or practices. And for me that was the whole point.[17]

While she still considers herself basically solitary, Kindlebee has recently ("within the last year") started to connect with other Neopagans on the internet. She has participated in one online ritual, and has been looking for ideas relating to ritual work:

I sometimes surf the net nowadays for spell ideas, and holiday celebration ideas. Some of the wicca/witchcraft sites that are interactive have seemed way too fantasy-oriented for me, "Hi my name is Crystal Cave and the goddess Lemshmknistrua called to me 10 years ago. I do shapeshifting and my power color is red..." etc. Gak!!![18]

Much like the festival arena, for Kindlebee the internet allows for an expression of religion which may not be ideal in outside life. "I am still 'in the closet' to a large extent. I only freely admit to being a witch [on a bulletin board], and to my boyfriend, his mom, his brother ... and a few close friends ... I mean *nobody* really knew until this year!!"[19]

There are, however, a variety of internet sites warning against the practice of Neopaganism, while chat rooms and bulletin boards set up for Neopagans (either permanent or transitory) are also fair game for those outside the religion. Although Neopagans on the internet are in less danger of personal harassment, the internet is not always a completely safe space. Neopagan chat rooms are regularly the target for "flamers," people who come in either to witness about another religion or accuse the chat participants of various things. In a Yahoo! chat room recently, I was surprised by the lack of this type of interruption, and asked if this was generally a "safe" place to chat. The responses were immediate, and all to the effect of "just wait."

On bulletin boards where Neopaganism is discussed, there are similar issues. In my own experience of boards where there is a mix of religions, Neopagan topics rarely go without negative comments, especially in the current political and religious climate of the United States.

> I have also been involved in discussions that take a rather anti-pagan stance, [although] whether they are harassment or not is foggy. Recently, during the debate about "God" being in the pledge of Alliegange [sic], I had several individuals tell me to just suck it up and say it anyway, which I refuse to do.[20]

Similarly, another Neopagan said she felt uncomfortable online "Particularly after the 9/11 thing. [I] kept hearing about being 'one of those' who was responsible for the whole thing happening because of my lifestyle choices that are abhorred by God."[21] These particular comments relate back to Pike's assertion that a great deal of harassment is tied to a conservative Christian segment who view Neopaganism as a threat to society.

There has been a great deal of research on alternative sexuality and flexible gender boundaries on the internet (Shade 2002). While a detailed survey of these texts is outside the possible scope of this paper, there are two issues I will briefly address, as they parallel the festival scene. Most obvious is the idea that one must self-identify gender while online; a person can choose to be female or male. "One of the more curious gender-bending practices that occurs is that a surprising number of men masquerade as women to seduce other men. While I've spoken to a few gay men who've tried this, more than a few straight men have become female for awhile to experiment with other men" (McRae 1996:249). The internet is, it would seem, a space to experiment sexually, in ways that a person might not attempt in normal life. In fact, an example like this shows something which would (at some point in the sex act) be impossible to carry off outside the realm of the internet.

The second point comes directly from my own research: the survey I posted on a small religion board was subsequently crossposted to at least two other places. I only noticed this when I began getting e-mails with "polyamory families" in the subject heading. Although all the boards the survey was posted to were small — and I expected few responses — at least half ended up being from the Polyamory board. My questions had not included alternative sexuality or families, but apparently the Neopagan population on this board was sizable.

Whether it is "in real life" or online, many Neopagans feel uncomfortable about being open about their religious choices. One quote from a recent e-mail aptly summarizes the issue of being "out":

> I have this bumper sticker that says "Witches' Parking Only: Others will be Toad." I taped it on the inside of my car window. I take it off whenever I have any dealings with the seller of the house I want to buy, because I don't want him to cancel the contract. So you might say that I have some internalized caution/censorship or just maybe a realistic sense of people's ignorance.[22]

It would be difficult to prove whether this concern is warranted or not. However, with the instances already discussed of violence against Neopagans in festival space, harassment is an ongoing concern for many Neopagans.

Normal Time and Sacred Time

One aspect of festival life researchers have focused on is the separation established between normal time/space — what Pike calls "mundania, and sacred time/space." At festivals, this delineation is quite obvious: one enters the festival site and is separated from the "normal" world. Within this boundary are a variety of other boundaries — specific rituals, specific places within any given festival site, and specific times. Even though some spaces within festival sites are "more related" to mundania than others (the merchants' row, for one), there is a clear division between the outside world and the festival space.

> Festivals become places separated from the everyday world not only because of their physical settings, but primarily because of the ways in which festival goers perceive them. Throughout festivals, participants work to make an experience set apart from their lives "back home." They create place myths: composites of rumors, images, and experiences that make particular places fascinating [Pike 2001: 21].

This delineation of time and space cannot be separated from the idea of *having a space* which I have discussed above — a space in which alternative groups can feel, for a time, as if they are part of a larger community. The spaces are made sacred, to some degree, because they signal a separation from the issues of mundania — these are places and times where it is "normal" to be Neopagan.

Similarly, most Neopagan Web sites make an attempt at a different "mood" on the internet. Many sites make full use of images and music to evoke a "separate" space: one example is "Wicca 101 @ Red Deer and Elenya's" (http://www.unc.edu/~reddeer/), which has an interesting gateway/home page. The design is based on a leaf-covered page, with a stone archway, burning sconces, and the message "Blessed Be to all who enter here...." The site is accompanied by Celtic music, and within the archway is an animated view of the current moon phase. The overall effect is much different from a basic information page; it attempts to create a "feeling" of sacred and separate space. These ideas lead quite naturally into a more detailed discussion of how the internet can be seen as a manifestation of the Neopagan world view.

Time and Space: The Internet as Worldview

After looking at similarities between Neopagan festivals and internet use, some of the specifics regarding the internet have already been covered: safety issues, flexible gender and sexuality boundaries, community formation, and sacred time/place. The similarities between "festival time" and "internet time" are important for showing *what* Neopagans use the Web for, but they do not fully explain *why* Neopagans use the Web in the first place.

With all this research on festivals and real-life events, the Web might seem to take second place to physical practice. It is my contention, however, that internet use is popular among this religious group because the internet itself both reflects and encompasses the Neopagan worldview. The third section of this paper will demonstrate that "the net" or "the Web" has been accepted and taken in by Neopagans because they see the very concepts behind it as extensions or demonstrations of their religious worldview.

Technology and Religion

The idea that advances in technology affect the worldview and practice of different religious groups is not a new concept. The most common example of this is the use of the printing press and subsequent changes to Christianity. As Brenda Brasher points out in *Give Me That Online Religion*,

> Little was it expected that the popularization of this communication technology would transform European religion, yet that is precisely what happened. As the printing press made the information formerly limited to rare and expensive texts more available and affordable, the fledgling industry gave birth to a new, more inclusive public [Brasher 2001: 14].

Similar changes in religious traditions can be seen with the introduction of television, radio, and films. To say, then, that the internet will affect religious traditions in different ways and at different levels is not a gigantic leap.

Brasher goes on to point out that the revolution of the printing press did more than simply make the text more available: it paved the way for religious dissent and change within the tradition.

> Before the technology of the printing press became widespread, religious authority in a mostly Christian Europe was solidly anchored in the hierarchically organized Roman Catholic Church. What was acceptably religious and what constituted heresy — the main building blocks of religion — was decided by religious authorities and trickled down to the populace on a need-to-know basis. With the advent of the printing press, Luther and other Christian dissidents had the means to challenge conventional religious norms — means that Luther, especially, exploited to the fullest [Brasher 2001: 15].

Brasher rightly questions whether one can attribute the changes in Christianity to the technology or to a reforming personality taking advantage of the technology, but both these options are relevant to a discussion of the Neopagan movement. Both aspects — the technology and the embrace of it — have occurred in the last decade with the internet and Neopaganism.

In fact, though Neopaganism is ostensibly a new religious movement, the use of media has been present in the tradition since the beginning. There are two aspects to explore here: First, the use of "new" media by Neopagan groups throughout their history to spread community: 'zines, a movement of home-produced, widely distributed magazines, were incredibly popular in the Neopagan community just before the widespread use of the internet. Second, I will look at the "creation" of new religious traditions from the use of popular culture. Here I will explore one group in particular: The Church of All Worlds, which took its very tradition from the popular book *Stranger in a Strange Land* by Robert Heinlein. I will look briefly at these two demonstrations of technology and media use before turning to the explosion of the internet in Neopagan culture.

'Zines hit their peak of popularity in the 1990s, with the advent of both cheaper computers and photocopying. When I first became involved with Neopaganism, one of the primary means of information were these homemade "newsletters"— from fairly cohesive publications such as Circle Sanctuary's offerings, to handwritten and photocopied "letters" from a Faerie commune in Northern California.

While the heyday of 'zines was short lived, they showed how alternative movements could take advantage of new (uncontrolled) technology: whereas before one would have to rely on publishers or have a great deal of money to make mass-mailings, the availability of desktop computers, printers, and photocopying made smaller groups able to contact larger segments of the population. This transitional step is another area I hope to explore further in the future, as it is a modern version of the changes that happened with the printing press. 'Zines show how availability of technology and autonomy of use can contribute to the spread of new ideas, and are a precursor to the same ideas regarding the internet.

The continued availability of publishing, however, had its own effects on Neopaganism. Many Neopagans are exposed to the religion through popular fiction, particularly novels with a Neopagan worldview or characters. Some of the most popular books cited are Marion Zimmer Bradley's *Mists of Avalon* and the writings of Mercedes Lackey. Science fiction and fantasy novels contribute by making people aware of "something else" going on in religion. For example, one Neopagan says that she started reading Mercedes Lackey and "[a]s part of her fan club, learned that she practiced neo-paganism and I started reading about it for a couple of years before I made the decision to practice."[23] This type of exposure is quite common in personal accounts of how an individual learned about Neopaganism. It will be interesting to pursue this in a context of dates: are the people who make this type of statement "older" practitioners, and with newer practitioners has the internet filled this role of initial exposure?

An extension of this initial exposure can be seen with the Church of All Worlds (CAW), which was formed in 1962, a year after Heinlein's publication of *Stranger in a Strange Land*. As writer Erik Davis describes it:

> Undergrads Lance Christian and Tim Zell were obsessed with Ayn Rand and Maslow's self-actualizing philosophy. Then they read Robert Heinlein's A Stranger in a Strange Land, which described the communal non-monogamist Church of All Worlds founded by the Martian exile Valentine Michael Smith. Grokking their deepest desires in the SF text, the two students and some female friends performed Smith's sacred water-sharing ritual, hopped in the sack, and founded a church. Later Zell renamed himself Otter, penned a prescient form of the Gaia hypothesis, and started using the word "Pagan" to describe CAW's increasingly earthy and eclectic religion. As Zell recently put it, "we're a sequel to a myth that hasn't even happened yet."[24]

This view of the world and religion demonstrated by the "founding" of CAW is an important mindset in general and for Neopagan ideas about religion. Discarding the notions of sacred text and linear history, Neopaganism plays with an entirely different worldview. "History" can in fact be created in the present, because religion is in relation to natural forces and not bound to a leader or to a singular text. The "foundational" text of CAW may be one particular book, but the group has used the book itself as a jumping point.

I will return to CAW in relationship to the internet below, but it is important to look first at how this fits into Brasher's ideas of religious change and revolution. That Neopaganism is a deviation from mainstream religious traditions is an obvious point; however, noting that technology has been the impetus for the spread of these traditions is very important. Certainly there are other factors involved — availability of mass transportation, for one — but in this case it seems to be widespread publishing, and now the internet, which has made Neopagan ideas spread, and spread quickly.

In the ARIS study it was noted that Neopaganism (and Wicca, specifically) have been growing exponentially:

> The fastest growing religion [in terms of percentage] is Wicca — a Neopagan religion that is sometimes referred to as Witchcraft. Numbers of adherents went from 8,000 in 1990 to 134,000 in 2001. Their numbers of adherents are doubling about every 30 months. Wiccans in Australia have a very similar growth pattern, from fewer than 2,000 in 1996 to 9,000 in 2001.[25]

With the undeniable presence of Neopaganism on the internet, I contend that this must be a major factor in the growth of the religion. It will take further research to establish the internet as a primary "tool" of Neopagan religious growth; an outline for this research would include surveys both online and in "traditional" circles as well as in-depth interviews. I believe from my beginning research that the technology itself, as well as the "reforming personality" type Brasher refers to will be important in the study of online Neopaganism. This is important because it cannot be discounted that Neopaganism is, to some extent, reactionary and revolutionary. Both in traditional texts and online, Neopaganism is put in direct opposition to other religions, specifically Christianity.

Moving to the Internet

To begin this final section, I return to CAW. The group has gone on to become freely internet-based, as stated at the CAW website:

> CAW may be the first religion to draw as much of its inspiration from the future as from the past, embracing science fiction as mythology with the same enthusiasm as we embrace the classical myths of ancient times. We are future-oriented, meaning we care about how we evolve and change, not only about how we got here and how we will come to an end. We embrace evolution, and in embracing the planet as a living organism, we embrace the evolutionary changes of the planet by bringing human consciousness into direct contact with the growing web of planetary consciousness through such things as the worldwide computer Internet.[26]

This statement shows that CAW is not just "using" the internet to further a religion; it is accepting the internet as part of the religion itself, as a part of the web of interconnectedness that CAW holds as a religious ideal. Unlike the Vatican website (www.vatican.va), the CAW is not simply looking to spread information about the faith and happenings, but to draw the internet in as part of that faith.

CAW, in its online magazine, *Green Egg*, has made it a point to look forward to what the future will bring for its group and other Neopagans.

> The next thirty years will be very different from the last thirty. What challenges will the Green Egg face? What kind of environment and social climate will it exist in? New technologies have already transformed our society and this process is only in its infancy. What kind of Green Egg for example, would exist in a world where we were routinely donning special headsets and entering the Internet in full virtual reality environments, appearing before our global kindred in simulated temples, stonehenges, initiatory caverns, sacred groves and fantasy settings heretofore unimagined, our projected electronic images outfitted in ritual regalia as well as physical forms of our own choosing, including those of mystical beings?[27]

As technology develops, the way we interact with others changes as well. In the world of fiction, this idea takes center stage in many different novels: Tad Williams's 1996 novel *Overland*, for example, describes a world in which research, personal interaction, and play is done almost entirely in the virtual reality *Green Egg* points to, although class levels continue to play a significant role in the quality of their lives.

> The actual citizens of the Inner District, those who had the money and power to commandeer their own private space in this elite section of the net, did not have the same restraints on their sims as visitors. In the distance Renie could see a pair of naked men with incredibly bulging muscles who also both happened to be bright candy-apple red and thirty feet tall. She wondered what the upkeep on *those* must have been, just in taxes and connection costs alone — it was much costlier to move a non-standard body through the simulations [Williams 1996: 40].

Class becomes the only identifiable mark of identity, and even that can be manipulated and overcome through underground means in this particular fictional world. Even with the economic limitations, the blurriness of gender and race is a new step.

Even though true virtual reality is in the future, the internet forms the same type of space. People have a *choice* of disclosure on the internet; if people do not meet in real life (IRL), one's identity is unquestionably what one makes of it. While we can look for clues to different identities in the context of dialogue, the only semi-limiting factors to truly creating identity are class and economics as they relate to the availability of technology. As Donna Haraway states in "Simians, Cyborgs, and Women,"

> we are now accustomed to remembering that as objects of knowledge and as historical actors, "race" did not always exist, 'class' has a historical genesis, and 'homosexuals' are quite junior. It is no accident that the symbolic system of the family of man — and so the essence of woman — breaks up at the same moment that networks of connection among people on the planet are unprecedentedly multiple, pregnant, and complex [Haraway 1991:160].

The internet has become one form of that timeless space/place in which the categories of gender, sexuality and class are beginning to be openly challenged.

Are these things "natural"? How can they be used by "nature-based" religions? There are in fact ideas which allow for a spread to (and on) the internet in the writings of (pre–Internet) Neopagans. Starhawk, in the Neopagan work *Spiral Dance*, published in 1979, says in a section on creating sacred space:

> In Witchcraft, we define a new space and a new time whenever we cast a circle to begin a ritual. The circle exists on the boundaries of ordinary space and time; it is "between the worlds" of the seen and unseen, of

flashlight and starlight consciousness, a space in which alternate realities meet, in which the past and future are open to us. Time is no longer measured out; it becomes elastic, fluid, a swirling pool in which we dive and swim. The restriction and distinctions of our socially defined roles no longer apply; only the rule of nature holds sway.... Within the circle, the power within us, the Goddess and the Old Gods, are revealed [Starhawk 1979: 71].

Nothing in this statement is contradictory to using the internet as a form of sacred space; in fact, the description Starhawk gives could be read as a *reason* for using the internet, although it was written a decade before its widespread use. What could be more "on the boundaries" of space and time than a nebulously defined "non-space-time"?

Erik Davis points this out in his exploration of Neopaganism and technology, saying that powerful new technologies are magical because they *function* as magic, opening up novel and protean spaces of possibility within social reality. They allow humans to impress their dreaming wills upon the stuff of the world, reshaping it, at least in part, according to the designs of the imagination. Davis characterizes Neopagans as "tinkerers," in a positive sense: a group whose members will use whatever is put in front of them to their own (religious) advantage. In what he calls "experimental spiritual pragmatism," he says that Neopagans "have thus learned to maneuver quite cannily between technoscientific categories and imaginative practice. And they have done so in part by replacing the religious question of belief with the hands-on exploration of embodied experience and altered states of consciousness" (Davis 1999:183). Delving into the internet for spiritual practice is simply another form of this type of "hands-on" experience, though perhaps without the literal "hands."

In *Give Me That Online Religion*, Brasher cites an example of what might prove to be a "typical" online Neopagan:

> Twenty-eight years old, single, and in her second year of graduate school studying for a Ph.D. in sociology at the University of Southern California, Julia introduced herself to her classmates as a "nonpracticing neopagan...." It was a memorable introduction, but not exactly accurate. Julia was in fact a practicing neopagan; however, she no longer met face-to-face with a coven ... or participated in the communal solstice rituals held in forests in the area. Instead, she had opted to be on the cutting edge of a new phenomenon. She was a practicing cyber-witch [Brasher 2001: 85].

Several questions remain unanswered in this section of Brasher's book, particularly why Julia would introduce herself as "nonpracticing." However, in the background that is given about Julia, one thing stands out: she reacts to the internet in a certain way, which leads her into the practice of cyberspace religion. "[S]he began reacting to cyberspace as if it were a technological sacred forest. Nestled in mystery, it seemed to her imbued with sacred qualities that made unique magical connections possible." This certainly isn't the reaction of all people, or of all Neopagans. It is, however, one way in which Neopaganism is moving in today's world, and Julia seems to fit quite well with what Davis would call a "technopagan."

Most forms of Neopaganism emphasize a communion with nature in their ideology and ritual. While accepting the internet as a means for that communion or worship definitely means reimagining what "nature" means, I do not see it as outside the scope of the Neopagan worldview. It may be more problematic from an outside perspective, simply because in the past "nature religion" has been the most common way for Neopagans to describe their own practice. In most Neopagan works, however, the ideas have been more subtle than a simple focus on the natural world — something which is difficult to get across in a brief conversation.

As an example, when I try to explain Wicca to someone, my focus is generally on defending against preconceived notions of devil worship, sacrifice, and the like. For this reason, my explanation is generally limited to "a focus on nature and the seasonal cycles, with the worship of a God and Goddess as personifications of natural principles." Even recently, when explaining my course on "History of Magic and Witchcraft," my comments to several other graduate students were limited because of the notions they brought into the conversation: jokes such as "are you doing a practicum on goat sacrifice?" made an in-depth explanation of the course almost an impossibility. Understanding how Neopaganism can function on the internet means looking more closely at the ideas behind the words "nature religion," and I will conclude this section by exploring more in-depth what this worldview might mean.

While Starhawk's *Spiral Dance* has a heavy focus on ritual for different seasonal holidays, she begins with a section on "The Worldview of Witchcraft." Here is where she explains the general principles which take one form in seasonal celebrations:

> The mythology and cosmology of Witchcraft ... is ... that all things are swirls of energy, vortexes of moving forces, currents in an ever-changing sea. Underlying the appearance of separateness, of fixed objects within a linear stream of time, reality is a field of energies that congeal, temporarily, into forms. In time, all "fixed" things dissolve, only to coalesce again into new forms, new vehicles [Starhawk 1979:32].

This idea, that the underlying principle is one of movement and change, means that the focus on rituals *within nature* is only one way of expressing the ideas of Witchcraft. In her "Ten Years Later" section (written in 1989),

Starhawk says outright that the mythology of Witchcraft is changeable. Commenting on the Wheel of the Year, from which her seasonal festivals are drawn, she says that: "Myths in the Craft are not graven in stone. The traditional tales have much to teach us, and we should be wary of changing them. But as we work with them and reflect on them, we may understand them in new images and language that reflects our own changes." Using a different "format" to explore these ideas is well within the worldview Starhawk states, and accepting the internet as a form of a natural principle of interconnectedness is one direction in which Neopagans are moving, as shown above in the CAW statement.

However, this does not work for all Neopagans. As Erik Davis points out,

> For the bulk of Pagans and magic users, online community plays second fiddle to spiritual experience. Paganism is an earth religion, after all, and its practitioners seek sacred communion on the material plane, in woods and deserts and black-lit basements, amidst unguents and drums and dancing flesh. This visionary materialism is worlds away from the incorporeal writing space of the Internet, and many Pagans, especially Goddess-oriented Wiccans, distrust the cyberspace obsessions of technopagans, fearing that the enthusiasm for cyberchat and virtual reality may simply reproduce the same disembodied and ecologically bankrupt tendencies of modern civilization that Pagandom otherwise so imaginatively resists [Davis 1999: 186].

Here again the paradox of "nature religion" and internet use comes to the fore. It is my contention that these ideas are *not* contrary, despite what Davis says about the division between "technopagans" and other Neopagans. It is valid to say that different people and groups use the internet for different reasons, and that not all of them would find online practice appealing. However, even groups of "Goddess-oriented Wiccans" are taking at least partial advantage of what cyberspace can offer: the Covenant of the Goddess, for example (www.cog.org) is a organization that specifically focuses on spreading information between Goddess covens, and uses the internet for that purpose. While they do not have online rituals, they have maintained a detailed Web site since the early days of the internet.

The festival scene, which I have used in part to explore the popularity of online Neopaganism, is obviously different from the internet scene. One is bodily, one is not. One is composed of face-to-face interaction on a level beyond what most Neopagans experience in their daily lives, a sharing of religion and ritual which is difficult to create outside such a space. Similarly, the concept of a real-world coven allows for personal interaction which is not the same as an online coven.

However, many of the characteristics of a sacred circle or a beloved coven can be achieved, in different ways, via the internet. The drawbacks are balanced, for a segment of the Neopagan population, by the way in which the internet allows for expansion: forming a coven which extends from the United States to Britain to Australia, and who can meet at any given time, is an experience of connection usually not available by other means. The ideal of a coven meeting "in perfect love and perfect trust" is not negated by the fact that it meets online. As Margot Adler describes a coven (again, writing before the influx of the internet),

> A coven simply means a group of people who convene for religious or magical or psychic purposes.... Most Wiccan covens work within a circle, "a portable Temple," as one Witch wrote to me. Certain groups in England have been known to set up a psychic "castle," and many Witches will tell you that their circle is really a sphere. The circle is the declaration of sacred ground. It is a place set apart, although its material location may be a living room or backyard. But in the mind the circle, reinforced by the actions of casting it and purifying it, becomes sacred space, a place "between the worlds" where contact with archetypal reality, with the deep places of the mind — with "gods," if you will — becomes possible. It is a place where time disappears, where history is obliterated. It is the contact point between two realities [Adler (1979) 1986: 109].

One of Adler's points, here, is that the physical location of the coven or the circle makes no difference; it is the intent of those casting the circle, and the space which is formed *mentally* which makes the (religious) difference. There has always been great variety in the types of spaces used for Neopagan practice; while there is still a great interest in practicing in a natural setting — borne out by the upsurge of interest in festivals — this type of practice need not be the only way. An example such as Circle Sanctuary (above) shows how Neopagans can combine (what is perceived as) "normal" Neopagan practice with the use of the internet. There is, and will continue to be, a great range of what constitutes Neopagan ritual. As Davis points out, some groups are more likely than others to embrace the concept of internet practice. This may be an area which needs further exploration: which subsections of Neopagans — and which age groups, in particular — are more likely to view the internet as religiously worthwhile?

A generation of people who rely on the internet for everything from games to research to dating will no doubt feel more comfortable about the idea of online religion in general. This was the case with Brasher's example of Julia, the "cyberwitch." Julia was already interested in Neopaganism, and — separately, at first — in computers and the internet. The discovery of a website, TIAMAT (Testing the Internet as a Magical Tool), is what Brasher cites as Julia's realization that Neopaganism and cyberspace could be combined.

Here is where the most work needs to be done for the future: an exploration of how Neopagans create or adapt rituals for online use. MUDs (Multi User Dimensions) and MOOs (Multi Object Oriented) are types of internet "areas" in which users can virtually move around, interact with a created environment, and interact with other people. There are a variety of differently themed MUDs and MOOs, including role-playing games. Moreover, chat rooms and bulletin boards are also among the many ways Neopagans are trying out cyberspace practice.

Conclusion

Neopagans have embraced the internet in different way. For some, it is merely a tool to communicate; for others it demonstrates one of the primary tenets of the religion: interconnectedness. The fact that I can discuss holiday rituals with a fellow Pagan in Australia — instantly — or participate in an online ritual while linked with people from five different countries is new and exciting. It is also *natural* in the sense that when I do these things, I am more connected with other Neopagans than ever.

The very terms with which Neopaganism has been defined — by researchers and practitioners alike — are problematic. The phrase "religion of interconnectedness," while a bit unwieldy, seems to more accurately describe Neopagan views than does "nature religion." "Interconnectedness" allows for an expanded view of the natural, along with the ideas of flexibility and self-definition which are important hallmarks of these religious traditions.

For a segment of the population — a segment which a number of Neopagans is drawn from, as I argued in the first section of this paper — the internet has been an alternative "space" in which to do almost everything. This does not mean that Neopagans are leaving nature behind, nor does it mean that even those Davis calls "technopagans" will rely solely on the internet for practice, forgoing any other type of interaction. The worldview of Neopaganism allows for, perhaps even calls for, adaptation and the creation of new types of ritual space. The internet as "web" is, for some Neopagans, an ideal way to explore the concept of interconnectedness, as well as being a space in which other beliefs can be realized in a new way.

The internet has allowed greater access to research and exploration for many people, on many topics. It is not surprising that religion is one of those topics, but it may seem surprising that a "nature-based" religion has been the one to take full advantage of the internet. However, by looking at the demographics and growth of Neopagan groups, at the parallels between the popularity of festivals and the internet, and by exploring the Neopagan worldview, it is quite clear that the internet is an ideal place for Neopagans to interact.

Printed References

Adler, Margot. *Drawing Down the Moon: Witches, Druids, Goddess-Worshippers, and Other Pagans in America Today*. Boston: Beacon, 1979.

Berger, Helen. *A Community of Witches: Contemporary Neo-Paganism and Witchcraft in the United States* (Studies in Comparative Religion). Columbia, SC: University of South Carolina Press, 1999.

Brasher, Brenda. *Give Me That Online Religion*. San Francisco: Josie-Bass, 2001.

Davis, Erik. *Techgnosis : Myth, Magic + Mysticism in the Age of Information*. New York: Three Rivers, 1999.

Foushee, Herman R. "Cult Sex: The Mass Media Reporting of Sexual Issues Surrounding New Religious Movements." In *Sex/Machine: Readings in Culture, Gender, and Technology: Indiana Series in the Philosophy of Technology*, edited by Patrick D. Hopkins. Bloomington: Indiana University Press, 1999.

Haraway, Donna. *Simians, Cyborgs and Women: The Reinvention of Nature*. New York: Routledge, 1991.

Hayles, Katherine. *How We Became Posthuman: Virtual Bodies in Cybernetics, Literature, and Informatics*. Chicago: University of Chicago Press, 1999.

Krxywinska, Tanya. "Hubble-Bubble, Herbs and Grimores." In *Fighting the Forces: What's At Stake in Buffy the Vampire Slayer*, edited by Rhonda V. Wilcox and David Lavery. Lanham, MD: Rowman & Littlefield, 2002.

McRae, Shannon. "Coming Apart at the Seams: Sex, Text, and Virtual Body." In *Wired Women, Gender and New Realities in Cyberspace*, edited by Lynn Cherney and Elizabeth Reba Weise. Seattle: Seal, 1996.

Pike, Sarah. *Earthly Bodies, Magical Selves: Contemporary Pagans and the Search for Community*. Berkeley: University of California Press, 2001.

Shade, Leslie Regan. 2002. *Gender and Community in the Social Construction of the Internet: Digital Formations*, Vol. 1. New York: Peter Lang, 2002.

Starhawk. *Spiral Dance : A Rebirth of the Ancient Religion of the Great Goddess*. San Francisco: Harper San Francisco, 1979.

Williams, Tad. *Otherland: City of Golden Shadow*. New York: DAW Books, 1979.

Non-Printed and Internet Sources

[1] Argentium G. Tiger, "Thoughts on Nature" http://www.annwnscauldron.com/agtiger/thoughts/Argentium_on_Nature.html

[2] "I Robot, You Jane" (1.08) quote from http://www.elvis42.cwc.net/scripts/buffy/season1/episode108.htm

[3] http://www.religioustolerance.org/wic_nbr.htm

[4] http://www.religioustolerance.org/wic_nbr.htm

[5] http://www.religioustolerance.org/wic_nbr.htm

9. There's No Place Like Home.html 227

6. TechnoPagans http://www.wired.com/wired/archive/3.07/technopagans.html
7. Falling Through the Net: Executive Summary. http://www.ntia.doc.gov/ntiahome/fttn99/execsummary.html
8. http://www.circlesanctuary.org/psg/memories/
9. Charlene Suggs, "Where I live during the Summer Solstice" at http://www.circlesanctuary.org/psg/memories/mem_livesolstice98.html
10. http://www.circlesanctuary.org/liberty/report/
11. http://www.branwenscauldron.com/
12. search conducted on Google using "neo-paganism" on 2/16/03.
13. http://www.thetowntalk.com/html/DF4605E8-38FA-4E18-9416-48EDAFCD9EF9.shtml
14. http://forerunner.com/champion/X0038.html
15. http://forerunner.com/champion/X0039_Child_Sacrifice_in_t.html
16. http://www.thetowntalk.com/html/DF4605E8-38FA-4E18-9416-48EDAFCD9EF9.shtml
17. Kindlebee, e-mail to author 2/16/03.
18. Kindlebee, e-mail to author 2/16/03.
19. Kindlebee, e-mail to author 2/16/03.
20. "Laura" letter to the author 2/20/03
21. "Frog" letter to the author 2/18/03
22. "Kindlebee, letter to the author 2/16/03.
23. e-mail to author, "Laura" 2/20/03.
24. Erik Davis, "Remains of the Deities: Reading the Return of Paganism" (Nov. 1993) http://www.levity.com/figment/neopaganism.html
25. http://www.religioustolerance.org/chr_prac2.htm
26. http://www.caw.org/articles/cawquest.html#13.
27. "The Myths of Oberon" from Green Egg, Vol.30 Issue 123, http://www.greenegg.org/Features/Oberon/123.html

10

Religious Conflict in the Periphery

Islam and Politics in Turkey

MUSTAFA SAATCI

Introduction

The role and status of religion in public discourse varies greatly in the core and peripheral states. While the former are secular and able to accommodate religious conflicts, including extremist movements, the latter are marked by the dynamics of prolonged ethnic conflicts which often incorporate religion as one of their primary constituents.

The prevailing disparity is a result of the historical development in which core states went through the nation-state formation process earlier, possibly beginning around the 18th and ending in the 19th century (Wallerstein 1974; Anderson 1979). Peripheral societies, on the other hand, had a different experience depending on whether they were colonized or not. While relatively strong states were able to stay independent and initiate the nation-state building process during the latter part of the 19th and early part of the 20th centuries, most of the colonized entities did not have the option until the second half of the 20th century.

The rise of the nation-state system has led to the tendency to eliminate multiethnic empires and societies and homogenize populations through various methods. One of the alternatives is to draw from a common history no matter how diverse it is, and to build upon it. Another path is to forge "imagined communities," new identities based on real or fictitious notions of the past (Anderson 1991).

As part of the project, statehood has been placing increasing demands on ethnic identities toward the formation of nationhood in the past 200 years, and, as a result, has created a contradiction between ethnicity and the state (Olzak 1998). The dialectic between ethnicity and the state has a dual dimension. The first originates from the proclivity in contemporary societies to substitute primordial ties with civil ties. This means that existing cultures, languages, and tribal or ethnic identities are thrust toward national affiliations and state-dictated cultural objectives. The other dimension involves the inconsistency between the geographic and ideological boundaries of states and ethnic groups that are located within them. This incongruity exists since the formation of modern states has not followed the logic of social or cultural patterns but rather the logic of markets and political organization. Furthermore, ethnic identities themselves are in a constant state of flux.

The critical issues facing Turkey today are ethnic and religious conflicts on the one hand, and, on the other, economic crises (Kasaba and Bozdogan 2000:1). While the two categories are closely linked at the empirical level, a distinction can be made analytically in that ethnic and class conflicts are intersecting yet separate planes, each with its own modus operandi. The status of Islam in present-day Turkey embodies many different influences and paradoxes that originated at the juncture of the transition from Ottoman Empire to Turkish Republic.

In particular, the discontinuity in the incorporation of religion to the state apparatus, including its ideological foundations as well as its role in the public domain, resulted in an array of discontent and resistance by various groups (Lewis 1968). The transition, in turn, was formulated by the expansion of the world system in the region and the emanating conditions that followed (Islamoglu-Inan 1987; Kasaba 1988). The establishment of the new Turkish Republic in 1923 out of the remains of the Ottoman Empire continued with an effort toward forming a Turkish nation-state. It has been, however, an experiment rather than a completed project, manifest in the magnitude and diversity of current crises.

Religious and ethnic discord involves Turks vs. Kurds, Sunnis vs. Alevis, Sunnis vs. other religious minorities, and secularism vs. fundamentalism. Furthermore, each of these pairs is not uniquely defined. Instead, they overlap to create many more subcategories of ambiguity and conflict while the ideological and social definitions of these groups are still being negotiated. For instance, while the majority of Kurds are Sunnis, some are Alevis. Similarly, Sunni Turks make up the core of Turkish society yet a significant number of them are Alevis. Consequently, there is a constant tension between the desire to find a common ground for nationalism and, at the same time, define the boundaries of each category within the ideological confines of the state.

The class conflicts, on the other hand, may be categorized into two areas. The first is the relationship between those who hold economic and political power such as the military, the bureaucratic and entrepreneurial classes, and those who lack power in any of its dimensions. The second is the competition and cooperation among the members of the powerful groups, which is quite significant in the peripheral context since capital is not as liquid or mobile and "rationalized" as it is in the core countries. The term liquidity in this context refers to the absence of extensive financial markets in which assets are shifted with relative ease and low cost. Rationalized capital, on the other hand, refers to the process of capital accumulation as an end in itself and through formal rationality at the social level.

The contradictory nature of class and ethnic positions is articulated in the efforts to gain access to the state through the political process. However, it is not easily accomplished since access to the state is blocked by various means such as cooptation, legal sanctions, intimidation, and physical force.

Given the legacy of its predecessor, it will be necessary to consider the political history of Turkey before any analysis of the current conditions is conceptualized. The final analysis, then, will combine the historical conditions and the more recent developments in Turkey by focusing on the state, religion, social classes, and the conditions under which they have transformed over time.

The Ottoman Empire and Islam

The origins of the Ottomans were modest. Continuing the outward migration movements from Central Asia that had begun in the 12th century, about 300 nomadic Turkish tribes migrated to western Anatolia in the 13th century (Kafadar 1995).

The area in which the Turkish tribes settled was at the southeastern frontiers of the Byzantine Empire where they met a large number of cultures and civilizations, some of them much stronger than themselves. Thus, their physical and cultural survival was dependent on the ability to gain control of their surroundings. Toward that objective, the Turks used two strategies: changing their religion to Islam, and intermarriage with the local populations. In the case of the Ottoman ruling family, intermarriages with the local Byzantine notables proved to be a much more rewarding enterprise since it enabled them to achieve political and economic power in a short period of time (Kafadar 1995).

The Ottomans' rapid ascendance to a dominant position, and their ability to expand resulted in a large and powerful empire. At its zenith in the 16th century, the empire controlled lands from Hungary to North Africa, and contained many different ethnic and religious groups. The success of the Ottomans was made possible, in part, by placing Islam at the center of the Ottoman society and establishing it as the raison d'être for the state while permitting non–Muslim populations to maintain their social organization and religious practices. However, religious freedom granted to non–Muslims had a number of clauses, most significant of which were higher taxation and exclusion from the political sphere. The Ottoman state Islam had a pivotal role in not only providing the spiritual, social, and institutional framework for the society during times of peace, but also in the justification of its expansionist policies.

In some ways, as some authors have argued, the Ottoman state was never a fully Islamic state in that to be able to accommodate the multiethnic structure of the empire it was necessary to be flexible and it was "achieved by developing a body of traditional law (orfi hukuk) which did not derive from religious law (the Sharia). Care was taken, however, that religious laws would not be openly violated" (Turan 1991:32–33). Military campaigns, for instance, were initiated, officially at least, for spreading Islam, thus disguised as "doing God's work."

In terms of political organization, the various dimensions of power were conjoined and vested with the sultan. He drew power from religion, initially by getting *fetva* (decree issued by high-ranking clergy) from the *ulema* (high-ranking clergy) for wars and other ventures, and later by assuming the title of the *caliphet* (highest Islamic ruler and authority), such that the caliphate was assumed by Selim I in the 16th century. The sultan was also the commander in chief of the armed forces and fought alongside of his soldiers, thus drawing organizational and charismatic powers.

The absolute power of the sultan continued from the time the empire was founded until the beginning of its decline in the second half of the 16th century. This does not mean that he was not challenged. On the contrary, as early as the 14th century "the state began to separate itself from the sultan by separating the state treasury from that of the sultan" and by establishing "state rules" instead of "sultans' rules" (Heper 2000:2).

During its descent, the distribution of power was divided between the sultan, the *ulema,* and the high-ranking officials of the military and bureaucracy, particularly the grand vizier and the janissary branch of the military. The sultans lost a significant portion of their power when they stopped actively participating in military campaigns beginning in the second half of the 16th century. Later, during the mid–19th century, the power shifted further in favor of the bureaucratic classes when sultans relinquished their powers almost completely and became symbolic figures rather than holders of real authority (Heper 1980:82). Another contributing factor was the reign of a series of incompetent, and in some cases mad, sultans. Their madness was caused by years of isolation and confinement to a room in the palace by their sultan brother, and the possibility of execution at a moment's notice.

This practice was instituted in the 17th century after the tradition of fratricide was abandoned. The efforts by some of the sultans to regain power were in vain since by then the other groups had become quite formidable and entrenched in their positions, powerful enough to dethrone or even execute the sultans.

Feeling the effects of economic and military pressure exerted by the strong states of Europe, the Ottomans unsuccessfully tried to modernize in the 18th century. However, the modernization attempts were limited to the military and war technology. It was not until the 19th century that broad reforms were initiated.

Between 1807 and 1908 there were extensive reform efforts in the military, the state, and social institutions. They included the establishment of military and medical schools, a general post office, ministries and the parliament, constitutional laws replacing sultans' orders, equal rights, taxes based on income, trial system for punishment, agricultural reforms, and secularization of the state (Lewis 1968). The changes, however, remained ineffective since they were implemented from top to bottom, and also were intended to change superficial elements in the society without altering its fundamental structure and social and economic relations.

Turkish Nation-State Formation

The real threat of losing Anatolia, the center of the empire, in 1918 when the Allied and Greek forces invaded it following World War I presented an urgent need for redefinition of both geographic borders and raison d'être of the state. Having succeeded in reclaiming independence in 1922 and forming the new republic in 1923 brought forward the recurrent question of what should come next.

The modernization efforts by the late sultans were now formulated into a nation-state formation project (Brockett 1998; Kasaba and Bozdogan 2000). It was carried out in two areas: the definition and role of the state, and national identity. The debate on state and nationhood could not be settled on a democratic or national platform since political stability and cohesion could not be guaranteed by taking an egalitarian and pluralistic approach. This meant that the formation of a national identity could not come from bottom to top, but had to be assumed by the state (Barkey 2000). Moreover, the meaning of "Turk" itself was vague and needed to be construed. It is possible to see the two periods as the same and one being the continuation of the other in some ways. However, the new Turkish Republic fits the definition of a modern nation-state, compared to the Ottoman Empire which was a world-empire.

Islam, being the prevailing principle up until that time, was one of the alternatives at the new juncture. The difficulty, however, was twofold: first, there were many non-Muslim *millets* (groups defined by religion and language), and *kavims* (ethnic groups or tribes) who did not want to be under Turkish control; and second, there were objections as to the role of Islam in the state's objectives. The distinction between *millet and kavim* was based on religion, language, and the size of the population. For example, Christian subjects were considered as *millets* whereas the Kurds were considered to be a *kavim*. The founders and the elite of the new state were aware of the failures of the past, and perceived Islam as an obstacle to the adoption of Western political, economic, and social standards. They also considered Islam a suspect in the possible restoration of the old system (Barkey 2000). Thus, Islam, either alone or attached to the revival of Ottomanism, was not considered as a viable option, and was replaced with other ideals and universals such as Turkism, modernity, and étatism, very similar to statism where the state plays the leading role in the planning and organization of the economy and society.

The removal of Islam from public domain had three critical consequences: first, at the individual level there was nothing to replace it in terms of moral code. In other words, Kemalism was no substitute for Islam (Mardin 1971: 198), in that Kemalism is a set of principles, outlined by Mustafa Kemal Ataturk, regarding the future course of modern Turkish society, yet decisively secular such that it constituted something separate from Islam as a religious force. The principles of Kemalism are republicanism, populism, secularism, reformism, nationalism, and statism. Second, it created a gap between the ruler and the ruled since Islam and Islamic institutions historically provided a bridge between the two groups. And lastly, Islam's role as the principal means and locus of social protest was also eradicated (Tapper 1991: 7).

The focus of the new state was on the formation of Turkish identity and nationalism, and the direction toward which Turkey would navigate. During the initial decades of the republic sweeping social, economic, and political reforms were initiated by the government of Mustafa Kemal Ataturk with the hope that they would accelerate the modernization of the society (Kucuradi 1995).

In 1924, the caliphate was abolished and unity of language in education was declared. In the following year the hat was introduced, replacing the fez, and activities by *tarikats* (religious sects) were banned. The combined effect of these changes was to produce widespread resentment and conflict. The ethnic and religious revolts in 1930 were a result of the developments between 1926 and 1929 during which a secular system of government was adopted, new civil laws were introduced giving women more rights, polygamy was outlawed, and a constitutional provision was added eliminating Islam as the state religion. Similarly, the bloody uprising in 1937 followed the changes in state policies, particularly in 1934, prohibiting religious attire in public and increasing pressure on ethnic groups, particularly the Kurds.

The founders of the new republic had made the erroneous assumption that all of the remaining groups in Turkey would converge to become Turks over time. They also had assumed, implicitly and explicitly, that Islam would be the dominant or the only religion, yet remain in the individual sphere of a secular state.

The sudden and large-scale shift away from religion coalesced with vigorous ethnic assimilation efforts, hence, creating a contradictory context between the state and ethnic and religious segments of the population. The government's other policies of replacing Islamic social and legal codes with Western codes, outlawing religious organizations, and making Turkish the official language exacerbated the relations between the state and populations (Barkey 2000). The alienation and ideological perforation between the state and religious and ethnic segments of the population continued throughout the latter part of the 20th century, although it was muted at times because of the continuing intolerance and suppression.

Secularism versus Laicism

There have been two significant developments in the revival of Islamic movements since Ataturk's death. First, secularism has been redefined by the state, and second, the movements have shifted from rural to urban origins. While the effects of the former are somewhat ambiguous, those of the latter are far more extensive and consequential.

Initially, laicisation was equivalent to secularism both in terms of definition and practice since Ataturk had intended to separate religion from the state and political domain and confine it to the individual sphere. As a result, Ataturk and other leaders implemented cultural and institutional reforms to reduce the role of Islam. Ataturk stated in his speeches that without changing the mentality inherited from the Ottomans and Islam there could be no progress, and that "the great Turkish nation ... has accomplished a revolution not only in its institutions but in its thinking as well" (quoted in Kucuradi (1995:45). According to one perspective, it was a cultural revolution carried out politically (Kucuradi 1995).

Over time, however, the two terms acquired different meanings after Ataturk's death. The government abandoned the concept of secularism for laicisation, which meant the subordination of Islam to state objectives, and active management of religious institutions and affairs by the state. The military, which has perceived itself as the guardian of the republic, played a crucial role in the redefinition of secularization, that it is not only a separation of religion and politics but also a detachment between religion and society (Yavuz 2000).

The relocation of Islam-based movements to cities, on the other hand, was a direct result of urbanization during the last three decades. Prior to the 1950s, the rural population outnumbered urban population, and the separation of religious from secular populations was mostly based on geographic location. For instance, in 1927, 12.5 percent of the population resided in cities with 20,000 or more inhabitants. In comparison, today 71 percent are classified as such (Kasaba and Bozdogan 2000: 5). Thus, the social distance between them was reinforced by physical separation.

The conditions after the 1950s took a different turn as increasing numbers of people migrated to major cities. For the first time, physical proximity became the main determinant of social distance and confrontation between the two groups. More importantly, it crystallized the contradictions between them, and, at the same time, increased the magnitude and intensity of Islamic movements.

The groups in power, by default, design and implement laws and policies against organized Islamic movements rather than Islam itself, especially when the religious segments seek access to the state through the democratic political process. The architects of current policies draw their justification from the legacy of Ataturk and his principles on the state and society, obscuring the underlying social inequalities in the process. One of the subtle ways to enforce homogenization may be found in the fact that birth certificates in Turkey include "religious affiliation." Just as significant is that it may not be left blank.

As a result, democratically elected governments by Islamic political parties have been removed from power by the military for reasons of national security. The latest incident was on June 18, 1997, when the military asked the coalition government of the Welfare Party to resign. In January 1998 the Constitutional Court closed it down permanently for violating the principle of laicism. The party's leader, Necmettin Erbakan, has been removed from power, banned from politics, and jailed a number of times throughout his political career.

At the institutional level, people with strong real or apparent religious affiliations have been forced out of government, civil service, and military positions. In addition, religious practices and attire have been banned in government offices, universities, and certain public spaces. The exclusion of religion is particularly enforced in the military structure. Military schools accept students after an exhaustive investigation of their personal and family backgrounds. Still, there are periodic "cleansing operations" through which officers suspected of fundamentalist tendencies are relieved of their commissions.

The government, indeed, violates the principles of Kemalism and secular government when necessary. For instance, after the military coup in 1980 the state de facto accepted Sunni Islam as the state religion by implementing policies to make religious education in schools compulsory rather than optional, increasing the role and power of the Directorate of Religious Affairs, and initiating the construction of additional mosques in Alevi neighborhoods.

In practice, the management of organized Islam is carried out by the government. The Directorate of Religious Affairs, "with a budget greater than the combined expenditures of five ministries" is financed and run by the government (Yavuz 2000:3). The agency is given the responsibility to manage Islam and religious organizations according to the needs of the state. Thus, the government organization controls all of the 80,000 mosques, and manages the imams as government employees.

The Ministry of Education, on the other hand, administers imam-hatip schools (secondary educational institutions with Islam as their organizing principle), manages the compulsory religion classes in all public schools, and publishes books and magazines with Islamic views.

Current Conflicts

The distribution of religious and ethnic groups in Turkey remains debatable. This is due to a number of reasons such as the role of assimilation, socially and geographically isolated locations of the groups, and the political reasons for inflating or deflating their size.

Estimates show that out of the 65 to 70 million people living in Turkey less than half a percent are Christian and Jewish, 12–18 percent are Kurdish, and the remaining 77–81 percent is divided among a number of different ethnic groups considered to be Turkish. The most significant of the groups is the Laz of the Black Sea Region, and Cherkes (Circassians). Others derive their ethnic identity from past and present groups in the Balkans, Central Asia, and Anatolia. There is also another category, perhaps half a percent of the total, consisting of smaller ethnic groups. The distribution of non–Muslim populations is such that there are approximately 60,000 Jews, 60,000 Armenians, and 130,000 Greeks. There is also a number of other small groups such as the Gypsies, Assyrians, and Yezidis.

The distribution of religious affiliation, on the other hand, is that about 65–67 percent of the population are Sunni Turks, 14–15 percent are Alevi

Turks, 12–13 percent are Sunni Kurds, and four to five percent are Alevi Kurds (Shankland 1999). The religious and ethnic groups were defined "loosely" during the time of the Ottomans since there was no need to do otherwise. Today, however, there is a need and tendency to clearly define the boundaries of each group. This has resulted in a frantic search for what each identity was and is, which, in turn, has led to various factions and centers of authority within each group. Among the Kurdish population, 80–85 percent are Sunni Muslims, and 8–10 percent are Alevis. The remaining is divided between the Shiites, Yezidis, and others. Also, each major group is further divided into sects. Some of these sects have beliefs and traditions containing elements of Christianity, pre–Christianity, and Islam.

The category of Muslim, hence, does not consist of a single, homogeneous group. On the contrary, the differences are so significant that they lead to exclusion and violent conflicts. The divisions within Islam are a result of various reasons. First, some sects were created over time by the personal and political struggles for power after Muhammed's death. Second, some were created for defining a national identity, such as Iran. And lastly, some were produced by the imposition of Islam onto the existing social systems of different groups in the region who accepted Islam while preserving some of their pre–Islamic beliefs and traditions. Even though there are subsects within the Sunni sect, it is one of the major categories in Islam, and can be placed in the first type of origin.

The Shiite sect was created by the shah of Iran in the 16th century who wanted to separate the Persians from the Arabs. The Alevi sect is, arguably, an example of the third type of formation. The term Alevi literally means those who follow Ali, one of the caliphs and Muhammed's son-in-law. It is a "blanket term" for a number of groups and traditions. There are various arguments over the definition of what Alevi means. Some state that they made up the peasant or landless class of Turkish populations who were subjected to the cruelty of the sultans and local landlords. Their rebellions resulted in their treatment and isolation as outcasts, and harsher punishments by the authorities. On the other hand, others argue that it is based on religious principles. As a group, Alevis in Turkey are more secular than others. For a detailed treatment of Alevi politics, see Erman & Goker (2000).

The Yezidis, for example, are pre–Islamic Zoroastrians, with many elements integrated from Islam, however regarded contemptuously as "devil worshippers" by both the Turkish and Kurdish Sunnis. The historical divisions between the Sunni and Alevi Kurds, manifested by the cooperation of Sunni Kurds with the Ottoman sultans against the Shiite Persians, continue even today.

In the last few decades, Turkey has experienced violent clashes between various groups. During the civil unrest between the early 1970s and 1980, which had both class and ethnic and religious components, approximately 1,500–2,000 people died each year. In 1978, a bloody clash between the Sunnis and Alevis in the city of Kahramanmaras resulted in tens of deaths. The armed conflict, on the other hand, between the Kurdish organization PKK and government forces that lasted from 1984 to 1999 claimed the lives of 26,418 people, resulted in many more injured, and also caused large out-migrations from the eastern region (Milliyet 1998:8). In the total, 4,049 were civilians, 5,121 were government security personnel, and 17,248 were those classified as terrorists.

More recently, during an Alevi cultural festival a mob of Sunni fundamentalists set the hotel housing Alevi guests on fire, killing 37 people in 1993. In a 1995 riot, incited by a drive-by shooting in a poor Alevi neighborhood and the indifference of the police to the incident, 16 people died, all Alevis (Milliyet 1993; 1995). Perhaps the most shocking incident occurred in January 2000, involving the discovery of a series of mass graves across the country "containing the tortured and mutilated bodies of more than 40 (mostly Kurdish) businessmen and moderate Islamic intellectuals who had been missing for several years" (Kasaba and Bozdogan 2000:5). According to the public opinion, as expressed by Kasaba and Bozdogan, "the radical Islamist organization Hizbullah, used by the government in the early 1990s as a pawn against Kurdish nationalists and supplied with weapons and ammunition from the state, was responsible for these gruesome murders" (Kasaba and Bozdogan, ibid.: 5). Despite extensive investigations, however, no connection has been established between the extremist groups and the Islamist parties.

Politics and Revival of Islam

For analytical purposes, it is possible to distinguish Islamic movements in Turkey into two categories: the "political Islam" and "Islam outside of politics." In reality, however, they continuously intersect, intertwine, and evolve.

Political Islam is characterized by the tendency to gain access to economic and social power through the political process. It synthesizes social class and religious or ethnic identity, and, thus, consists of diverse groups of individuals and organizations.

The class dimension involves two groups, "white Turks" versus "black Turks" (Yavuz 2000). According to Yavuz, black Turks and Kurds include "socially conservative, pious Muslims; a large sector of the Kurdish population; the economically excluded sector of the population who live in shantytowns; and Muslim merchants and industrialists in Anatolia who run small and medium-sized enterprises" (2000:13).

The new economy also fostered an Islamist elite that is different than

10. Religious Conflict in the Periphery

the masses of devout Muslims. This group can be divided into the following categories: 1) Successful businessmen who live modestly; 2) New Muslims who enjoy the benefits of their wealth; 3) Islamist Yuppies who waver between the first two poles (White 2002:48).

The "white Turks," on the other hand, include capitalists, the bureaucratic class, and the highest-ranking members of the military. The exclusions by the white Turks are aimed "to protect and preserve their political and economic hegemony against the black Turks and Kurds, and to exclude them from the privatization process" (Yavuz 2000:31). The government is the medium of conflict by the two classes for which the political process provides the means of access to power.

In the current context, the concept of "Islam outside the political domain" denotes the status and efforts of the remaining Muslim groups who are in the minority, but not necessarily insignificant in numbers. Historically, they have been kept outside the power structure and excluded from social negotiations.

The most significant group in this category is the Alevis, who traditionally have been a close ally to secularist forces since the role of Islam in Alevi social and political organization has never been important by any measure (Erman and Goker 2000). During the last few decades, however, the growing pressure on Alevis, with government support, demanding to abandon their beliefs and practices and yield to the principles of Sunni Islam has resulted in a backlash, and increased their political involvement by acquiring a more active agenda in Turkish politics.

The most apparent government pressure may be observed in the construction of thousands of new mosques in Alevi neighborhoods since the 1980s. Even though the project was mostly carried out by the elected Sunni Islamic governments, it would not have been possible without the approval and encouragement of the "guardians of the Republic." Their motive, perhaps arguably, had more to do with the imposition of the state-approved sect of Islam on the minority groups, which would serve toward further homogenization of the society, rather than as a precursor to tolerance for Islamic politics.

The urbanization of Alevi populations contributed greatly to their political mobilization as well as to the need to define their historical and ideological boundaries. Before their mass urbanization, Alevis had an isolated existence in which social identity was defined by local communities, and culture was transmitted through oral narratives. The urban life, however, threatened the bases of their identity, and necessitated a shift to written and uniform traditions.

Prior to the coup in 1980, Alevi politics were defined by their urban and class positions. However, as argued by Erman and Goker (2000), since the 1990s they have shifted the bases of their identity toward cultural and religious characteristics because

> Since the 1980s, Alevis have been experiencing downward mobility politically and economically. The significance of the unionized working class has declined parallel to the decline in the real wages, so they are economically worse off as a social group. Now a new dimension has been added to this downward mobility trend; since a large number were employed by Social Democratic municipalities, their jobs are often threatened or taken away by the new right-wing incumbents [Ayata, quoted in Erman and Goker 2000: 2–3].

Thus, paradoxically, the growing class disadvantage of the Alevis has compelled them to incorporate ethno-religious components into their identity and politics.

Class Structure and Social Inequality

The main contributor to the shift in objectives regarding religion and politics has been the deepening class conflicts. The widening of the gap between upper and lower classes, economic and political crises, and the inability to resolve them have created conditions in which many contradictions are located.

One of the most important problems facing Turkey is its inability to manage the economy. High levels of inflation, unemployment, nonofficial economy, inefficient government sector, corruption, and income inequality have had paralyzing effects. The relative size and role of government in the economy also play a key role in the instability of the society. The government maintains a significant role in the production and distribution of goods and services in that, first, it directly participates in production and employment through the state enterprises, and second, it has the ability to determine the size and activities of the private sector by laws and regulations.

The distribution of income and wealth in Turkey has gone through fundamental changes in the past two decades, moving toward greater inequality (Hirsch 1970; Boratav 1966; Bulutay, Timur, and Ersel 1971; Dervis and Robinson 1980; Celasun 1986). The declining fortunes of the middle and lower classes originated from two different sources. On the one hand, they were excluded from the "export boom" and also from the multiplier effects of domestic public and private spending mostly financed by external debt. In addition, high inflation rates that persisted for three decades had a profound effect on the living standards of salaried and working classes. To quote White, "Different social groups carried a disproportionate share of the burden and benefits of the new economy. [It] created great wealth for some, while the lives of industrial and agricultural workers, retirees, public sector workers, and other people on a fixed income became more precarious" (White 2002: 41–42).

Table 1.1: Sources of income, percent distribution

	Agriculture	Wages/Salaries	Other
1965	35.8	27.0	37.2
1970	31.1	31.2	37.7
1980	23.9	26.7	49.4
1985	17.8	19.5	62.7

Source: Hansen (1991): page 292, Table 6–14.

According to Barkey (1990), during the decade 1980–1990 real wages have declined 30 percent and 50 percent for private and public sector employees, respectively. As shown in Table 1.1 the share of income from wages and salaries has declined from 27 percent in 1965 (even though it briefly increased between 1965–1970 to 31.2 percent) to 19.5 percent in 1985. During the same period, on the other hand, income from "other" sources increased from 37.2 percent to 62.7 percent. The latter category includes income from self-employment, interest and investments, and other sources.

Referring to the data in Table 1.2 Hansen (1991) reports that despite their shortcomings, the available data reveal a rather polarized distribution of income. It shows a Gini coefficient of around 0.50, implying a relatively high income inequality. In addition, the shares of different quintiles have changed over time. For instance, the lowest quintile's share was reduced from 4.2 percent in 1963 to 2.6 percent in 1983.

Table 1.2: Income Distribution, Selected Years 1952–1983

Survey Year	Gini Coefficient	Lowest Quantile	Highest Quantile
1952	n.a.	n.a.	n.a.
1963	0.56	4.2	61.0
1968	0.56	3.0	60.0
1973	0.50	3.5	55.3
1978	0.51	2.8	54.7
1983	0.52	2.6	54.9

Source: Hansen (1991): page 276, Table 6–6.

Table 1.3: Share of income accruing to families under poverty line

	Nation	Agriculture
1973 survey	38.4	49.1
1983 estimate	29.9	51.3

Source: Hansen (1991): page 288, Table 6–15.

A study by the State Planning Organization (1996) found that income inequality grew further during the 1990s. According to the report, the share of the top 20 percent increased from 49.9 in 1987 to 54.9 percent in 1994. The share of the bottom 20 percent decreased from 5.2 percent to 4.9 percent during the same period. The incomes of the middle classes also declined, from 35 percent to 31 percent. The geographic distribution of incomes was also unequal in that the large cities in the western and southern parts of the country had greater share in the total.

The distribution of wealth, on the other hand, is most likely to be more unevenly distributed than income, given its highly concentrated structure in general. It is reflected in the economic and geographic concentration of business enterprises. In 1980, for instance, the 500 largest industrial concerns accounted for 49.4 percent of all manufacturing sales (Barkey 1990). In the total 79 units were owned by the government as well as the 12 largest. Out of the remaining 421 privately owned enterprises, 253 were located in Istanbul, recording more than 61 percent of sales by private sector, and 62.4 percent of capital. Collectively, the 421 enterprises accounted for more than 70 percent of private sales and capital in Turkey.

What is significant in terms of concentration of wealth is that even though the large private enterprises are open to the public for ownership, they are mostly owned and controlled by a small number of families. Also, the joint and interlocking ownership of banks and other businesses makes it possible to use public funds for individual businesses. For example, a holding company may own a bank which, in turn, may own shares of or lend money to the parent company by using the deposits held by the public.

Aside from the higher inequality of income and wealth, class systems in peripheral countries are different in other ways compared to core countries. One such difference is the vagueness in the definitions and determinants of class boundaries. In peripheral societies rapidly changing social and economic conditions result in constantly changing class dynamics and uncertainty. For instance, persistent high inflation rates and liquidity crises lead to reallocation of wealth, and also increase future uncertainty.

Conclusions

The role of religion in contemporary Turkey has been rather paradoxical. On the one hand, Islam has provided individuals with a means of spiritualism and social cohesion. And, as an integral part of individual philosophy and social identity, it furnishes Turkish nationalism with much-needed impetus. On the other hand, it is excluded from the public sphere, especially when presented in the form of organized, collective action. Thus, Islam resides in both inclusion and exclusion, simultaneously.

Islam also synthesizes the class conflicts between the privileged and the masses. There is, however, no consistency in this characteristic of Islam either. While the Sunni version is practiced by the majority and recognized and supported by the government, the Alevi version is adhered to by a minority of other Turks and Kurds who are subjected to cultural and political discrimination. In addition, the class boundaries of these groups are not uniquely determined by ethnicity alone.

In the final analysis, a recurring question is the possibility of a fundamentalist Islamic state in Turkey. The answer is no, if history is taken to be the greatest determinant of the future. The voting patterns and cultural practices of Turkish society also support this contention. They collectively show that in the opinion of the majority Islam should remain subordinate to individual and nationalist goals.

The current conditions transpire within the expansion of the world economy and the nation-state formation process as part of its historical development. In this regard, an important issue facing the peripheral countries is the dilemma that is built into their development and globalization project in that the resulting ethnic and class conflicts cannot be resolved within what is available to them. More specifically, the crystallization of opposing social identities and deepening class conflicts cannot be reconciled in a political system alien to democracy, host to oppressive traditions and institutions, and, more importantly, located at the lower part of the world's hierarchical structure. In the case of Turkey, and many others with similar conditions, another alternative is the breakdown of the nation-state, which is always possible but highly unlikely.

References

Anderson, Benedict. *Imagined Communities*. London: Verso, 1991.
Anderson, Perry. *Lineages of the Absolutist State*. London: Verso, 1979.
Andrews, Peter A. *Ethnic Groups in the Republic of Turkey*. L. Wiesbaden: Reichert, 1989.
Barkey, Henri J. "The Struggles of a 'Strong' State." *Journal of International Affairs* 54: 87–101, 2000.
Barkey, Henri J. *The State and Industrialization Crisis in Turkey*. Boulder, CO: Westview Press, 1990.
Berkes, Niyazi. *The Development of Secularism in Turkey*. Montreal: McGill University Press, 1964.
Boratav, K. "Turkiye'de Kisisel Gelir Dagilimi ve Planlama Teskilatinin Arastirmasi [Distribution of Personal Income in Turkey and the Study of Planning Organization]. *Journal of the Faculty of Political Sciences* 20 (1996). Ankara.

Brockett, Gavin D. "Collective Action and the Turkish Revolution: Towards a Framework for the Social History of the Ataturk Era, 1923-38." *Middle Eastern Studies* 34 (1998): 44-65.
Bulutay, T., S. Timur, and H. Ersel. *Turkiye'de Gelir Dagilimi 1968* [Income Distribution in Turkey 1968]. Ankara: Ankara University Publications, 1971.
Celasun, M. "Income Distribution and Domestic Terms of Trade in Turkey." *Studies in Development* 13 (1986): 193-216. Ankara: METU.
Dervis, K., and S. Robinson. "The Structure of Income Inequality in Turkey 1950-1973." In Ozbudun, E., New York: Holmes and Meier, and A. Ulusan. *The Political Economy of Income Distribution in Turkey: 1950-1973*. 1980.
Entessar, Nader. *Kurdish Ethnonationalism*. Boulder, CO: Lyenne Reiner, 1992.
Erman, Tahire, and Emrah Goker. "Alevi Politics in Contemporary Turkey." *Middle Eastern Studies* 36 (2000): 99-115.
Gellner, Ernest. *Nations and Nationalism*. Ithaca, NY: Cornell University Press, 1983.
Gökalp, Ziya. *The Principles of Turkism*. Leiden, Netherlands: E.J. Brill, 1968.
Gülalp, Haldun. *Nation State Formation: A Study of the Turkish Revolution*. Ph.D. Dissertation. Department of Sociology, Binghamton University, NY, 1991.
Gurr, Ted. *Minorities at Risk: A Global View of Ethnopolitical Conflicts*. Washington, DC: United States Institute of Peace Press, 1993.
Hansen, B. *The Political Economy of Poverty, Equity, and Growth: Egypt and Turkey*. Oxford: Oxford University Press, 1991.
Heper, Metin. "The Ottoman Legacy and Turkish Politics." *Journal of International Affairs* 54 (2000): 63-80.
_____. "Center and Periphery in the Ottoman Empire: With Special Reference to the nineteenth Century." *International Political Science Review* 1 (1980): 81-105.
_____, and M. Selcuk Sancar "Is Legal-Rational Bureaucracy a Prerequisite For a Rational-Productive Bureaucracy?" *Administration & Society* 30 (1998): 143-163.
Hirsch, E. *Poverty and Plenty on the Turkish Farm: A Study of Income Distribution in Turkish Agriculture*. New York: Columbia University Press, 1970.
Huri Islamogu-Inan, ed. *The Ottoman Empire and the World-Economy*. London: Cambridge University Press, 1987.
Izady, Mehrdad R. *The Kurds: A Concise Handbook*. Washington, DC: Taylor and Francis, 1992.
Kadioglu, Ayse. "The Paradox of Turkish Nationalism and the Construction of Official Identity." *Middle Eastern Studies* 32 (1996): 177-194.
Kafadar, Cemal. *Between Two Worlds: The Construction of the Ottoman State*. Berkeley, CA: University of California Press, 1995.
Karabelias, Gerassimos. "The Evolution of Civil-Military Relations in Post-War Turkey, 1980-95." *Middle Eastern Studies* 35 (1995): 130-152.
Kasaba, Re_at. *The Ottoman Empire and the World-Economy*. Albany, NY: State University of New York Press, 1988.
_____, and Sibel Bozdo_an. "Turkey at a Crossroad." *Journal of International Affairs* 54 (2000): 1-16.
Keyder, Ça_lar. "Social Structure and the Labor Market in Turkish Agriculture." *International Labor Review* 128 (1989): 731-44.
_____. *The State and Class in Turkey: A Study in Capitalist Development*. London: Verso, 1987.

Kramer, Heinz. "Turkey Toward 2000." *Brookings Review* 17 (1999): 32–37.
Kreyenbroek, Philip G., and Stefan Sperl. *The Kurds: A Contemporary Overview*. London: Routledge, 1992.
Kucuradi, Ioanna. "Secularization in Turkey." *Free Inquiry* 16 (1995): 45–48.
Kushner, David. *The Rise of Turkish Nationalism: 1876–1908*. London: Billing and Sons, 1977.
Landau, Jacob M. *Pan-Turkism: From Irredentism to Cooperation*. Bloomington, IN: Indiana University Press, 1995.
Lewis, Bernard. *The Emergence of Modern Turkey*. 2nd ed. London: Oxford University Press, 1968.
Mango, Andrew. "Turkey: The Urge to Reform." *Middle Eastern Studies* 37 (2001): 195–220.
_____. "Ataturk and the Kurds." *Middle Eastern Studies* 35 (1999): 1–22.
Mardin, _Erif. "The Ottoman Empire." In *After Empire: Multiethnic Societies and Nation Building*. Edited by Karen Barkey and Mark von Hagen. Boulder, CO: Westview Press, 1999.
_____. Religion and Social Change in Modern Turkey. Albany: SUNY, 1989.
_____. " Ideology and Religion in the Turkish Revolution." *International Journal of Middle East Studies* 2 (1971): 197–211.
Mason, Whit. "The Future of Political Islam in Turkey." *World Policy Journal* 17 (2000): 56–70.
Milliyet Turkish daily newspaper. June 30, 1998: 8.
_____. July 3, 1993:1.
_____. March 12, 1995: 1.
Mutlu, Servet. "Ethnic Kurds in Turkey: A Demographic Study." *International Journal of Middle East Studies* 28 (1996): 517–41.
Olzak, Susan. "Ethnic Protest in Core and Periphery States." *Ethnic and Racial Studies* 21 (1998): 187–217.
Öz, Baki. *Alevili_in Tarihsel Konumu* [Historical Status of the Alevis]. Istanbul: Der Yayınları, 1995.
_____. *Osmanli'da Alevi Ayaklanmaları* [Alevi Revolts in the Ottoman Empire]. Istanbul: Ant Yayınları, 1992.
Shankland, David. *Islam and Society in Turkey*. Cambridgeshire: Oethen, 1999.
Smith, Anthony D. "Towards a Theory of Ethnic Separatism." *Ethnic and Racial Studies* 2 (1979): 21–35.
Soysu, Hale. *Kavimler Kapısı-1* [The Gate of the Ethnicities-1]. Istanbul: Güney Yayıncılık, 1992.
State Planning Organization. *A Comparison of the 1994 Temporary Results of the Income Distribution Survey with the Results of the 1987 Income Distribution Survey*. Ankara: DPT, 1996.
Tapper, Richard, ed. *Islam in Modern Turkey: Religion, Politics and Literature in a Secular State*. London: I.B. Tauris, 1991.
Tezcan, Nuran, ed. *Atatürk'ün Yazdı_ı Yurtta_lık Bilgileri* [Citizenship Manual Written by Atatürk]. Istanbul: Der Yayınları, 1994.
Tuncay, Mete, and Erik Jan Zurcher. *Socialism and Nationalism in the Ottoman Empire: 1876–1923*. London: British Academic Press, 1994.

Wallerstein, Immanuel. *Historical Capitalism.* London: Verso, 1983.
_____. *The Capitalist World Economy.* Cambridge: Cambridge University Press, 1979.
_____. *The Modern World-System I.* New York: Academic, 1974.
_____ et al. "The Incorporation of the Ottoman Empire into the World-Economy." In *The Ottoman Empire and the World-Economy.* Edited by Huri _slamo_lu-_nan ed. London: Cambridge University Press, 1987.
White, Jenny B. *Islamist Mobilization in Turkey.* Seattle: University of Washington Press, 2002.
Yavuz, M. Hakan. "Cleansing Islam from the Public Sphere." *Journal of International Affairs* 54 (2000): 21–38.

11

The Virgin Mary Versus the Monkeys

Deana Weibel

"The Virgin Mary Versus the Monkeys" sounds like the title of a sacrilegious science fiction film of the 1950s that has fallen into well-deserved obscurity. However it is, in fact, an apt characterization of the current tension that exists between secular and religious forces in Rocamadour, a small village centered around a Roman Catholic shrine in the Lot department of south central France. In this paper I will describe Rocamadour's history as a pilgrimage destination, its rebirth as a tourist center and the effect that this tourist presence, encouraged by such attractions as *La Forêt des Singes* (the Monkey Forest), has on the overall secularization of what has always principally been a religious space.

The specific circumstances of Rocamadour's origins as a site of Catholic pilgrimage are unclear, but the first written mention of the site was in a papal bull written by Pope Pascal II in 1105 C.E. The shrine, a series of seven churches and chapels built roughly halfway up a 140-meter cliff overlooking the Alzou River and its valley, was the subject of a dispute between the monks of Marcilhac-Sur-Cele and those of Saint-Martin-de-Tulle. The former order had been given charge of Rocamadour, but the latter claimed that the shrine's management had been abandoned, inciting them to request control of the potentially very lucrative pilgrimage destination. Eventually the Pope sided with the monks of Tulle and they helped Rocamadour develop into one of the most important sanctuaries of medieval Europe.

During its heyday in the 12th and 13th centuries, droves of pilgrims came to the shrine, including such notables as Saint Louis and his mother, Blanche de Castille. The principal object of veneration at the shrine was a crudely carved wooden statue of the Virgin Mary, believed to date from the 11th century or earlier, although Rocamadour's wooden figure of the Virgin

Mary has never been scientifically dated. The site was considered a significant location for honoring the Virgin, but was somewhat unusual because of its lack of a relic.

In 1166, however, this oversight was corrected when builders unearthed a perfectly preserved body of a man near the chapel dedicated to the Virgin Mary. His state of preservation indicated his likely sainthood, but his identity was a mystery. Although French legends linked him to the biblical figure Zaccheus (Chauveau 1998), he was eventually dubbed Saint Amadour, after the site where he was found. This allowed *Roc Amadour* to be understood as "Amadour's Rock" when its true derivation was most likely *Roca Majeur*, or "Great Rock."

I will not take the time in this relatively short article to explore the time that passed between the 13th and 20th centuries, except to note that Rocamadour fell into disrepair by the 15th century, but was renovated during the zeal for all things Marian that took place in France during the 19th century. The pinnacle of Rocamadour's popularity, though, would not be reached until the 20th century, when railroads and highways made travel into rural France convenient and a new emphasis on leisure and holiday travel made vacations into the countryside particularly fashionable.

After World War II, travel throughout France became a popular pastime for the French and foreign visitors alike. Rocamadour, which is very close to the department of the Dordogne and its famous river, began to grow increasingly popular as a *site*. This term refers to locations that are visually dramatic and picturesque. Rocamadour's motto throughout most of the 20th century was "*Le deuxième site de France*," ("France's second site") following a poll that recognized Rocamadour as the second most popular tourist destination in the country, following only Mont Saint Michel. Despite its growing secular importance (mostly due to its proximity to dramatic caverns like the *Grotte des Merveilles*, the *Grottes de Lacave* and the *Gouffre de Padirac*), it remained a significant Marian shrine. Although it was somewhat eclipsed as a religious destination by its newer, more glamorous neighbor, Lourdes, to the south, such Marian festivals as the Assumption saw an influx of pilgrims to the locale every year. Secular visitors notwithstanding, Rocamadour's principal identity was as a religious site.

This began to change in 1974 when a troop of Barbary macaques was brought to Rocamadour from Morocco in an effort to provide the endangered animals with a safe haven in a suitable climate. The park was established within a forested section of the commune of Rocamadour, just a few kilometers from the shrine itself. Its proprietors opened *La Forêt des Singes* to the public and it was an immediate success. Tourists began to arrive at the park where, for a few francs, one could feed a handful of popcorn to the clever, amusing monkeys who roamed the wooded grounds.

11. The Virgin Mary Versus the Monkeys

The success of the Monkey Forest led to copycat establishments, the first being *Le Rocher des Aigles* (Eagles' Rock), set up in 1978. This park featured a variety of birds of prey visible in a zoo-like setting, who performed aerial shows several times a day. Unlike the monkeys, raptors, especially falcons, enhanced Rocamadour's new touristic image as an authentic medieval village.

By the time I arrived for my first leg of fieldwork in 1997, Rocamadour was also home to an aquarium, a "Bee House" where honeybees could be observed (and their honey purchased in jars or baked into cakes), a "Fairy Railroad" show, and a museum of mechanical toys. The nearby town of Gramat got into the act with its own zoo, and in the year 2000, a new park, Prehistoligia, featuring huge replicas of dinosaurs, was built five kilometers from Rocamadour in neighboring Lacave.

Despite its high level of secular tourist activity, Rocamadour remains a significant religious site in its region of France. Daily masses are held, of course, and the basilica is an important location for special ceremonies in the Cahors diocese. Rocamadour hosts formal processions twice a year. On August 15, the day of the Assumption, and on September 8, recognized by the locals as the Virgin Mary's birthday, groups consisting of community members and visitors meet at a small medieval church on Rocamadour's *Hospitalet* level, where the resident nuns and priests distribute candles encircled by prayer-marked paper shades. Singing hymns in chorus, the pilgrims descend into the Alzou Canyon, make their collective way up the *Grand Escalier* (the Great Staircase), which has over 200 steps, and links Rocamadour's main shopping street near the bottom of the canyon with the churches halfway up the cliff. They finish their procession with a special mass in the basilica in honor of the Blessed Virgin. The eight days surrounding September 8, from the Sunday preceding it to the Sunday following it, constitute a "Marian Week," with individual days set aside for child pilgrims, retired pilgrims, handicapped pilgrims, etc.

While the continued religious use of the shrine is apparent if one knows where to look for it, most secular tourists seem to be unaware that it exists. This makes Rocamadour somewhat distinct from other pilgrimage locales in France, as a comparison with the more famous Lourdes will illustrate.

Lourdes is a relative newcomer to the French pilgrimage scene, having taken on its status as a Marian apparition site in 1858, more than 700 years after Rocamadour's pilgrims began to arrive. Bernadette Soubirous, an impoverished 14-year-old, reported that a beautiful lady appeared to her a number of times, resulting in the miraculous manifestation of a spring whose water, the community discovered, had the power to heal.

Word of this apparently supernatural healing water began to spread, and the town of Lourdes quickly became France's preeminent pilgrimage destination. Pilgrims required places to stay, food to eat, and souvenirs to purchase, and so establishments providing for each of these needs were created. Most of these places took names that demonstrated their connection to the religious character of Lourdes and its origins, such as "*Le Palais de Rosaire*" ("The Rosary Palace") and "*Le Berceau de Bernadette*" ("Bernadette's Cradle"), and generally featured religious objects for sale. Because of this tendency to emphasize Bernadette's story and the church's presence, visitors to Lourdes, whether there as pilgrims or tourists, cannot help but be aware of the town's religious significance.

Rocamadour, however, comes across as a place where religion is only secondary, if it is emphasized at all. Most of its shops, particularly those on the main street, sell decidedly secular objects, like leather belts and purses, lace tablecloths, hunting knives, and pewter dishes. Rather than highlighting Rocamadour's status as a shrine, its stores tend to draw attention to its romanticized image as a medieval village. When restaurant menus or store signs do refer to the site's connection to pilgrimage, they focus almost exclusively on the pilgrims of this glorified past.

The Hotel Ste. Marie, for example, has a menu board in front of its restaurant featuring a traditional pilgrim of the Middle Ages. He is dressed in a light brown robe with a dark brown cape, carries a walking stick, and sports a customary wide-brimmed hat. Interestingly, his purse is marked with a scallop shell, identifying him as a pilgrim whose destination is not Rocamadour, but Santiago de Compostela, in northern Spain. He is certainly not a contemporary pilgrim, and while he can be found in Rocamadour, he is apparently just passing through on his way to a more important shrine. Rocamadour is located between two of the main French routes leading to Santiago de Compostela and pilgrims heading to Spain often do cross over, passing through Rocamadour.

During my fieldwork in Rocamadour, I had the chance to discuss the shrine's mostly non-religious nature with many shopkeepers, restaurant owners, and others whose income depended on the presence of tourists. I found that most wished to keep Rocamadour as secular as possible. A merchant in a shop that sold ceramics and table linens said that most sellers there believed that the *français moyen* (average French person) was not particularly religious and would not wish to spend his vacation in a place that overtly emphasized Catholicism. By downplaying its religious character, I was told, Rocamadour was better able to ensure its popularity as a tourist attraction, but at the cost of its reputation as a spiritual center.

The notion that the "average French person" is more secular than religious is borne out in the French almanac *Pour Comprendre les Français: Francoscopie 2003*. This volume reports that a 2002 study by *La Croix*/CSA showed that while the majority of the French population considers itself to be Roman Catholic, 7.2 percent of these identify themselves as practicing regularly, 20 percent identify themselves as practicing occasionally, and fully 44.2 percent identify themselves as nonpracticing. Another 20.9 percent of the French population identify themselves as being without religion (Mermet, p. 280). It is unsurprising, with figures like these and a growing awareness that France is becoming more secular, that those who rely on income from Rocamadour's tourists would prefer to present a more secular face.

Others at Rocamadour, however, especially members of the clergy and the town's older citizens, view the shrine's loss of its religious focus as something undesirable. After all, Rocamadour's reputation has always been based on its history of pilgrimage. In an attempt to remedy the situation, the clergy of Rocamadour and its surrounding diocese, with the cooperation of the Office of Tourism, have begun efforts to draw tourists away from the secular shops to the shrine section of the site.

On Wednesday nights during the summer, for instance, Rocamadour's basilica hosts a concert series featuring various live musicians playing religiously themed music. The promise of a concert, especially a free one, on a summer evening, certainly succeeds in attracting both tourists and locals to the shrine level of the site. The Office of Tourism also makes an effort to promote Rocamadour as a religious location. Among the many fliers the office displays, promoting such things as cave exploration at the Gouffre de Padirac or the delicious honey cakes available at the Bee House, are pamphlets suggesting that visitors undertake a "one-day pilgrimage" at the shrine. The Office of Tourism's employees told me that these fliers are among the slowest to be taken by visitors, or at least need to be replenished less often than most of the others.

Despite a perceived lack of interest by the public, the Office of Tourism has shown an increased enthusiasm for promoting the religious nature of Rocamadour since it joined *L'Association des Villes Sanctuaires en France* (the Association of Sanctuary Towns in France), which unites the tourism offices of several shrine locales, including Lourdes, Nevers, and Chartres, in a stated effort to improve the knowledge of all visitors, whether tourists or pilgrims, about the spiritual significance of these places. Each participant in the association works to promote the others, so that membership, theoretically, increases the number of visitors to all of the shrine towns.

The Office of Tourism's focus on Rocamadour's religious nature is recent, but the diocese of Cahors has been working for much longer to attract visitors to Rocamadour's church section. Probably the costliest project with this goal was the renovation of the *Musée d'Art Sacré* (Museum of Sacred Art), completed in 1995. The museum, formerly known as the *Musée du Trésor* (Museum of the Treasure), is also called the Francis Poulenc Museum. When it reopened in 1995 it was dedicated to Francis Poulenc, who composed his *Litanies to the Black Virgin* over just one night after a dramatic conversion experience in the Notre Dame chapel.

The museum, which houses religious art and objects not just from Rocamadour, but also on loan from the clerical storehouses of surrounding communities, was hollowed out during its renovation, turning its original medieval interior into something very modern, while retaining its original exterior. When the idea to renovate the museum was proposed, it seemed promising to the diocese's treasurer, but the more religious citizens of Rocamadour are frequently very critical of the result, describing it as a money pit or simply a disaster. The museum, while improved, has failed in its efforts to recoup its costs. Because the renovations were so expensive, admission to the museum was set at a rather high price. This has backfired, leaving the Francis Poulenc Museum nearly empty on most days, even during the summer tourist season. Its conspicuous underuse makes it stand out as a symbol of diocesan misjudgment.

Another scandal associated with the museum is that Francis Poulenc's original copies of his *Litanies to the Black Virgin*, while part of Rocamadour's collection, are apparently locked away from public view. The pages on display inside the museum are actually photocopies of the original, I was told by distressed museum workers. These workers, mostly young women who are often art history students undertaking summer employment at Rocamadour, took the museum's lack of success very personally. One of them, Millie, complained that when visitors approached her it was often only to ask where they could find the monkeys.

Other businesses owned by the diocese have fared better than the Museum of Sacred Art. The *Magasin de Pelèrinage* (Pilgrimage Store) is the only shop located on the church courtyard and the only establishment at Rocamadour that specializes in religious goods. The store is often packed with customers, particularly after special masses, and sells postcards, games, and costume jewelry in addition to rosaries, religious books and music, and statues of saints.

The castle overlooking Rocamadour's cliff and a home built up against the cliff wall called the *Maison à Marie* (Mary's House) are also owned by the diocese. When I was conducting my fieldwork, it was common for rooms in both to be rented out to groups from other dioceses that had come to Rocamadour on pilgrimage, permitting a certain amount of profit. The diocese has also installed coin-operated doors that require payment before letting visitors out onto the castle's 13th-century ramparts. It is clear that the diocese of Cahors, just like Rocamadour's local merchants, has a stake in increasing the number of people who visit the site.

Despite the usual cooperation that takes place between Rocamadour's secular and religious partisans, at least on the level of working to accomplish certain common goals, there are occasionally clashes between the groups. When Father Chauny, a relatively young and idealistic priest, became Rocamadour's rector in 1997, he vowed to bring a religious tenor back to the shrine area of the site by forbidding dogs and people wearing shorts from entering the church courtyard. He also declared that all garbage cans would be removed from the spaces surrounding the chapels.

As could be expected, Rocamadour's shopkeepers protested passionately. If visitors were barred from entering the church courtyard, for whatever reason, they would not be able to move freely between the shops at the top of the cliff and those nearer the canyon floor. Father Chauny, outnumbered, eventually had to make do with the removal of the garbage cans, although employees in both the Pilgrimage Store and the Museum of Sacred Art, which are located in the church courtyard, grumble that this actually causes more problems than it solved.

Now that Rocamadour's current situation of push and pull between its sometimes overlapping religious and secular forces has been described, how can it be understood in terms of anthropological understandings about pilgrimage? Victor and Edith Turner, in their *Image and Pilgrimage in Christian Culture*, describe how a typical shrine is likely to function and change, based on their work and that of other ethnographers at pilgrimage centers. The Turners borrow the term "entelechy" from the discipline of philosophy, using it in this context to refer to the "immanent force controlling and directing (the) development" of a shrine (Turner and Turner, p. 25). Normal shrine entelechy begins with a miraculous event, religiously important incident, or a significant discovery of some kind, like the apparitions of the Virgin Mary that Bernadette is said to have seen at Lourdes. Word of the occurrence begins to spread and people come to visit the location where the happening took place. As more and more people journey to the now-sacred spot, hotels, restaurants, roads, etc. are built to accommodate the pilgrims.

The Turners use an "organism-environment field" model to describe the typical result of shrine entelechy. The "organism" refers to the sacred aspects of a pilgrimage destination, such as relics, religious buildings, or miraculous objects. The "environment field" consists of the organism's support system — the secular developments that help a sacred center function. At Lourdes, for example, the organism would include the basilica, the grotto where the apparition is understood to have appeared, and the miraculous healing spring. The environment field, on the other hand, would be comprised of such phenomena as the hotels, the train station, and even Internet tour organizers that help would-be pilgrims arrange their voyages. Shrine entelechy, as described by the Turners, seems to go primarily in one direction, from a smaller system to a larger system, unless a shrine falls into disrepair.

The entelechy of Rocamadour, however, seems to have gone in a direction unanticipated by the Turners. It started out the way they would have predicted, with the Notre Dame chapel, the statue of the black Virgin and the *Grand Escalier* being central to Rocamadour's existence. The appearance of mills and inns during the Middle Ages and hotels, stores, and restaurants today, also seems to confirm that Rocamadour's entelechy is on course. It could be argued as well that attractions like the Fairy Railroad, Eagles' Rock and the Monkey Forest are merely part of the supporting environment field that surrounds the shrine.

But are these amusements truly playing only a supporting role? It seems instead that the appearance of the Monkey Forest marked the beginning of an era when Rocamadour's very reason for being began to change. If the organism is the underlying reason for a shrine, and the environment provides its support, it would appear that the organism would, by definition, be more essential than the environment in the continued existence of a shrine.

If we look at Rocamadour from this perspective, however, the situation is different from what we would expect. If the Notre Dame chapel housing the black Virgin were shut down, most of the approximately 1.5 million people who come each year to the site would probably still come. All indications at Rocamadour suggest that people principally go to the town to soak up the secular medieval atmosphere, watch the falcons, and feed the monkeys. If these attractions are only the supportive environment field, then something unanticipated is taking place.

If, conversely, the tourist attractions were shut down and only the sacred aspects of Rocamadour were preserved, it seems safe to say, given the current situation, that the number of visitors to Rocamadour would decline substantially. It is clear from this example that the essential center of the town, its organism, is made up of the various tourist attractions. The sacred chapels, holy objects, and other religious paraphernalia now appear to have been relegated to the periphery, perhaps having even become part of a structure that supports the secular tourism. These religious features have turned into an object of curiosity for the typical visitor to Rocamadour, not the actual destination.

Another indication that Rocamadour's organism has shifted is that its environment — the hotels, restaurants, etc. — are now clearly supporting tourism rather than pilgrimage. Rocamadour's reason for existing, its essential aspect, is secular now, not religious. This is a shift in entelechy unaccounted for by the Turner model.

To further demonstrate just how decidedly the shrine's balance has shifted, I will give an example I discovered during my most recent visit to Rocamadour, in January 2003. The castle that overlooks the cliff, which I noted earlier has customarily been used to house groups of pilgrims, has been given a new purpose. It is still owned by the diocese of Cahors, but has been given the name *Le Relais des Remparts* (the Inn of the Ramparts) and is operating now as an ordinary hotel. The fact that the diocese itself has started to support tourism at the expense of pilgrimage is a good indication of just how much Rocamadour has changed.

While I have argued that the Turners' model of shrine entelechy appears to have problems when applied to Rocamadour's circumstances, their contention that a shrine will never disappear but will instead lie dormant may hold some merit here, albeit in a way that probably would not have occurred to them. During my research I found that the chapel housing the black Virgin statue, the cliff itself and other parts of the church complex were being utilized by pilgrims other than the Catholic pilgrims for whom they were intended. Unlike at Lourdes, where the religious aspects of the site are interpreted for visitors through explanatory placards, store names, and the continuous presence of members of the clergy, Rocamadour's religious complex can be explored at will and has no visible official interpretation. To learn about the shrine's story, one must take a diocese-organized tour or ask a nun or priest at the visitors center during its sporadic operating hours.

This state of affairs appears to have made the site very attractive to visitors who could be described as having "New Age" proclivities. I interviewed individuals who went on pilgrimage to Rocamadour in order to evoke the Goddess, pray to the cliff wall or stalagmites, search for sources of microwaves and "tellurian" energy, and gather perceived supernatural emanations from the shrine into objects or even their own bodies.

In addition, many New Age books and Web sites about sacred locales include Rocamadour. The shrine's black Virgin statue is very highly regarded in these spheres, and is variously interpreted as the Virgin Mary, Mary Magdalene, Isis, a variety of other pagan goddesses, and Mother Earth.

Still, this new use of the shrine is far outweighed by the presence of secular tourists, and Rocamadour's increasing focus on tourism may eventually make the site less attractive even to these alternative pilgrims. Unless the Turners' model is correct and the shrine's religious partisans are able to reassert Rocamadour's Catholic identity, it appears likely, as strange as it may sound, that the monkeys will eventually prevail over the Virgin Mary.

References

Austen, H. I. "Pele and the Hawaiian Islands." In *Earthwalking Sky Dancers: Women's Pilgrimages to Sacred Places*, edited by L. Castle. Berkeley: Frog, Ltd, 1996.
Begg, E. *The Cult of the Black Virgin*. London: Penguin Books Arkana, 1996.
Bull, M. G. *The Miracles of Our Lady of Rocamadour: Analysis and Translation*. Woodbridge, Suffolk, UK: Boydell, 1999.

Chauveau, M., ed. *Rocamadour: Une Cité en Équilibre.* Saint-Cirq-Lapopie, France: Carnets de Notes, 1998.
Coleman, S., and J. Elsner. *Pilgrimage Past and Present in the World Religions.* Cambridge: Harvard University Press, 1995.
Cranston, R. *The Miracle of Lourdes.* New York: Image, Doubleday, 1988.
Eade, J., and M.J. Sallnow, eds. *Contesting the Sacred: The Anthropology of Christian Pilgrimage.* London: Routledge, 1991.
Eisler, R. *The Chalice and the Blade: Our History, Our Future.* San Francisco: Harper San Francisco, 1988.
Hamilton, M. *Incubation or The Cure of Disease in Pagan Temples and Christian Churches.* London, England: W.C. Henderson and Son, St. Andrews Simpkin, Marshall, Hamilton, Kent, 1906.
Heelas, P. *The New Age Movement: The Celebration of the Self and the Sacralization of Modernity.* Malden, MA: Blackwell, 1996.
Khalsa, P. S., ed. *A Pilgrim's Guide to Planet Earth: A Traveler's Handbook and New Age Directory.* London: Wildwood House, 1981.
Larkin, M. *Religion, Politics and Preferment in France since 1890: La Belle Epoque and its Legacy.* Cambridge: Cambridge University Press, 1995.
Mermet, G. *Pour Comprendre les Français: Francoscopie 2003.* France: Larousse, 2002.
Poux, D. *Rocamadour: Great Pilgrimage Center.* Albi, France: As du Coeur, 1991.
Preston, J. J. "Spiritual Magnetism: An Organizing Principle for the Study of Pilgrimage." In *Sacred Journeys: The Anthropology of Christian Pilgrimage,* edited by A. Morinis. Westport, CT: Greenwood, 1992.
Rocacher, J. *Rocamadour et son Pèlerinage: Étude Historique et Archéologique* Vol. 2. Toulouse, France: Edouard Privat, 1979.
_____. *Rocamadour: Un Prêtre Raconte la Roche Mariale.* Paris: Les Editions d'Atelier, 1999.
Rogers, S. C. *Shaping Modern Times in Rural France: The Transformation and Reproduction of an Aveyronnais Community.* Princeton, NJ: Princeton University Press, 1991.
Seel, P. *Rocamadour: La Croix, La Secte et Le Serpent.* Dire-Lot, 73, 1998.
Selby, B. *Pilgrim's Road: A Journey to Santiago de Compostela.* London: Little, Brown, 1994.
Sevin, M. *Pourquoi Partir? Partir en Pèlerinage,* 466. 1992.
Sigal, P. A., ed. *L'Image du Pèlerin au Moyen Âge et sous l'Ancien Régime.* Gramat, France: Association des Amis de Rocamadour, 1994.
Starbird, M. *The Woman with the Alabaster Jar: Mary Magdalen and the Holy Grail.* Santa Fe, NM: Bear & Company, 1993.
Thornburgh, R. *Never Look Back: Tramping to Rocamadour.* Dorset: Pharisaios, 1994.
Turner, V. T., and E. L. B. Turner. *Image and Pilgrimage in Christian Culture: Anthropological Perspectives.* New York: Columbia University Press, 1978.
Vernette, J. *Le Nouvel Age: À l'Aube de l'Ere du Verseau.* Paris: Pierre Tequi, 1989.
_____. Les *Pèlerins du Labyrinthe de Chartres.* Esprit et Vie: L'Ami du Clergé, 1990. 11(25), 353–358.
Webb, D. *Pilgrims and Pilgrimage in the Medieval West.* New York: St. Martin's Press, 1999.
Weibel, D. *Kidnapping the Virgin: The Reinterpretation of a Roman Catholic Shrine*

by Religious Creatives (Doctoral Dissertation): University of California at San Diego, 2001.

_____. "The New Age and the Old World: The Interpretation and Use of European Shrines by Religious Creatives." *Maria: A Journal of Marian Studies*, 2(2) (2002): 81–87.

_____. "The Energy We Call the Goddess: The Religious Creativist Use of a Roman Catholic Shrine." *Maria: A Journal of Marian Studies*, 2(2) (2002): 88–94.

_____. "Controlling Chance, Creating Chance: Magical Thinking in Religious Pilgrimage." *The Journal for the Academic Study of Magic* 1 (2003): 161–178.

Zimdars-Swartz, S. L. *Encountering Mary: Visions of Mary from La Salette to Medjugorje*. New York: Avon Books, 1991.

12

Martyrdom and Violence in Sikhism

The Transfer of Embodied Experience Through Witnessing

RORY G. MCCARTHY

In June of 1984, the Indian army surrounded the Harmander Sahib, or the Golden Temple, in Armitsar, a city in the Indian state of Punjab. In what became widely known as Operation Bluestar, troops laid siege to this most sacred shrine of Sikhism, hoping to drive out a small band of armed militants. Inside, charismatic religious leader and radical political activist Sant Jarnail Singh Bhindranwale was aware that death was at hand. When his followers encouraged him to escape the complex through a back door with his life intact, he reportedly replied, "Baba Deep Singh came so far to give his head at this place, and I am privileged to be able to give mine right here" (Mahmood, 1996:40). Baba Deep Singh, a religious scholar and brave warrior from the heroic period in Sikh history (the 18th century), had led an army to free the Golden Temple from invading Muslim forces. In the battle, his head was severed from his body, yet he continued fighting, head in one hand, sword in the other, until he reached the occupied shrine. The story of Baba Deep Singh is one of ultimate sacrifice, and the importance of his martyrdom for Sikhs rivals that of Joan of Arc for Catholics. When the dust settled after Operation Bluestar, Sant Bhindranwale's lifeless body remained inside the Golden Temple, but his name was given immortality as a martyr. Whether or not he uttered these famous words, his death had an immediate impact on the Sikh community, and the state of India.

In the 11 years following the death of Bhindranwale, countless Sikhs died in an armed struggle for independence in Punjab, a struggle that was countered harshly by the Indian government. Torture, forced disappearance, and police harassment came to typify day-to-day life for many Sikhs. Exploding bombs and gunfire echoed through the villages in Punjab, stirring up fear in the hearts of both Sikhs and Hindus, who were witnessing an ever-increasing gulf developing between the two communities. Pictures of Bhindranwale began to appear in the homes of Sikhs around the world, his long flowing beard and deep blue turban shrouding a face, calm and serene. As a martyr, he was brave and unwavering in the defense of his faith, and in the pursuit of justice, right up to the very end. To Hindus, this image came to represent a criminal and a feared enemy of the state, a terrorist whose radical fundamentalism threatened the stability and future of India as a nation. These fears were not exclusive to Bhindranwale's image, however, because a violent terrorist might be lurking behind the serene face, and flowing beard of any *amritdhari* Sikh (Mahmood, 1996).

This tale of death and martyrdom is a compelling anecdote for contemporary anthropology for a couple of reasons. First, it illustrates how notions of religion, identity, and nationalism become interwoven with history and tradition to constitute a political struggle. Second, it demonstrates how these struggles become incorporated, illustrated, and understood through the body, both figuratively and literally. Thus, martyrdom as a tradition becomes an excellent analytical tool for understanding how culture is experienced, and expressed through the body. It also shows how power expressed at a microlevel, through violence against an individual body, has implications for power struggles at the macrolevel, in this case in the form of an independence movement. In this paper, I will demonstrate, through an analysis of the Sikh tradition of martyrdom, how power is expressed, and then appropriated by a community that sees itself in a constant struggle to maintain an existence in the face of perceived oppression and persecution. Also, I will illustrate how images, such as paintings, and more recently photographs, have acted to transfer this moment of struggle for power, enacted on the bodies of both historic and contemporary martyrs, to a viewing audience.

The Body as Location

It has long been understood that the body is an important factor in understanding a culture and its practices. Ritual, initiation, and rites of passage — aspects of culture that have a strong bodily component — have all been at the center of anthropological inquiry since the earliest days of the discipline. However, it remains a fairly recent theoretical development to look at the body as a location where culture is experienced. While many see the origins of this notion of embodied culture in the work of Marcel Mauss

(Csordas 1999; Turner 1996), most would agree that the first attempt to extract cultural understanding directly from an analysis of the body lies in the work of Mary Douglas (1966, 1970). Douglas' ideas about symbolic bodily practices reflecting larger social concerns pushed the body to the forefront of anthropological inquiry. Equally important to our understanding of an anthropology of the body can be found in the work of French philosopher Michel Foucault. Citing Foucault, Alter (2000) points out that the body is a location for power, as well as a location where power struggles play out, and larger cultural themes of compliance or resistance are expressed. Nowhere is this power struggle more obvious than in violence carried out by one human being against another. When that violence is imbued with its own cultural symbolism or meaning, such as in the cases of torture and martyrdom, struggles for power taking place in this bodily context become compounded.

In *Discipline and Punish*, Foucault (1995) argues that before the emergence of modern forms of power, the sovereign exercised power over a population through public torture and execution. The criminal, whose unlawful activity was a direct challenge to the power of the state, was often punished for that challenge in a very public manner. The punishment enacted directly on the criminal's body was a manifestation of the consolidated power of the sovereign. The severity of bodily punishment and the public nature of the event served to remind those viewing the execution of an existing hierarchy of power that placed them all at the mercy of the sovereign. Foucault argued that the crime was treated as an act of war, and the punishment could be analyzed in terms of the defense of territorial boundaries (ibid).

Martyrdom is often the end result of similar expressions of power, through violence enacted on the body. The religious martyr, whose death symbolizes a commitment to faith, often finds expression of that commitment through bodily suffering at the hands of a more powerful "sovereign." While the martyr may suffer a fate similar to Foucault's criminal, there is something inherently different in the relationship between these victims of torture and their executioners. While some punishment takes place behind closed doors, the ultimate aim of the execution of the criminal is to make public the transgression against the state (ibid). Through a public reading of the charges, an acceptance of responsibility by the criminal, and pleas for mercy and forgiveness, a public execution acts to legitimize the authority of the sovereign through legitimizing the expression of violence on the body of the transgressor. There is agreement between the sovereign, the criminal, and viewing public that the punishment, and the power exercising it, are legitimate.

With the public execution of the martyr, there is a fundamental difference. The martyr is often treated as a criminal, but the crime is not ultimately expressed as a transgression against the state, but as one against a divine authority. Thus the power relations being expressed on the body of the accused are arranged in a less direct manner. Here, transgression against divinity is punished by human hands. The martyr, unlike the criminal, refuses to accept responsibility for the act of transgression, thereby choosing death rather than accepting guilt. Fenech (2001) argues that this choice is key to understanding the difference between Foucault's model of sovereign power and power as expressed on the body of the religious martyr. The condemned has a choice between religious conversion and death. The choice of death over conversion, like the execution itself, is made public. Thus, the martyr, the executioner, the sovereign, and the audience are all aware of the choice being made (ibid). The refusal of the martyr to recognize his or her own actions as transgressions against a divine power works to undermine the legitimacy of that power. To choose death usurps the authority of both the divine, and the sovereign power carrying out the act of punishment. Therefore, power expressed through these acts is transferred from the sovereign into the body of the martyr. Likewise, the spiritual authority of the martyr's own conception of divinity is infused with power, expressed through the suffering of the martyr. The martyr's possession of that power, however, is short lived. How does the community, represented by that martyr, appropriate this transferred power? Here, we must understand the role of the witness in these power struggles as they are expressed on the body of the martyr.

Embodiment as a Paradigm?

The rise of anthropological investigations into the role of the body in understanding culture took place in a larger theoretical move away from structural thinking about culture, and its dissemination. Combining Douglas' work on the body with new appreciations of agency, phenomenology, and existential experience, theorists such as Csordas (1990), Turner (1995), and Jackson (1998) began to see culture less as a grand narrative, and more in terms of the experiential. Embodiment, as described by Csordas (1990, 1999), came to include an understanding of culture as experienced, and expressed by the individual, through that individual's body. This understanding is largely informed by the work of Merleau-Ponty and Bourdieu (Csordas, 1990; Turner; 1995; Jackson, 1998). It is not my intention here to open up a full discussion of the implications of theories of embodiment, but rather, to limit the discussion to the embodiment of cultural experience. Csordas (1990), in his article "Embodiment as a Paradigm for Anthropology," argues that culture can be best understood through an analysis that employs a collapse of the dualities that typified the structural approach. This collapse of dualities, including mind/body and subject/object, is inherent in the embodiment approach to understanding cultural phenomena. And because embodiment places the body at the gateway to cultural experiences, it is through understanding individual bodily experiences that we can understand culture.

A problem arises when a cultural tradition such as martyrdom is introduced. If embodiment is rooted in the individual's experiencing of cultural phenomena through the body, then it would seem the martyr's experience would die with him. However, this does not appear to be the case. The martyr experiences an appropriation of power, and a consolidation of identity through the ultimate sacrifice of self, both of which are then transferred into the martyr's community. An oppressed community, then, obtains strength through its martyrs, and acquires a consolidation of group identity that can be linked to the actions of those figures. When that oppressed group is embroiled in a struggle for autonomy, a tradition of martyrdom becomes an important means of expressing the need for that autonomy, a means of rallying the troops around the cause (Mahmood 1996; Pettigrew 1992; Spencer 2000). How is it that the experiences of the martyr manifest themselves in the martyr's community? It is through witnessing the act of martyrdom.

According to Veena Das (2000), witnesses of violence can utilize the loss associated with the act to redefine themselves in the world, to create a new notion of themselves as subjects, one which is continually reconstituted by the memory of that violence. In viewing the violence carried out on the body of the martyr, the witness can imagine his own death. From this vantage point, the power usurped by the martyr can be utilized to strengthen the resolve of the endangered group, instilling it with a sense of communal cohesion or solidarity. Here, the strength of will, bravery, and faith of the religious martyr can be transferred, and embodied by others. And here, the injustice and persecution directed at the endangered group can be condemned.

Sikhism: A Tradition of Martyrdom

While a theoretical discussion of how a tradition of martyrdom can foster the embodiment of a transitory power, traced from the sovereign through the body of the martyr and into the larger community of the oppressed, is interesting, it provides little utility if it cannot be grounded in some historical and ethnographic evidence. The Sikh faith provides an excellent case study for two reasons. First, Sikhism has a long tradition of martyrdom, reflecting conceptions of a religious existence marked by constant oppression. Second, a recent struggle for autonomy in Punjab has resulted in a fusing of the past with the present, bringing this tradition to the forefront of group identity, and adding new names to the list of important martyrs within the Sikh faith.

The term used within Sikhism for a martyr is *shahid* (or *shaheed*), a term borrowed from Islam, meaning "witness" (Axel 2001; Fenech 2001; Mahmood 1996). While the Muslim use of the word most often refers to being the witness to one's faith, Sikh appropriation of the term alters its meaning. For Sikhs, shahid means one who, as witness, testifies against injustice. For this reason, the martyr within Sikhism is an individual who is an "exemplar of virtue, truth and moral justification" (Fenech 2001:7). Therefore, according to Fenech (2001), martyrdom results in liberation from the cycle of existence, of birth and rebirth, and culminates in an eternal union with God, referred to in the Sikh faith as *Waheguru*, or *Guru*. Mahmood argues, however, that martyrdom within Sikhism is not a means to an end, but rather a *"willingness to give one's head ... not the outcome, but the process"* (1996:34; emphasis in the original). Regardless, though a concept of a living martyr does exist within Sikhism, it is most often death that earns the title shahid (Fenech 2001). Thus, the tradition of martyrdom becomes the intersection where all ideals within Sikhism merge. "For Sikhs, a reference to Sikh martyrs is, therefore, a reference to the ultimate embodiment of heroism, defiance, endurance, loyalty, fearlessness and altruism" (Fenech 2001:39).

This tradition, with its incorporation of multiple religious ideals, was initially transmitted through stories and song. *Dhadhi jathas*, musicians who traveled the Punjabi countryside singing songs about the military exploits of the Gurus and the military leaders of the post–Guru period, became the transmitters of the tradition of martyrdom (Fenech 2001). These musicians were known to include, in their repertoire, songs about contemporary struggles, creating new figures associated with the tradition of martyrdom. After Operation Bluestar, songs praising the actions of Sant Jarnail Singh Bhindranwale, and others recently martyred, were spread by dhadhi jathas. Interestingly, the Indian government banned the performances of these songs, both old and new, after the events of 1984 (ibid).

Other means of maintaining this tradition are present in artistic renderings of the martyrdom of historical figures. Painted in graphic detail, these paintings often show the martyrs in the midst of extreme bodily torture, maintaining a serene, blissful expression that typifies the ideal (Axel 2001; Fenech 2001; Mahmood 1996). This art, depicting the martyrdom of famous figures such as Bhai Mani Singh, as well as large-scale massacre at the hands of Mughals, the British, and most recently the Indian Army during Operation Bluestar, has a power that cannot be denied. Mahmood (1996:189) describes this art as follows: "In their very gruesomeness, these paintings, drawings and photos assert themselves in a room; they are impossible to ignore, and intrude in conversation, meditation, and everyday activities. Their potency derives only in part from blood; it derives also from their unwillingness to be masked, covered, or distorted ... it is a kind of witness that will allow no one to rest."

These artistic renderings of the embodied moment of martyrdom can be found in children's books, magazines, and on calendars and Internet Web pages (Axel 2001; Fenech 2001). Likewise, they can be found on the walls in many gurdwaras (Sikh houses of worship), and in the homes of Sikhs both in India and abroad (Axel 2001; Mahmood 1996). Also widespread are more formal portraits of these martyrs. The prevalence of these images, and the familiarity of the associated meaning attributed to them, thus acts to constantly remind Sikhs of their precarious place in the world. A history of oppression and persecution, embodied by the viewer of this art, or the listener of these songs and stories, is made more poignant by a present-day struggle for independence. Thus, direct links can be made between the Mughals and the government of the state of India, just as links are drawn between the historical martyrs and the contemporary victims of violence, torture, and execution.

While there is some debate regarding the historic centrality of martyrdom to the Sikh identity (Fenech 2000; Oberoi 1994), the writings of Guru Nanak, the founder of Sikhism, are most often cited as the basis for a tradition of martyrdom. One of the most famous passages written by Guru Nanak reads as follows: "If you want to play this game of love, come to my street with your head in your palms" (Mahmood 1996:33). It is this reference to humility and grace that is most often associated with Guru Nanak. It is this same passage that later came to be interpreted as legitimizing martyrdom as a form of spiritual expression (ibid). It is this idea of giving one's head, in the literal sense, that was typified by Baba Deep Singh, Sant Bhindranwale, and countless others; a conceptualization of the figurative that came to be taken as literal.

However, it is the fifth guru, Arjun Dev who is generally agreed upon as the first Sikh to be martyred (Mahmood 1996; Pettigrew 1992; Singh 1999). In a tale of extreme bodily torture, and amazing strength of will, Guru Arjun Dev is reported to have been forced to sit on a steel plate, heated over a fire, while burning sand was poured over his entire body. He was forced to sit in a large pot of boiling water, and finally drowned in a nearby river. He is reported to have sat blissfully silent throughout the entire ordeal, never wavering in his convictions (Mahmood 1996; Singh 1999). Guru Arjun Dev claimed, "the true test of faith is the hour of misery" (quoted in Mahmood 1996:38), a supposition he embodied during his own torture and execution. It is this notion of the Sikh martyr calmly embracing death, attributed to Arjun Dev, which looms large in the Sikh imagination (Mahmood 1996).

The martyrdom of Guru Arjun Dev had a profound effect on the still-new religion of Sikhism. His son and successor as religious leader, Guru Hargobind, began a process of militarization of the faith by donning two swords, which he named *miri*, for temporal authority and *piri*, for spiritual authority (Axel 2001; Mahmood 1996; Singh 1999). These two swords are still closely associated with Sikhism, in the form of a symbol, known as a *khanda*. Hargobind is also credited with fostering the notion of the *sant-sapahi*, or "saint-soldier," a concept that Mahmood argues has become so closely associated with Sikhism, that for some, the two are interchangeable. Over time, this association of Sikhism with militarism, rooted in the concept of the "saint-soldier," has culminated in the formation of the *Khalsa* by the 10th and final living guru, Guru Gobind Singh (Axel 2001; Mahmood 1996).

In the Khalsa the process of militarization begun by the sixth guru was fully realized, a process that many Sikhs argue has origins in the words of Nanak, not merely the actions of Hargobind or Gobind Singh (Axel 2001; Mahmood 1996). Upon initiation into the Khalsa, which means "Brotherhood of the Pure," a Sikh is required to adopt the wearing of five external signs of the faith. These signs, known as the five "K's," have come to typify the modern Sikh identity, even though the wearing of them is only required of *amritdharis*, or Khalsa initiates. The symbols include unshorn hair, a comb, a steel bangle, a particular style of undergarment, and a sword or dagger. Each has particular significance, both in terms of religious doctrine and military preparedness (Axel 2001; Mahmood 1996; Singh 1999).

Many trace the origins of these signs back to Gobind Singh's creation of the Khalsa, in 1699, where they were implemented as a means of ensuring that "Sikhs would not be able to shirk their duty to defend their faith by blending unnoticed into the crowd" (Mahmood 1996:45). However, several recent scholarly publications have called the authenticity of this claim into question, arguing instead that the Five K's were promoted by a religious reform movement, known as the Singh Sabha, which attempted to consolidate a Sikh identity by eradicating what they saw as "un-Sikh" or "Hindu" elements from the practices of the community during the late 19th century. It is worth noting that the Singh Sabha is also credited by some for having established the centrality of the Sikh tradition of martyrdom (Fenech 2001; Oberoi 1994).

While all five articles are expected to be worn by both male and female initiates, Axel (2001) has argued that it is the long beard and the turban that have come to be most closely associated with Sikhism, keeping in mind that it is the more visible amritdhari identity that most people outside the community recognize as being Sikh. The result has been twofold, with the Sikh identity becoming both masculinized and fragmented (ibid). However, in recent years, some North American Sikh women have begun to wear a turban, something previously uncommon among the female ranks of Sikhism, thus appropriating one aspect of this highly masculinized identity (Mahmood and Brady, 2000).

A discussion of contemporary notions of identity within the Sikh community is important to understanding the tradition of martyrdom for a couple of reasons. First, links between the modern Sikh identity and the developments of Hargobind and Gobind Singh, both of whose fathers were martyred, draw the tradition of militarism, as expressed in the Khalsa, and that of martyrdom close together. In fact, militarism and martyrdom are often thought of as part of a single historical trajectory. Second, this association of amritdhari identity with its tradition of militarism, engendered a recognition that to wear one's faith outwardly was to open oneself up to potential harm, in the form of martyrdom. Thus a connection between amritdhari Sikhs and the historic Sikh martyrs, while not explicit, is inherent in the modern Sikh identity.

Nowhere is this connection between the amritdhari and the martyr more evident than with the rank and file of the Khalistani movement in Punjab during the 1980s and 1990s. As mentioned earlier, the death of Sant Jarnail Singh Bhindranwale and the fallout of Operation Bluestar had a profound effect on day-to-day life in Punjab (Mahmood 1996). Guerrilla organizations, drawing links between their own actions, and those of the historic martyrs, found validation within the Sikh community. Also, the notion that death brought about by fighting injustice, an ideal associated with the Sikh tradition of martyrdom, encouraged many young men to join the movement and risk their lives to right the ultimate wrong that was Operation Bluestar (Pettigrew, 1992).

Martyrdom was important to the maintenance of the various Khalistani guerrilla organizations for other, equally important reasons. The Indian government responded to the Khalistani movement quite harshly, adopting numerous counterinsurgency tactics that blatantly violated human rights. The result was widespread use of torture, forced disappearances, and staged gun battles between security forces and militants (Mahmood 1996). Because of the close association between the amritdhari Sikh and the image of the "saint-soldier," even men not active in the struggle found themselves detained and tortured (Axel 2001; Mahmood 1996, Pettigrew 1992). Therefore, the entire Sikh community felt an oppression, or persecution equivalent to that experienced by the early Sikh martyrs, further strengthening the connection. This connection is best expressed in an interview with a victim of police torture, conducted by Cynthia Mahmood:

> In our daily prayers we remember all our Sikh martyrs during the Mughal period, those who went through terrible hardships. They were cut to

pieces, made to survive on a small loaf of bread, and they withstood all those tortures. I used to think, "What type of people were they?" and while I was in the movement there was sometimes a little thought in the back of my mind that if the time came, would I be able to behave as those brave Sikhs, my ancestors, did? But finally when I went through it, it was not me but those other Sikhs who were sustaining that. It seemed that they were taking the pain with me. I felt then the satisfaction of knowing that with Guru's grace I was able to pass the test of being a Sikh [quoted in Mahmood 1996:37].

Clearly, the connection between the Khalistani militant and the historic Sikh martyr is more than one of surface identity. This man, tortured by the Punjab police, came to embody the tradition of martyrdom, feeling a sense of power otherwise denied to him by the fact that his torture and his choice were hidden from public view.

Likewise, Axel (2001) argues that photographs of torture victims, distributed widely during the movement, and now found on countless Internet Web sites dedicated to Sikhism, act to constitute the Sikh diasporic identity. Axel argues that violence propagated by Sikh militants, and against Sikhs by the government of India, as represented in art, photographs, and narratives, have come to shape an understanding of what it means to be Sikh, for Sikh and non-Sikh alike, at home and, more importantly, in the diaspora. These pictures also work to create a link between historic Sikh martyrs, the contemporary victims of torture, and the international Sikh community, a link made possible by the very existence of a tradition of martyrdom. In other words, the witnessing of torture, as experienced through viewing Web pages, and downloadable pictures, can act as a conduit for the transfer of the embodiment of martyrdom, both past and present. The sense of oppression, persecution, and reactive bravery, all written on the body of the photographed victim, transcend the moment of the act, and constitute the identity of the viewer (Axel 2001). Thus, the Sikh identity, forged at an intersection of perceived history, religious tradition, and present-day political circumstance, is embodied in the victim of torture, and transferred to the viewer. The viewer, made witness by closeness of these images to his own existence, comes to embody the moment, and the power associated with it.

Conclusion

What can be learned from an analysis of martyrdom as an embodied cultural practice, which by its very nature transfers the embodied experience to a larger community, helping to strengthen a group's resolve against a perceived threat? There is a great deal to taken from such an analysis, not only in terms of anthropological curiosity, but also in terms of a practical understanding of the world in which we live. In terms of anthropology, there is interesting work being done in the realm of identity formation, nationalism, and diaspora studies which can be enriched by an inclusion of the body as a viable location for cultural expression, and thus for anthropological research.

Outside of the walls of academia, there is much to be learned from such studies. In reality, the world is becoming increasingly polarized through processes of economic expansion and cultural misunderstanding. In many parts of the world, dissatisfaction and hostility are being expressed in terms of ethnic and religious nationalism, and the inevitable conflicts that accompany such developments. While the Khalistani struggle for independence has subsided, in terms of direct military action, there still exists within the Sikh community varying degrees of nationalist sentiment and desire for increased autonomy. Similarly, religious and ethnic conflicts exist in Kashmir (Mahmood 1996), Sri Lanka (Spencer 2000), Northern Ireland (Feldman 1991), and elsewhere.

Understanding what motivates people to be willing to sacrifice themselves for such causes should be paramount within the social sciences. This is not to say that a paper on the embodiment of a tradition of martyrdom provides the answers necessary to solve these problems. In fact, martyrdom, as a cultural tradition may have very little impact on how many of these conflicts develop and sustain themselves. However, to summarily dismiss the activities, which grip the headlines and our consciousness, as being the work of "evil" madmen, cowards, or fundamentalists with no regard for life is to not fully appreciate the complexity of the issues that drive these movements. Social science in general, and anthropology in particular, has the capacity to evaluate these issues in a manner from which we would all benefit. Realizing that individual experience, through the body, acts to constitute communal identity, as well as cultural practice is an important first step in addressing these issues.

References

Alter, Joseph S. *Gandhi's Body*. Philadelphia: University of Pennsylvania Press, 2000.
Axel, Brian Keith. *The Nation's Tortured Body*. Durham: Duke University Press, 2001.
Csordas, Thomas J. "Embodiment as a Paradigm for Anthropology." *Ethos* 18 (1990): 5–47.
Csordas, Thomas J. "The Body's Career in Anthropology." In *Anthropological Theory Today*, edited by Henrietta L. Moore Pp. 172–205. Malden: Blackwell, 1999.
Das, Veena. "The Act of Witnessing." In *Violence and Subjectivity*, edited by Veena Das, Arthur Kleinman, Mamphela Ramphele and Pamela Reynolds. Pp. 205–225. Berkeley: University of California Press, 1999.

Douglas, Mary. *Purity and Danger.* New York: Praeger, 1966.
_____. *Natural Symbols.* London: Barrie and Jenkins, 1970.
Feldman, Allen. *Formations of Violence: A Narrative of the Body and Political Terror in Northern Ireland.* Chicago: University of Chicago Press, 1991.
Fenech, Louis. *Martyrdom in the Sikh Faith.* London: Oxford University Press, 1999.
Foucault, Michel. *Discipline and Punish.* New York: Vintage Books, 1995.
Jackson, Michael. *Minima Ethnographica.* Chicago: University of Chicago Press, 1998.
Mahmood, Cynthia Keppley. *Fighting for Faith and Nation.* Philadelphia: University of Pennsylvania Press, 1996.
Mahmood, Cynthia, and Stacy Brady. *The Guru's Gift.* Mountain View: Mayfield, 2000.
Oberoi, Harjot. *The Construction of Religious Boundaries.* Chicago: University of Chicago Press, 1994.
Pettigrew, Joyce. "Martyrdom and Guerrilla Organization in Punjab." *The Journal of Commonwealth and Comparative Politics* 30 (1992): 387–406.
Singh, Patwant. *The Sikhs.* New York: Knopf, 1998.
Spencer, Jonathan. "On Not Becoming a 'Terrorist.'" In *Violence and Subjectivity*, edited by Veena Das, Arthur Kleinman, Mamphela Ramphele and Pamela Reynolds. Pp. 120–140. Berkeley: University of California Press, 1999.
Turner, Brian S. *The Body and Society,* 3rd ed. Thousand Oaks: Sage, 1994.

13

Catholicism Recycled

The New Age in Poland

Dorota Hall

In this chapter I will address the issue of the reinterpretation of Catholic elements in the Polish New Age Movement. For a social researcher, the New Age Movement is a difficult subject to investigate. In Poland, it is socially constructed through friendship networks, and its ideas draw from diverse areas of culture and society, which produce unique beliefs and practices that appear quite eclectic to the outsider.

In Poland, even identifying New Age adherents is exceptionally difficult. From the sociological point of view it is very problematic to mark a boundary between what is traditional Catholicism in its specifically Polish manifestation, and what is New Age Catholicism, because Catholicism past and present and secular and religious Polish culture are so intertwined. On top of this, the Polish New Age movement draws from traditional as well as innovative Catholicism, and also from numerous other non–Polish, non–Catholic religions, cultures, and forms of spirituality. Given the Polish commitment to Catholicism and its close relationship to Polish nationalism and cultural history, New Agers in Poland do not often reveal themselves openly as such. Furthermore, even those committed to New Age spirituality do not distance themselves from Catholicism publicly or personally. Thus, New Ageism in Poland takes a specifically Polish form, such that adherents sometimes remain substantially within the mainstream, while some would be outside the mainstream. Thus, both conceptualization and measurement are problematic.

Polish ideological pluralism admits some variations in Catholic views, but at the same time, Polish New Agers seem to be dutiful in adhering to many traditional Catholic rituals. As a result, it is impossible to gauge precisely the scale of the New Age phenomenon in Poland. Statistical questionnaires have proven unreliable, and qualitative studies indicate the presence of change, but not the extent. Thus, this paper offers some initial insight as the basis for more extensive conceptualization and research, both in regards to the Polish context, and similar changes in religion throughout the Western world.

Background

Poland is overwhelmingly Catholic. More than 90 percent of Poles declare themselves as Catholics. However, such data does not take up the question: what does it mean for somebody to identify as Catholic? In the winter of 2002, Polish sociologists of religion published results of their studies conducted within the international research project known as RAMP — Religious and Moral Pluralism. Composed of researchers from 14 European countries, RAMP compared dimensions of religiosity and morality in different European states. One of the principal findings concerning Poland is that religious belief is highly individualized, while at the same time Poles dutifully adhere to traditional Polish-Catholic ritual and remain strongly identified with the Catholic Church (Borowik and Doktór 2001) as an institution. Let this apparent paradox be the background for the following discussion of New Age in Poland.

Conceptualization

I treat the New Age as a phenomenon of the contemporary culture founded on a holistic vision of the world. It is a way of thinking, believing, and acting premised on the "parapsychological" aspects of mind, primarily from the religious ideas of the East (Buddhism, Hinduism, Taoism) and on various unorthodox currents of Christianity, Islam, Judaism, and a broad, typically folkloric category called "esoteric knowledge."

Conducting my cultural investigation, I have treated New Age first as a peculiar kind of social association, which assembles people based on an individualistic self-development and personality transformation, within a mystical, transcendent social-cultural context. This context derives from an admixture of Christianity with Eastern mysticism, as well as so-called occult and nontraditional Western beliefs, such as channeling, crystal meditation, and spiritual healing (Bowman and Sutcliffe 2000).

Investigation

Parallel with the RAMP research, I conducted an ethnographic study concerning their visions of existence, both temporal and transcendent, in the New Age culture in Poland. The studies lasted two years and I was assisted by students of the Department of Ethnology and Cultural Anthropology at Warsaw University. We conducted a participant observation of New Age activities and many interviews on the subject of energy (in a spiritual sense) as the main spiritual category used by New Agers.

Importantly, our interviewees had achieved typically a secondary education, more or less equivalent to a U.S. high school education. Thus, the picture of the Polish New Age that I will sketch below does not involve those of higher education or intellectual elites. My students and I searched for respondents in places imbued with the cultural manifestations of New Ageism — in shops and galleries offering "esoteric accessories" in Warsaw, at esoteric festivals, and among participants of yoga courses or other educational activities that emphasize the possibility of immediate and spiritual self-enhancement. We also gathered many interesting observations and opinions beyond our immediate research objectives, some of which are more immediately relevant and which we thus discuss as part of this research.

Findings and Discussion

"The prayer in church ... people shouldn't repeat formulas thoughtlessly as they do, but their prayers should flow directly from their hearts" [interviewee 1]. Very often and in different ways our respondents expressed their dissatisfaction with the tedious ritual of religious experience during church practices. In Poland, such critiques do not concern a theoretical abstraction, but relate to what are very real phenomena supported by real observations. The authors of the RAMP report called attention to the ritualism of religiosity in Polish society (Borowik and Doktór 2001). Less than 10 percent of Poles do not attend the church. This percentage contrasts with other European countries generally where regular churchgoers constitute roughly 50 percent overall (Borowik and Doktór 2001:148) and less than 20 percent in some Western European countries specifically (Bruce 2002). More than 75 percent of Poles take part in the mass at least once a month (Borowik and Doktór 2001:132–133) and 95 percent of all the adults in Poland declare membership in the Catholic Church (Borowik and Doktór 2001:68). At the same time, only a scant percentage of people uphold Catholic religiosity as part of their personal convictions, although they attend church regularly. Again, the apparent paradox between devout practice and minimal belief arises.

13. Catholicism Recycled

New Agers we interviewed have noticed the divergence between following religious practices on the one hand and being really emotionally engaged in them on the other. At the same time, however, they are themselves facing a similar dilemma. For example, they told us about their fascination with the religions of the East, but simultaneously they stipulated that they are Catholics or at least Christians:

> My interest for Eastern religions gives me deep satisfaction. I feel this is the right path for me. Here you can learn how to be the master of your own body and mind. You can achieve indifference to suffering and independence from the changeable conditions of the external world. But I'm aware of being a Catholic and I'm not going to accept conflicting views [interviewee 2].

It is obvious that the interviewee has her own definition of what is Christian or Catholic, and as a representative illustration, we see that the apparent contradiction between churchgoing, church dogma, and ritual compared to individual belief does not trouble New Agers.

However, it is uncanny that she felt the urge to specify her belonging to the Catholic community. This phenomenon seems to be very characteristic for the Polish landscape of religion. In the beginning of the '90s, many sociologists, largely inspired by Luckmann (1967), predicted that many Poles would resign from their religion as an institution and the religious ritual would descend to the level of invisibility. There were certain premises for such a view. The Communist era had ended and there was a rise of ideological pluralism. Since that time there was no need for identification with the Catholic Church for political reasons (during the '80s church attending was a manifestation of sympathy for the political opposition such as the Solidarity movement and Lech Walesa). But it now appears that the '90s did not bring significant changes in the ritual sphere or on the level of social identification with Catholic religion. Thus, ideological pluralism coexists with a general yet decisive declaration of being a Catholic. The move away from the church has concerned a part of the elites but not Polish society in general.

New Age adherents have expressed their attachment to the traditional religion in different ways. Usually it has assumed a form of justifying their opinions. One of the respondents claimed: "The theory that Jesus Christ comes from cosmos doesn't deny the principles of [Catholic] belief. He comes from the other world" (interviewee 3). New Agers have tried to combine their own philosophies with the Christian outlook as if they did not want to be found apostates. Very often they called on the authority of the Bible in order to justify their views, despite the fact that some quoted situations were not exactly the same as in biblical scripture. One of the litho-therapeutists (a type of spiritual healer) said: "Stones are related to planets and the zodiac. The Bible tells us about it. In St. John's Apocalypse we have it specified by name" (interviewee 4).

Another interviewee claimed: "Therapy with stones is nothing occultist. What did Moses have when he was approaching the Ark [of the Covenant]? He wore a beautiful robe with 12 various precious stones" (interviewee 5).

Very often Polish New Agers make creative efforts to combine Catholic motifs with threads from other religions. For example, some of the interviewees claimed that after death the soul descends to purgatory but then it comes back to Earth, improved, in the new incarnation. The Om mantra, very popular among New Age advocates, also has been involved in the same type of interpretations:

> The world came into existence from the Om, the primary vibration of cosmos, because "In the beginning the Word already existed" [interviewee 6]. Another says that "Om is a symbol of a union of all the subtle energies. The prayer Om connects sublime energy of a man with cosmic subtle energies. The Christian Amen is the same as Om" [interviewee 7].

Many elements of non–Christian religions hold equal status with Catholic tradition. For example: "An angel is the same as Hindu deva" (interviewee 8). There are many Bible motifs that New Age adherents have interpreted through their own convictions. For example: "Agnihotra is a ritual which you can find in every religion. Shepherds were feeding a sacred fire while Jesus was born. This fire was a symbol of consciousness and the Holy Spirit" (interviewee 9).

New Agers believe that every person can do miracles, the problem is only that he or she does not know or does not remember about it. They are not astonished then at the miraculous skills of Jesus Christ. They relate stories about him enthusiastically, but without any particularly Christian piousness: "Jesus Christ was able to walk on the water. This is the question of the refined mind and deep contact with all the elements" (interviewee 10). Sometimes New Age sympathizers cited the words of Jesus and explained them in terms of their own views. One of the respondents claimed that every word and every thought had its own unique power (some much more than others) and could produce an effect on the physical level. From this perspective, one woman said: "Jesus said that human beings cannot live by bread alone, but they live with every word they speak. Thus everybody should be conscious and aware of every word and thought, even the least significant ones" (interviewee 11). The quoted phrase actually has a different meaning in the Bible, which says: "Human beings cannot live by bread alone, but need every word that God speaks" (Matt. 4:4). New Agers often take elements of the Bible, arguably out of context, to support their own agenda, although usually they have done so unconsciously and quite sincerely.

There are not many Poles who are Bible readers. Polish religiosity is anti-intellectual to a high degree (Borowik and Doktór 2001:110) and it holds true for the New Agers in our study as well. The most important thing here is to understand the role of the Bible in this context. It might suggest that New Age adherents do not challenge the Christian tradition which, in some respects, seems compatible, or which they make compatible through their own interpretation. The issue as to whether Polish New Agers understand or apply the Bible correctly from a scholarly standpoint they see as irrelevant to the practitioner.

Whether they read it or not, New Agers freely interpret the Bible, often enthusiastically, and the most popular New Age interpretations of the Bible have been expressed in terms of energy and power, which also constitute the central categories of spirituality for New Agers. Our interviewees referred to God as "the highest" or "the most sublime" energy that exists. God was seen by them as the primary source of energy, a source of existence for the whole world. The world itself was seen as energy, too — New Agers explain that physical matter has "slower" or "lower" vibrations than the invisible or transcendent aspects of existence. Thus, according to New Age adherents there is no qualitative difference between God and creation, it is only the question of "faster" or "higher" energetic vibrations in transcendent realms, and "slower" or "lower" energy in the mundane world.

Using the language of energy and vibration, our subjects expressed the idea of holism. The same language served them to express their belief in the possibility of self-development, too: "For someone to be on the spiritual path is to make his or her own energy more subtle" (interviewee 12). New Age culture offers many practices that express their concept of holistic but nevertheless vague spirituality, as for example "making someone's energies more subtle" to help them relax or gain enlightenment. Vegetarianism, very popular among those who identify themselves with New Age ideas, was also interpreted in terms of energy and vibration, in contradistinction with scientific or traditional perspectives. Meat, for example, has "stout" vibration, so if someone wants to progress along the spiritual path, one should forsake it. Otherwise, stout energy binds the individual to earthly existence.

Similarly, sections of the Bible that describe human contact with God ("the highest energy") were also understood in terms of energy: "Moses was at Mount Sinai and he was talking with God. That means he had the possibility to ascend to the higher energy level" (interviewee 13). The vision of nonpersonal, God as energy-essence, of course, is not a Christian idea, but it is more or less permissible in Poland among the religious population who identify with Catholicism in essence, and not necessarily with the Catholic Church as the sole legitimate representative and authority of Catholicism. This allows for a kind of ideological pluralism yet still within Catholic traditionalism and Polish culture. The concept of God as energy correlates with the more general notion that God exists as a mysterious, transcendent power.

Thus, the issue of theological compatibility by itself does not interest us so much as the question of how it functions in the context of Polish ritualized religiosity which stresses church attendance and participation in religious ceremonies. One may conclude that it functions very well. There were not many New Age respondents who disavowed categorically their participation in the mass or the acceptability of traditional rituals. The problem is again how they interpret their activity in the field of Catholic religion. Usually Polish New Agers prize all New Age currents which stress traditional celebrations. Many Sai Baba followers, for example, have emphasized with pleasure that at the Sai Baba center in India none of the celebrations of any denomination is neglected, so they have the possibility to observe Christmas there or they have Sai Baba's consent to celebrate it at home.

But the meaning of Christmas was interpreted by many New Age interlocutors differently than in the customary Catholic tradition. Although ritual is not an issue, the meaning of Christmas is. The birth of Jesus Christ has been often treated as a metaphor which expresses the possibility of the birth of God's consciousness in man. So New Agers take part in the ritual of Christmas mass obligatorily as the majority of the Polish community does, but they interpret the significance and meaning of the ceremony in accordance with their own concepts. Moreover, they readily participate in many other strictly Catholic events, but similarly attribute different meanings. Some of them go to Czostochowa, the most significant Catholic pilgrimage center in Poland, every year to adore the holy icon of the Mother Mary.

As always, New Age advocates have their own, very non–Catholic interpretation of what happens in the temple when the icon emerges into public view:

> When trumpets play the image emerges from behind the covers as the light comes from the darkness. The light from the darkness is the same as God in Hinduism. It means that a cover is a symbol of matrix, a form that we have to transcend and then we are elected, we can be one with God. The image reminds us of that truth [interviewee 11].

The next question is how New Age adherents understand the space of the church where they pray or take part in masses. A typical respondent said that

> There is a small church in Szczyrk [a village in southern Poland]. I felt very good there. I felt very powerful, very good and beneficial influence of the energy, it really strengthened me. I was doing it consciously, I was just gathering this energy, because I felt it was helping me and regenerating me [interviewee 14].

New Agers commonly interpret Catholic churches and shrines as "power-points." New Age adherents intend this literally. They believe that some special points on the Earth emit a powerful, spiritual energy. They have mentioned sacred places of traditional cultures as Eliade indicated them: mountain peaks, river sources, some trees and groves, caves, and temples (Eliade 1949). Catholic edifices likewise hold special power, in particular the old ones. New Agers believe that in former times priests who decided to build a church were able to point at places distinguished by the special power and that same power makes itself felt today. Moreover, the magical vision of the world that New Age adherents represent lets them understand churches as places where all the energy from all the performed prayers are gathered. One of the New Age interlocutors claimed: "In my opinion the prayer such as 'Our Father' has its peculiar power. These are the words of love, they bring positive forces" (interviewee 15).

These forces have been understood in a very material sense. According to the general opinion of New Agers, the ardor of intentions of those who were praying in churches for centuries still remains there. It makes the space of a church more powerful and favorable to the spiritual transformation of those who stay there. The participation in mass has been seen in those terms, too: "We attend the church because it's the power-point, isn't it? Maybe the power is bigger when a number of people comes. Because then the energy is more powerful, more substantial" (interviewee 16).

Moreover, the same beliefs that induce New Age adherents to visit churches also guide them to avoid places where negative power might be gathered. The usual example of such a negative place, not recommended for lengthy visits, is Auschwitz. For New Agers, substantial negative energy has accumulated at Auschwitz, because of vast suffering that occurred there.

New Age adherents who attend the church are disposed to the reception of energy sensations. "I like going to the church. I sit down there and I just experience. I don't listen to the priest, he can speak whatever he wants to but I just feel the subtle energies of the Eucharist" (interviewee 17). Such pronouncements are common in New Age circles and there is no need to add that they do not reflect a traditional or doctrinal Catholic approach. They rather mirror contemporary tendencies to concentrate on precognitive experience as the essential form of reception of the world (Bauman 1995). New Agers have stressed the experiencing of religious enchantments — the flow of life energy, just as they have associated power-points (churches among them) with the possibility of a deep feeling of transcendent spiritual experience.

There are other elements of ritualized Polish religiosity besides church attendance. One of them is practice of church ceremonies such as baptism and the wedding ceremony. New Age respondents often avow performing them and they have explained it again in terms of energy. Moreover they have seen baptism or the other sacraments as one of many energetic events in someone's life that instills sacred power. Yet contrary to traditional Catholic doctrine and Polish culture, New Agers regard reiki initiation or other mysticist traditions as spiritually equal to Catholic practices.

New Age adherents often interlace traditional Catholic practices with practices of contemporary or non–Western origin. Reiki, one of many alternative therapies very popular in Polish New Age circles, seems to be a good example here. Reiki masters teach that the therapeutist should precede every treatment by entering into contact with positive cosmic energy. Many masters recommend the Our Father prayer for this purpose. They believe that by the power of these words, healing energy flows down on the therapeutist and through him or her and into the patient. Many other New Age techniques integrate Christian ceremony. For example, one of the bioenergotherapeutists who was setting an installation against disadvantageous energies in New Agers' houses told all the housemates to make the sign of the cross. According to him it was necessary for putting the installation into operation.

Traditional religious accessories are also entangled in the New Age energetic vision of the world. Respondents said, for example: "I've got an amulet. I've got a rosary and this is my amulet. I always keep it with me and it protects me from bad energies" (interviewee 18). And similarly, "I have a pendant on my neck, a cross. This is my amulet" (interviewee 19). Particularly Catholic objects have also been seen in the broader context of the sacred symbols of other religious traditions:

> All the time I have my amulets with me. They protect me from disadvantageous vibrations. I've got six stones, Om symbol and the medal of St. Bernard. And that is all for today but I'm going to buy new, additional stones and a pendant of Atlantis [interviewee 20].
>
> It's very important to have an amulet. It might be a consecrated medal. It doesn't have to be beautiful or expensive but it has to contain a spirit. A consecration gives power, such a spirit, to it [interviewee 21].

Almost 90 percent of Poles have "a cross, a medal or the other sacred object" as it was formulated in the RAMP questionnaire (Borowik and Doktór 2001:138). There is tradition of placing crosses in Polish flats or houses, or other Catholic symbols. Popular culture has provoked a custom of arranging home altars where images of Jesus Christ, saints, and angels might be situated. New Agers practice this popular tradition, although their altars include many more religious symbols than the Catholic ones. New Age altars remind their owners of the sacred reality and the necessity of spiritual transformation. They facilitate contact with "subtle energies" and also evoke them:

You can create your own power-point all by yourself. You choose a nook in your room and there you put a symbol which you associate with the highest energies, let's say the Mother of God. You can place a figure of elephant there or whatever you believe in. A candle is good because it increases energetic vibrations. And this will be your place for connecting with cosmos. Everyone can create such a clear place with the highest energy [interviewee 22].

There are many elements of the New Age culture that might be associated with popular religiosity. This popular, folk-based sensibility has been deeply rooted in Poland — a country where many roadside shrines exist and attachment to the ceremonial dimension of religion is easy to observe. Poland never accomplished a radical disenchantment of the world as Weber argues about the West, nor the rationalization of society, especially not in religion, as Protestant culture much more profoundly established in the West (Weber [1905] 2002). Rather, Polish culture, especially in the religious realm, has always remained decidedly enchanted, always committed to the mysteries of faith. Polish New Age adherents understand Catholic enchantment through the language of energies and powers. There is a certain continuity in both visions — the New Age worldview affirms Polish-Catholic mystery even as it integrates it with other traditions.

Conclusions

Polish New Agers do not challenge Catholicism explicitly. However, they have contributed to a reinterpretation in popular notions of Catholicism. Within New Age, all traditions are subject to reinterpretation; although New Agers are serious about spirituality, they tend to have little regard for tradition, which they often treat with lightness, and very often with facetiousness. Personal experience overrides tradition, or we might say, as does Kubiak (2002), that New Agers accept tradition on a individual basis, often very innovatively. For example, the figure of Jesus as the thaumaturgist and healer is very characteristic for the New Age culture in general, not only for the Polish manifestation of it. Given the centrality of Catholicism to Polish culture, it has been the focus of especially intense reinterpretation. However, Catholicism returns the favor and exerts its presence on the Polish New Age movement very distinctly.

List of Interviewees

1— male, age about 50, bioenergotherapeutist, met in his own studio of alternative medicine in Warsaw, autumn 2001;

2 — female, age 30, yoga and reiki adept, met in studio of ma-uri massage in Warsaw, summer 2000;
3 — female, age about 30, met in W_siory in northern Poland where the old stone circle, so-called power-point, is, summer 2001;
4 — female, age 45, litotherapeutist, met in her own studio of litotherapy in Warsaw, autumn 2000;
5 — female, age about 50, litotherapeutist, met in her own studio of litotherapy in Warsaw, winter 2001;
6 — male, age about 40, leader of a therapy with music workshop in Warsaw, autumn 2001;
7 — female, age about 50, author of a book about *agnihotra*, met in Warsaw, autumn 2000;
8 — male, age about 30, met in an esoteric gallery in Warsaw, winter 2001;
9 — male, age about 50, leader of an *agnihotra* workshop in Warsaw, spring 2001;
10 — male, age 31, met in an esoteric gallery in Warsaw, winter 2001;
11 — female, age about 40, bioenergotherapeutist and astrologist, met in an esoteric gallery in Warsaw, autumn 2001;
12 — female, age about 30, Silva Method and reiki adept, met in Warsaw, winter 2001;
13 — female, age about 50, owner of an esoteric gallery in Warsaw, met there, autumn 2000;
14 — female, age 23, bioenergotherapeutist, met in a studio of alternative medicine in Warsaw, spring 2001;
15 — female, age about 50, met in an esoteric gallery in Warsaw, summer 2001
16 — female, age about 55, met in an esoteric gallery in Warsaw, summer 2000;
17 — female, age about 40, Art of Living leader, met in Warsaw, summer 2000;
18 — female, age about 55, yoga adept met in Warsaw, summer 2000;
19 — male, age 23, healed by bioenergotherapy, met in Tarnobrzeg (southern Poland), summer 2001;
20 — female, age 38, met in an esoteric gallery in Warsaw, spring 2001;
21 — male, age about 30, met at alternative medicine fairs in Warsaw, spring 2001;
22 — female, age 42, reiki adept, met in Warsaw, summer 2000.

References

Bauman, Zygmunt. *Ciao i przemoc w obliczu ponowoczesno ci* [Body and Violence in Postmodernity]. Warsaw: Toru, 1995.
Borowik, Irena, and Tadeusz Doktor. *Pluralizm religijny i moralny w Polsce* [Religious and Moral Pluralism in Poland]. Kraków, 2001.
Bruce, Steve. *God is Dead: Secularization in the West.* London: Blackwell, 2002.
Bowman, Marion, and Steven Sutcliffe, eds. *Beyond New Age. Exploring Alternative Spirituality.* Edinburgh: Edinburgh University Press, 2000.
Eliade, Mircea. *Traité d'historie des religions.* Paris: Alcan, 1949.
Kubiak, Anna. *"Prodigal Son." Identity in Transformation. Postmodernity, Postcommunism and Globalization,* edited by M. Kempny and A. Jawowska. New York: Praeger, 2002.

Luckmann, Thomas. *The Invisible Religion. The Problem of Religion in Modern Society*. New York: Basic Books, 1967.
Trimble, Shawn Michael. "Spritualism and Channeling." In *America's Alternative Religions*. Albany, NY: SUNY Press, 1995.
Weber, Max. *The Protestant Ethic and the Spirit of Capitalism*. 1905. Reprint, Los Angeles: Roxbury, 2001.

About the Contributors

Alyssa Beall is completing her Ph.D. studies at Syracuse University. Her ongoing interest in religion focuses on Neopaganism, both in more traditional contexts and recent innovative contexts. Her latter research finds expression in this volume, as she examines use of the Internet and electronic media as a means of virtual community building.

Charles M. Brown, a professor of sociology at Albright College in Reading, Pennsylvania, has been active for years in the study of religion, with several papers and presentations to his credit. Professor Brown can legitimately claim the title of "expert" on evangelical Christianity and its relationship to, and production of, popular culture. His work considers the interaction of belief, economics, and cultural products within the ever-changing spectrum of contemporary pop culture.

Dorota Hall is a doctoral candidate at the School for Social Research in the Institute of Philosophy and Sociology, Polish Academy of Sciences in Warsaw. Her approach combines the intellectual rigor of philosophy with the empiricism of sociology. Her interest in religion arises from the rapid social change in Poland and Eastern Europe after the fall of Communism.

Titus Hjelm has a unique perspective on popular culture. In addition to his position in the Department of Comparative Religion at the University of Helsinki, Finland, Titus also plays in a heavy metal band named Thunderstone, and thus has an ongoing interest in religion in popular music, as both a scholar from the outside and a participant on the inside. Like many scholars, Titus sees an injection of religiosity into issues that are otherwise typical social or, in the case of his chapter here, criminological issues. Crime is not new, and neither are religion-based explanations for it, but the two have not been put together for decades. Thus, his work looks at a trend found throughout late modern society, the religionization of social and political issues.

Maruq F. Khan is a sociology Ph.D. student at Loyola University, Chicago. Her current research interests include social movements resisting gender and patriarchal norms in the Muslim world; Muslim identity construction vis-à-vis Islamic full-time schools in America; and the impact of civil liberties violations on an immigrant Pakistani community in Chicago in the wake of 9/11.

Agnieszka Koscianska is a graduate student in sociology at Warsaw University in Poland. Her contribution comes from her recent comprehensive study of a new charismatic movement in Poland, within the context of rapid Westernization in the post–Communist world. Poland and Eastern Europe generally has become a dynamic and vigorous creator of new religious movements, and Agnieszka's ongoing work considers the synthesis of Polish and imported religious and cultural traditions.

Lauren Langman is a professor of sociology at Loyola University of Chicago. He has long worked in the tradition of the Frankfurt School of Critical Theory, especially on issues of alienation and relationships between culture, politics and psychosocial. His most recent publications include a special issue of *American Behavioral Politics* devoted to the presidency in a television age. He has also published on the alternative globalization movements, and the many forms of identity that emerge in the current age from fundamentalist to the extremes of body modification; more recently, he has published several book chapters on Islam and fundamentalism.

George N. Lundskow of the Department of Sociology at Grand Valley State University in Allendale, Michigan, approaches religion through ethnographies, which he has conducted on new evangelical and Neopagan communities. His interest range from contemporary movements to ancient religions, most recently on Zoroastrianism and its contributions to Judaism, Christianity, and Islam. Through history and ethnography, Professor Lundskow examines the social construction of belief and practice and its concurrence with social change and the relates of the age, so to speak, as people strive for meaningful existence.

Rory G. McCarthy of the University of Pittsburgh's Department of Anthroplogy looks to the experience of oppressed groups as a means to understand the religious experience. Although many studies have told us much about religious beliefs and practices in routine occurrence, the same people under the stress of persecution and even execution tells us even more about faith. His chapter here represents one such case, that of Sikhism, but the conclusions here may perhaps have broader applications. Devotion and faith are here found in the moment of greatest threat, especially the threat of death.

Michael R. Ott, also a member of the Department of Sociology at Grand Valley State University, in Allendale, Michigan, studied with Rudolf Siebert, and thus receives his pedigree from a very distinguished and accomplished mentor. Professor Ott's recent book, *Max Horkheimer's Critical Theory of Religion*, examines the treatment of religion in the Critical Theory tradition, and his contribution here expands the discussion even further. Like the Critical Theorists who preceded him, such as Theodor Adorno and Max Horkheimer, Ott's interests range beyond the theoretical, and toward practical applications of sociology within the context of contemporary debates on important social issues.

Mustafa Saatci comes originally from Istanbul, Turkey, and teaches in the Department of Sociology at the University of Maine. In contrast to the recent trend that religion is finding its way back into secular life, Professor Saatci considers the opposite trend in Turkey, that the state is claiming Islam as parts of its secular bureaucracy. Beyond this, his research interests include migration, ethnic identity, and globalization. He is currently working on a book about Turkish migrants in the United States.

Rudolf J. Siebert, originally from Germany, is one of the foremost experts on Critical Theory and the Frankfurt School. Professor Siebert, who teaches in the Department of Sociology at Western Michigan University, has amassed an impressive array of work over his long and continuing career. With numerous publications to his credit, his major accomplishments include extensive theoretical volumes in diverse areas: religion, philosophy, science, theology, and important social concepts such as freedom, power, and love. Professor Siebert's work draws from, and is in turn relevant to, a variety of disciplines, and his vast output of books and articles speaks to timeless questions for the ages, as well as issues particular to contemporary society.

Deana Weibel received her Ph.D. in anthropology from the University of California at San Diego for research into pilgrimage conducted in Rocamadour, France, and Chimayó, New Mexico. She is currently living in Grand Haven, Michigan, and is an assistant professor of anthropology at Grand Valley State University in Allendale, Michigan.

Mark P. Worrell teaches sociology at the University of Kansas, Department of Sociology, and Kansas City Art Institute, Department of Social Sciences, positions that allow him considerable opportunity to stretch out from the conventions of traditional sociology departments. His work draws from a range of theorists and empirical work, across all times and places in history. Worrell's substantive interests focus on the intersection of religion, class, money, and power, as well as the issue of authority in ostensibly free and democratic societies.

Index

action and ethos 191
Adler, Margot 203
Afghanistan 138
Alevis 237
alienation 20, 55, 70, 74
Al-Qutb 144
Al-Wahab 144
Amalfi codes 139
Amritdhari 259
Amritharis 265
Anti-Christ 38
Anti-Semitism 21; indicators of 26–28; types of 22–25
apocalyptic affinities 125
apocalyptic radicalization 134
apocalypticism 119–123, 126, 129; lyrical dimensions 129; religious themes in 121–123; secular themes in 122–123; visual dimensions 128
Aquinas, Thomas 39
Arab secularism 151–153
Assembly of God 91
Attaturk, Mustfa Kamel 233
authoritarian personality 50, 80
authoritarianism 7, 12, 75–76, 78, 83

Baba Deep Singh 264
bellum omnium contra omnes (the war of each against all) 40
Benjamin, Walter 45, 101
Berger, Peter 78
Bhai Mani Singh 263
Bhindranwahe 264
bio-energy therapy 278
Birmingham School 194

Black Turks 238
Bourdieu, Pierre 14
bourgeois (pertaining to the bourgeois class): Christianity 108; morality 45–46, 106; religion 43, 102; society 53, 107
bourgeoisie 39, 48
Branwen's Cauldron 208
Buffy the Vampire Slayer 201
Bush, George W. 40, 49, 50, 60–61, 91, 108

Caliphate 138
Calvary Church 72, 91
Calvinism 28
Camp Sister Spirit 212
Catharina of Siena 162
Catholic faith 160
Catholic visions 161
cemetery vandalism 177ff.
channeling 271
charisma 12, 16, 162, 170
Chauny, Father 253
child sacrifice 211
Christian Coalition 71
Christian faith 61
Christian identity 78
Circle Sanctuary 207, 217, 224
civil society 47
class (economic) 63, 82, 101, 109–110, 220, 240
Copernicus, Nicholas 38
Coughlin, Father Charles 48
counter-revolution 65
critical theory 39, 44, 55, 57, 59, 60, 75, 77, 84, 97, 99, 105

287

crystal meditation 271
cult police 183
cyber witch 224

Darwin, Charles 38
David (king) 174
death of God 19
Deliverance (rock band) 130
democratization 32–34
demythologization 44, 48
Descartes, Renee 54, 97
devil worship 222
Dhadhi Jathas 263
dialectic of productive function 7
The Divine Mercy 162, 167, 172
Djibouti 138
Double-God 21
Durkheim, Emile 7, 10, 90, 141

Egypt 154
embodiment, theory of 261
energy vibration (spiritual) 275
enlightenment 139
entelechy 253
esoteric knowledge 271
essentialism (as applied to gender) 144
evangelicalism 127
The Exorcist (film) 117

Faerie Commune 217
faith 111
Fatima, Lady of 160
Faustina (saint) 161
Fellowship of Christian Athletes 69
festival space (analytical concept) 210, 213
Festival time (analytical concept) 202, 206, 210, 211
fetishism: of commodities 8, 10, 19, 105; ideological 32
Fichte, Johann Gottlieb 44
First Great Awakening 70
Foucault, Michel 260
Fox News Channel 50
Frankfurt School 37
French religiosity 250
Freud, Sigmund 7, 38, 39, 51
Fromm, Erich 39, 51, 80, 85, 140
front end/back end disproportionality 192
functionalism 107

fundamentalism (religious) 78, 104, 138, 153, 171
Future Society 42, 43, 50, 63, 66

Galileo 38
Gardner, Gerald 71
gender 209, 214, 215
Ghandi, Mahatma 42
Globalization 145, 151
Golden Rule 41, 45, 59
Gouffrede Padirac 248
Graham, Billy 126
Grottes de Lance 248
Grottes des Merveilles 248
Guru Nanak 264

Habermas, Jürgen 39, 44, 58
handfasting 212
Haraway, Donna 220
Hare Krishna 177
Hegel, Georg Wilhelm Friedrich von 7, 43, 44, 50, 52, 55, 97
Heinlein, Robert 217
Hermander Sahib 258
Hildegarda von Bingen 162
historical materialism 100
Hitler, Adolf 50, 102
Hobbes, Thomas 52
Holy Spirit 174
homology 194
Horkheimer, Max 39, 51, 97, 99, 101–112
horror cult 179
human energy field 169

Ibn Khaldun 142
imagined community 228
International Monetary Fund 110
Islamic feminism 156, 158
Islamocracy 154, 156
Italehti 177, 190

Jesus Christ 131, 174
Jouissance 30

Kant, Immanuel 44, 54
Khalistani Guerrillas 266
Kierkegaard, Søren 56–57
King, Martin Luther 42
Kurds 238

labor markets 146

Index

Lammas 199
Led Zeppelin 117
Legion of Small Knights 163
Lex Talionis 41
litho-therapy 273
Luddites 141
Lughansad 199

mafia capitalism 50
magic 203
mana 12, 16
Manilow, Barry 117
Marcilhac-Sur-Cele 247
Marcuse, Herbert 39, 51
Martin-de-Tulle (saint) 247
martyrdom 260
Marx, Karl 7, 8, 38, 51, 53, 105, 141
mediated sociality 178
millets 233
modern animism 105
modern society 195
modernity 97, 139, 144, 154, 233
modernization 145, 148, 151, 153, 232
money 19–22
monkey forest 249
moral value 47
morality 45, 49, 184
Morocco 154
Mortification (rock band) 130, 131
motivation and ethos 185–190
MTV 85
Mundania 210, 214
Musée d'Art Sacré 251
Muslim feminists 149
Muslim intellectuals 148–150

nature 40, 199
negative theology 58
neofundamentalism 70, 73, 79
neopagan demographics 202, 218
neopaganism 69–70, 72
Neumann, Franz 52
New Age Catholicism 270
New Age Religion 169, 270, 273
New Age Spirituality 208
New Religious Movement 209, 216
New World Order 59
Newton, Sir Isaac 38
Nietzsche, Friedrich 38, 39, 59, 140
Nigeria 138
Nixon, Richard 39

Operation Bluestar 258, 263, 266
Orenda 17
The Other 23, 27, 57, 59, 105, 111
Ottoman Empire 230
Ottoman State 231

Pagan Academic Network 209
pagan census 207
pagan community 87
pagan spirit gathering 208
pagan tea house 200
Palestinian women 153
pentacostalism 71, 91
Persian Gulf War 40
Plato 52
Polish Catholic Church 270
Polish Catholic ethnocentrism 171, 174
Polish Catholic mystery 279
Polish nationalism 164, 172
Polish religiosity 275, 277
Polish religious demographics 271
Polish religious opinion 272
political Islam 238
Popper, Carl 52
positivism 104, 112
Power-God-Money thesis 11
power points 277
productivity (character type) 85
progressivism 110
Promise Keepers 69, 72, 75, 78, 84, 88, 91

Quranic discourse 148–149

rationalization 139, 142
Reagan, Ronald 39
reformation 139
Reiki 278
religion: ambiguity of 99; critical theory of 107; dialectic of 99; functionalization of 42; future of 106; ideology of 103; relation to authority 77; relation to science 54; return of 38
religionization 195
religious revival 69
Renaissance 139
ressentiment 140, 142
revolution 65
riddles of providence 39
Rocamadour 247
Rumsfeld, Donald 50

Saatananpalvonnan monet kasvot (The Many Faces of Satan) 187, 193
Sacrament (rock band) 129
sacred space 214, 223
Satan 130
Satanic ethos 186–187, 192
Satanic evil 187
Satanic ritual 212
Satanic symbols 181–183
Satanism 117, 176, 182–185, 197, 213; perspective of Church employees 184–187; perspective of youth 189–191; relation to criminality 185–187
Saudi Arabia 144
Schelling, Friedrich Wilhelm Josef von 44
Schmidt, Carl 40
Second Vatican Council 171
Self: affirmation of 75; negation of 75
September 11, 2001 42, 147
sexuality 215
Shahid 263
Sharia (Islamic Law) 139, 149
Shiite 237
Sikh Identity 264
Singh Sabha 265
Sister Zofia 162, 164, 167
social character 81; dysfunctional 82; fundamentalist 83; neopagan 85; relation to belief 86
Soros, George 50, 54
Sotto Voce 145
stage theory 140
Starhawk 220, 222
Stranger in a Strange Land 217
stratification 240
Stryper 119, 124
Sudan 138
Sultan 231
Sunnis 237
Surplus and Excess thesis 9

surplus, theory of 8

Taliban 138
Tarikat 233
technopagan 201, 222, 223, 225
Ten Commandments 111
Teresa of Avila 162
theodicy 41, 45, 56
tradition, power of 141
transubstantiation 18
true believer 130
Turkish ethnic demographics 236–237
Turkish religious demographics 236
Turkish republic 232

Ulema 231
utopianism 64

value 8, 28; theory of 17
Vengeance (rock band) 118, 125
Virgin Mary 164, 174, 247, 249, 253, 255
Visible Divinity 11, 20

Wahe Guru 263
Wakan 18
wealth distribution 242
Weber, Max 7, 10, 92, 139, 141
White Turks 238
wicca 71
witch 208
witchcraft worldview 222
World Bank 110
World Trade Organization 110

Yemen 154
Yezidis 237

Zanan 155
Zizek, Slavoj 18
Zoroastrians 237

www.ingramcontent.com/pod-product-compliance
Ingram Content Group UK Ltd.
Pitfield, Milton Keynes, MK11 3LW, UK
UKHW041927140426
5217IPUK00014B/349